The Animal Who Writes

Composition, Literacy, and Culture

David Bartholomae and Jean Ferguson Carr, Editors

The Animal Who Writes

a posthumanist composition

Marilyn M. Cooper

University of Pittsburgh Press

Chapter 2 is based in part on a chapter titled "Being Linked to the Matrix: Biology, Technology, and Writing" that appears in *Rhetorics and Technologies: New Directions in Writing and Communication*, edited by Stuart A. Selber, published by the University of South Carolina Press (2010). This material is being used with the permission of the publisher.

A version of chapter 5 originally appeared as "Rhetorical Agency as Emergent and Enacted," in *College Composition and Communication* 62, no. 3 (2011), pp. 420–49. Copyright © 2011 by the National Council of Teachers of English. Used with permission.

A version of chapter 7 originally appeared as "Listening to Strange Strangers, Modifying Dreams," in *Rhetoric Through Everyday Things*, edited by Scot Barnett and Casey Boyle, University of Alabama Press, 2016, pp. 17–29. Used with permission.

Published by the University of Pittsburgh Press, Pittsburgh, Pa., 15260
This paperback edition, Copyright © 2025, University of Pittsburgh Press
Copyright © 2019, University of Pittsburgh Press
All rights reserved
Manufactured in the United States of America
10 9 8 7 6 5 4 3 2 1

Cataloging-in-Publication data is available from the Library of Congress

ISBN 13: 978-0-8229-6759-0
ISBN 10: 0-8229-6759-6

Cover photo: Marilyn M. Cooper
Cover design: Alex Wolfe

Publisher: University of Pittsburgh Press, 7500 Thomas Blvd., 4th floor, Pittsburgh, PA 15260, United States, www.upittpress.org

EU Authorized Representative: Easy Access System Europe, Mustamäe tee 50, 10621 Tallinn, Estonia, gpsr.requests@easproject.com

*Dedicated to my mother and father,
Margaret S. Cooper and Edwin L. Cooper,
whose love and support made everything possible*

Contents

Acknowledgments
ix

Abbreviations
xi

Introduction
3

1. Enchanted Writing
19

2. Writing as Entangled
45

3. Writing as Making
76

4. The Dynamics of Becoming
106

5. The Agency of Writing
127

6. The Creativity of Writing
157

7. Ethical Persuasion
189

Conclusion: Good Writing Is Well Made
221

Notes
235

Works Cited
249

Index
265

Acknowledgments

I have many creatures to thank, many of whose stories are entangled in the chapters of this book. The pair of peregrine falcons nesting on the Portage Lift Bridge, whose antics, and their four nestlings, viewable on a nestcam, distracted me as I worried through chasing down errant citations. My energetic, voluble border collie Scout who managed not to distract me all the time. The equally energetic reviewers of the manuscript, Tom Fox and Thomas Rickert, who detailed extensive, collegial suggestions that inspired a great deal of needed revising. The long cold Keweenaw winter that kept me inside so that I would keep writing. Two books without which I could never have worked out my proposal of enchanted writing: Isabelle Stengers's *Thinking with Whitehead* and Karen Barad's *Meeting the Universe Halfway*. That dragonfly that buzzed into my car one summer. My brother John, most sincerely, for all his help and support.

Thanks to the English Department at the University of Louisville for awarding me the Thomas R. Watson Distinguished Visiting Professorship and to Michigan Technological University for a yearlong sabbatical, both of which gave me time to read and think. Thanks to Casey Boyle for inviting me to speak about this work at the Western States Rhetoric and Literacy Conference in Salt Lake City, and to Matt Newcomb who also invited me to speak about this work at the State University of New York, New Paltz. Thanks to Ciro Sandoval who introduced me to the work of Humberto Maturana and Francisco Varela. And very special thanks and love to Joe Roberts, with whom I taught the Marcuse first-year writing classes at Michigan Technological University.

Thanks to friends and colleagues who supported me with stimulating and encouraging words: Scot Barnett, Gary Bays, Carl Blackman, Robin Brown, Jill Burkland, Kevin Cassell, Jack Dunning, Paula Dunning, Patricia Freitag Ericsson, Moe Folk, Randy Freisinger, Gayle Gaskill, Diana George, Nancy Grimm, Tom Grimm, Byron Hawk, Erik Hayenga, Daniel Hendrickson, Carl Herndl, Diane Price Herndl, Jill Hodges, Bruce Horner, Johndan Johnson-Eilola, Debra Journet, Stephen Jukuri, Kate Latterell, Nancy Leonard, Bill Leonard, Min-Zhan Lu, Dennis Lynch, Scott Marratto, Carolyn Miller, Tony O'Keeffe, Laura Pennington, Wayne Pennington, Stuart Selber, Cindy Selfe, Dickie Selfe, Diane Shoos, Marty Smith, John Trimbur, Victor Villanueva, and Anne Wysocki.

Special thanks to the peeps in my exercise class for keeping me energized: Andrea Bourne, Peg Gale, Lou Helman, Patty Lins, Marge Shanette, and our leaders Sarah Fuhrman and the indomitable Terry Smythe.

Also special thanks to the students in the graduate seminar I taught at the University of Louisville: Alicia Brazeau, Carrie Kilfoil, Brice Nordquist, Shyam Sharma, Mike Sobiech, Ryan Trauman, John Vance, Caroline Wilkinson, and Mark Williams, and to the students in my final graduate seminar at Michigan Technological University: Keshab Acharya, Liz Coyne, Megan Gray, Lindsay Hingst, and Dan Lawrence. Thanks to the rhetoric reading group at Michigan Tech who read chapter 1 and engaged me in a most useful intra-action: Oren Abeles, Andrew Fiss, Nic Gerstner, Karla Kitalong, Wenjing Liu, Abraham Romney, Marika Seigel, and Hua Wang.

Finally, I am endlessly grateful to Josh Shanholtzer, my editor at the University of Pittsburgh Press, for his support and patience.

Abbreviations

Tim Ingold

BA	*Being Alive*
M	*Making*
PE	*The Perception of the Environment*

Stuart Kaufmann

HU	*At Home in the Universe*
I	*Investigations*

Bruno Latour

MC	*On the Modern Cult of the Factish Gods*
PH	*Pandora's Hope*
PN	*Politics of Nature*
RS	*Reassembling the Social*
WM	*We Have Never Been Modern*

Isabelle Stengers

TW	*Thinking with Whitehead*

Alfred North Whitehead

AI	*Adventures of Ideas*
AE	*The Aims of Education*
CN	*The Concept of Nature*
MT	*Modes of Thought*
PR	*Process and Reality*
RM	*Religion in the Making*
SMW	*Science and the Modern World*

The Animal Who Writes

Introduction

Edward Hoagland writes:

> I'd lie on my back on a patch of moss watching a swaying poplar's branches interlace with another's, and the tremulous leaves vibrate, and the clouds forgather to parade zoologically overhead, and felt linked to the whole matrix, as you either do or you don't through the rest of your life. And childhood—nine or ten, I think—is when this best happens. It's when you develop a capacity for quiet, a confidence in your solitude, your rapport with a Nature both animate and not much so: what winged things possibly feel, the blessing of water, the rhythm of weather, and what might bite you and what will not. (49–50)

Perhaps it was because my father was a freshwater ecologist and we spent a lot of time on lakes when I was a child that I know this feeling of being linked to the whole matrix and that it is deeply sedimented into my thinking. Much of this book was written at my camp on Lake Superior,[1] the Big Lake, and a lot of my thinking was done as I walked along the beach or in the woods, distracted or inspired by the loons who called to my border collie and by the redstarts, black-throated green warblers, and yellowthroats in the trees whose colors and calls commanded my attention. This is the place I feel most connected; this is where I write from.

This is a book about writing and the teaching of writing.[2] Writing comes from someplace, but it also takes you places. In my quest to think anew about why writing matters and how we can best help students to become good writers, I stray far from the bay that shelters the small community of composition and rhetoric scholars to troll the deep waters of complexity theory and process philosophy, hoping to catch concepts I can cross with the mid-water concepts of scholars in anthropology and sociology of science who have also been fishing those deep waters and bring them back into my small community. This is no longer such an adventurous quest, though as Alfred North Whitehead argues, there are always adventures to be had: others in composition and rhetoric have also been fishing these same waters. The world of scholarship always mirrors that of the wider eco/socio/cultural/economic world, and scholarship in all communities now exhibits characteristics of ecosystems like Lake Superior in which everything is connected, or entangled, in Hoagland's whole matrix, all busily intra-acting and trading their stuff.[3]

It was a long trip, and many concepts dear to composition and rhetoric fell prey to the sharks of continental philosophy and complexity theory, if not devoured at least substantially transformed: the writer as an autonomous human subject and sole agent of writing; writing as essentially a conscious, cognitive, and rational means of communicating, representing, and interpreting the world through linguistic texts. As Collin Brooke and Thomas Rickert point out, "both process and postprocess theories rely on essentially humanist assumptions about what writing is, how it occurs, how it is received, and how it is taught" (163). They allow that postprocess theory did attempt to move beyond the assumption of the autonomous subject but remained committed to "a linguistically mediated sociality that obscures more basic, even fundamental relations to technology and materiality" (164). A look at what Thomas Kent recently wrote about postprocess theory reveals its humancentric and linguistic bias. He differentiates postprocess from process theories by emphasizing that writing is not something to be learned but an action of producing comprehensible texts, which necessitates triangulation "with the world and with other language users who inhabit that world" (xvii–xvii). Thus writing is a "doubly hermeneutic" activity: since texts "represent someone's interpretation of the world ... when we confront a text ... we must interpret someone else's interpretation" (xv). As writing is "a kind of communicative interaction" (xviii), it is social: it requires not just a solitary writer but at least two actors, a writer and reader. But in Kent's vision, both actors are human with everything else in the world being merely a reference point, something to be interpreted through language. This understanding of writing has been challenged by several movements inspired by the vision of the world as a matrix of linked beings.

Posthumanism, new materialism, and the nonhuman turn from epistemology to ontology challenge the assumptions that writing is simply a cognitive activity of symbol use; that humans are the only agents involved in the activity of writing; and that writing is an activity that is dominantly directed to understanding, or as Kent says, interpreting the world. Attempting to rework Kent's definition of postprocess, Byron Hawk argues that a "posthuman image of the world ... includes humans but decenters them in relational models of assemblage and expression" ("Reassembling" 77). Diane Davis argues for "an affectability or persuadability [that] operates irrepressibly and below the radar" of reason and "that precedes and exceeds symbolic intervention" (*Inessential Solidarity* 36). Posthumanism is a repudiation of what Rosi Braidotti calls universal humanism, in which "subjectivity is equated with consciousness, universal rationality, and self-regulating ethical behaviour" (15) and to which she opposes a posthumanist subjectivity that is "materialist and vitalist, embodied and embedded, firmly located somewhere" (51). Writers are not just disembodied brains working with symbols but rather, as Hawk says, bodies that "occupy material situations that are in constant motion, interpret those flows through bodily knowledge and expression as much as language, and contribute to those assemblages by participating in their public gathering" ("Reassembling" 77). Writers are affective and kinetic as well as cognitive bodies that learn about and participate in their worlds through all these modalities.

New materialism further decenters the human writer. Diana Coole and Samantha Frost note that "materialism has remained a sporadic and often marginalized approach," for thinking about matter usually seems to inspire instead the emergence of superior idealities believed to be fundamentally different from matter: "language, consciousness, subjectivity, agency, mind, soul" (1–2). They argue that it is now time "to give material factors their due in shaping society and circumscribing human prospects" (3). As Brooke and Rickert say, "The world and its objects are essential to the ability to think, speak, write, make, and act" (168). Scholars in composition and rhetoric are now recognizing such things as language, word-processing technologies, and databases as tools that distribute the activity of writing across multiple agents. Even further, nonhuman beings and things are recognized as agents in themselves. Bruno Latour calls them actants, and Scot Barnett and Casey Boyle describe them as "vibrant actors, enacting effects that exceed (and are sometimes in direct conflict with) human agency and intentionality" (*Rhetoric* 2). Finally, as Barnett and Boyle explain, rhetoric has joined with other "humanities" disciplines in a nonhuman turn from epistemology to ontology: "Rhetoric is conceived as more than just a knowledge-making praxis; at the same time, it is thought to constitute ways of being and ways of being-with-others-in-the world" (*Rhetoric* 9). Writing is no longer conceived of as an epistemic or even a socio-epistemic practice of understanding the world but rather as a behavior of intra-acting in the world in which writers participate in their own and the world's emergence.

I have contributed to furthering these ideas that have been flowering in rhetoric and composition, ideas that writing is a process of the world's becoming; that the agents of writing are not just human animals but all living and nonliving entities, and especially, increasingly, technologies; and that humans are animals who write, not so very different from other living beings in how we feel and think and act. Humans are not the masters of the world, much less of the universe. This loss of humancentricity can be disheartening, even frightening. Still, as Karen Barad says, we do have a role to play.[4] By embracing our entanglements we can learn to meet the universe halfway: "Intra-acting responsibly as part of the world means taking account of the entangled phenomena that are intrinsic to the world's vitality and being responsive to the possibilities that might help us flourish" (Barad 396).[5] As intra-action, writing is inescapably an ethical practice, what Barad calls a worldly ethics: an ethics that is "not about right response to a radically exterior/ized other, but about responsibility and accountability for the lively relationalities of becoming of which we are a part" (393). Whitehead envisions it as an openness to the "vivid immediacy" of specific entanglements (PR 341). Whitehead was terrified, as Isabelle Stengers says (TW 333), of the "trick of evil" (PR 223) in which the embrace of "what everyone knows" overpowers vivid immediacies, obliging them to "fade into night" (PR 341). Writing ethically, I argue, entails developing habits of paying attention to the relationalities of becoming and always entertaining the possibility that "what everyone knows"—and what you believe—might be wrong.

This understanding of humans as entangled participants in the becoming of an ever-changing world emerges from a radical rethinking of the foundations of Western thought that has been developing over the past century and that is now coalescing into a coherent, if not yet common, vision, a vision I refer to as enchantment ontology.[6] It is a vision that is responsive to the overriding challenges of our times—globalization, late capitalism, and climate and technological change—challenges that require that we take account of our intimate entanglement with other beings, things, and forces, that we understand all entities including ourselves as not prior to these entanglements but as emerging from them in an ongoing becoming, and that we recognize this emergent process of making in which we participate as writers and rhetors as one of the sources of novelty and complexity in the world.[7]

From my long and often adventurous "fishing" trip in conferences and lectures and college classes, in writings by various scholars, and in walks along Lake Superior, I've brought back these answers.[8] I think writing matters because it is the way we make things that are meaningful to and have important effects on ourselves and others of all kinds. I think we can best help students become better writers by encouraging them to adopt and hold to habits that enable them to make meaningful things. I've been working on this project for a long time. I've made a theory that I believe in, that has changed the way I think about writing (and about other kinds of making), and that I hope will have meaningful effects on you who read the book. Most of my work has not been in "getting the words right," as Hemingway said about finishing the ending to *A Farewell to Arms*, but in more creative work that was essential in making this theory: paying attention to how making watercolors changed the way I look at the world; how training my dog involved a certain kind of trust; how an unexpected meeting with a dragonfly sparked an aha moment and helped me understand Whitehead's concept of propositions.[9] Pondering what Marcel Detienne and Jean-Pierre Vernant say about the how the helmsman "pits his cunning against the wind" (20) while watching a kite surfer leap waves. Arguing with a colleague about the importance of rationality in arguments. Daydreaming in the morning when I woke up, before I sat down to another day at the computer. All the work that's sometimes referred to as prewriting and is anything but. It wasn't brainstorming or invention, either, because I wasn't looking for ideas to fill up a thesis, but mixing my feelings and thoughts with those of disparate others, human and nonhuman. I'm sure these experiences sound familiar—but are these the activities commonly thought of as central to writing? And are the habits that lead to such activities taught in composition courses?

Kent argues that "the production of texts constitutes the writer's raison d'être" (xvii). I argue instead that the overriding purpose of writing is rather to make things like consumer protection policies, techniques for 3-D printing of prosthetic hands, alliances between environmental groups, theories of writing, and, yes, even facts.[10] As Latour argues, facts are not discovered out in the world but are carefully and laboriously made with a lot of work, over time, using various techniques or methodologies, through the efforts of many agents intra-acting in institutional (and other) communities ("Textbook Case" 95). This intra-active work, and not validation by reference to the "real world," is what distinguishes facts that are thus "well made" (cf. MC).[11] Latour focuses on how scientists make facts, but his description applies as well to other writers such as reporters who work together using journalistic methods of interview, document searching, and cross-checking to make "real news" unlike the "fake news" that is the product of fancy. Writing is creative in this sense: it adds new things to the world (Whitehead), including entities (Barad) as well as artifacts—it remakes writers as well as the world—and thus creates an ever more complex cosmos (Kauffman).[12] We make ourselves and our worlds in our writing, and even though we are never masters of the outcome, we are responsible for and accountable to what we make. We can participate in the emergence of what Latour calls a good common world, the best of all possible worlds, even though we often fail to do so.

As many writing teachers note, students who are cognizant of how school works largely agree with Kent in seeing what they make in writing courses simply as texts whose only purpose is to be evaluated, which quite reasonably attenuates their level of engagement. Nora Bacon, who taught in one of the earliest service learning programs at Stanford University, suggests that because students participating in these projects have a "real" audience and can make "a genuine contribution to the community organization," they are "highly motivated and thoroughly engaged in their writing" (41). Linda Adler-Kassner, Robert Crooks, and Ann Watters observe that "in the most successful cases, such as the one related . . . by Nora Bacon, participants in service projects make the crucial transition from students to writers" (2). When students work with others to make things that matter, they begin to understand what writing ethically involves.

Rosemary Arca suggests that it is not just providing students with a "real" audience or even helping them understand that they can make a contribution that turns students into writers.[13] More important is their intra-action with those others they "serve" who are quite different from them and who are also engaged in shaping and accomplishing the purpose of the writing that emerges out of the project. Arca says, "When we acknowledge our interconnectedness, we recognize how we can effect change, and then we seek to serve. When we serve, we realize that our service is changing not only the focus of our service but also ourselves" (133). Students who understand that they are working *with* other agents and not just *for* some passive unfortunates come to understand their roles—and themselves—differently, not as all-knowing missionaries who have nothing at stake in the outcomes they work toward but as engaging with others to make changes in the world and, in turn, in themselves.

Connecting students with real audiences and changing the venue of teaching as is done not only in service learning but also in approaches that focus on public writing begin to align writing pedagogy with the tenets of enchantment ontology,[14] but more needs to be done and can be done in traditional courses. We can help students to develop habits of writing well, habits that will allow them to make good policies, alliances, facts, and so forth. Habits of writing well are habits of intra-action that help writers to pay attention to their entanglements with other beings, technologies, institutions, and forces, and to how they can work with them creatively and how they affect and are affected by them. The habits I offer bear some similarity to the "habits of mind" detailed in the *Framework for Success in Postsecondary Writing*, but my goal differs; habits of mind, instead of ways of paying attention to entanglements, are ways of approaching learning (*Framework* 1). In addition, while my habits of writing well are ways of doing things, the *Framework*'s habits of mind are attributes or abilities. So, for example, I describe the habit of wonder as a habit of asking questions and speculating, while the *Framework* describes the habit of curiosity as "the desire to know more about the world" (1). In defining habits, I follow Aristotle's understanding of *hexeis* as elaborated by Joe Sachs; habits are "an active having-and-holding that depends upon the effort of concentrating or paying attention" (*Nicomachean* xii). They involve an active comportment toward the world, an awareness of something that matters in a particular way. Such an awareness is not necessarily conscious, though it is available to consciousness, and not dominantly cognitive but affective. They are learned by practicing them consciously, but they become, as Sachs says, "an active condition, a way in which we hold ourselves, having taken hold deliberately of the feelings and dispositions that are in us merely passively" (ix). For example, Barack Obama's disposition to mediate differences, to seeing common themes in the midst of an arguing bunch, became a habit of centered flexibility, a way of acting that then felt to him as the thing to do.[15] The habits of writing well I offer are ethical ways of intra-acting, practices that respect differences and strive for creativity—for example, making good decisions.

Enchantment ontology inspires a focus on how all writing begins in intra-action and is realized through accountability for what comes to be in the process. It is an ontology that requires a major shift in how we understand reality and ourselves. Instead of a world made up of bounded individual entities, enchantment ontology envisions individuals as entangled in intra-active phenomena from which they co-emerge contingently in an ongoing process of becoming. Change is not the result of intentions and planning, but emerges continually as parts of the universe affect one another. Everything is made new in every moment. In chapter 1, I describe these shifts as involving three assumptions: (1) parts of reality are entangled in intra-active phenomena from which emerge individual entities; (2) reality is a process of unceasing and contingent change in which everything is always in the process of becoming; and (3) novelty is immanent, inevitably emerging in a self-organizing world. These assumptions—entanglement, becoming, and creativity—also envision the universe as a single system, a cosmos, not divided into the separate realms of nature and society. Commenting on the hybrid phenomenon of the ozone hole over Antarctica, Latour says, "A single thread links the most esoteric sciences and the most sordid politics, the most distant sky and some factory in the Lyon suburbs, dangers on a global scale and the impeding local elections or the next board meeting" (WM 1).

Michael Pollan relates an incident that nicely illustrates the vision projected by enlightenment ontology. When a set of tornadoes came through his hometown, a forty-two-acre forest of old-growth white pines near the center of town was reduced to a pile of fallen timber. The forest, called Cathedral Pines, had been enjoyed by the residents as a popular place for hiking and Sunday outings and weddings and had been preserved as a national landmark owned by The Nature Conservancy. A dispute, framed in terms that pit humans against nature, arose over what to do about the catastrophe. As Pollan considers the history of Cathedral Pines, however, what to do does not seem to come down to a simple choice between attending to the desires of humans or the "laws" of nature. Cathedral Pines was not a true wilderness, untrammeled by man. It had been logged twice, clearcut by the first settlers and selectively logged for hardwood a hundred years later, producing a pure stand of pines. The option of leaving the forty-two acres to restore itself through the process of forest succession turns out to be just as conditioned by man—the imported Norway maples from residents' yards might take over the area instead—and just as subject to contingent factors like an increase in the deer population or floods that would result in a forest of spruce or a tangle of Japanese honeysuckle, another species imported by man. The "law" of forest succession turns out to be "a human construct imposed upon a much more variable and precarious reality" (183). The option of actively restoring the forest leads to the conundrum of which of the past versions of the forest to choose: the mixed species forest the settlers encountered or the pure stand of pines that took over after the logging? Indeed, the forest had been changing over its entire history: "Just since the last ice age alone . . . tree species forced south by the glaciers migrated back north . . . Indians arrived and set their fires . . . the large mammals disappeared . . . the climate fluctuated" (186). Concluding that clearly the actions of man and of nature cannot be disentangled, that the forest is always changing and becoming a new forest through complex intra-actions, Pollan turns to the garden "as a place with long experience of questions having to do with man *in* nature" (190). Our idea of a garden, he argues, is no different from any of our other ideas of nature—wilderness, resource, ecosystem—all are "an indissoluble mixture of our culture and whatever it is that's really out there" (191). The best we can do is to "Consult the Genius of the Place," as Alexander Pope advised landscape designers, which comes down to paying attention to what will grow in a particular kind of area (not palm trees in the area that was Cathedral Pines). And we can exercise our human nature and act for "our well-being and survival as a species" and for the well-being of other forms of life on which we are dependent, which involves acting with restraint in the battle against nature's weeds, storms, and plagues. Pollan says, "Attentiveness to nature can help us attune our desires with her ways" (195). Just as Barad says, "We can learn to meet the universe halfway . . . taking account of the entangled phenomena that are intrinsic to the world's vitality and being responsive to the possibilities that might help us flourish" (396).

Conceiving writing in line with the assumptions of enchantment ontology requires equally large shifts in how we understand rhetorical concepts central in teaching writing. In chapters 2 through 7, I develop my understandings of technē, agency, and persuasion and offer habits of writing well that they inspire. Chapter 2 details how the understanding of writing as thinking has changed: the thinking involved in writing is no longer limited to rational conscious thought nor is it a process internal to individual brains or bodies. Writers are embodied and enworlded—or, better, entangled with others in the phenomenon of writing. Work in cognitive ethology, cybernetics, and neurology has led to an understanding of cognitive behavior as what beings do in the world. All living beings, Jacob von Uexküll argued, are subjects: they exercise their characteristic modes of perception and action to make their living and their world. The tick perceives the odor of butyric acid given off by a dog's skin glands and drops onto the dog, where it scurries around through the fur until it perceives the warmth of bare skin and commences to drink blood. This behavior is a functional cycle, Uexküll says, not a mechanical response (*Foray* 50): the tick notices the odor and acts on it, just as, he says, a gourmet may notice and pick out raisins from a cake (53). Barad says, "Knowing is not a play of ideas within the mind . . . knowing is a physical practice of engagement" (342). Humans, like all living things, think by intra-acting with others in functional cycles of perception and action that depend on senses and feelings more often than on conscious thought.

I call humans the animal who writes to emphasize that writing is a behavior very like other animal behaviors, not only simple behaviors like the tick's but more recognizably in extended systems of cognitive ecologies, which involve tools and language. Bernard Stiegler conceives of tools and language as arising not from impressing a mental image on flint or by creating a symbol to refer to it but from an intra-action between cortex and material. As an early hominid works flint, what happens is a "meeting of matter whereby the cortex reflects itself" in the flint, a "movement of their mutual coming-to-be" (*Technics 1* 141). This is what Barad calls an agential cut, "*an agentially enacted ontological separability within the phenomenon*" (175), from which a distinction that did not preexist the intra-action emerges. Tools and language emerge from intra-actions between living beings and materials, tools from materials like flint, language from the material of perception and experience. I will argue that both tools and language are instruments of making, or technē.

When reworked through the assumption of entanglement, technē becomes a correspondence as in exchanges of letters, an ongoing entanglement involving not only makers and tools and materials but also things and forces, a "dance of animacy" (Ingold, M 100–2). Writers make research reports, for example, with the tools of language and images and the materials of data, experiments, and observations. In chapter 3, I argue that the technē of writing is better conceived with reference to the practical intelligence of mētis and phronetic technē than to epistēmē. Joseph Dunne retrieves phronetic technē as an unofficial Aristotelean concept from Aristotle's examples of aberrant technai such as navigation and medicine where "success is to be achieved . . . not so much by keeping one's gaze fixed on the preconceived form which one will impose on the material, as by a flexible kind of responsiveness to the dynamism of the material itself" (256). Distinguished from poiesis, which is activity directed toward an end, phronesis is practical knowledge, aligned with mētis in emphasizing experience and perceptiveness rather than rules. Unlike mētis, however, which required scheming and cunning in dealing with the ungoverned contingency of the practical world, phronesis is the wisdom, or character, of an ethical person, "a person who knows how to live well" from long personal experience (Dunne 244). Thus a phronetic technē relieves mētis of the implication of making as a struggle of man against nature (Whitehead's bifurcation of nature), and endows the maker instead with the wisdom that comes from long experience. Like phronetic technē, Ingold's theory of making abandons hylomorphism and the bifurcation of nature, and like mētis it abandons any notion of an unchanging sphere of being and of true and definite knowledge. Also, just as mētis and phronetic technē involve bodily comportment (hexis), Ingold sees making as relying on habits, bodily "capacities of movement and feeling that have been developed through a life history of past practices" (BA 58).

As an example of writing as making, we meet in chapter 3 the plant biologist Nicholas Harberd who kept a notebook of his activities for a year. We follow him through the countryside to observe a single thale-cress plant and to visit a nearby nature reserve, and we hear of his work on two research projects and of his writing of the papers that came out of the research. His account exhibits three useful habits of writing as making: close observation of the subjects of the writing; connection of observations, experiences, memories, and feelings through patterns; and wonder: speculating and asking questions. Wonder is an especially valuable habit of enchanted writing, as it is a felt recognition that something is important, or as Barad says, how in intra-action something has come to matter.

Chapter 4 elaborates the ongoing process of becoming. Gilles Deleuze and Félix Guattari say that becoming "concerns alliance"; it is a "contagion" (238, 241). Stiegler, as discussed in chapter 2, calls it a "mutual coming-to-be" (*Technics 1* 141). Whitehead conceives it as a concrescence in which an entity infects "its environment with its own aspects" while at the same time "the aspects of all things enter into its very nature" (SMW 94). Individuals are always becoming depending on the intra-actions they enter into, though they do also endure as a "route of antecedent occasions" over time (Whitehead, PR 43). John Holland observes cities, immune systems, and ecosystems in which "patterns in time" arise out of nonlinear interactions in a continuous becoming (*Hidden Order* 2). And Gunter Kress defines writing as a process of "transformative engagement in the world, [and] transformation constantly of the self in that engagement" ("Gains" 21). Becoming shifts our understanding of change. We are accustomed to think of influential individuals or significant writings as the engines of change, and we overlook the long, convoluted, intra-active processes by which writing comes into existence and influences us and by which individuals develop the commitments and happen into moments or positions that enable their writing to have substantial effects. Philosophers like Whitehead, scientists like Holland, and linguists like Kress and many others instead understand change as driven by complex, entangled, everyday phenomena and therefore inescapable, nonlinear, and contingent.

In thinking about writing, the most important aspect of becoming is the way intentions, purposes, plans—and even writers themselves—do not exist prior to writing but rather emerge in the process of writing. Writing and the agents of writing are intra-active phenomena. Writers intra-act with aspects of the immediate situation minute by minute without reasoning about what they are doing, unless something goes wrong. They may consciously and unconsciously form intentions and purposes in writing, they may change them in the course of writing, and they may formulate and reformulate plans before, during, and after writing, but these intentions, purposes, and plans function more like transient orienting devices (GPS) than like the instructions for assembly of Ikea furniture. Gilbert Simondon understands individuals in the same way, as a process of individuation: "a partial and relative resolution manifested in a system that contains latent potentials and harbors a certain incompatibility with itself" ("Genesis" 300). As a process, individuation interweaves permanence and change, the attainment of a partial resolution along with an instability that harbors potentials. Writers emerge as new entities along with their writing.

Reconceiving the relation of permanence and change as complementary rather than dialectical and individuals as emergent within metastable complex systems allows me to redefine agents and agency in chapter 5. Neither the modernist autonomous subject nor the postmodern socially determined subject can serve as a model for an enchanted understanding of writers as agents. Agents are not determined by social structures; they do act and make a difference through their intra-actions. But unlike modernist subjects, they do not act with conscious intentions, and their actions cannot determine the difference they make. The enactive approach to the study of mind describes the process by which neural systems create meanings through intra-action: nonconscious acting into the world followed by conscious perception of and considering of the consequent meanings. Just as the tick notices the odor of butyric acid and acts on it, neural systems actively and creatively respond to emotions and sensations rather than being determined by them. The neuroscientist Walter Freeman explains that "this dynamic system . . . is the agency in charge, not our awareness, which is constantly trying to catch up with what we do" (139). In the sense that our actions, ensuing from our emotions, are always our own, we act with free will; agency is grounded in the actions of individuating entities.

Jeffrey Nealon as well as Carl Herndl and Adele Licona have defined agency on the model of Michel Foucault's power relationship, but Nealon still conceives of agency as a form of resistance. He argues that an agent is simply a person who acts, and he decries approaches in which "agency is a code word for a subject performing an action that matters, something that changes one's own life or the lives of others" (102). Foucault, though, says that a power relationship further requires that it open up "a whole field of responses, reactions, results, and possible inventions" ("Subject" 220). Thus, I argue that agency always does have effects: it opens up possibilities and by doing so changes lives in ways that matter—it's just that it isn't either a free or determinate action of a conscious subject. Agency is a relation, an entangled intra-action, in which agents are acting and becoming together. Agency is productive in the way that Foucaldian power is productive and it is creative in the way Whitehead's concresence is: it is an intra-action that produces possibilities.

As an example of productive agency, I consider Barack Obama's speech on race delivered in his 2008 campaign for the presidency. Obama saw the speech not just as a political necessity but as a "teaching moment," an opportunity to mediate seemingly irreconcilable racial tensions and misunderstandings. He narrated incidents from his life as reflecting both the problems and possibilities involved in racial tensions in the country and rather than offering a solution, he offered a choice that left up to his listeners the decision to act. His speech demonstrates three habits of productive agency that Obama adopted as he became, over time, the individuating entity that he was on that day: a centered flexibility that impels him to mediate differences; a recognition of the wider import of his personal narrative; and a mode of addressing others as agents acting out of their own subjective experiences. These habits evince dispositions to trust in living values that can be modified without losing their personal value, to see one's own experience as shaped by intra-actions with other beings in the world, and to understand one's listeners as people who also act out of their living values and yet can be open to embracing change.

In chapter 6 I argue for writing as a creative intra-active process, an adventure of ideas "in which one does not feel oneself to be the master of what one writes, but where writing forces one to think, to feel, and to create" (Stengers, TW 354). Michael Carter has also argued, based on Whitehead's process philosophy, that writing is essentially creative. Our readings of Whitehead, and consequently our versions of the creativity of writing, differ in instructive ways. He understands creativity as arising from a dialectical tension between order and disorder and values creativity as an aspect of individual being: the writer's enjoyment of being creative. In contrast, I understand creativity as arising in reciprocal intra-action, and value creative writing as pragmatic: serving external rather than intrinsic purposes, it makes real material differences in the world. Adhering to dialectics that hold differences in tension, Carter misunderstands how new entities arise in Whitehead's notion of concrescence. Propositions, "one of the major inventions of Whitehead's philosophy" (Stengers, TW 396), explain how change is always emerging in writing, how writing always has effects that need to be taken account of.

A proposition is a version of the feeling "this is important" with variable specifications of *how* it is felt to be important. Whitehead calls propositions "lures for feeling" and relates them to the miracle of creation as described in Ezekiel. He says, "These subjective ways of feeling are not merely receptive of the data as alien facts; they clothe the dry bones with the flesh of a real being, emotional, purposive, appreciative" (PR 85). Stengers relates it to the phenomenon of hypnosis in which the hypnotist does not command but suggests a possibility: "This is a path suggested to the new 'you' made to emerge by the addressing, by which the corresponding 'I' will verify its own existence" (TW 462). What is felt in entertaining a proposition begins with the awareness of "the marked contrast between the actual and the possible that Carter says characterizes the enjoyment of creativity (133). But entertaining a proposition doesn't stop with awareness; it is followed by a conscious activity directed to a real, specific possibility. Propositions pose insistent questions of the "what if" type: what if that's a tiger? As the question merely poses a possibility, it doesn't determine the answer; that is up to the entity entertaining the proposition. For example, Irene Pepperberg describes an intra-action with Alex, the grey parrot she worked with for many years. Inspired by Bernd Heinrich's experiments with ravens, she tested Alex to see if he could figure out how to retrieve a nut hanging on a string from his perch. She had previously tried the experiment with a younger parrot who immediately pulled up the string to get the treat, so she was surprised when, after putting Alex on the perch, he looked at the nut, looked at her, and said, "Pick up nut." Pepperberg replied, "No, Alex, *you* pick up nut." Alex looked back at her and said, "Pick up nut!" He wouldn't do it. Alex's behavior offers a proposition. His "failure" is important—surprising—in that he has previously exhibited many impressive skills. What if this is a failure? Pepperberg had to think about Alex's proposition for several years before she concluded something that was equally surprising. She noticed that Alex often sent research assistants scurrying around to fulfill his demands for things he wanted—"Want corn . . . want nut . . . wanna go shoulder . . . wanna go gym"—and she realized that "Alex's 'failure' . . . was not a black mark on his intelligence. . . . It was a measure of his sense of entitlement, his expectation that I would do as he asked" (150–52). Propositions are not intentional communications. They offer possibilities. Alex does something new and Pepperberg observes a new significant behavior.

Propositions "miraculously" bring about changes without determining what the changes will be. They are especially valuable not only in understanding how writing is creative but also in understanding how to listen across differences. Alex and Pepperberg correspond with each other, as Ingold would say; they enact an answer to Donna Haraway's question about training with her dog Cayenne: "What are we to become?" (*When* 221).

How to listen across differences is the focus of chapter 7, where I rethink persuasion as an intra-action in which interlocutors are changed, consciously and unconsciously, through the expression and entertainment of propositions. I see persuasion as inherently ethical, crucially dependent on considering other creatures as strangers and paying attention to their specific presences. The shift in understanding persuasion I am proposing is a major shift in the style of engagement that persuasion involves. Instead of focusing on rhetors' intentions, I focus on all participants' actions in persuasive encounters, how they affect each other unconsciously and consciously in intra-action and what new possibilities emerge. Ethical persuasion takes seriously the importance of others' narratives, commitments, attachments, beliefs, and habits that do not provide an identity but a hold on experience that might change, or become modified, and that cannot "be explained away, for instance through the appeal to something in common" (Stengers, "Ecology" 189). Successful—ethical—persuasion is simply persuasion in which people change in ways that do not harm them.

Describing Hannah Arendt's take on public discourse, Patricia Roberts-Miller says, "Good thinking requires that one *hear* the arguments of other people . . . it is not a discourse in which one announces one's stance; participants are interlocutors and not just speakers; they must listen . . . it must be a world into which one enters and by which one might be changed" ("Fighting"

593). Persuasion depends on listening to others, and so I offer three habits of listening: assuming there are creatures to listen to; letting creatures be in themselves in one's relations to them; and exploring new styles of listening. I use the term "creatures" here in Whitehead's sense to mean all things that are created—and all creatures are involved in persuasion. Comportment toward the other as capable of and often (though not always) desiring to address you is the most important habit. Krista Ratcliffe says that refusing to listen by "pretending the 'desire to be heard' does not exist, hoping it will disappear, or waiting for someone else to handle it" needs to be transposed "into a self-conscious desire for receptivity" (29). It is also a matter of attention, of acknowledging the presence of another creature and being aware of how it is affecting you. Letting creatures be in themselves means paying attention to the other creature as a specific instance of a specific individual in a specific time and place. It means not assuming or imagining that the creature is just like you, or a lot like you, or just like someone else you know or have read about, or just like all others of that ilk—that you understand or can easily come to understand the creature. (Remember how long it took Pepperberg to realize what Alex was doing.) Exploring new styles of listening means adopting or inventing new ways to get into discussions, ways that might be especially helpful with creatures quite strange to you. Latour calls such styles of listening speech prostheses: they rely on interacting in media other than language, such as through experimental apparatuses.

In this final chapter, you get to meet lots of strange creatures engaged in mostly successful persuasive encounters. No dragonflies or hummingbirds are harmed as they encounter humans; no human is harmed by his cochlear implant; no atom of cobalt is harmed by the geochemist who studies them in Antarctic lakes. None of the disparate humans involved in a dispute over a forest in Indonesia comes to any harm. And no one in the riotous crowd Bobby Kennedy addressed in Indianapolis on the night of Martin Luther King's assassination was harmed—and neither was he.

Polite persuaders do not try to understand or identify with others, but instead offer and entertain possibilities, and they often do so, as did Alex, in the form of propositions, tales that might be told, or in the form of choices that may suggest new paths. Polite persuaders also accept the test posed by encounters with others by considering what is demanded by their own hold, as did Pepperberg in pondering why Alex "failed" the test she gave him. It's not good manners or tolerance or empathy or understanding that makes ethical persuasion polite. Instead, polite persuasion requires embracing the habit of belief and trust in what other creatures can do, the habit of respect for the different holds other creatures have on experience, and embracing the habit of both offering and entertaining propositions that take account of the entangled phenomena that are intrinsic to the flourishing of us all.

In the conclusion I address the ethics of and suggest some approaches to teaching enchanted writing. The explicit purpose of writing courses is to intra-act with students in ways that bring about changes in their understanding of and behavior in writing. Ethical persuasion augmented by features of epideictic discourse allows teachers to intra-act with students in ways that promote the values of enchanted writing. Enchantment ontology values writing because it makes the world what it is and values differences because they enable writers to create possibilities that change the world. Epideictic discourse praises "common values" that "are not put into question," values that command unconditional fidelity (Perelman 132). Ethical persuasion adds the requirement that these values not be inculcated in ways that require students to relinquish their experienced values. Students are only asked to understand writing as a valuable behavior. In writing courses, students are invited to join a community in which they make writing that is important to them and about which they make their own decisions.

Thus, the primary goals of writing courses should be to help students find something that is important to them, that offers propositions they are impelled to explore, and to encourage them in ethical habits of well-made writing. I design courses to be lures for feeling, with readings that challenge or outrage them or with topics so multifaceted and complex that they cannot fail to find something in them that they feel strongly about. I emphasize the value of writing by taking their writing seriously, by listening carefully to their ideas, by asking questions, and by pointing out problems in their recommendations, policies, or constructions of facts. I introduce habits by simply telling students that these are things that writers do, and I trust them to adopt habits they find useful.

Writing begins in a feeling of importance and it takes you places, to new possibilities. It does so over and over as you make writing, not just at the "beginning." Even in a very short writing—Bobby Kennedy's speech, barely six minutes, or a short note of condolence—what is important and how it is important occupies the most attention as writers intra-act with feelings, memories, language, other creatures, changing themselves and others moment by moment. These intra-actions are not preparation for writing but the essence of writing. Through stories and suggestions—and arguments I hope have been polite—I have tried to offer a proposition that I hope you will entertain: what if all our intra-actions with other creatures served to invite them to adopt the ethical habits of writing well?

1

Enchanted Writing

Enchantment ontology suggests new, unfamiliar ways to think about what writing is and what we are doing when we write, ways of thinking that can be hard to change, especially for those of us in the West. It suggests that writing is not an epistemic or even a socio-epistemic practice of interpreting the world but rather a behavior of intra-acting in the world, not a behavior dominantly driven by intentions or purposes but rather by responding to possibilities that arise through intra-actions, and finally not a behavior governed by effectiveness or efficiency but rather by creativity and accountability. Our habitual focus on specificity, purpose, and the effective communication of information in writing makes it difficult to perceive how all writing begins in intra-action and is realized through accountability "for what materializes, for what comes to be" (Barad 361) in the telling. These are the aspects of writing that enchantment ontology inspires us to focus on.

Robin Wall Kimmerer's essay "In the Footsteps of Nanabozho: Becoming Indigenous to Place" (*Braiding Sweetgrass*) demonstrates how habits of writing such as paying attention to and corresponding with all kinds of other beings, being open to learning from intra-actions, and connecting the past and present can generate possibilities for new futures. In her essay, Kimmerer, a botanist and member of the Citizen Potawatomi Nation, muses on the situation of immigrants as she walks through a spruce forest to a bluff over the Pacific Ocean, an area new to her. She tells of her encounters with the unfamiliar beings she corresponds with and relates them to the Anishinaabe story of Original Man (Nanabozho), who, as the last of all beings created, is also an immigrant. From these intra-actions, a new way of thinking about immigration and becoming indigenous arises, and her writing creates and accounts for this realization. Her new understanding of becoming indigenous also derives from her connections of her present situation with the origin story of Nanabozho. As she explains, for her people, time is not linear, and such "stories are both history and prophecy, stories for a time yet to come" (207).

Kimmerer tells how Nanabozho received instructions from the Creator "to walk in such a way 'that each step is a greeting to Mother Earth,'" which he understood to mean that he should learn the true names of all the beings, not so that he could master them but so that he might learn from them (206).[1] As Nanabozho greeted all the beings, they greeted him in return and he began to feel at home. As Kimmerer walks in the Pacific Coast forest where "no one knows [her] name," she follows Nanabozho by greeting "my Sitka Spruce grandmother" whose "swaying foliage is constantly murmuring to her neighbors"; she says the spruce will "eventually pass the word and my name on the wind" (206). "Names are the way we humans build relationship, not only with each other but with the living world" (208), Kimmerer says. The immigrant human and native plant are now corresponding, to use Tim Ingold's term for a kind of intra-action in which beings pay attention to one another by "moving along together" in "a dance of animacy" (M 106–7). As Ingold observes, the pattern is the same as in written correspondence, writing and reading, writing and responding.

Sitting under the sitka spruce and listening to the wind, Kimmerer ponders how immigrants might become indigenous to place. As she walks back to the trail, she recognizes a plant she had not noticed before, an immigrant from the east: the common plantain, called by the Potowatomis "White Man's Footstep" and by Linnaeus *Plantago major*, which refers to the sole of a foot. Plantain followed the white settlers west, and everywhere else they went, and made itself at home. Unlike other nonnative plants like loosestrife and kudzu that "have the colonizing habit of taking over others' homes and growing without regard for limits," plantain is a good neighbor: "Its strategy is to be useful, to fit into small places, to coexist with others around the dooryard, to heal wounds" (214). After five hundred years, plantain became a naturalized member of the community. Kimmerer remembers that, just as for Nanabozho, "the plants are our oldest teachers" (213). Out of her intra-action with her "old friend" plantain emerges a new possibility: maybe human immigrants could "follow the teachings of White Man's Footstep" (214). It is "by honoring the knowledge in the land, and caring for its keepers [that] we start to become indigenous to place" (210).

Kimmerer says that her book offers "a braid of stories meant to heal our relationship with the world" (x). Stories, even when they do not address humans' estrangement from the natural world, best exemplify the intra-active and creative aspects of writing. Rather than informing readers, stories engage readers by suggesting a path for them to follow, as Ingold explains: "The telling of stories is an education of attention.... To tell, in short is not to explicate the world, to provide the information that would amount to a complete specification, obviating the need for would-be practitioners to inquire for themselves. It is rather to trace a path that others can follow" (M 110). Ingold sees stories not as fictional accounts but as means of teaching, as do many Native American communities (cf. Basso 57–60). By tracing a path, pointing out "where to go and what to look out for" (Ingold, M 110), they encourage the habit of paying attention.

Introducing her book that addresses "the possibility of life in capitalist ruins," Anna Lowenhaupt Tsing also emphasizes the importance of being open to intra-actions. She asks, "What do you do when your world starts to fall apart?" and answers, " I go for a walk, and if I'm really lucky, I find mushrooms" (*Mushroom* 1). She argues that finding oneself "without the handrails of stories that tell where everyone is going and, also, why" (2), one can realize that "there are still pleasures amidst the terrors of indeterminacy" (1). Coming upon mushrooms that "pop up unexpectedly" reminds her of how indeterminacy engenders "multiple futures [that] pop in and out of possibility" (viii). She comments, "The uncontrolled lives of mushrooms are a gift—and a guide" (2), and she hopes her readers will follow where they lead her. Her writing thus begins not with intentions but with intra-actions: her response to the specific "autumn aroma" of matsutake mushrooms and the different stories this entanglement engenders.

Assumptions of Enchantment Ontology

Kimmerer's and Tsing's books not only highlight the enchanted aspects of writing, they also exhibit the central assumptions of enchantment ontology that are crucial to understanding this shift in perspective. When I began introducing the idea of how enchantment ontology could reorient our thinking about writing, I realized that it was not easy for others to grasp how great a shift it required. Responses of those attending my presentations and presentations of similarly oriented colleagues left us puzzling: why don't they get it? Though enchantment ontology has been developing over the past century, it still offers radical challenges to Western thought, challenges to the sharp division between the human and natural worlds, to essential and unchanging forms as the basis of reality, and to change as a difficult process involving external causes. Instead, it assumes:

> **Entanglement:** parts of reality are entangled in intra-active phenomena from which emerge individual entities;

Becoming: reality is a process of unceasing and contingent change in which everything is always in the process of becoming; and
Creativity: novelty is immanent, inevitably emerging in a self-organizing world.

These assumptions also envision the universe as a single system, a cosmos, not divided into the separate realms of nature and society.

As Kimmerer relates how she and Nanabozho learn from the teachings of other beings, she affirms that humans are entangled in the cosmos, corresponding with sitka spruces, plantains, the sounds of the wind, the story of Nanabozho. His story is part of the intra-action, the past entangled with present and future—Nanabozho's footprints "lie on the path behind us and on the path ahead" (207)—and is changing, becoming, along with Kimmerer and other entities in the intra-action. And her realization of how immigrants can become indigenous demonstrates the creativity of intra-action. The assumptions describe overlapping aspects of enchantment ontology, not a linear process, and Tsing's recognition of the positive aspects of indeterminacy encapsulates how the assumptions work together: when entities are understood not as essential and separate unities but as constantly intra-acting and becoming, possible futures continually "pop in and out of possibility."

The concept of entanglement goes beyond the posthumanist acknowledgment of the existence and relevance of other beings and cultures in dispelling the specter of the rational, free man as the universal condition of human existence. Entanglement is not just a way of saying that we're all in this together, that everything is connected in causal chains. As Karen Barad explains, it is a perspective drawn from quantum mechanics, which understands "the primary ontological unit to be *phenomena*, rather than independent objects with inherent boundaries and properties" (333). Subjects, objects, and agents emerge from specific phenomena of novel becoming, which entangle some "parts" of the material world, a process Barad calls intra-action. All "entities" change and become something else in intra-action; Donna Haraway, who calls this process reciprocal induction,[2] describes her training with her dog Cayenne as "partners-in-the-making through the active relations of co-shaping, not [as the interaction of] possessive human or animal individuals whose boundaries and natures are set in advance of the entanglements of becoming together" (*When* 208).

The ongoing becoming of entities through intra-action is captured in Alfred North Whitehead's concept of concrescence: "The actual world is a process, and . . . the process is the becoming of actual entities . . . also termed 'actual occasions'" (PR 22). Concrescence is the "production of novel togetherness": "The novel entity is at once the togetherness of the 'many' which it finds, and also it is one among the disjunctive 'many' which it leaves; it is a novel entity.... The many become one, and are increased by one" (21). Whitehead asserts, "*How* an actual entity *becomes* constitutes *what* that actual entity *is*. ... Its 'being' is constituted by its 'becoming'" (23). Each entity, as an actual occasion, is a specific, unique holding together of disparate entities. Concrescence is somewhat analogous to Martin Heidegger's equally enigmatic notion of the fourfold, in which things come to presence through gathering aspects of the world "into something that stays for a while: into this thing, that thing" ("Thing" 172). The bridge "*gathers* the earth as a landscape around the stream"; it "escorts the lingering and hastening ways of men to and fro, so that they may get to other banks and in the end, as mortals, to the other side"; the bridge is an actual entity that "*gathers* to itself in *its own way* earth and sky, divinities and mortals" ("Building" 150–51). Whitehead says, "In their natures, entities are disjunctively 'many' in process of passage into conjunctive unity" (PR 21). In the "creative advance" of concrescence, a novel entity, the one, arises from a gathering of some of the many already existing actual entities and thereby adds one more entity to the world.

Creativity follows logically from the first two assumptions: the singleness of reality in which entanglement results in a continual and irreversible becoming of new entities. Intra-action, or concrescence, explains the creativity inherent in the cosmos. Change and creativity are no longer seen as motivated by some external cause but are events in which multiple agents participate and for which they are jointly responsible. Everything is becoming as intra-acting entities respond to one another and "trade their stuff," as complexity theorist Stuart Kauffman puts it (HU 129). Complex systems theory, which developed in computing, biology, and other fields in the mid-twentieth century, explains how "order for free" emerges from intra-action with no need for central control or separate instigating agents. Many more entities are acknowledged as agents, or actants, as Bruno Latour calls them, since agency is understood as involving affective entanglements rather than conscious purpose.

The understanding of systems as open, entangling natural and social systems, also distinguishes enchantment ontology from social constructionism and most versions of postmodernism which, in contrast, assume a divide between natural and socially constructed realms. Arguing forcefully against the bifurcation of nature into "the nature apprehended in awareness and the nature which is the cause of awareness," Whitehead maintained that perceiving the red sunset is "not an action of nature on the mind. It is an interaction within nature" (CN 31). The experience of "the red glow of the sunset" is as much a part of nature as are "the molecules and electric waves" by which science explains the glow (28). Kimmerer also recognizes what she learns from intra-acting with plants as on a par with what she knows from studying them scientifically. Thus when Humberto Maturana and Francisco Varela say that "every act of knowing brings forth a world" (*Tree* 26), they do not mean that our minds or society or culture creates a representation of the world, an alternate or shadow world with a tenuous connection to reality, a world of infinite and endless relativity.[3] As Barad says, "Realism, then, is not about representations of an independent reality but about the real consequences, interventions, creative possibilities, and responsibilities of intra-acting within and as part of the world" (37). Steven Shaviro, too, observes that the pragmatic consequences of Whitehead's and Gilles Deleuze's rejection of essentialism are quite different from the aporias of the deconstructionists and the polite conversation of Richard Rorty (*Without Criteria* 145–46). For process philosophers, "evanescence, becoming, incessant novelty, and 'perpetual perishing' do not make reference and grounding impossible. Rather, these experiences are themselves our fundamental points of reference" (Shaviro, *Without Criteria* 151). All our experiences tell of what we know about the world and support our becoming. In writing as in living, we intra-act within one world, and our intra-actions create the patterns in time that compose our world.

In what follows, in order to more fully elucidate how enchantment ontology reorients our understanding of writing, I trace its origins in complexity theory and process philosophy. I then contrast my approach with that of two other scholars in rhetoric and composition who also draw on versions of enchantment ontology. And finally, I address the question of how habits such as paying attention and being open to possibilities can transform effective writing into enchanted writing.

Origins of Enchantment Ontology

The roots of enchantment ontology go deep into Western intellectual history.[4] The assumption of a single reality can be traced at least to the end of the nineteenth century as thinkers in both the sciences and humanities began undermining what Latour famously called the modern constitution, the rigorous distinction between human society and nonhuman nature that defines the project of humanism, in favor of a vision of "the common production of societies and natures" (WM 141). In the nineteenth century, Charles Darwin, along with Lamarck and Alfred Russel Wallace, unsettled the belief in the great chain of being by suggesting that species arise and die out in interaction with each other and their environments. At the turn of the twentieth century, a group of German-speaking scientists comprising the "Wholeness" movement argued that viewing "phenomena less atomistically and more 'holistically,' less mechanistically and more 'intuitively' . . . could lead to the rediscovery of a nurturing relationship with the natural world" (Harrington xii). As they said, "It would 'reenchant' the world," voicing the idea long before Morris Berman's best-selling book (Harrington xii). Wholeness began with Hans Dreisch's fin-de-siècle revival of vitalism and was elaborated not only in the work of scientists such as Jacob von Uexküll but also in the process philosophy of Henri Bergson and Alfred North Whitehead. Uexküll's observations of how organisms interacted with their environments to create functional circles, or "soap bubbles," later inspired Heidegger's concept of being-in-the-world, Maurice Merleau-Ponty's notion of the intercorporeal self, and, in part, Deleuze's concept of affect.[5]

Uexküll, in turn, had been inspired by Immanuel Kant, who, in the *Critique of Judgment*, had suggested that humans in the mode of aesthetic response interact with the world much as do other animals. The aesthetic subject, as Shaviro describes it, "neither comprehends nor legislates, but only feels and responds . . . this subject is itself *informed* by the world outside, a world that (in the words of Wallace Stevens) 'fills the being before the mind can think'" (*Without Criteria* 13). William Connolly suggests that Kant also saw animal behavior as not simply driven by natural laws but as purposive, like that of humans. An organism, according to Kant, "exists as a natural purpose . . . [it] is both cause and effect, both generating itself and being generated by itself ceaselessly" (249; qtd. in Connolly, *Fragility* 106).

As Anne Harrington explains, Uexküll's concept of a functional circle uniting organism and environment arose out of his close study of these openings in Kant's thought: "It now seemed self-evident to him that every animal, every living thing, far from being a passive product of an external world . . . was also, in fact, an active *creator* of its own 'external reality'" (41). For Uexküll, every living thing, all organisms, human and nonhuman, are *both* products and creators, and reality is the experiencing of this process. In his *Theoretical Biology*, he extends this idea to encompass scientists themselves, arguing that "Nature imparts no doctrines: she merely exhibits changes in her phenomena. We may so employ these changes that they appear as answers to our questions" (ix). The natural world responds to the natural scientists' questions, just as the garden responds to the gardener, creating "doctrine" (theories) and beauty and sustenance. For Whitehead, Uexküll's functional circles coalesce into nature as a system of interrelated and responding attributes, much as it does in Deleuze (see Buchanan 174–76).

Whitehead also cleaves to the second assumption of enchantment ontology, the understanding of change as an arc of becoming: "It is nonsense to conceive of nature as a static fact, even for an instant devoid of duration. There is no nature apart from transition, and there is no transition apart from temporal duration" (MT 152; and see CN 54). Whitehead got the idea of duration from Bergson, who conceived of time as no longer "a mere quantitative measurement" but rather "an inner principle of existence" (Shaviro, *Without Criteria* 76). Bergson argues that existence is a matter of change: things that do not change do not endure. Thinking of time as a neutral succession of instants strung on a cord is an illusion of consciousness, an abstraction from our inner experience of time, which is duration: "The continuous progress of the past which gnaws into the future and which swells as it advances . . . all that we have felt, thought and willed from our earliest infancy is there, leaning over the present which is about to join it, pressing against the portals of consciousness that would fain leave it outside" (4–5). We cannot relive any past moment because we cannot erase our subsequent formative experiences. Thus time is irreversible; each moment "is something new added to what was before" (Bergson 6). What is true of human existence is also true of everything in the universe, he argues, concluding, "The universe *endures*. The more we study the nature of time, the more we shall comprehend that duration means invention, the creation of forms, the continual elaboration of the absolutely new" (Bergson 11). As Shaviro says, with the notion of duration, "becoming is liberated from static being, and the new can be privileged over the eternal" (*Without Criteria* 76). The continual elaboration of the absolutely new—creativity—is the third assumption of enchantment ontology, the positing of change as immanent and inescapable rather than resulting from final purpose or human intention—or from divine intervention.

In general terms, the emergence of novelty can be traced from the dawn of Western thought in Heraclitus and Aristotle through Darwin's vision of the evolution of "endless forms most beautiful and most wonderful" (450) and to complexity theorist Kauffman's observation that "the universe in its persistent becoming is richer than all our dreamings" (I 138). Creativity, Whitehead says, is "the ultimate metaphysical principle . . . the advance from disjunction to conjunction, creating a novel entity other than the entities given in disjunction" (PR 21). As Isabelle Stengers points out, it is not to be confused with "an underlying impulse" (TW 256). Creativity is not a power belonging to entities but the basis of their existence, the process through which they become what they are through affecting and being affected by other entities, as Deleuze suggests and as Benedict de Spinoza proposes: "The striving by which each thing strives to persevere in its being is nothing but the actual essence of the thing" (75). Whitehead says creativity "is the pure notion of the activity conditioned by the objective immortality of the world"; like Aristotle's "matter," "It is that ultimate notion of the highest generality at the base of actuality" (PR 31).

The emergence of novelty from the activity of the world—"the advance from disjunction to conjunction"—is not limited to living entities nor has it been addressed only by philosophers and biologists. Jane Bennett, drawing on Spinoza and Deleuze, emphasizes that "creative vitality" is harbored not only by living organisms but also by material things (*Vibrant* 125n11). Fritjof Capra, in his account of the development of complex systems theory, notes the early and little-known work of the medical researcher, philosopher, and economist Alexander Bogdanov who advanced a general systems theory in 1912–17: "Bogdanov shows how organizational crisis manifests itself as a breakdown of the existing systemic balance and at the same time represents an organizational transition to a new state of balance" (45). Bogdanov's work anticipates physicist Ilya Prigogine and chemist and philosopher Isabelle Stengers's analysis in 1984 of how order arises out of chaos: "In far-from-equilibrium conditions we may have transformation from disorder, from thermal chaos, into order. New dynamic states of matter may originate, states that reflect the interaction of a given system with its surroundings. We have called these new structures *dissipative structures* to emphasize the constructive role of dissipative processes in their construction" (12). Their example of "entities formed by their irreversible interaction with the world" (95) is Michel Serres's analysis of turbulence, which forms through spontaneous, unpredictable deviations in the rate of speed of a river as it encounters rocks or a steeper slope (141).

Prigogine and Stengers credit Whitehead as articulating the basis for their description of the new physics: "Whitehead . . . demonstrated the connection between a philosophy of *relation*—no element of nature is a permanent support for changing relations; each receives its identity from its relations with others—and a philosophy of *innovating becoming*. In the process of its genesis, each existent unifies the multiplicity of the world, since it adds to this multiplicity an extra set of relations. At the creation of each new unity 'the many become one and are increased by one'" (95; quoting Whitehead, PR 21). Whitehead's articulation of permanence and change offers a mode of thinking he calls an adventure of ideas. Understanding becomes a matter of composing entities, events, and meanings, rather than of comprehension. His approach is constructivist not in the sense of being arbitrary or contingent, a "mere construction," but in the sense of "a construction that 'is able to hold,'" that provides a way of addressing a situation that inspires questions "that shed light on features that are important to each situation" (Stengers, TW 18–19). Whitehead says, "Understanding is never a completed static state of mind. It always bears the character of a process of penetration, incomplete and partial" (MT 43). Oppositions or contradictions do not resolve into a higher unity, as in the Hegelian dialectic; rather both participate in "the creative advance into novelty," each as "the instrument of novelty for the other" (Whitehead, PR 349).

Enchantment in Rhetoric and Composition

As I mentioned in the introduction, I am not the only or even the first rhetoric and composition scholar to draw on a version of enchantment ontology to reorient our thinking about writing.⁶ To sharpen the focus of my project, I now consider how it relates to two salient examples of this work: Louise Wetherbee Phelps's *Composition as a Human Science*, and Thomas Rickert's *Ambient Rhetoric*. I am particularly interested in contrasting the focuses and the theoretical frameworks of their projects with mine.

Published in 1988 and drawing on Stephen Pepper's contextualist theory and on quantum physics, *Composition as a Human Science* offers a surprisingly early and percipient presentation of the fundamentals of enchantment ontology: reality is understood as an event including both nature and society and characterized by change; entities are "mutually defining and transactive" (32); observers are "participants in the reality they observe and [also] creators of it" (142). Citing Prigogine and Stengers, Phelps observes, "Within such a system emergent novelty, unpredictable new orderliness, becomes possible" (33). Still, as she addresses her central question of what kind of discipline composition studies is (or should be) and subsidiary questions of what writing is and what teaching writing involves, she limits herself to the social realm of discourse, the dynamism and intersubjectivity of writers and readers co-constructing meanings through the medium of texts. For Phelps, writing begins in the cognitive interactions among writers, readers, and texts rather than in the affective intra-action of entities of all kinds in the world. In line with her project of defining composition as a discipline whose imperatives are "to develop or synthesize organized knowledge about human experiences of writing . . . and, as a praxis based on this knowledge, to cultivate personal growth in literacy and discursive consciousness" (75), she understands contextualism as an "epistemic revolution" in the human "way of knowing" (40).

Phelps's cognitive and epistemic approach follows naturally from her reliance on Paul Ricoeur's version of phenomenology and on Fritjof Capra's and Gary Zukav's treatment of the "new physics" in which, "human consciousness," though "embedded" in the world (23), plays the "creative role . . . in constituting reality as the phenomenal world of everyday experience" (142). She does emphasize that the single subject cannot solipsistically constitute reality; she follows Charles Taylor in describing "social reality as a sphere of communal, experiential meanings, constituted and expressed largely through language" (Phelps 166) that also includes, as Calvin Schrag argues, background experienced totalities—"facts of perception, practical activity, and sociopolitical action [that] are already ways of comprehending the world" (Phelps 23).

The interaction between the observer and this human world—as well as the interaction between writer, reader, and text—is "discursive and hermeneutical in character" (166), a conscious, cognitive, "communicative transaction" (198).

This is a subtle and persuasive characterization of the intersubjective creation of meanings and of social reality in writing. What it does not account for—excusably, given Phelps's focus and theoretical framework—is the creativity of the world beyond human consciousness, a creativity that is not consciously intended but is an important part of the behavior of writing, if not of discourse, which, according to Phelps, is "the act of conscious subjects" (198). The novelty Prigogine and Stengers talk about emerges from complex systems, not from conscious human intentions; it emerges in intra-action, or concrescence, in preconscious material reality, which as Barad claims, cannot be separated from the social world of meanings: "Matter and meaning cannot be dissociated. . . . Mattering is simultaneously a matter of substance and significance" (3).

Speech act theory made a move toward recognizing the preconscious aspects of linguistic interaction, as Ricoeur acknowledges. J. L. Austin posited the notion of the perlocutionary act as an act of affecting the hearer in some way, but it is downplayed in his discussion in favor of the locutionary and illocutionary acts because it is not conventional and often unintentional (103, 107). Ricoeur goes farther: he excludes the perlocutionary act from discourse because of its affective character: "The perlocutionary act is precisely what is the least discourse in discourse. It is the discourse as stimulus. It acts, not by my interlocutor's recognition of my intention, but sort of energetically, by direct influence upon the emotions and the affective dispositions" (Ricoeur 132–33; qtd. in Phelps 151). The difference between illocutionary and perlocutionary acts is the difference between conscious cognitive intentions and preconscious affects, which are contingent intrusions into the ideal of successful communication—and which are an important source of creativity in discourse of all kinds.

While Phelps is concerned with defining the discipline of composition, I begin instead by asking, why does writing matter? I take my direction from Whitehead's process philosophy and Barad's reading of quantum physics,[7] both of which center on the ontological question of what is real rather than the epistemic question of how we come to know reality and both of which are resolutely affective rather than humanist and cognitive in orientation. Thus, instead of seeing writing as the intersubjective creation of meanings that represent or interpret the world, I focus on the affective intra-actions among humans and other entities that precede and create the possibility of the construction of new meanings. I claim that writing matters because it constitutes not just the reality of human experience but creates material entities or phenomena that are added to the entangled cosmos, entities that make a meaningful difference. I contend that it is with this fundamental creativity that writing begins.

The different consequences arising from defining writing as a cognitive communicative transaction and defining it as an affective innovating becoming are illuminated in the contrast between Ricoeur's and Whitehead's treatment of contradictions. Phelps describes Ricoeur's "third way" as a dialectic "strategy for opposing two sides of a polarity in order to discover the limits of each, often through a third term" (190). This dialectic strategy draws attention to the constitutive relation between the sides of the polarity—how structure and event, for example, depend on and limit each other—but Ricoeur's is a dialectic that does not resolve, instead infinitely postponing a synthesis and leaving the terms in a "living tension" (Phelps 190). Thus, for example, Ricoeur comes to an understanding of language as "the 'incessant conversion' of structure and event into one another in discourse" where the third term mediating the polarity is the articulated word, which "makes the sign actual, but also" returns "the event to the system" (Phelps 196). Phelps explains: "The polysemy of the lexicon is nothing but a record of the history by which context makes words mean . . . in speech the word is constantly charged with new use-values, but its possible values at any given moment are constrained (though indefinitely) by existing values laid down or sedimented in the system" (196). For Ricoeur novelty is attributed solely to human consciousness (the writer or speaker) which is constrained by and then assimilated into the linguistic system. Dialectic is an interpretive method that can enable a deep understanding of conflictual relationships—how linguistic structure limits the creativity of the discourse event—but it cannot easily account for the creation of new entities, new words, new meanings.

Whitehead addresses the relation of structure and event as the relation of permanence and change. For Whitehead, opposites are not static poles in conflict, they do not limit each other, nor do they exist in a "living tension" within a third term. They are instead contrasting processes, both participating in "the creative advance into novelty," each as "the instrument of novelty for the other" (PR 349). Permanence is associated with the enjoyment of the completed unity, the many becoming one, and change with the appetition for the potential that increases the many by one. The illusion of opposition between permanence and change (or structure and event) is converted into a contrast, and the process celebrates both appetition and enjoyment in the creation of new entities (PR 348).

Whitehead's treatment of oppositions as contrasts was motivated by an ethical stance that is important in understanding why I argue for writing as fundamentally creative. Stengers explains that Whitehead was "terrified" by the "trick of evil," professional habits (associated with the industrial revolution) that insisted on compliance, that relied on asserting one side of a polarity as true or good and thereby suppressing doubt and curiosity about the possibilities of the other side. His adventure of ideas, his speculative philosophy, was an attempt to transform those stultifying professional habits by mobilizing the possibilities that lurk in the interstices of contradictions (TW 333). Professional habits and creative habits respond to interstices differently, as Stengers explains: professional habits behave like a cement wall while creative habits behave like a wall of dry stones. "Cement rejects the interstices in which the weed grows that will one day crack it open. . . . But the wall of dry stones is not defined against the interstices; the latter belong to it just as much as the stones that make it up. . . . Whitehead's wager is that we can learn [habits] that enable us to celebrate together both the obstinate stones and the interstices that will transform them into preconditions for what will eventually displace them" (TW 274–75). Accepting the interstices as contrasts rather than contradictions enables societies to move beyond insisting on "what everyone knows to be true," and beyond the deadlock of dialectic, whether resolved or in tension, to discovering what could be possible. The trick of evil can only be overcome when "what was felt as intolerable be accepted, canalized, admitted to infect its social environment, making it capable of original responses" (TW 333–34). Instead of understanding the polarities of permanence and change as a living tension, Whitehead's speculative philosophy posits a living process of the creation of mattering and meaning together: the newly created entity—perhaps the path of stepping-stones that the collapsed wall becomes—is material and matters.

In addition to the two imperatives that Phelps assigns to the discipline of composition—to develop organized knowledge about writing, and to cultivate growth in literacy—she notes that "some would add" a third imperative: "to make literacy an effective force for social critique and change" (75). I hold to a revised version of this imperative. Phelps was rightly wary about social critique, for in the 1980s, the "social turn" in composition had spawned practices of "critical pedagogy" that often verged on indoctrination of students into particular ideological positions.[8] Critique is not an effective method for bringing about change. Whitehead's understanding of how contrasts create new possibilities offers instead a positive way that writing can effect change not only in society but in the world.

Published in 2013, twenty-five years after Phelps's book, Thomas Rickert's *Ambient Rhetoric* significantly furthered the increasing interest in enchantment ontology in rhetoric and composition. Though he focuses on rhetoric while I focus more on writing, his theoretical framework is very similar, with differences mainly in emphasis. Rickert's project, as stated in his introduction, is to offer "a more comprehensive understanding" of rhetorical theory and practice as ambient (3). He argues that rhetoric is ontological and material, a human modality of bringing about change through being-in-the-world in a responsive way, just as I argue that writing creates worlds through intra-action in the world. He defines ambient rhetoric as "*a responsive way of revealing the world for others, responding to and put forth through affective, symbolic, and material means, so as to (at least potentially) reattune or otherwise transform how others inhabit the world to an extent that calls for some action*" (162). For Rickert, as for me, rhetoric and writing begin in the first assumption of enchantment ontology: ambience and attunement refer to the "presymbolic persuadability" of the world that entanglement produces.[9] In his focus on responsiveness and transformation, he emphasizes as well the second assumption of enchantment ontology: becoming, or change. But in drawing on Heidegger's notions of dwelling and disclosure (revealing), he does not focus as much on the creation of new entities and new possibilities as I do in drawing on Whitehead's notion of the concrescence of actual entities.

Attunement refers to the specific ways we are entangled in the world: "It indicates one's disposition in the world, how one finds oneself embedded in a situation ... [that] results from the co-responsive and inclusive interaction that brings out both immersion (being with) and specificity (the way of our being there)" (Rickert, *Ambient Rhetoric* 9). To emphasize, attunement is not something we do; we *find* ourselves in, or as Heidegger says, we are thrown into, the world. "We are always already attuned; there are only changes in attunement" (9). Disclosure, or revealing how we are embedded, is also not solely a result of human agency; rather, "Being-in-the-world discloses. That is to say, there is a mutually conditioning amalgam of humans, animals, environment and things that co-responsively produce disclosure, including, necessarily, the forms of disclosure that render these entities as what they are for one another, ... something akin to relational conditioning as yielding being-together-in-the-world" (183). Disclosure reflects the process Haraway calls reciprocal induction, which produces "partners-in-the-making through the active relations of co-shaping" (*When* 208), extended here to that mutually conditioning amalgam that produces the larger social structures of ways of being.

Heidegger argues that dwelling is the human way of being; it discloses "the manner in which we humans *are* on the earth" ("Building" 145). Arguing that dwelling and building derive from the same Old English and High German verb *Bauen*, Heidegger observes that to dwell, which means "to remain, to stay in place," also means to build, and that "both modes of building—building as cultivating . . . and building as the raising up of edifices—are comprised within genuine building, that is dwelling" ("Building" 144–45). Rickert explains that dwelling "conveys active comportments toward the world . . . enacted less as the perpetuation of mastery and control than as a 'letting be' that spares, preserves, and cultivates human beings in the world or, just as important for Heidegger, cultivates world as part of what already entails human being, namely, the manner in which we dwell" (34). He also argues that ambient rhetoric is "integral to our dwelling in the world": "rhetoric is revealing and doing—doing as revealing and revealing as doing" (33). He elaborates: "Instead of being only the most conscious, willed aspects of discursive production, rhetoric reveals and constitutes the informational environment within which we flourish, even as it works in and through both the existent informational situation and the local material environs" (34). He offers the sustainable way of being of the residents of Toronto Island, in Ontario, as an example of dwelling: the island "gathers and is gathered by the fourfold" so that it is "integral to the unique character of dwelling there" (266). The residents "free their island to be what it is precisely by attending to the island as an island," not as a resource or a preserve; this freeing is the comportment that is the essence of dwelling (267–68). Dwelling thus implies an ethical stance that Rickert, in his conclusion, connects with Barad's conclusion that "a delicate tissue of ethicality runs through the marrow of being" (Barad 396).

I, too, argue that writing involves not just conscious, willed discursive production but an active comportment toward the world, a paying attention that is not a matter of mastery, but a letting be, though for me, paying attention is not "a freeing to let something be what it is" (268) but rather a freeing to let something become what it can become in intra-action. And I, too, follow Barad in arguing that entanglement in the world bestows an ethical onus. Rickert quotes from the final paragraph of *Meeting the Universe Halfway* that begins with the sentence I quoted above, but he elides from Barad's penultimate sentence something that distinguishes her stance from Heidegger's. Rickert's quotation ends: "Meeting each moment . . . is an ethical call" (271). The full sentence reads as follows: "Meeting each moment, being alive to the possibilities of becoming, is an ethical call, an invitation that is written into the very matter of all being and becoming" (396). Where Heidegger focuses on dwelling as an ethical way of being, as "genuine building," Barad focuses on responding to the possibilities of becoming.

Rickert addresses this difference in his conclusion, acknowledging that in his emphasis on dwelling as preserving and cultivating places as "material-social-hermeneutic" ecologies, he may have seemed to be ignoring a "countercurrent" of "movement and change, hybridity and otherness" (272). He argues:

> It is important to balance an attendance to what is present with an attendance to what withdraws and to what the future brings so that we are open to whatever further disclosive possibilities may become manifest.... We should seek neither static being nor endless becoming but the resting of both trajectories within rhetoricity itself. In other words, we need to understand disclosure as something always ongoing and transforming in accordance with the play of being-in-the-world, attuned simultaneously to what matters to us now while mindful that we cannot take reality for the simple presence of beings as they seem. (280)

His argument for balancing attendance to what is present with attendance to what withdraws would seem to accord well with Whitehead's reconfiguring of the contradiction of permanence and change into a process of concrescence that celebrates both enjoyment and appetition in the creation of new entities, especially as it aligns with Whitehead's fear of the tyranny of "what everyone knows to be true." But Heidegger's notion of revealing as the play of disclosure and withdrawal remains focused on the essence of things, their Being, and not on the creativity arising from intra-action. While disclosure frees something to be what it is, concrescence creates new entities, new possibilities.

In his lengthy consideration of disclosure in *Parmenides*, Heidegger explains that disclosure is not simply the opposite of concealment: "Instead, the dis-closure [Ent-*bergen*] is at the same time an en-closure [*Ent*-bergen], just like dis-semination, which is not opposed to the seed, or like in-flaming [*Entflammen*], which does not eliminate the flame [*Flamme*] but *brings it into its essence*" (133; emphasis added). Disclosure doesn't simply reveal what was hidden; it brings it fully into active being, as in the dissemination of seed. The enclosure in which a being attains to Being is the open, a space in which humans see the truth of Being: "Because he has the word, man, and he alone, is the being that looks into the open and sees the open in the sense of αληθες [truth]" (155). Rickert allows that, as Heidegger argues, animals cannot get a sense of being as Being, but he argues that they can practice rhetoric "in activities that are, in some fashion corresponding to crowlike ways of disclosure" and thus that "disclosure is worldly" (173, 281). But what, then, can be meant by saying disclosure frees something to be what it is?

Rickert refers to Barad's reading of Niels Bohr, which demonstrates that "what we call physical reality is inseparable from the measuring or observational apparatus that renders something as what it is," and says, "Disclosure is itself ontological, and there are no simple, determinate, and preexisting objects—or *concepts*—independent of observation" (283). But his conclusion to this line of thought—"complex dances of mutual interaction are not aftereffects of already existing objects but rather the necessary precondition for the particular 'look' and 'stand' of an object" (283)—is not quite the position Barad is arguing for.

When Barad argues that "the primary ontological unit is not independent objects with inherent boundaries and properties but rather *phenomena*" (139), she is not concerned with objects; she is intent on shifting attention from objects to the phenomena through which material articulations of the world (things, beings, concepts) come to matter. This is the difference she draws between interactions and intra-actions: "*Phenomena are the ontological inseparability/entanglement of intra-acting 'agencies'*" through which "particular concepts (that is, particular material articulations of the world) become meaningful" (139). She elaborates: "*phenomena are differential patterns of mattering* ('diffraction patterns') produced through complex agential intra-actions of multiple material-discursive practices or apparatuses of bodily production, where *apparatuses are not merely observing instruments but boundary drawing practices—specific material (re)configurings of the world—which come to matter*. These causal intra-actions need not involve humans" (140). She concludes: "The world is an open process of mattering through which mattering itself acquires meaning and form through the realization of different agential possibilities" (141). In Barad's account, intra-action creates new meaningful articulations; meanings are not disclosed from the hidden depths of what an object is, from an object's fulsomeness, what Graham Harman calls its "grand dark abundance" (125; qtd. in Rickert, *Ambient Rhetoric* 200), or revealed from depths harbored by the world (Rickert, *Ambient Rhetoric* 213). They are not aspects of an essential entity that were withdrawn from presence, as Rickert implies in his analysis of the community of Toronto Island: "The island is never brought fully to presence, since part of it withdraws, and that withdrawal is also important" (260).

Also thinking in part with the quantum theory of Niels Bohr, Whitehead, too, emphasizes how intra-action produces new entities in an ongoing way. Although earlier I said that Whitehead's notion of concrescence was somewhat like Heidegger's notion of the fourfold, there is a difference. While in the fourfold, aspects of things come to presence, concrescence is instead the intra-active "production of novel togetherness" (PR 21). Whitehead asserts, "*How* an actual entity *becomes* constitutes *what* that actual entity *is*. . . . Its 'being' is constituted by its 'becoming'" (PR 23). It creates itself by means of its prehensions of other entities—"this self-functioning is the real internal constitution of an actual entity" (PR 25)—a process that is characterized as a decision: Stengers says, it "'decides for itself': thus, and not otherwise" (TW 263). Whitehead says that "decision" "is used in its root sense of a 'cutting off,'" a separation of what matters from what does not, "an activity procuring limitation" (PR 42–43), in other words, what Barad calls a boundary drawing practice. "The satisfied actual entity embodies a determinate attitude of 'yes' or 'no'" (PR 212). This is the phase in concrescence of the enjoyment of the completed unity, but it is followed again by appetition, as the one rejoins the many that it left. "The real internal constitution of an actual entity progressively constitutes a decision conditioning the creativity which transcends that actuality" (PR 43).[10]

Like Barad, Whitehead thus emphasizes the phenomenon of becoming over being, referring to actual entities also as "actual occasions" (PR 22) or "events" (SMW 194) that arise as reconfigurings of the world. Also like Barad, he emphasizes that what is created is a new mattering or value: an event is "the realization of a definite shape of value . . . a matter of fact which by reason of its limitation is a value for itself; but by reason of its very nature requires the whole universe in order to be itself" (SMW 194). Entities have value and meaning in themselves, but their values and meanings arise from their relations to the whole universe.

The shift from focusing on objects to focusing on phenomena or events of becoming is crucial to understanding "the complex dances of interaction"—or rather of intra-action—that Rickert refers to. Rickert's position is not as resolutely focused on things as Harman's is, but he still risks the quandary Harman falls into of not being able to account for how objects relate to one another, or "touch"; in other words, how they change. In a debate with Latour at the London School of Economics, Harman says, "Things are not just placed in vacuum-sealed bubbles that never touch. They do touch. And that's what has to be explained. Given that an object by analysis reveals that it should be something that withdraws from all relations (at least by my analysis) then you just have to figure out that there is this paradox. Because, on the one hand, objects seem like they should be isolated, and yet relations and events do occur" (Latour et al., *Prince* 70). Latour's answer is simple: "Things-in-themselves are actually things that you reach, which is always a paradox" (*Prince* 71). Earlier in the debate, Latour says he is puzzled by how Harman seems to understand Latour's position on this so well in the first part of *Prince of Networks* (Harman's book about Latour) but in the second part shoehorns it "into a problem which involves an alternative between a thing that would be made of its relations and a thing that would be made of its inner intimacy" (43–44). Latour follows Whitehead in rejecting both options: "For me it's precisely because of the irreducible singularity (which you sometimes call the inner kernel of things) that they have to be translated without ever emptying their kernel" (43). For Latour as for Whitehead the irreducible singularity of an object is the event of its actual occasion, which is continually being translated in its trajectory of becoming. Things are inexhaustible because they are always becoming something else in intra-action. They are created *through* relations, but they do not consist only *of* relations. Rickert emphasizes the need to be "open to whatever further disclosive possibilities may become manifest" (*Ambient Rhetoric* 280), but Heidegger's emphasis on the Being of entities cannot account for how those possibilities arise. Whitehead's concept of the propositions that arise in concrescence enables him to articulate a process of positive change.[11]

To sum up how my project differs from Rickert's, I suggest revising his definition of ambient rhetoric into a definition of enchanted writing: "Enchanted writing *is a responsive and responsible way of* creating [not *revealing*] *the world through intra-action* [not *for others*], *responding to and put forth through affective, symbolic, and material means, so as to (at least potentially)* invite others to create new possibilities through entertaining propositions [not *reattune or otherwise transform how others inhabit the world*] that may inspire new ways of acting [not *to an extent that calls for some action*]." Rickert and I agree that enchantment ontology draws attention to how rhetoric and writing arise from affective entanglement in the world, but while he focuses on affective persuasion, I focus on a form of persuasion that creates new entities and new possibilities. Ambient rhetoric focuses on reattuning others in order to persuade them to inhabit the world differently, while enchanted writing focuses on how interlocutors create new meaningful entities through intra-action. Ambient rhetoric reattunes others as a call for action, while enchanted writing invites others to participate in creating new futures.

In line with this difference, I argue in chapter 6 for rethinking persuasion as a "polite modification of dreams," an action that "does not aim at awakening, leaving the cave. It is itself a dream, a storytelling: to learn 'inside' the Platonic cave, together with those who live and argue within it. Not in the hope that the false appearances will gradually yield their secrets, but in the hope that these 'appearances,' if they are appreciated in their affirmative importance, might be articulated into fabulous contrasts" (Stengers, TW 516). Storytelling, as I said earlier, offers a path for others to follow. It is polite in that it respects the differences of others "insofar as their habits constitute a world for them" (TW 517). Politeness is not to be confused with tolerance, as Stengers insists: "Civilized conversation, to speak with Richard Rorty" avoids serious conflict by indulging "in well-bred—that is, without consequence—language games," renouncing "everything that might compromise their belonging to the same world" (TW 513). Polite persuasion, instead, involves habits of paying attention and being open to the world in order to celebrate differences as contrasts that can inspire new ideas and ways of being in the world.

Habits

In the introduction I argued that writing well is making things that are meaningful to and have important effects on ourselves and others of all kinds. Writing well requires developing habits as active dispositions to pay due attention to the world, reaching out to grasp the world in a way that still lets beings and entities become through their own decisions. Good writing habits require attunement, an active prehension of other entities that enables writers to create and entertain propositions—"tales that might be told"—that are meaningful and matter to other entities. They are serial practices that innovate responses—written and otherwise—in the specific ecologies in which beings are entangled.

This understanding of habits departs rather a lot from the common usage of "habit" as Joe Sachs explains in the introduction to his translation of Aristotle's *Nicomachean Ethics*. He complains of the common translation of *hexis* as "habit": "Every implication of the English word is wrong" (xii), he says. "Habitual action need not be chosen knowingly, and it does not have a flexible constancy but a mindless uniformity . . . [it is] only a passive and mechanical response to a superficial sameness in outer circumstances" (xiii–xiv). Aristotle, he claims, is not talking about "habit—*ethos* in Greek—but character: êthos" (xiv). Aristotle does relate habit and character in this way: "Excellence in character comes into being as a consequence of habit, on account of which it even gets its name by small inflection from habit" (*Nicomachean* 21–22). Sachs cautions that by good character Aristotle does not mean "a set of socially approved habits," nor simply "a pre-existent natural capacity"—what is often conceived of as a person's true nature. The "crucial and necessary factor that brings a virtue into being . . . is the deliberate contribution of the person who comes to have it, the *hexis*" (*Nicomachean* 22n). Aristotle says, "The virtues come to be present neither by nature nor contrary to nature, but in us who are of such a nature to take them on, and to be brought to completion in them by means of habit" (*Nicomachean* 22). Sachs notes that Aristotle allows that "habituation has to work on a natural capacity already present" (*Nicomachean* 47n), but "we decisively determine the *hexeis* that come to be ourselves . . . *hexis* . . . [is] an active condition, a way in which we hold ourselves, having taken hold deliberately of the feelings and dispositions that are in us merely passively" (*Nicomachean* ix).

What Aristotle means by habit here—that it is a being at work—is apparent as he describes the process of bringing virtues to completion: "We do take on virtues by first being at work in them . . . people become, say housebuilders by building houses or harpists by playing the harp. So too, we become just by doing things that are just" (*Nicomachean* 22). Sachs notes that "being at work," *hexis*, derives from the verb *echein*, which means "to have something . . . or to be something in an enduring and active way," and thus *hexis* is "an active having-and-holding that depends upon the effort of concentrating or paying attention" (*Nicomachean* xii). He argues that Aristotle believes "that we are only open to the world" by being in an active state, "by the effort of holding ourselves ready" (*Nicomachean* xii).

When Kimmerer recognized the plantain on the trail, which she had not noticed when she passed this way earlier, as an "old friend," she was open to the world and actively paying attention. Her recognition was "not intellectual," not conscious, but it was active, a being-at work, an awareness of "an object of peculiar type with its own particular ingression into nature" (Whitehead, CN 155). As an indigenous woman and a botanist, she habitually holds herself ready to pay attention to particular entities in the world which she sees as her relatives: her "Grandmother Sitka," her "old friend" the plantain," and her "new neighbors—giant firs, sword ferns, and salal" (213). She names the plants she encounters, for "names are the way we humans build relationships" (208). Encountering plants who are strangers, she turns off her "science mind and names them with a Nanabozho mind . . . not *Picea sitchensis* but *strong arms covered in moss*" (208) in order to focus on "looking even closer" to see if she has "gotten it right," just as Nanabozho was instructed to "learn the names of all the beings . . . to discern their true names" (208). She recognizes the plantain with both her people's name for it, "White Man's Footstep," and its scientific name, *Plantago major*, both of which refer to its nomadic habit. The situation and the events surrounding the encounter between Kimmerer and the plantain also condition her felt recognition of the plantain as nonnative. Here in a Pacific Coast forest, both she and the plantain are strangers, immigrants like Nanabozho, who was "the last of all beings to be created" (205).[12]

The emergence of the plantain as an immigrant is an "outcome of the habit of experience," which is, Whitehead observes, common to all "complex living organisms" as a condition for their survival (CN 155–56). Habits of experience involve an active comportment toward the world, not a "a passive and mechanical response," but an awareness of something that matters in a particular way. Such an awareness is not necessarily conscious, though it is available to consciousness, and not dominantly cognitive but affective: it is, as I said, a felt recognition. Stengers instances a rabbit turning its head toward a noise as aware that the noise may have an important meaning and bolting when the noise is revealed as "a predator" (TW 31). She comments that a "habitual gesture" like this "does not 'lack' anything, but it is different from a conscious gesture" in that it "translates other urgencies [such as survival] than those, presupposing language, of having to account for what one 'means'" (TW 349). Habits of experience also are not mindlessly uniform but exhibit the flexible constancy that Sachs sees in *hexeis*. Stengers says "the goal is not to penetrate" the experiences of other human beings or animals "but to think on the basis of the 'habits' that enable us to say 'a rabbit' or 'a sociologist,' that is, to evoke a style of experience or adventure that is endowed with a certain stability" (TW 26). Kimmerer does not mindlessly register the presence of a plantain, but reaches out to grasp the ingression of a particular plantain into a specific experience located in a specific place and chain of events.

Habits of experience are wagers concerning the world; they testify to the existence of something in the world: "The existence of a mountain climber testifies to the fact that in general, the side of a mountain offers reliable footholds" (TW 88). The habit of mountain climbing depends on mountains being the kind of thing that offers footholds to humans, just as the habit of botanizing testifies to the existence of various plants with differing effects on other beings. Habits of experience validate perceptions of the world as direct experiences, not as representations constructed in the mind. Whitehead argues that recognition of objects is a "non-intellectual relation of sense-awareness which connects the mind with a factor of nature without passage" (CN 143). As Latour says, things-in-themselves are actually things that you reach. Whitehead does refer to this connection as a disclosure: "In sense perception nature is disclosed as a complex of entities whose mutual relations are expressible in thought without reference to mind" (CN 4–5). But as Stengers explains, he does not mean by it that the goal of paying due attention "is to experience something hidden, latent, and implicit, which would be more 'true,' in one way or another, than our usual perceptions" (TW 46). Instead, she says, for Whitehead, "The goal is never to go 'beyond' usual experience but to transform it, to make what usually 'goes without saying' matter" (TW 46). What matters does not precede the encounter; it is a new entity that emerges in the encounter.

Kimmerer's recognition of the plantain as an immigrant is a transformation of it into something that matters. As Whitehead says, "Recognition is that relation of mind to nature which provides the material for the intellectual activity" (CN 143). The encounter has produced what he calls a proposition. Propositions are not verbal statements, but rather are experienced, or entertained, as a feeling of a break in continuity. On seeing the plantain, which her focus on her "new neighbors" had prevented her from noticing before, Kimmerer says, "I am stopped in my tracks" (213). Whitehead says, "The primary mode of realization of a proposition in an actual entity is not by judgment, but by entertainment. A proposition is entertained when it is admitted into feeling. Horror, relief, purpose, are primarily feelings involving the entertainment of propositions" (PR 188). He emphasizes that entertainment of propositions results not in a change in the look and stand of an object, but a new entity: "When a non-conformal proposition is admitted into feeling . . . a novelty has emerged into creation . . . it is new, a new type of individual, and not merely a new intensity of feeling" (PR 187). Propositions are "tales that perhaps might be told about particular actualities" (PR 256). Stengers says, "As a lure—'what might be' said, or felt, about particular actual entities—[a proposition] raises a question" (TW 413).

Propositions are entertained not only by human beings but also by other beings, though, as with Heidegger, language does play a role in distinguishing how humans entertain propositions. Stengers explains that language does not enable humans to judge what is objectively true, "to manipulate the pros and cons" logically using descriptive statements; instead language elaborates propositions into a speculative adventure: "Speculative language should be able to induce not the reaction of a rabbit becoming aware that this grey shade is what we call a wolf, that it is a convinced 'it matters!' but a speculative adventure entailing questions such as 'how does it matter?' 'does it really matter?' 'what if I accepted that it does not matter?' 'how did it come to matter?' unrealized ideals then shaping our experiences" ("Whitehead's Account" 54). Rabbits entertain propositions as a feeling; they are aware of the event and its meaning, but they do not proceed to speculate about it. Speculation marks the entrance of conscious thought into the entertainment of propositions.

As she thinks about how the plantain matters, Kimmerer draws on other preceding events in her walk. She had been remembering that when Nanabozho arrived, he had "many paths to follow, made by all those whose home this already was" (206) and that they would be his teachers in ways "to become native to his new home" (207). But she notes that Nanabozho's instructions have been forgotten, and she asks, "What happens when we truly become native to place, when we finally make a home? What are the stories that lead the way?" (207). Comparing what she knows of the habits of plantain to those of other immigrants, both human colonizers and plant species from abroad, "that do *not* make themselves welcome on a new continent" (214), she realizes that plantain, by becoming "so well integrated," is now naturalized, just as are human immigrants when they become citizens. Her good habits of actively paying attention and of being open to the teachings of other entities in the world have led her to a speculative adventure that results in a new response. Casey Boyle observes that in the serial practice of habits "we do not withdraw a prior experience to fit with an event but are habituated by having had to resolve related events and become disposed toward composing fitting responses" (545). Habits arise in and are perpetuated and elaborated in ongoing experience.

Good habits don't truly become a part of us, as Aristotle says, until they are put in action and become, well, habitual. Ingrained practices (or habits) are, as Whitehead says, "the way the mind reacts to the appropriate stimulus in the form of illustrative circumstances" (AE 27); they are responsive to the specifics of a situation and are thus material behaviors. Just as Aristotle argues that one must knowingly choose *hexeis* "being in a stable condition and not able to be moved all the way out of it" (26), William James argues that one acquires habits through ongoing attention and effort to convert feelings and dispositions into action: "A tendency to act only becomes effectively ingrained in us in proportion to the uninterrupted frequency with which the actions actually occur, and the brain 'grows' to their use" (125). He urges us to "*Keep the faculty of effort alive in you by a little gratuitous exercise every day*" (126). Sachs observes that for Aristotle, a "crucial necessary factor that brings a virtue into being . . . is the deliberate contribution of the person who comes to have it" (*Nicomachean* 22n). Aristotle thus distinguishes habits from feelings and predispositions; habits are actions, actions that are knowingly chosen and held to for their own sake (*Nicomachean* 26–28). This ongoing effort is as crucial in doing good writing as it is in bringing virtue into being. Good writers need to not only choose but also enact and hold to habits that create speculative adventures.

Whitehead introduces habits of experience to emphasize that sense-awareness—"the red glow of the sunset"—is an intra-action within nature, not something distinct from what we know about nature—"the molecules and electric waves" that account for the phenomenon. Actively attending to the direct felt experience of the world enables humans to participate in "the creative advance" of nature (MT 151). His objection to "professional habits" was that by valuing abstractions over and to the exclusion of concrete facts, they obstructed creativity: "professionalised knowledge . . . produces minds in a groove . . . to be mentally in a groove is to live in contemplating a given set of abstractions. . . . Thus in the modern world, the celibacy of the medieval learned class has been replaced by a celibacy of the intellect which is divorced from the concrete contemplation of the complete facts" (SMW 197). He refers to a well-known rhyme about the Master of Trinity College, Cambridge—I am Master of this College / And what I know not / Is not knowledge—as an example of what leads to the "trick of evil" discussed earlier. "This attitude is always prevalent in the learned world. It sterilizes imaginative thought, and thereby blocks progress" (MT 43). Writing in the 1920s in *Science and the Modern World* and *The Aims of Education*, Whitehead was particularly concerned about how this attitude permeated educational practice and restricted social progress, arguing that the successes of rationalism in western European thought had revealed limitations that "call for a renewed exercise of the creative imagination" (SMW 208).

He asserts that "the central problem of all education" is "the problem of keeping knowledge alive, of preventing it from becoming inert" (AE 5). What students most need to discover is that abstractions are useful only to the extent that they help one understand one's experience, "that stream of events which pours through . . . life" (AE 2). Utilizing an abstraction means "relating it to that stream, compounded of sense perceptions, feelings, hopes, desires, and of mental activities adjusting thought to thought, which forms our life," and when abstractions are not utilized in this way, they are "positively harmful" (AE 3). Stengers comments that this is how teaching "vivid" ideas differs from teaching "dead" ideas, "the former setting the students' minds in motion, and the latter being synonyms for indoctrination and passivity" (TW 141). Being at work, actively paying due attention to the concrete facts of experience, allows students to create new entities through entertaining propositions that set their minds in motion.

Boyle also argues that habits build up capacities for taking hold of situations, of responding to the world in ways that are useful. Repetition of practices, he argues, does not increase individuals' agency but rather their capacity, a term that, "with its etymological connections to taking hold," shifts "from abilities inherent to humans to the ecology of entanglements between entities" (Stormer and McGreavy 5; qtd. in Boyle 545).[13] Boyle also suggests that serial practices thus imply an ethic: "A serial practice is not simply a choice of a particular style but is the adoption of a style of engagement, an ethic in developing capacities for becoming affected by others as much as affecting others" (548). Habits of paying due attention to events and entertaining propositions mark the adoption of this style of engagement. They are practices of *hexis*, an active having-and-holding that depends on paying attention and that through the effort of holding oneself ready enables one to be open to the world. This style of engagement suggests a kind of ethic that, as Boyle says, "does not impose moral ideas but works within a given situation to develop *good practices*" (548)—and, I would say, good habits of writing.

Stengers observes that Whitehead follows James in affirming both "the creator's trust and the power of habit": "Educators must trust the creative character of what they are charged with transmitting, and, although they are concerned with the difference between good and bad habits, they cannot denounce habit as such" (TW 139). Habits are built up of experiences that have succeeded in providing specific footholds and their importance must be respected: "Others' dreams, like yours, are created according to the means of their own adventure" (TW 518). New "good" habits do not drive out old "bad" ones; instead they coexist, expanding the kinds of footholds in the world. Instancing physicists who judge a poet's description of a sunset as subjective, Stengers explains: "What is aimed at by an 'ethical modification,' in this case, is not 'modified' physicists, having become able to reconcile what has bifurcated. It is simply physicists capable of celebrating the adventure they inherit in its singularity, without turning the 'physical reality' of the electromagnetic waves emitted by the sun into 'the' objective version, in opposition to which all other versions must be defined . . . their 'ethics' remain indeed those of physicists. . . . They have 'simply' acquired the good habit of dreams that do not turn them into the thinking head of humanity" (TW 515–16). Thus when Kimmerer acquired the habits that made her a botanist, she was not required to nor did she relinquish the ethical habits that made her indigenous. Her habits were not contradictory but contrasting; both enabled her hold. She imagines Nanabozho and Linneaus walking together in a forest, discussing the names for things: "They're both so enthusiastic, pointing out the beautiful leaf shapes, the incomparable flowers . . . Linneaus lends Nanabozho his magnifying glass so he can see the tiny floral parts. Nanabozho gives Linneaus a song so he can see their spirits" (209). Stengers says, "The question is no longer of knowing 'who is right,' but of what each one of them has 'done' with the vivid experience that nourished them all" (TW 141).

The good habits of writing I offer in chapters 3, 5, and 7 are offered as ethical in this sense. They are habits of addressing difference, paying attention to differences, being open to them, accepting them as engendering propositions that can lead to new possibilities. They do not instruct writers in how to respond, just to accept the test constituted by the encounter with the other. Like virtues, they do value particular behaviors, or actions, but, like acting justly, they are very short on specifics. As with acting justly, there are some people who do not believe in the importance of paying attention to others, but I think it is difficult to find a society or culture that doesn't in some sense see it as a good thing.

I also offer these habits not as replacements but as supplements to other habits of good writing, such as those in the *Framework for Success in Postsecondary Writing*. I do, however, consider the habits I offer as crucial in doing writing that testifies to the importance of our intra-actions in an entangled world and to our accountability for how we respond. They are habits as *hexeis* that actively pay due attention to experience and mobilize possibilities by letting entities be what they are becoming and letting them show what they can do.

2

Writing as Entangled

While enchanted ontology developed throughout the twentieth century and intensified in the work of scholars across humanistic and scientific disciplines in the twenty-first century, discussions about writing by scholars, policymakers, and the lay public for the most part remained firmly fixed in the Enlightenment. In 2003 the National Commission on Writing emphasized that "writing, properly understood, is thought on paper . . . [and] also thought on screen." They went on to argue that "writing is best understood as a complex intellectual activity that requires students to stretch their minds, sharpen their analytical abilities, and make valid and accurate distinctions" (13). The position they were arguing against here is the common assumption that writing is merely the transcription of thought, that a writer first thinks something up and then writes it down, bringing the transcendent mind into the material world. The process movement in the teaching of writing in the 1960s had expanded the realm of writing to include the generation of thought on paper (or reexpanded the realm, as invention had been part of classical rhetoric). Today, most writers—and most writing teachers—would agree that writing is a complex cognitive activity. But most also still cling to the Cartesian understanding of thinking as the activity of a rational individual mind, a mind separate from the body, emotions, and the world outside. As a writer of a letter to the editor of my hometown newspaper lamented, "We have become the victims of the emphasis on the body, i.e. feelings, emotions, etc. with little attention to our minds. But our mind is what makes us human, while the adaptation of technology to express ourselves dehumanizes us in a serious way" (Jegstrup).

From the beginning of Western philosophy, attempts have been made to distinguish humans from all other forms of life and especially from animals. Although many abilities or characteristics have been adduced as the source of human exceptionalism—Jacques Derrida lists "speech, reason, experience of death, mourning, culture, institutions, technics, clothing, lying, pretense of pretense, covering of tracks, gift, laughter, crying, respect, etc.—. . . *all of that*" (*Animal* 135)—the most prevalent of these have been language, technology, and cognition in the sense of rational conscious thought. Kenneth Burke says that humans are "symbol-using" animals (*Language* 3); Andy Clark says that humans are "natural-born cyborgs." But exceptionalism, especially as furthered by language and technology, has come to be seen as a not-so-progressive project. Max Horkheimer and Theodor Adorno delineated how language and technology as enabling humans to master nature (and their fear of the unknown) paradoxically led to human subjectification to the word and the technical apparatus as well as creating an alienated self: "The identical 'I' of Homer could be seen as primarily the result of a mastery of nature carried out within the individual. This new self trembles within its thing-self—a body—once the heart has been rebuked" (48n). Humans came to distrust language, which "must discard the claim to be like . . . [and] to know" nature (18), and to fear technology: "Men expect that the world . . . will be set on fire by a totality which they themselves are and over which they have no control" (29). In short, the disenchantment of nature—the separation of humans from other animals (and other entities) as masters of nature through rational thought, language, and technology—was destructive both to ourselves and to the world: Horkheimer and Adorno's postulate that "the fully enlightened earth radiates disaster triumphant" (3) is echoed, more subtly, in Heidegger's notion of Enframing, and less subtly in popular culture (for example, the *Terminator* films)—and in popular opinion, as in the letter to the editor I quoted above, which argued that "technology is a prosthesis, meaning that we are no longer entirely human" and that "the impact of science, i.e. technology, on education" will cause us "to lose that which makes us human" (Jegstrup).

Rational conscious thought, language, and technology are all involved in writing, but they do not account for what is most important about writing nor does possessing them distinguish humans from other living beings. By saying humans are the animal who writes, I want to emphasize that humans are animals and that writing is a behavior very like other animal behaviors—and increasingly like "smart" technologies. One effect of the commitment to a cosmos that entangles human and nonhuman beings is that humans are placed firmly back among everything else in the world as embodied and enworlded.[1] As Glen Mazis says, "Our embodiment, which is an ongoing fluid meshing with things, people, and events around us, is the way into the world, and the way of having a world, and the primary way of being human or animal" (39). I argue that the behavior of writing springs from this ongoing fluid meshing, from entanglement in the world. Katherine Hayles says that "embodiment is contextual, enmeshed within the specifics of place, time, physiology, and culture, which together compose enactment" (*How* 196). Humans and other beings intra-act in many ways—ways that the Enlightenment taught us to think of as separate: action, feeling, cognition—and all are enactions, inextricably mental and physical, all having material effects in the world.

Studies in cognitive ethology, cybernetics, and neurology have undermined the belief that writing is merely thought on paper, thought on screen. We know that the thinking involved in writing is not only not limited to rational conscious thought but is as much a behavior as any action or feeling. We think with our bodies—and not just with our brains—and everything we make, from texts to technologies, are material entities entangled in one reality. Nor is thinking a process internal to individual organisms. We think with others (humans and nonhumans) in intra-acting with them: with axes as we chop wood, with GPS as we try to find our way, with border collies as we herd sheep—and with the sheep too. Like all other animals, humans spin out their relations and weave them into the meshwork of their existence (Ingold, M); through their characteristic modes of perception, action, and interaction, they shape the *Umwelts* they inhabit (Uexküll, *Foray*). As Hayles also says, "Embodiment is the specific instantiation generated from the noise of difference" (*How* 196). Like all other beings, we create our worlds—and ourselves—through the entanglements of our living and of our writing.

From Axes to Scanning Tunneling Microscopes

Gregory Bateson observes that thinking about thinking in this way is difficult as it requires us to revise who we think we are and how we relate to other beings. He says that he knows intellectually that when, for example, he cuts down a tree, "a total system, tree-eyes-brain-muscles-axe-stroke-tree" is involved in the process, and this total extended system "has the characteristics of immanent mind" (317). In such distributed cognitive systems, agents and objects and tools blur together, but still, for Western people, the belief in a delimited self and object is strong: "*I* don't know how to think that way . . . If I am cutting down a tree, I still think 'Gregory Bateson' is cutting down the tree" (462). Margaret Syverson reacted similarly when she took Edwin Hutchins's courses on distributed cognition: "Suddenly thinking was revealed as not simply a matter of logical processing neatly managed by a brain in splendid isolation but as a complex ensemble of activities and interactions among brains, hands, eyes, ears, other people, and an astonishing variety of structures in the environment, from airplane cockpits to cereal boxes to institutions" (xiv). Bruno Latour, in his review of Hutchins's book *Cognition in the Wild*, was more blunt: the central point of the study, he says, is that "cognition has nothing to do with minds nor individuals" ("Cogito" 56). He adds that Hutchins might have gone on to apply this analysis not only to "mere" navigation processes but as well to the discoveries of "higher minds" like Galileo and Mercator, concluding: "Laboratories think, communities discover, disciplines progress, instruments see, not individual minds ("Cogito" 61). The work in distributed cognition, which I will discuss further below, highlights the entanglement of cognitive processes in humans, other beings, and technologies, and it also suggests that focusing on individual entities cannot account for the generation of ideas, discoveries—or of writing. As noted in chapter 1, entanglement necessitates focusing on the intra-actions that comprise phenomena and on thinking and writing as enactments.

Karen Barad argues, "Knowing is not a play of ideas within the mind of a Cartesian subject that stands outside the physical world the subject seeks to know . . . knowing is a physical practice of engagement" (342). Like Bateson, she emphasizes the magnitude of the shift in thinking about thinking required, in her case, by the implications of Niels Bohr's interpretation of quantum physics: "It may not be too much of an exaggeration to say that every aspect of how we understand the world, including ourselves, is changed" (23). Barad avers that boundaries and properties of entities—selves, objects, concepts—do not precede intra-actions but are produced in phenomena by "agential cuts" that create meaningful material articulations. Objects do not exist outside of intra-actions, and in different intra-actions they have different boundaries and properties. Take the blind person's stick, a popular meme in such discussions. Bateson notes how the stick confuses "the localization and boundaries of the self": "Where does the blind man's self begin? At the tip of the stick? At the handle of the stick?" (318). Maurice Merleau-Ponty used the same example to explain how instruments become incorporated into bodies in use (143), and Bohr used it to explain how subject-object boundaries shift depending on how someone intra-acts with the stick: "When the stick is held loosely, it appears to the sense of touch to be an object. When, however, it is held firmly, . . . the impression of touch becomes immediately localized at the point where the stick is touching the body under investigation" (99; quoted in Barad 154). It's important to remember that a stick is never just a stick; it is never "outside" entanglements, which do not have to include humans.[2]

Barad offers a more complex example of how intra-actions enact meaningful cuts in reality as she discusses the use of a scanning tunneling microscope (STM) to image and move single atoms.[3] As Don Eigler, a physicist at IBM's Almaden Research Center, moves a single atom of gadolinium, the STM alternates between being an instrument of moving and one of scanning: the STM scans a surface for the gadolinium atom, then lowers its tip, consisting of a single atom, closer to the surface and "picks up" the gadolinium atom by bonding with it. The STM is then raised and moves the atom to a new location, drops it, and then pulls back and scans the surface to verify that the atom has moved. The gadolinium atom is alternately a part of the surface being scanned and part of the STM tip as it is being moved. And in moving the atom with the STM, Eigler becomes a nanotechnologist, just as Donna Haraway and Cayenne become partners-in-the-making in their intra-action in agility training. Barad observes, "The key . . . is not representing, but intervening; not simply the imaging of atoms, but the ability to manipulate them" (356). Through this intra-action, the atom becomes real: not just a concept or an image, but something that has through this procedure demonstrably been moved. It has taken on the meaning of a movable.

Barad emphasizes that instruments like the STM are not to be considered merely as tools, "human-constructed laboratory instruments," but rather are "specific material configurations (dynamic reconfigurings) of the world that play a role in the production of phenomena" (335). Bohr, too, like Whitehead (who maybe learned it from Bohr) believes that *"we are a part of that nature that we seek to understand"* (Barad 26). Specific dynamic material configurations—material practices—do not bridge a "gap" between human concepts and the world; they produce real phenomena. Barad extends Bohr's analysis to discursive practices as also material configurations, practices that *"causally* produce specific material phenomena" that matter, both materially and meaningfully. "Material-discursive practices" dynamically enact cuts that determine "boundaries, properties, and meanings" (335). These practices are not linguistic, and "meaning is not a human-based notion; rather, meaning is an ongoing performance of the world in its differential intelligibility . . . a matter of differential responsiveness, as performatively articulated and accountable, to what matters" (335). The final scan that verifies that the atom has been moved is what Barad means by accountability. Material practices have effects that are measurable as marks on bodies that can be accounted for, in the sense of verification but also in the sense of responsibility, because "it matters which cuts are enacted; different cuts enact different materialized becomings" (361). When I say we create worlds in writing, I mean that we participate in the creation of material meanings that matter, that have effects, and that we are held accountable for our participation.

A Memo

How might Barad's agential realism enable us to understand writing differently, as a phenomenon of entangled intra-acting agencies? A mundane writing event: a memo written in response to a request from the dean for proposals that would improve student retention.[4] Producing a memo involved intra-actions among the assistant head of the department, the department head, the director of the graduate program, the director of the writing program, and the coordinator of the writing center as well as the dean.[5] Their intra-actions were largely oral, in meetings and in private conversations in hallways and offices and homes, though several of them wrote drafts or parts of drafts. Their conversations focused not simply (and not much) on retention but more broadly on what the assistant head called "a Gordian knot of problems" facing the department that circulated around the problem of staffing. These problems were material concerns: any decisions about how to staff the writing program would enact cuts about who mattered and how. At stake were part-time faculty's employment as well as financial support for graduate students. Students in writing classes deserved well-trained instructors and suitable class sizes. The working conditions of writing center coaches depended on a well-trained writing center staff too. The Conference on College Composition and Communication and the Council of Writing Program Administrators had positions on staffing writing programs that many of the participants, especially the director of writing studies, felt accountable to. Full-time faculty, especially untenured faculty, needed research release time. Not inconsequential and also of substantial material concern were the professional engagement and investment in the writing program of the current part-time instructors, many of whom had been teaching in the program for years and several of whom were related to the participants in this writing event.

Writing the memo was not an activity in the mind of the writer of the final draft (the assistant department head) or even in the minds of the other participants. It involved instead the intra-actions of these material concerns as they were enacted by those involved in writing the memo and the rest of the department members (and others) as they were drawn into the intra-actions. It's important to emphasize that individuals are entangled in specific ways and that they always change in intra-actions. Just as the atom became a movable and Eigler became a nanotechnician in his work with the scanning tunneling microscope and Kimmerer and the plantain became immigrants in the intra-action I discussed in chapter 1, new properties materialize in intra-actions.

The memo that was sent did not directly address any of the concerns about staffing. It proposed some plans to improve the first-year writing sequence, requested funding to implement these plans, and recommended that excellent teaching be provided "by involving faculty from all ranks in the regular teaching" of the first-year writing courses. Though the writing program did later receive more funding, it was not in response to this memo, and no more full-time faculty became involved in teaching writing. Thus it might be thought that this writing event was a failure, or inconsequential. But it did have effects: as the participants wrote and exchanged drafts, discussed, worked, and socialized together, their personal and professional relationships were restructured as well as their commitments to writing students, graduate students, and other faculty. Subsequently, the department initiated the practice of offering part-time faculty yearly contracts, but part-time instructors were also eventually phased out in favor of graduate student instructors. Clearly, these effects did not arise solely from this writing event, but the writing was a factor and those who participated in the consideration of who mattered and who didn't were held accountable.

Writing Is a Material Practice

Considering a writing event as a phenomenon highlights its status as material practice in the world rather than as the manipulation of representations in the mind. In this sense, writing can be considered to be a form of thinking, as long as we think of thinking as material. Doing so is crucial because it obviates the "gap" that prevents writing and thought from having any purchase on reality. Cognition is not a process in which the mind conceives of actions and then directs the body to execute them but rather is, as Tim Ingold says, "integral to the functioning of an entire system of perception and action constituted by the nexus of relationships set up by virtue of the immersion of the agent in his or her environment" ("Tool-use" 433). Francisco Varela, Evan Thompson, and Eleanor Rosch refer to embodied cognition as enactive, explaining that cognitive systems "do not operate by representation. Instead of *representing* an independent world, they *enact* a world" (140). Rejecting the Enlightenment construction of the mind as a mirror of unchanging nature (see Rorty), they define cognition as "knowing how to negotiate our way through a world that is not fixed and pregiven but that is continually shaped by the types of actions in which we engage" (144).[6]

It was Uexküll's pioneering work in animal behavior that forced a reconsideration of how "the body enter[s] into relation with, and creation of, the environment" (Buchanan 3). Uexküll's argument that animals should be thought of as subjects rather than physiological machines entails that cognition should be more broadly defined as perceiving and acting and that in this sense all animals think. Humberto Maturana's research with Gabriela Uribe and Samy Frenk on color vision in pigeons offers empirical support for understanding cognition in this way. They discovered that the patterns of activity in the pigeons' retinas had no one-to-one relationship with the wavelengths of the light striking the pigeons' retinas. Instead, the patterns of activity in the retinas correlated with the pigeons' discriminations of color (Maturana and Varela, *Autopoesis* xv). Maturana explains that these experiments led to his insight that the nervous system is a system that operates on itself through making changes in its structure in response to its interactions with the environment rather than by operating on representations or "information" obtained from the environment. He concludes that the phenomenon of structural coupling requires a change in the formulation of questions about cognition,[7] from the question "'How does the organism obtain information about its environment'" to the question "'How does it happen that the organism has the structure that permits it to operate adequately in the medium in which it exists?'" (*Autopoesis* xvi). How is it that the tick (Uexküll's famous example), out of all the odors in its environment, responds only to the odor of butyric acid? How is it that our visual experience of the world is continuous despite the easily demonstrable blind spot that results from the lack of light sensitivity in the area of our retinas where the optic nerve emerges? To say that our minds screen out or repress our blind spots is as excessive an explanation as to say that ticks' minds sort through all incoming odors looking for butyric acid. Maturana's new question suggests a simpler answer: through patterns of interaction over time our nervous systems have become structured so that they do not respond to the lack of stimuli in that area of our retinas—"*we do not see that we do not see*," as Maturana and Varela say (*Tree* 19)—and ticks' nervous systems have become structured in such a way that they respond only to the odor of butyric acid.[8]

Through structural coupling, all extant organisms have modified their structures congruently with changes in the environment, and this ongoing history is what enables them to continue to operate adequately, or in other words, to live. Maturana concludes that "*Living systems are cognitive systems, and living as a process is a process of cognition*" (Maturana and Varela, *Autopoesis* 13). Later, he offered a fuller statement: "That which we human beings call cognition is the capacity that a living system exhibits of operating in dynamic structural congruence with the medium in which it exists. It does not matter if the living system observed is an insect or a human being. We may ask ourselves whether the knowledge that the living system exhibits is learned or instinctive, but our assessment is the same: namely, if we see a living system behaving according to what we consider adequate behavior in the circumstances in which we observe it, we claim that it knows" (Maturana, "Autopoesis" 26). The difference between learned and instinctive behavior, he explains, has only to do with the historical origin of the behavior: both arise from structural coupling, but learned behavior is attributed to the restructuring in the development of individual systems (ontogenesis), while instinctive behavior is attributed to the inheritance of evolutionary changes (epigenesis).

Another source for the idea that cognition is a material practice rather than internal to minds is Ludwig Wittgenstein's argument with Augustine, in which he claims that the meanings of words arise from their use. He imagines a simple protolanguage used by a builder and his assistant: "A is building with building-stones: there are blocks, pillars, slabs, and beams. B has to pass the stones, and that in the order in which A needs them. For this purpose they use a language consisting of the words 'block,' 'pillar,' 'slab,' 'beam.' A calls them out;—B brings the stone which he has learnt to bring at such-and-such a call" (sec. 2). This language is learned by training B to respond to the words in particular ways: Wittgenstein asks, "Don't you understand the call 'Slab!' if you act upon it in such-and-such a way?" (sec. 6). B has learned the use of the words and that is all he or she needs to know to understand and play this primitive language game. Wittgenstein asks, "Now what do the words of this language *signify*?" and answers with yet another question: "What is supposed to shew what they signify, if not the kind of use they have?" (sec. 10). He finally states, "The term 'language-*game*' is meant to bring into prominence the fact that the *speaking* of language is part of an activity, or of a form of life" (sec. 23).

Paleoanthropologist Alison Wray suggests that language originated in a protolanguage like Wittgenstein's builder's language that consisted of holistic utterances that later, through recursion as Maturana would say, developed into symbols. Some animal communication, too, seems to be like this protolanguage, emerging out of coordinating behavior rather than from acts of referring. An example often cited comes from the study of the alarm calls of vervet monkeys in Africa who give one of three types of alarm calls when they see one of their three main predators—leopards, eagles, and snakes. Like Wittgenstein's builder, the monkeys respond to these calls with behavior: they climb into trees in response to the leopard call, dive into bushes in response to the eagle call, and stand up and look around in response to the snake call (Donald Griffin 158). Thus animal behaviorists conclude that the calls might better be translated in behavioral rather than referential terms: for example, "Behave in a way to avoid a snake," rather than, "There's a snake."

Like Wittgenstein (sec. 38), Maturana argues that language is not a matter of denotation but of language games, or what Maturana calls "the flow of the coordination of behaviors" ("Nature" 462). We do not use language to communicate; instead, communication is a post hoc observation we make about interactions in which language arises. He says, "If we see that in the flow of the interactions between two persons there are coordinations of behavior, we say that there is communication between them" ("Nature" 462). Seeing language as an instrument of communication mistakes the result for the cause, he explains: "Human beings can talk about things because they generate the things they talk about by talking about them. That is, human beings can talk about things because they generate them by making distinctions that specify them in a consensual domain" ("Biology" 56).

He offers an example of a woman hailing a taxi by meeting the gaze of a taxi driver and making a circular hand gesture: the gaze initiates a coordination of behavior consummated in the hand gesture, a learned coordination of the behaviors of getting attention and committing to hiring ("Nature" 463). In this coordination of coordinating behaviors, the object, the taxi as a carrying device, arises. In other domains the taxi may arise as something else—an art object, say—or may not be individually distinguished—if it arises as part of a traffic jam, for instance. As Barad would put it, it acquires different "properties" in different intra-actions. Such domains of interobjectivity are consensual not in the sense of being agreed-upon, but in the sense of a "coherent transformation of behavior of two or more organisms as they live together, [which] occurs as an unintended result of that living together" ("Nature" 463). In sum, he says, "We literally create the world in which we live by living it" ("Biology" 61).

Different Beings, Different Behaviors

If all living beings think—and in the sense discussed above, we must admit that even microorganisms do—why don't they all exhibit the same behaviors? And to what extent are these behaviors different? Also, if writing is thinking, should we also admit that in this sense, all living beings write? Despite Darwin's emphasis on the continuity between human and animal behavior, even most Western biologists have been careful to avoid any taint of anthropomorphism in their descriptions of what they observe.[9] But studies in cognitive ethology, a field initiated by Donald Griffin, have demonstrated that nonhuman animals exhibit self-awareness, form conscious plans, and communicate semantic information to each other (vervets, chickens, and honeybees, for example) and to humans (honeyguides and dogs). Griffin rejects "the customary assumption that if some behavior has been genetically programmed [i.e., is instinctual], it cannot be guided by conscious thinking" as "not supported by any solid evidence" (254). Antonio Damasio argues that the neural foundations of self are shared by all vertebrates, and that humans differ only in having a more complex cortex (*Descartes' Error* 243). Even Daniel Dennett, who denies consciousness to nonhuman animals, allows that the difference is not absolute: "While a bat, like even the lowly lobster, has a biological self, it has no selfy self to speak of... *or at most a negligible one*" (448; emphasis added). This is not to say that there are no differences between human cognition and that of others.

One difference many focus on as important in human cognition, apparent in the quotations in the preceding paragraph, is consciousness, but recent work in neurology reveals that consciousness is only one part of cognition, and not the largest part. Hayles distinguishes conscious and "new unconscious" cognition from nonconscious cognition based on awareness: conscious cognition is the focus of awareness while new unconscious cognition operates below awareness but is accessible to awareness (she regards the Freudian unconscious as a subset of the new unconscious). Nonconscious cognition is inaccessible to awareness but supports conscious cognition in integrating bodily representations and sensory inputs, processing information much faster than conscious cognition, recognizing more complex and subtle patterns, and making inferences that influence behavior and influence priorities. Hayles is most interested in nonconscious cognition, as she notes the "not accidental" parallels between it and the technical cognition exhibited by digital technologies that also support human cognition (*Unthought* 10–11), which I will discuss later. A lot, but not all, of the cognitive behaviors of nonhuman animals are considered to be nonconscious—although as Griffin suggests, evidence of consciousness is difficult to find—and plants and microorganisms are generally considered to exhibit nonconscious cognitive behavior.

Differences in kinds of cognition may not be as helpful as humanists might believe, however, in arguing for what human and nonhuman animals can do. Frans de Waal points out the significant distinction between mechanism and function in animals (as always including humans, remember): it is very common for animals to achieve the same end (function) by different means (mechanism). Forgetting this, he says, results in misleading conclusions "when the mental achievements of large-brained animals are questioned by pointing at 'lower' animals doing something similar . . . 'If wasps can do it, what's the big deal?'" (73). His example is facial recognition, once thought to be solely a human achievement, now disproved by studies of not only apes and monkeys but also crows, sheep, and paperwasps, the latter of which have only minuscule sets of neural ganglia—and also by octopuses (Godfrey-Smith). A more intriguing example of the mechanism/function distinction was recently reported in *The Atlantic*: a slime mold, a brainless unicellular organism that can fuse into a single-celled plasmodium, has been able to replicate the Tokyo rail system when presented with a petri dish containing a map with bits of food standing in for urban centers. The article explains: "If one part of the plasmodium touches something attractive, like food, it pulses more quickly and widens. If another part meets something repulsive, like light, it pulses more slowly and shrinks. By adding up all of these effects, the plasmodium flows in the best possible direction without a single conscious thought. It is the ultimate in crowdsourcing" (Yong).

Yong comments: "Human designers had created that network to be as efficient as possible; the slime mold had done the same, but without any brainpower." The brainpower of "less civilized" humans is also commonly denigrated in a similar way: witness the "less rational" (but more efficient) route of Broadway in New York City, which cuts across the grid of numbered streets and avenues as it follows the path of the Algonquin Wickquasgeck Trail. Conscious rational thought is not the only way to achieve worthwhile designs, nor does it always produce the best ones.

The way entities use different physical mechanisms to achieve the same ends can also be observed in computers and robots, as Lucy Suchman argues: "Interaction between people and machines requires essentially the same interpretive work that characterizes interaction between people, but with fundamentally different resources available to the participants" (180). Mazis notes that the assumption that a machine, unlike a human or nonhuman animal, is a "'mere object'—it has no relationship to its environment" (49) is no longer valid. The shift in artificial intelligence and robotics toward embodied intelligence, like the shift away from the Cartesian notion of the disembodied mind, has led to robots with distributed systems that allow them to learn through interacting with their environments, machines like the Roomba vacuum cleaner that navigates itself around the room by sensing and reacting to obstacles and the dirtiness of the floor. Mazis cites work by Juyang Weng and colleagues who have been training robots through interacting with them: "after a human pushes the SAIL robot 'for a walk' along corridors of a large building, SAIL can navigate on its own in similar environments while 'seeing' with its two video cameras. After humans show toys to SAIL and help SAIL's hand to reach them, SAIL can pay attention to these toys, recognize them, and reach them too. To allow SAIL to learn autonomously, the human robot-sitter lets it explore the world on its own, but encourages and discourages behaviors by pressing its 'good' button or 'bad' button" (Weng et al. 600). Using feedback from the environment and from its human companion, SAIL can act competently in its world: it thinks, in Maturana's sense, even though, as Hayles comments, it "can never be fully alive" (*Unthought* 22). Its structures of perception, action, and interaction—video cameras, buttons—and its experiences differ, but its behaviors are similar.

All living beings think in the sense of operating in dynamic congruence with their surroundings and other beings, but differences in sensorimotor capacities, biological and psychological structure, and histories of interactions with others and with their environment can produce differences in cognitive behaviors. Uexküll's noting of differences in sensory apparatuses led to his explanation of how different species bring forth different worlds through their living. He strikingly illustrates the worlds of various animals with drawings that contrast what humans would perceive in the animal's surroundings with what the animal would perceive. For example, in the illustrations of a scallop on the seafloor, the predatory starfish that in the human view is clearly visible on a nearby rock is completely invisible in the scallop's view. Uexküll explains that scallops only respond to movement: "The scallop's eyes are set to pick up neither form nor color, but only a certain speed of movement, which corresponds exactly to that of its enemy" (*Foray* 82–83). As Varela, Thompson, and Rosch conclude, "Cognition depends upon the kinds of experience that come from having a body with various sensorimotor capacities, and . . . these individual sensorimotor capacities are themselves embedded in a more encompassing biological, psychological, and cultural context" (173).

Differences in cognitive behavior can arise among closely related species due to differing experiences over time as the behaviors become canalized, or inherited. Vilmos Csányi and his colleagues at Eötvös University in Budapest attribute differences between dogs' and wolves' cognitive behaviors to differences in their history of interactions with humans, which they, like Maturana, assert arose both in ontogenesis and epigenesis. In one study, they tested their hypothesis that dogs' preference for looking at humans could be the basis for dogs' "surprisingly good" performance at communicative tasks. To control for the effects of socialization to humans, they raised a few wolf pups in close contact with humans from before when their eyes were open and a few dog pups in the same way, then compared their behavior on tasks performed in the presence of their adoptive humans. They trained the wolves and dogs until they could perform a task (opening a bin or pulling a rope to obtain food) and then made the task insoluble (by locking the bin or tying off the rope) and tested them again. When faced with the insoluble task, dogs looked back at their humans earlier and spent more time gazing at them. In a report on Csányi's research published in *The Chronicle of Higher Education*, the differences are described in a less restrained way: "In experiments where the rope was anchored, the dogs tried a couple of times, then turned to their masters for assistance or cues. The wolves, by contrast, continued yanking on it until exhausted, never once giving their caretakers so much as a glance" (Woodard). Csányi and his colleagues conclude that "preferential looking at the human seems to be a genetic predisposition in dogs, as it was difficult to induce this behavior in wolves even after intensive socialization," and they surmise that this predisposition "provides the foundation on which developmentally canalized complex communicative interactions can emerge between man and dog" (Miklósi et al. 764–65; Csányi 102–7).[10]

John Bradshaw hypothesizes that modern dogs may have descended from a subgroup of wolves who were "able to form social bonds with humans," which, he argues and Csányi's experiments demonstrate, is the "most striking difference between dogs and wolves today" (51). My dog Pegeen all too regularly solicited my help: when her favorite ball would roll under the sofa, she would look at me, look under the sofa and back at me, and would utter short yelps until I got up and retrieved the ball for her. (On walks, she would also look back at me when she encountered something worrisome, like an approaching stranger or a bear in the woods, as if to ask, "What should I do now?") These observations illustrate how a simple behavior—paying attention to humans—can scaffold more complex behaviors over time as beings continue to interact with each other.

Even language, the most cherished characteristic of humanness,[11] also consists of a set of behaviors exhibited by many nonhuman animals. In their discussion of who has language, Mark Hauser, Noam Chomsky, and W. Tecumseh Fitch note that research on speech perception has "surprisingly . . . turned up little evidence for uniquely human mechanisms special to speech, despite a persistent tendency to assume uniqueness even in the absence of relevant animal data" (1574). They discuss an array of behaviors that are constitutive of language—discriminating and producing speech sounds, vocal imitation, using abstract concepts, attributing mental states to others, referential signaling, and recursion—all of which have been exhibited, to some extent, in some nonhuman animals. Only recursion (a process "that takes a finite set of elements and yields a potentially infinite array of discrete expressions" [1571]) might possibly be unique to humans, and one or two other behaviors are more certain or more developed in humans. Current data about attributing mental states to others preclude "any firm conclusion" (1576); about referential signaling (as in the vervet monkeys I discussed earlier), they find that human words "have only weak analogs or homologs in natural animal communication systems, with only slightly better evidence from the training studies with apes and dolphins" (1576). Even with recursion they find that some animals, including cotton-top tamarins, exhibit specific behaviors that underlie the ability to recursively embed phrases within other phrases. Reviewing research that demonstrates the use of recursion in visual domains, they suggest that recursion may have evolved in animals more generally "to solve other computational problems such as navigation, number quantification, or social relationships" and, if so, "it is possible that other animals have such abilities, but our research efforts have been targeted at an overly narrow search space" (1578).[12]

Hauser explains such differences by hypothesizing that animals possess mental tool kits, the contents of which may vary. Some tools (like object permanence) may be common to many animals and others may be unique or specialized. He sees tool kits as a product of natural selection, developed in response to social or ecological pressures. After carefully reviewing studies of the numerical behaviors of lions, rats, pigeons, chimpanzees, parrots, and monkeys—some of which are quite impressive—he concludes that many animals make quantity distinctions (one, few, many), and some (chimpanzees and parrots) apparently can be taught to pick out the required number of objects up to five (they have a number category), but none clearly have a number concept—none understand that 1-2-3-4-5 is an extendable sequence. Why might this be? Hauser suggests, "In nature, animals confront situations where relative, rather than absolute quantification is required"—larger or smaller quantities of food, fewer or more members of a competing pack—and thus "it seems highly unlikely . . . that animals living under natural conditions would confront ecological problems that would select for greater numerical competence" (328–29).

Humans, like other animals and robots, have tool kits of cognitive behaviors that overlap but are not the same from being to being. James Paul Gee describes capital D Discourses, which he defines as *"saying (writing)-doing-being-valuing combinations,"* as "identity kits" that are acquired "by enculturation ('apprenticeship') into social practices through scaffolded and supported interaction with people who have already mastered the Discourse" (526–27). He emphasizes that "Discourses are ways of being in the world; they are forms of life which integrate words, acts, values, beliefs, attitudes, and social identities, as well as gestures, glances, body positions, and clothes" (526). The metaphor of tool kits is useful in emphasizing how ways of being in the world characterize differences among beings, but it has some drawbacks. Hauser's description of mental tool kits as consisting of "specialized devices" in the brain (15) implies that they are fixed and autonomous entities, possessions rather than mutable behaviors. And, thus, which is more worrisome, they imply that cognitive behaviors precede their enaction, as already established programs that recruit beings. Ingold similarly cautions: "The assumption that for people to speak they must first 'have' language, or for people to use tools they must first 'have' technology—or indeed for people to engage in intelligent activities of any kind they must first 'have' intelligence" (PE 407) prevents us from understanding that "skill . . . is a property not of the individual human body as a biophysical entity, a thing-in-itself, but of the total field of relations constituted by the presence of the organism-person, indissolubly body and mind, in a richly structured environment" (PE 353). Ingold here echoes both Varela and Griffin in arguing that structures alone do not account for differences in cognition but rather the ongoing interactions among sensorimotor structures—which are themselves interacting and restructuring—and among them and everything else in the richly structured and structuring environment. As Michel Foucault says of power, cognitive behaviors are enacted relations, not possessions ("Subject" 219) or properties. Cognitive behaviors are what beings do in the world, not a means by which they take in or reflect on or express the world.

Inspired by George Kennedy's article "A Hoot in the Dark," published in 1992, as well as by the increase in studies of animal cognition, many rhetoricians (after a longish hiatus in which Kennedy's article was considered a "'wild,' perhaps savage" assertion "that animals—not just human ones—practice rhetoric" [Hawhee, "Toward" 82; quoting, in part, Vitanza ix]) have recently turned to animal studies to contest the Western tradition that defines rhetoric as a "specifically human enterprise" (Davis, "Some Reflections" 275).[13] Reviewing rhetorical behaviors that have been documented in animals, Diane Davis avers, "There is no single, indivisible line between 'the human' and 'the animal,'" and she argues that compiling "rhetorical bestiaries," like those contained in the special issue of *Rhetoric Society Quarterly* she is responding to, "could be one strategy of attunement, one way for rhetoricians to begin to approach the complex differential relations obscured by the presumption that 'human' and 'animal' name ontologically discrete domains" (278, 279). She especially cites Debra Hawhee's recent work analyzing Aristotle's "zoological texts" as "reanimating a crucial engagement with bodily intelligence at the very heart of our legacy" (280). In this work, Hawhee observes that "nonhuman animals turn up in rhetoric's theoretical and instructional texts when sensation matters the most, thereby bringing rhetoric to its—or the—senses" (*Rhetoric* 2). My interest in animal and technical cognition is inspired by some of the same motives, suggesting that embodied cognitive behaviors involved in writing are not exclusively human and that "sensation, feeling, and emotion" offer "positive counterparts to rationality and reason" as cognitive behaviors (Hawhee, *Rhetoric* 7) that demand attention in the study of writing and the teaching of writing. Like Davis, I also have emphasized the complex intersections of human and nonhuman cognition here and in my consideration in chapter 1 of how humans and rabbits entertain propositions. But I am also especially interested not just in what cognitive behaviors human and nonhuman beings have demonstrated but also in what they can do when offered the chance to be interesting.

An intriguing recent study reported that lab-dwelling ravens "can plan for the future outside behaviors observed in the wild" (Milius 9). Ravens, like all corvids, are notoriously clever birds, but they do not use tools much in the wild, nor do they trade for food. But in tests similar to those done on nonhuman apes and young children, they "selected a rock useless at the moment but likely to be useful later for working a puzzle box and getting food," and also picked "a tool instead of a ho-hum treat when the tool would allow them to get a fabulous bit of kibble 17 hours later" (9).[14] I discuss similar examples of what animals can do in chapters 6 and 7 where I consider the creativity of writing in more detail. Do nonhuman animals write? They certainly do create worlds in their living and, like humans, respond to possibilities of new behavior.

Cognitive Ecologies

Work in distributed cognition has tended to focus on technology, from the simple extended systems involved in the use of tools like axes to those involved in high-frequency trading. In drawing attention to the "total field of relations" that skill relies on, Ingold also echoes scholars working in various disciplines who conceive cognition as behaviors that weave together brains, bodies, tools, objects, other beings, and institutions in ways that modify their modes of existence. Bateson emphasizes that it is the "total system that has the characteristics of immanent mind" (317); Hutchins argues that it is the "system of person-in-interaction-with-technology [that] exhibits expertise" (155); Latour describes how networks or chains of reference enable "the propagation of representations through various media" ("Cogito" 57); Haraway postulates cyborg beings (*Simians* 151–52); and Clark examines extended minds (*Natural-Born Cyborgs*). Hayles calls these systems cognitive assemblages, but she distinguishes them from Latour's networks (and from Deleuze's assemblages): "A cognitive assemblage emphasizes the flow of information through a system and the choices and decisions that create, modify, and interpret the flow" (*Unthought* 116). She also emphasizes the role of "cognizers within the assemblage that enlist these affordances and direct their powers to act in complex situations" (116), ruling out some material agents and forces as cognizers. Although I accept some of the distinctions she is making (cement certainly is a different kind of agent than a digital personal assistant), I prefer to recognize systems like Latour's networks and Ingold's meshworks of forces and beings as well as cognitive assemblages as cognitive ecologies in which information, choices, and decisions are not the only or most prominent determining forces. Cognitive ecologies represent a mode of entanglement, less intimate than that proposed by Barad, but still emphasizing interactions among all kinds of agencies.

Bateson ascribes his understanding of mind as a total system as developing from his nascent understanding of feedback in cybernetic systems through his participation in the first Macy Conferences on Cybernetics in 1942 where he met with Warren McCulloch and Julian Bigelow. He realized that "obviously there are lots of message pathways outside the skin, and these and the messages which they carry must be included as part of the mental system whenever they are relevant" (458). The mental system operates through feedback from outside the nervous system; for example, when a man is cutting a tree with an axe, "Each stroke of the axe is modified or corrected, according to the shape of the cut face of the tree left by the previous stroke. This self-corrective (*i.e.,* mental) process is brought about by a total system, tree-eyes-brain-muscles-axe-stroke-tree; and it is this total system that has the characteristics of immanent mind" (317). Bateson insists that this system is not contained inside the individual body or self: "The total self-corrective unit which processes information, or, as I say, 'thinks' and 'acts' and 'decides,' is a *system* whose boundaries do not at all coincide with the boundaries either of the body or of what is popularly called the 'self' or 'consciousness'" (319).

Hutchins developed his theory of distributed cognition in his ethnographic study of navigation on navy ships. He describes how a variety of instruments are used in fixing the position of a ship: a telescopic sighting device (an alidade) linked to a gyrocompass provides a three-digit bearing reading on a particular landmark; a bearing log records the bearing; and a one-armed protractor (hoey) enables the bearing number to be related to the chart. He argues that the instruments, rather than amplifying human cognitive processes, "*transform* the task the person has to do" by translating bearing readings into a visualization where "the path to the solution is apparent" (155). He concludes that this understanding gives new meaning to the term "expert system":

> Clearly, a good deal of the expertise in the system is in the artifacts (both the external implements and the internal strategies)—not in the sense that the artifacts are themselves intelligent or expert agents, or because the act of getting into coordination with the artifacts constitutes an expert performance by the person; rather, the system of person-in-interaction-with-technology exhibits expertise. These tools permit the people using them to do the tasks that need to be done while doing the kinds of things the people are good at: recognizing patterns, modeling simple dynamics of the world, and manipulating objects in the environment. (155)

Clark calls these technologies problem-solving artifacts or cognitive shortcuts that "effectively transform complex problems into ones that the biological brain is better equipped to solve" (*Natural-Born Cyborgs* 77), and he argues that using these artifacts is "the distinctive way human brains [create] extended cognitive systems whose computational and problem-solving profiles are quite different from those of the naked brain" (78).

Hutchins goes on to explain that when a team participates in fixing a position, the interactions and communications among them also become part of the system. Although members of the team all know the overall goal of the activity, they each have different kinds of knowledge and different access to knowledge and action due to their relative experience and physical position in the navigation spaces. The organization of the work of the team is partly specified in the ship's procedures that explain for each team member what to do in what situations, but when situations vary from the limited range specified in the procedures (which is often) crew members negotiate together the meanings and applications of the procedures, pass on needed information to crew members who aren't in a position to obtain it, and sometimes perform part of the actions that are the responsibility of another crew member. Hutchins remarks: "We can think of the team as a sort of flexible organic tissue that keeps the information moving across the tools of the task. When one part of this tissue is unable to move the required information, another part is recruited to do it" (224). People and instruments work together, all as parts of a system, and the expertise, or the cognitive behavior of the system, is immanent in the system as a whole.

Like Clark, Latour notes that keeping information moving across components in the system translates or reformats tasks into simpler or easier tasks by delegating more of them to "other actors in the setting, either humans or non-humans" ("Cogito" 57). He also points out that it is not only the tasks that are transformed. So too are the "*very lightly equipped human subject . . . who might have internalized some parts of the process*" ("Cogito" 56) by learning new behaviors. And so too are the artifacts, which he says are transformed by being entered into a new "mode of existence" ("Textbook Case" 101) as, for example trees or cliffs become landmarks when they are used in navigation.

Latour provides an extended example of the transformation of artifacts in his study of the work of a team of scientists in Brazil. A geographer, a botanist, and a soil scientist were attempting to discover whether, in an ecotone, the forest was advancing on the savanna or retreating from the savanna's "merciless encroachment" (PH 26–27). The forest is "rendered as a diagram" through the botanist's marking of study tracts and the soil scientist's marking of transects that cross the extremes of soil types (43). Soil becomes samples loaded into a box divided into cubical containers (a "pedocomparator"); when the provenance of each sample is noted on the side of each cube and the soil is defined by color, "the earth becomes a sign" (49). With the comparisons of samples from across the forest-savanna ecotone thus made easier, and with further propagation through other summatory diagrams and finally to a text, the soil has passed from the mode of existence as the living support of the forest-savanna ecotone to the mode of existence of representing the ecotone in a scientific inquiry. As Latour says about an exhibit of fossilized bones of ancestors of modern horses, "At the intersection with [scientists] . . . their former selves had been shunted . . . into [scientific] pathways" (PH 24).[15] In these accounts, Latour, like Barad, foregrounds an important implication of understanding cognition as behavior that is immanent in systems: that humans can no longer be considered to be the sole agents in the universe. Now everything is an actant, including inanimate objects like soil and horse fossils; all kinds of things participate in cognitive behaviors.

If it is difficult, as Bateson says, to think of cognition as extended when talking about chopping down trees, it is even more difficult when talking about writing. The commonplace understanding of writing in Western cultures, arising from the equation of writing with thinking, is that it is a solitary, individual, and internal practice (see Brodkey 54). But although writers in the process of inscribing are often not in physical proximity to other people, they are never alone with their thoughts: they are at the very least continually interacting with language and writing technologies and texts and thus always writing and thinking with others. Scholars of writing have argued for the past fifty years that all writing is fundamentally collaborative, at least in the respect that it responds to other writings (intertextuality), and often concretely, especially in workplace settings (such as laboratories, as Latour observes). Like understanding a writing event as a phenomenon, thinking of writers as always enmeshed in cognitive ecologies conceives it as a mode of reciprocal induction or coordination of behaviors: writers are perceiving, acting, responding, and being transformed in interaction with technologies, other people, and other beings and things that are also perceiving, acting, responding, and being transformed.

The most obvious examples of cognitive ecologies of writing are the everyday ones that underlie definitions of writing as social action: families making shopping lists use pen and paper or checklists (or personal digital assistants) to translate nearly empty salt containers or a list of ingredients in a recipe into a transportable reference that can be translated back into a full shopping cart; citizens petitioning government institutions go door to door or set up tables in shopping malls with printed statements including lines for signatures—or post statements online where others can sign with a click. How technologies transform tasks and shunt people and things into different pathways is often overlooked in such writing behaviors.[16]

A more striking example of a system of writer-in-interaction-with-technology that exhibits expertise is provided by a professional writer, Steven Johnson. He describes a "tool for thought" he has been using in his writing, a sophisticated indexing software that works on an archive of the writer's writings and notes and excerpts from the writer's reading. Johnson explains that the software (DEVONthink) not only searches on specific words but also "learns associations between individual words, by tracking the frequency with which words appear near each other." He describes how in working on a book project that involved the history of the London sewers, he ran a search on "sewage." Among the results, he also received references to "waste," a word that often occurs with "sewage," including a quote about how calcium waste products were repurposed into bones in the evolution of vertebrates. Johnson comments:

> That might seem like an errant result, but it sent me off on a long and fruitful tangent into the way complex systems—whether cities or bodies—find productive uses for the waste they create. It's still early, but I may well get an entire chapter out of that little spark of an idea.
>
> Now, strictly speaking, who is responsible for that initial idea? Was it me or the software? It sounds like a facetious question, but I mean it seriously. Obviously, the computer wasn't conscious of the idea taking shape, and I supplied the conceptual glue that linked the London sewers to cell metabolism. But I'm not at all confident I would have made the initial connection without the help of the software. The idea was a true collaboration, two very different kinds of intelligence playing off each other, one carbon-based, the other silicon.

Like the instruments of ship navigation or the collections of soil samples, DEVONthink translates the task into one Johnson is good at. Just as the pedocomparator allows the soil scientists "to discern emerging patterns that no predecessor could see" (Latour, PH 38), DEVONthink allows Johnson to see a connection that helps him develop his book. All of the technologies of propagating and indexing writing allow for this kind of invention. As Latour says, discoveries arise out of cognitive ecologies, not from the isolated mind of a writer.

Other writers are more often recognized as parts of cognitive ecologies. A particularly interesting example can be found in the history of the writing of the disputed texts of Mikhail Bakhtin. Biographers Katerina Clark and Michael Holquist argue that Bakhtin was most probably the author of many of the writings published under the names of Pavel Medvedev and Valentin Voloshinov, but they explain that the three men discussed their ideas together frequently. They all recorded the results of these discussions along with other thoughts in extensive notebooks in which they worked out their ideas, and Clark and Holquist find it "highly likely" that much of the material in the disputed texts came from Bakhtin's, Medvedev's, or Volishinov's notebooks and was published variously under one or more of their names for political reasons. If we think of the notebooks and the published texts as technologies or tools of writing, we can see the three writers as a team that, as Hutchins says, "keeps the information moving across the tools of the task." And "when one part of this tissue is unable to move the required information," for political or other reasons, "another part is recruited to do it." Clark and Holquist point out that the problem of the disputed texts might have amused Bakhtin, for it goes to the heart of questions his theory strives to address: "Does authorship amount to preparing a manuscript for publication? Does it amount to translating ideas into a form and vocabulary acceptable for publication? Or does it mean providing the original ideas, along with the highly idiosyncratic vocabulary in which they are couched?" (169) As his questions make clear, writing is always an extended and distributed form of cognition.

Cognitive ecologies are systems in which what are habitually thought of as separate realms—mind and body, subject and object, human and other, culture and nature—are entangled with one another in the process of becoming. Many scholars argue that the creation of more complex and extended cognitive ecologies is what qualitatively distinguishes humans from other animals. Hauser, Chomsky, and Fitch assert that "no species other than humans has a comparable capacity to recombine meaningful units into an unlimited variety of larger structures, each differing systematically in meaning" (1576); Andy Clark asserts that "we—more than any other creature on the planet—deploy nonbiological elements (instruments, media, notations) to *complement* our basic biological modes of processing, creating extended cognitive systems whose computational and problem-solving profiles are quite different from those of the naked brain" (*Natural-Born Cyborgs* 78); and Kathleen Gibson argues that the construction of rich cognitive complexes is definitive of humans: "Other animals possess elements that are common to human behaviors, but none reaches the human level of accomplishment in any domain—vocal, gestural, imitative, technical, or social. Nor do other species combine social, technical, and linguistic behaviors into a rich, interactive and self-propelling cognitive complex" ("General Introduction" 7–8). Gibson's first claim is rather anthropocentric, depending as it does on setting humanlike behaviors as the measure of levels of accomplishment.[17] But her second claim accords with the others in seeing the distinction as dependent on the complexity and extensiveness of cognitive ecologies.

Latour also notes that the networks humans construct have become more complex and extended in the modern period, but he argues that this does not represent "a vast saga of radical rupture" (WM 48): "To be sure, the innovation of lengthened networks is important, but it is hardly a reason to make such a great fuss" (WM 124). For Latour, the human has always been the mediator or intersection of nature and society, subject and object: "A weaver of morphisms—isn't that enough of a definition? . . . By seeking to isolate its form from those it churns together, one does not defend humanism, one loses it" (WM 137). The *anthropos*, he says, cannot be threatened by machines or objects, for "it is made of them as much as they are made of it. It has defined itself by multiplying things" (WM 138). Humans have never been modern, he says: "We have never stopped building our collectives" (WM 115).

I side with Latour in observing that the length and complexity of cognitive ecologies is not something to make a great fuss over. Many ecologies that do not include humans are equally extended and complex, far beyond human control and understanding—forest ecologies that include microrhizomes and microorganisms as well as flora and fauna and soils and minerals and interactions with climatic forces, for example. I also agree with Latour in seeing the *Homo* genus as having been involved from very early on with technology. The *anthropos* is a weaver of morphisms, a maker, as I will discuss in chapter 3. Though humans are not the only tool and language using animals—octopuses use coconut shells as portable shelters, chimpanzees and crows use twigs to retrieve food, sea otters use stones carried on their chests to smash shellfish, and alligators and crocodiles balance sticks on their noses to lure birds (de Waal), and apes and monkeys as well as chickens and other birds, prairie dogs, and meerkats among others use vocal languages while many other organisms use chemical signals—that this behavior has been important in our development is testified to by the work of André Leroi-Gourhan, who inspired what Derrida calls the human adventure that began with the first flaked tool in the Olduvai Gorge.

Becoming the Animal Who Writes

Kenneth Burke argues that language is not essentially a tool: "Language is a species of action, symbolic action—and its nature is such that it can be used as a tool" (*Language* 15). I have been similarly arguing that language is behavior and not a thing, but as I claim that it is a behavior of coordinating behaviors and not essentially symbolic, I see language and tools as sharing a lot in common. Certainly, language is not a tool in the sense of being an instrument, but neither are tools best understood in this way. Ingold argues that "both tool-use and speech are, for humans, forms of intelligent activity ... [they] are used to mediate an active engagement with the environment rather than to assert control over it" ("Tool-use" 431–33). Hutchins, too, sees both tools and words as mediating technologies: they "do not stand between the user and the task. Rather, they stand with the user as resources used in the regulation of behavior" (154, and see 299–300).

Back in 1964, the French paleoanthropologist André Leroi-Gourhan made much the same observation, equating tools and language as "the expression of the same intrinsically human property" (113). He argues that human evolution was driven not by the increasing cognitive sophistication of the brain but rather by structural coupling between the skeleton and technology and language. Tools did not spring from the brain of early humans; instead, they "seem to have possessed their tools in much the same way as an animal has claws. They appear to have acquired them, not though some flash of genius which, one fine day, led them to pick up a sharp-edged pebble and use it as an extension of their fist (an infantile hypothesis well-beloved of many works of popularization), but as if their brains and their bodies had gradually exuded them" (106). The discovery of tool manufacture and use in human ancestors who had yet to acquire the proportionally giant brains of *Homo sapiens* argues against the development of technology as a rational cognitive achievement. Instead, tools seem to have arisen out of physical and kinetic coordinations between agents and their environment: they emerge in behaviors of shaping rather than being instruments designed for shaping.

Language does not leave as clear a fossil record as do stone tools, and despite careful study of the anatomy of early human skulls, paleoanthropologists can ascertain no more than a possibility of the capacity for articulate speech in early species of *Homo* (see Klein 207, 220, 234, 514–17). But Leroi-Gourhan argues that "as soon as there are prehistoric tools, there is a possibility of a prehistoric language, for tools and language are neurologically linked and cannot be dissociated within the social structure of humankind" (114). Thus he argues that these early tool users also had a form of language, a language he describes as holistic and context-bound, like Wittgenstein's and Wray's protolanguages, as "operating sequences limited to the expression of concrete situations, at first concurrently with them and later involving the deliberate preservation and reproduction of verbal sequences going beyond immediate situations" (115–16). For Leroi-Gourhan, technology and language, present in *Zinjanthropus* 1.75 million years ago, are what define the human; he says, "From the earliest moment at which we pick up the trail, the human is something other than a monkey" (116).

In place of the ape-man depicted in the opening of *2001: A Space Odyssey* who ponders a large bone before using it to smash up his surroundings (and then throws it in triumph up into the sky, where it comes down as a space shuttle), Leroi-Gourhan gives us an image of early human use of tools as ready-to-hand. His argument focuses on Louis Leakey's discovery of primitive tools surrounding remains of *Zinjanthropus* in the Olduvai Gorge in 1959, which necessitated a rethinking of the then common view of human ancestors as intelligent apes. *Zinjanthropus*, from the neck down, looked human, not apelike, with an upright posture and normal-length arms. Only the long face with prominent orbital ridges was apelike, and due to this skull configuration, *Zinjanthropus* had a very small (though recognizably human) brain (about half the volume of *Homo sapiens*). Leroi-Gourhan proposes that bipedal locomotion and erect posture freed the hands for grasping and the face for speaking and restructured the skull; when the skull is attached vertically rather than horizontally to the spinal column, it is freed from "the mechanical stresses of mandibular traction and suspension of the head" and the volume of the cranial vault increases (45). In *Zinjanthropus* this process is nearly complete, and so in place of an intelligent ape, we have a rather unintelligent human ancestor who nevertheless uses tools. Leroi-Gourhan characterizes *Zinjanthropian* technicity as "extremely simple," and comments, "The state it implies is one of technical consciousness to which, however, we must not apply our own yardstick. It is undoubtedly less of a risk to see human technicity as a simple zoological fact than it would be to credit *Zinjanthropus* with a system of creative thought. The countless millennia during which his industry remained unchanged—conditioned, as it were, by the shape of his skull—disproves the latter hypothesis" (92). About one million years separates the Oldowan technicity of *Zinjanthropus* from the Acheulean technicity of the Archanthropians, and it took yet another 650,000 years or so to arrive at the Mousterian technicity of the Neanderthals, which Leroi-Gourhan characterizes as that of "a highly developed technical intelligence" nearly indistinguishable from that of "any technician of a more recent age" (102). Though Neanderthals still had prominent orbital ridges, the back of the cranium had expanded, and Leroi-Gourhan comments that "leaving aside the detail (admittedly an important one) of the smallness of the prefrontal areas, the brain of Neanderthal man largely corresponded to ours, particularly in the number of cells in the middle cortex" (99)—the middle cortex being significant because it is the location of language processing.

Leroi-Gourhan describes technical intelligence as increasing, though slowly, throughout this long history, and he emphasizes in particular an innovation in Archanthropian toolmaking. The addition of a second series of actions—creating shaped flakes rather than the single sharp edge arising from a single blow—"was more than simply the addition of something new"; it "implied a good deal of foresight on the part of the individual performing the sequence of technical operations," for it involved shaping the tool to match "a shape that must be preexistent in the maker's mind" (97). Still, he argues, "we can hardly escape the conclusion that the phyletic series can have included only a very few Archanthropians of genius, for the industrial stereotype remained unchanged for several hundreds of thousands of years" (97). Only with the Mousterian technicity of the Neanderthals did the pace of technological development accelerate, testifying, he argues, to "the first upsurge of new aptitudes of the brain that both counterbalance and stimulate technicity" (107).[18]

Leroi-Gourhan's ideas (and Derrida's interpretation of them) inspired Bernard Stiegler's theory that "the invention of the human," a being who exhibits what Burke calls the reflexive or second-level aspect in tool and language use, began at that moment of Archanthropian innovation. But Stiegler significantly shifts Leroi-Gourhan's understanding of that moment. Rejecting his assumption that "a shape . . . must be preexistent in the [tool]maker's mind," Stiegler asks, "*Where is the memory of the stereotype kept, if not in the material trace of the stereotype in which the preexisting tool itself consists, repeated, duplicated by its 'maker' and guiding the latter much more than being guided by him or her?*" (Technics 1 158).[19] Stiegler argues that it is the material trace, the flint, and not an image in the mind that conserves epigenesis: "what Heidegger calls the already there . . this past that I never lived but that is nevertheless my past" is "sedimented" in the flint (Technics 1 140–41). The transmission of the already-there is only possible because the trace is material, "the organized albeit inorganic matter that the trace always is—be it a matter of tool or of writing" (Technics 1 141). As the Archanthropian works the flint, what happens is a "meeting of matter whereby the cortex reflects itself" in the flint, a "movement of their mutual coming-to-be" (Technics 1 141). This reflection, or exteriorization as he also calls it, is not a matter of taking something that was inside (an image in the mind) and putting it outside. The "interiority" of the brain and the "exteriority" of the flint tool arise at the same time in "a singular process of structural coupling" between the cortex and the flint "in the course of which the differentiation of the cortex is determined by the tool just as much as that of the tool by the cortex" (158).[20] It is a moment of reciprocal induction in which, as in Gilbert Simondon's notion of the transductive relation and Barad's notion of intra-action, the structures—differentiation of the cortex and the flint tool—do not preexist the relation.

Understanding this "exteriorization" in terms of structural coupling and intra-action allows us to understand tools and language as mediating an individuating cognitive ecology, and to understand writing—composing with both words and tools—as a behavior not of minds but of cognitive ecologies that entangle parts of the world in a reciprocal becoming. Clark argues that "our cognitive relation to our own words and language (both as individuals and as a species) defies any simple logic of inner and outer" (*Supersizing* 59), and Latour agrees, asking, "Is the referent what I point to with my finger outside of discourse, or is it what I bring back inside discourse?" (PH 32). Internal reflection on thoughts, Burke's reflexive second-level aspect and Clark's second-order cognitive dynamics, arises in cognitive ecologies and is internal to the system, not the property of an isolated mind. Like Burke, Clark sees it as "a good candidate for a distinctive human capacity and one that may depend on language" (*Supersizing* 58). But just as Hauser, Chomsky, and Fitch suggest that recursion is not exclusive to language, also occurring in visual behavior, Stiegler sees reflection not merely in symbolization but more generally in technology. Clark's description of reflection matches Stiegler's and applies equally to tools: "In creating the object, we need have no thoughts about thoughts, but once it is there, the opportunity immediately exists to attend to it as an object in its own right. The process of linguistic [and technological] formulation thus creates the stable attendable structure to which subsequent thinkings can attach" (*Supersizing* 58–59). Cortex and flint, internal speech and external language, reflect each other in a phenomenon of entanglement that makes us human, although still very much like many other animals.

Stiegler's argument owes a lot to Derrida, who uses Leroi-Gourhan's account of the origin of the human to argue against the metaphysics of presence and the theory of writing as inscription. He applauds Leroi-Gourhan's refusal to equate writing with "the simple possibility of the *graphie* [the sign] in general" (*Grammatology* 84). Instead, he says, Leroi-Gourhan invokes "the notion of *program*," which Derrida insists is "intelligible only in terms of a history of the possibilities of the trace as the unity of a double movement of protention and retention"—roughly speaking, anticipation and memory (*Grammatology* 84).[21] He comments, "This movement goes far beyond the possibilities of 'intentional consciousness.' It is an emergence that makes the *grammè* appear *as such* (that is to say according to a new structure of nonpresence) and undoubtedly makes possible the emergence of systems of writing in the narrow sense" (*Grammatology* 84). For Derrida, writing is not limited to the inscription of signs but is defined by the temporalized trace: "The trace, arche-phenomenon of 'memory' . . . belongs to the very movement of signification" (*Grammatology* 70). He explains: "[The] trace is the opening of the first exteriority in general, the enigmatic relationship of the living to its other and of an inside to an outside: spacing. The outside, 'spatial' and 'objective' exteriority . . . would not appear without the grammè, without differance as temporalization, without the nonpresence of the other inscribed within the sense of the present, without the relationship of death as the concrete structure of the living present" (*Grammatology* 70–71). As Derrida says here, alluding to Heidegger, and as he famously explains in his argument with John Searle, the trace is not only a spatialization (inside/outside) but also the temporal structure of being-in-the-world. It is memory and anticipation inscribed in the present: as an identifiable shape, it can be iterated, but because it can be iterated it has no essential unity. The trace is always in process, its possibilities always deferred—this is differánce: "A written sign . . . is a mark that subsists, one which does not exhaust itself in the moment of its inscription . . . by virtue of its essential iterability, [it] can always be detached from the chain in which it is inserted or given without causing it to lose all possibility of functioning, if not all possibility of 'communicating,' precisely. One can perhaps come to recognize other possibilities in it by inscribing it or *grafting* it onto other chains" ("Signature Event" 9). Thus in Derrida's reading, Leroi-Gourhan's account of "the human adventure" is an account of the history of writing: "a stage or an articulation in the history of life—of what I have called differánce—as the history of the *grammè*" (*Grammatology* 84). Differánce defines the structure of the *grammè*, which Derrida argues underlies the programs that Leroi-Gourhan refers to: "One cannot think them without the most general concept of the *grammè*" (*Grammatology* 84).

Leroi-Gourhan understands programs as operating sequences, sequences of gestures and tools or words organized "by means of a 'syntax' that imparts both fixity and flexibility to the series of operations involved," a syntax "suggested by memory" that emerges "as a product of the brain and the physical environment" (114). He uses this definition to argue that species differences are not due to "higher" animals relying less on instinct but are simply a matter of them having more plastic operating sequences that he insists "must be interpreted as a liberation, not from instinct, but from the fixed sequences established at the confluence of the individual's internal biological environment and the exterior . . . the nervous system is not an instinct-producing machine but one that responds to internal and external demands by designing programs" (221). Picking up Leroi-Gourhan's expression, Derrida argues for a liberation that is continuous with rather than a rupture from biological behavior: the emergence of the grammé is "a 'liberation of memory,' . . . an exteriorization always already begun but always larger than the trace which, beginning from the elementary programs of so-called 'instinctive' behavior up to the constitution of electronic card-indexes and reading machines, enlarges differánce and the possibility of putting in reserve" (*Grammatology* 84). And, just as Hauser, Chomsky, and Fitch do not restrict recursion to humans, Derrida does not deny the possibilities of the trace to nonhumans: "These possibilities or necessities, without which there would be no language, *are themselves not only human*" ("Eating" 116).

The human adventure begins with a moment that does not mark a permanent or clear break with other life forms. Programs, as Leroi-Gourhan's discussion suggests, are no more fixed entities than anything else; even the elementary programs of instinctive behavior evolve as flexible organisms-in-their-environments respond to internal and external demands. The concepts of the gene and heredity, those elementary programs of so-called instinctive behavior, have been revised by scholars in the new discipline of evolutionary developmental biology (Evo Devo). As Sean Carroll explains, the discovery that most of the genes that participate in organizing bodies are the same in most animals means that they cannot be the sole cause of the differences between arthropods, insects, and vertebrates, or between humans and nonhuman animals (9). Just as Derrida argues that the trace does not specify a singular meaning, Susan Oyama argues that "genes do not create traits according to a plan written in their very structure, even by operating on conveniently available raw materials" (43) and that the "information" carried by genes is not a code but rather a "certain disposition and use" of energy and matter (40). As Carroll says, "The evolution of form is not so much about what genes you have, but about how you use them" (153). Development results from "a complex of interacting influences, some inside the organism's skin, some external to it, and including its ecological niche in all its spatial and temporal aspects, *many of which are typically passed on in reproduction*" (Oyama 39). What is passed on through the generations is the same as what influences the development of the individual: the whole individuating system that involves not only genes, zones, and switches but also ecologies, climates, geologies, societies. Oyama concludes: "What is programmed, committed, or determined, switched or triggered, depends on external considerations that are as causally basic to the design of the phenomenon as internal factors" (40–41). Carroll describes how the same two genetic proteins that are used to make gills in crustaceans are used in insects to make wings (176). Sounding very Derridean, he argues, "Genes in the tool kit are important actors in this picture, but the tool kit represents only possibilities, not destiny" (165).

What this means in terms of the becoming of the animal who writes is just what we find: the program of exteriorization that resulted from the interaction of cortex and flint continues to evolve into more complex programs as the internal and external demands of being human change. As is noticeable in some of the passages I have quoted from Leroi-Gourhan, one of the reasons he refuses to ascribe intelligence to early humans is the slowness of the development of technology, which, he argues, is evidence of technicity as a "zoological fact" (106). Later evolution of *Homo sapiens*, driven by "the gradual development of the frontal and prefrontal areas appears to have entailed a progressively growing faculty for symbolization" (107), and evolution through symbolization, as Stephen Jay Gould has explained, is incomparably faster than biological evolution. Gould asserts that "human uniqueness" rests on cultural evolution: "Whatever one generation learns, it can pass to the next by writing, instruction, inculcation, ritual, tradition, and a host of methods that humans have developed to assure continuity in culture (325).[22] Stiegler describes this new form of evolution as epiphylogenesis—"a passage from the genetic to the nongenetic" (*Technics 1* 138)—emphasizing the inescapable meshing of biology, language, and technology: "Epiphylogenetic memory, essential to the human being, is technics: inscribed in the non-living body" (*Technics 2* 4).

Stiegler is concerned that "the seizure of control of epiphylogenesis by transmission technologies" has reduced the already-there to "calculations of amortization and productivity" (*Technics 2* 222), which will lead not to a future becoming but to entropy (*Technics 2* 224). Simondon and Latour are more hopeful. Simondon argues that the technical mentality has already produced "coherent and usable schemas" (Cartesian mechanism and cybernetics) in the cognitive domain and can also do so in the domain of voluntary action through the new twentieth-century "multifunctional network" that unites humans, nature, and technology ("Technical Mentality" 20, 22). The key, he says, is to "open" technical objects so they can continue to function instead of becoming obsolete: "If one imagines an object that, instead of being closed, offers parts that are conceived as being as close to indestructible as possible, and others by contrast in which there would be concentrated a very high capacity to adjust to each usage, or wear, or possible breakage in case of shock, of malfunctioning, then one obtains an *open* object that can be completed, improved, maintained in the state of perpetual actuality" (24). He argues that opening is "the perfection of the technical mentality" (24). In contrast with what he calls the "technocratic attitude" (see Heidegger's notion of Enframing) and what Stiegler laments as reducing epiphylogenesis to economic calculations, technical mentality becomes a mode of entanglement creating new parts of the world.

Latour, a big fan of Simondon, considers all objects—not just the objects like handmade jugs that Heidegger discussed—to be "born things" ("Why" 247), arguing that they are "simultaneously *made* through a complex history, and [are] new, real, and *interesting* participants in the universe" (234). He cites as an example computers, which if considered correctly "cease to be objects defined simply by their inputs and outputs and become again things, mediating, assembling, gathering many more folds than [the four specified by Heidegger]" (248). He refers to Turing's famous essay "Computing Machinery and Intelligence," which muses on the future of computers: Turing distinguishes between subcritical minds, which respond to an idea with "less than one idea" and supercritical minds, which respond with "a whole 'theory' consisting of secondary, tertiary, and more remote ideas," and then wonders, "Can a machine be made to be super-critical?" (454; qtd. in Latour, "Why" 248). And so they have: George Dyson reports that on first visiting Google, he realized they were "building a very large distributed AI, much as Turing had predicted," and he thought, "my God, this is not Turing's mansion—this is Turing's *cathedral*" (qtd. in Kelly 122). And so can humans, Latour says, if we understand that "the critic is not the one who debunks, but the one who assembles" ("Why" 246). Aligning critique with Simondon's technological attitude, he says that we, too, can become supercritical. If we approach objects as things we can touch, explain, and deploy in the collectives we gather, we can generate "more ideas than we have received, inheriting from a prestigious critical tradition but not letting it die away" (248).

We have inherited a past that we never lived, a way of making that we can choose by being open to its possibilities. Foucault once suggested that "maybe the target nowadays is not to discover what we are, but to refuse what we are. We have to imagine and build up what we could be" ("Subject" 216). Writing is a material practice, an embodied behavior, creating cognitive ecologies through the intra-action of entangled parts of the world that reciprocally create them anew.

3

Writing as Making

In introducing a song about a ship captain, Gordon Bok says, "He knew the mind of a boat; he knew what the damn thing was thinking." Tim Ingold comments, "It is curious how books have minds of their own. All their authors can do is to find the ways they want to go, and follow them" (M xi). What does it mean to say that a six-thousand-foot freighter has a mind and thinks? That books have minds of their own and ways they want to go? Are we to believe that boats and books have intentions and agency? Navigating a boat and writing a book are both technē, or making, modes of entanglement. Rejecting the hylomorphic vision of technē as the implementation of an agent's image, plan, or intention in the material world, Ingold argues that making instead is a "dance of animacy" (M 100), a correspondence as in exchanges of letters, an ongoing entanglement involving not only makers and tools and materials but also things and forces. The captain acts in correspondence with the boat, which acts in correspondence with the waves, which acts in correspondence with the wind, which acts in correspondence with the water and the boat and the captain's actions—a perfect dance of animate co-responses. Rather than mastery, making is a mode of becoming. "Everything there is . . . has its trajectory" (M 81); books are always in the process of becoming, just as much as authors and captains and boats and waves, and they become in the "form-creating systems" their entanglements create. Making, as Ingold describes it, embraces all three assumptions of enchantment ontology: everything is always in the process of becoming, all trajectories of becoming are entangled with others, and as a result novelty is inevitably emerging. But Ingold emphasizes the entanglement of entities in making as an intra-action—or as he says a correspondence—among, not a mastery of, entities, forces, materials, and tools.

I will have more to say about intentions and agency in chapter 5. In this chapter I argue that writing is making in the way Ingold thinks of it, that it is better referred to the notions of mētis and technē (especially phronetic technē) than to epistēmē.[1] Marcel Detienne and Jean-Pierre Vernant define mētis as "intelligence which operates in the world of becoming" (44), a world "of change and of that which never remains the same as itself" (307), and Joseph Dunne argues for an alternate Aristotelian phronetic technē "whose responsiveness to the situation is not fully specifiable in advance and which is experiential, charged with perceptiveness, and rooted in the sensory and emotional life" (355). Phronetic technē also has ethical overtones—it is a determinate shaping that confers value and meaning—and thus it resonates with Karen Barad's injunction that we meet the universe halfway.

Mētis, Technē, and Making

Accounts of practical knowledge in early Greek mythology and philosophy associated with the concepts of mētis and technē, suppressed in the dominant tradition of Western thought, have similarly been neglected until recently in Western rhetorical studies (cf. Atwill; Dolmage; Hawhee, *Bodily Arts*). Detienne and Vernant, describing mētis as "an intelligence which, instead of contemplating unchanging essences, is directly involved in the difficulties of practical life" (44), argue that "there can be no place for mētis" in the fourth-century Greek philosophical tradition: "In the intellectual world of the Greek philosopher, in contrast to the thinkers of China or India, there is a radical dichotomy between . . . the sphere of being, of the one, the unchanging, of the limited, of true and definite knowledge . . . [and] the sphere of becoming, of the multiple, the unstable and the unlimited, of oblique and changeable opinion" (5).[2] Noting how for over ten centuries, the practical intelligence that underlay the "skills, know-how and activities as diverse as weaving, navigation and medicine . . . [had been] a permanent feature of the Greek world" (307), Detienne and Vernant argue that it was at the hands of "the philosophers, the professional experts where intelligence was concerned"—Plato, and to a lesser extent, Aristotle—that "the qualities of mind which go to make up mētis . . . were thrust into the shadows, erased from the realm of true knowledge" (4). In the end, "*Sophia* becomes contemplative wisdom and ceases to refer to the knowledge of the skillful craftsman" (315).

Likewise, Janet Atwill notes that technē is "defined against virtually every distinguishing feature of traditional Western humanism" (7).[3] She, too, blames Plato for this legacy, arguing that "the scholarly neglect of Aristotle's domain of productive knowledge bears witness to the power of the philosophical paradigm to obscure alternative, situated standards of knowledge and value" (10–11). She argues that in ancient Greece, technē was "a distinctive form of intelligence" (48) "defined by its relation to situation and time" (7) and thus associated with both mētis and kairos. But by the time of imperial Rome, thanks to Plato's distinction between true and false knowledge, technē had devolved into "a neutral tool" in rhetoric and other realms of arts and crafts.

Ingold does not refer directly to these distant antecedents of his account of making, but comparing what he argues for with Detienne and Vernant's account of mētis and Dunne's account of Aristotle's phronetic technē illuminates both what has endured from this tradition and what has changed. Most obviously, Ingold retains focus on the intelligence of the particulars of practical life, an intelligence that comes from experience, arguing, in fact, that the craftsman is superior to the theorist in that she allows "knowledge to grow from the crucible of our practical and observational engagements with the beings and things around us" (M 6). Just as mētis and technē are defined as intelligences that operate in a realm of instability and difference, Ingold sees making as the intelligence necessary for living in a sphere of becoming—but for him this is not *a sphere* but reality, for indeed everything is "created in movement" (M 85). And just as mētis and phronetic technē involve bodily comportment (hexis), Ingold sees making as relying on habits, bodily "capacities of movement and feeling that have been developed through a life history of past practices" (BA 58), although Ingold emphasizes that dexterous skills are not preexisting properties but are called forth by "the gestural synergy of human being, tool and raw material" (PE 352). Though the concepts of concern are the same—practical intelligence, experience, becoming, embodied movement—Ingold's theory of making abandons not only hylomorphism but also the bifurcation of nature and any notion of an unchanging sphere of being and of true and definite knowledge.

In his discussion of technē and phronesis in Aristotle's works, Dunne notes that Aristotle's "official" concept of technē omits key features instantiated in some of Aristotle's examples of technē and that those features are pretty much what Detienne and Vernant associate with mētis: a highly prized "talent for making out against the odds of greater strength, a talent which combines 'flair, wisdom, forethought, subtlety of mind, deception, resourcefulness, vigilance, opportunism, various skills and experience acquired over the years ... [and] is applied to situations which are transient, shifting, disconcerting and ambiguous, situations which do not lend themselves to precise measurement, exact calculation or rigorous logic'" (Dunne 257; quoting Detienne and Vernant 3–4). Detienne and Vernant also notice this, allowing that, in contrast to Plato, "for Aristotle, 'practical intelligence' at least retains in its aims and in the way it operates many of the features of mētis" (4). Aristotle distinguishes two kinds of nontheoretical knowledge: productive knowledge (poietike) and practical knowledge (phronesis), and for the most part he associates technē with productive knowledge. Productive knowledge involves making (poiesis) and is concerned with the specific kind of activity that is directed toward an end (kinesis), as in the arts of building or cobbling. Aristotle says, "All art is concerned with coming into being . . . with contriving and considering how something may come into being . . . and whose origin is in the maker and not in the thing made" (*Nicomachean* vi.4).[4] What is in the maker is knowledge of the form that is to be made: "From art proceed the things of which the form is in the soul" (*Metaphysics* vii.7). Productive knowledge is knowledge of the forms, of "general rules" (Dunne 259; cf. 250). Practical knowledge involves a different kind of activity—acting (praxis)—a kind of activity "whose end . . . is realized in the very doing of the activity itself" (energeia), as in "the conduct of one's life and affairs"; it is the wisdom, or character, of an ethical person, "a person who knows how to live well" from long personal experience (Dunne 244). Aristotle says, "A young man with practical wisdom cannot be found . . . [because] such wisdom is concerned not only with universals but with particulars, which become familiar with experience, but a young man has no experience, for it is length of time that gives experience" (*Nicomachean* vi.8). For Aristotle, productive knowledge was superior because its universality and explanatory power made it more like theoretical knowledge, whereas practical knowledge, or wisdom, remained firmly rooted in the experience of particulars.

Dunne, however, notes a difficulty here in that knowledge of universals does not lead to practical effectiveness, which Aristotle acknowledges: "If, then, a man has theory without experience, and knows the universal but does not know the individual . . . he will often fail" (*Metaphysics* i.1). Dunne comments that in Aristotle's official concept of technē, "We do not get any sense of a making that is itself intelligent, endowed with a know-how which is learned and actualized in the very process of making" (285). But this is exactly the sense of making that Dunne says informs Aristotle's examples of aberrant technai such as military strategy, navigation, and medicine, where "success is to be achieved . . . not so much by keepings one's gaze fixed on the preconceived form which one will impose on the material, as by a flexible kind of responsiveness to the dynamism of the material itself. It is sensitivity or attunement rather than mastery or domination that one strives for" (256). He notes the "*affinity* between practical knowledge (phronesis) and the philosophically orphaned technai" (257–58), quoting Aristotle on how, in matters of conduct and of health, accounts of particular cases "do not fall under any art or set of precepts, but the agents themselves must in each case consider what is appropriate to the occasion, as happens also in the technē of medicine or of navigation" (*Nicomachean* ii.2). Dunne thus argues that Aristotle implies that the intelligence involved in technai like medicine and navigation is analogous to that involved in phronesis, or living well—"so much so, indeed, that *they can scarcely be said to be technai at all*" (258). Phronesis, Dunne argues, mediates "the universal and the particular in a way that puts a premium on experience and perceptiveness rather than on formulated knowledge" (273). Thus wedding the phronetic mode of action (praxis) to mētis-like technai, Dunne finds in Aristotle an unofficial concept of phronetic technē, a technē short on formulated knowledge and grounded in the particulars of human praxis. At the same time, as Dunne observes, Aristotle relieves these technai of the moral deviousness associated with mētis: "Part of Aristotle's achievement ... was to bed into his conception of ethical knowledge—i.e., the knowledge of a character which is oriented to the good—much of the suppleness and flexibility which were already well recognized as requirements in areas such as oratory and politics as well as in navigation or hunting" (260–61).

Practical knowledge was regarded as inferior to theoretical knowledge in Greek philosophy because it was the knowledge of workaday humans rather than the gods (and philosophers). It was the knowledge allotted to the weak, who needed deviousness and trickery to succeed against uncertainties and hostile forces. Detienne and Vernant refer to the "art of the sophist who, in contrast to the philosopher whose wisdom is directed toward the world of ideas, embodies the scheming intelligence of the man of *mētis*, plunged into the world of appearance and Becoming" (45). Michel de Certeau's notion of tactics, whose "space is the space of the other . . . an art of the weak" (37), was inspired by mētis. And Dunne notes that we learn from the myth of Prometheus that "all the technai were divine gifts to creatures who, without them, would have remained nakedly exposed to 'ungoverned contingency' or tuchē [chance]" (255). He comments, "The life of contemplation is self-justifying, [but] it is not, however, in the human world in which we live, self-sustaining" (242). Intelligence that allowed one to understand and cope with the sphere of becoming was necessary and even good when it was employed to achieve such things as ethical character, justice, health, and safety. But philosophers aspire to attain the true knowledge of the sphere of being, a sphere superior to the everyday world of becoming.

This value-laden two-sphere framework distantly presages Alfred North Whitehead's concept of the bifurcation of nature, which he observed seemingly makes knowledge of reality impossible. Neither of the two "systems of reality" that nature bifurcates into are knowable: the entities that supposedly are really in nature are available only as conjectures, such as electrons defined by speculative physics, and what we "know" of nature are only dreams, the "byplay of the mind," perceptions caused by whatever is out there in nature (CN 30). In Greek philosophy, humans are in the same situation: what is really out there are the forms that reside in the sphere of being, accessible only to philosophers, and humans, confined to the practical world of becoming, know only illusions. But Whitehead argues that we can and do know what we experience in nature: our experience *is* our knowledge. Ingold illustrates this in his conception of the weather-world. To expand a discussion he was having with his students about how a landscape is perceived, he took them to a beach on a stormy day. He describes what they experienced: "The noise of the breakers . . . invaded our auditory awareness: we did not just hear them; we heard *with* them. Far from being disclosed to us as targets of perception, waves, wind and sky were present as an all-enveloping experience of sound, light and feeling. . . . The breaking waves *were* their sound, not objects that make a sound; the wind *was* its feel, not an object touched; the sky *was* light, not something seen in the light" (BA 134). He concludes, "The experience . . . *is* light, sound and feeling, not something we obtain" by perceiving objects (BA 134). The sphere of becoming is not a sphere of illusion but the experienced world in which successful comportment requires the attributes of phronetic technē, "a flexible kind of responsiveness . . . sensitivity or attunement rather than mastery or domination" (Dunne 256). These are not, however, attributes that are mostly associated with mētis.

Ingold describes experience in the world as a "dance of animacy" in which "bodily kinaesthesia interweaves contrapuntally with the flux of materials within an encompassing, morphogenetic field of forces" (M 101). In contrast, mētis operates in a world in which humans are locked in combat with an external nature, managing recalcitrant materials and controlling hostile forces. Mētis is "an intelligence . . . directly involved in the difficulties of practical life with all its risks, confronted with a world of hostile forces which are disturbing because they are always changing and ambiguous," where "sickness and argument are forces just as hostile and disturbing as the sea, fire or molten metal" (Detienne and Vernant 44, 307). Confronted with a constantly changing and unpredictable world, humans must become like their opponent: quick, supple, malleable, adapting to events, seizing the kairotic moment: "It is thus that the helmsman pits his cunning against the wind so as to bring it safely to harbour despite it. . . . It is this way of conniving with reality which ensures [the] efficacy" of mētis (Detienne and Vernant 20–21).

Conniving with reality does not involve experiencing waves, wind, and sky as did Ingold and his students on the beach. Rather it is a tactical way of dealing with a powerful world, as Detienne and Vernant explain:

> There are many activities in which man must learn to manipulate hostile forces too powerful to be controlled directly but which can be exploited despite themselves, without ever being confronted head on, to implement the plan in mind by some unexpected, devious means: . . . for example, . . . the art of the pilot steering his ship against winds and tides, the verbal ploys of the sophist making his adversary's powerful argument recoil against him, . . . and the sleights of hand and trade secrets which give craftsmen their control over material which is always more or less intractable to their designs. (47–48)

Manipulation, exploitation, and control are the activities of mastery, which is the signal attribute of the hylomorphic model of making.

Hylomorphism also harks back to the split between the sphere of being and the sphere of becoming. Ingold succinctly describes it as "the logic of inversion . . . deeply sedimented within the canons of western thought" (BA 68) by which the "animacy of the lifeworld" is split into internal designs (forms, mental schemas) that determine the ephemeral structures and behavior of beings and things in the world. This is the model that underlies Aristotle's official version of technē, the bringing into being of things "whose origin is in the maker and not in the thing made" (*Nicomachean* vi.4). As I discussed in chapter 1, enchantment ontology, in contrast, assumes that entities are always emerging from processes of reciprocal induction among maker, materials, and forces rather than existing in advance and impressed on or induced in organic and inorganic material.

As an anthropologist, Ingold has for at least the past fifteen years consistently applied this precept to understanding the making activities of native peoples and other beings.[5] He does not disallow that there is friction involved in making: "It is precisely where the reach of the imagination meets the friction of materials, or where the forces of ambition rub up against the rough edges of the world, that human life is lived" (M 72). But he also does not see humans as struggling against the rest of the world, and indeed not even as the sole actors involved in making. Unlike mētis, which is characterized by "a whole gamut of operations in which the intelligence attempts to make contact with an object by confronting it in the guise of a rival, as it were, combining conniving and opposition" (Detienne and Vernant 6), Ingold's making is a process of *working with* materials and forces. Ingold says, "The forms humans build . . . arise within the currents of their involved activity, in the specific relational contexts of their practical engagement with their surroundings . . . a process of *working with* materials and not just *doing to* them, and of bringing form into being rather than merely translating from the virtual to the actual" (BA 10). He describes an experiment he engaged in with students to explore this thesis that "even if the maker has a form in mind, it is not this form that makes the work. It is the engagement with materials" (M 22). On a beach they used willow branches to make baskets by sticking lengths vertically into the sand in a circle, tying them at the top, and then weaving other lengths horizontally around the circle. Ingold comments: "Many students were surprised by the recalcitrant nature of the material . . . the willow did not want to be bent into shape. . . . Then we realised that it was actually this resistance, the friction set up by the branches bent forcibly against each other, that held the whole construction together. The form was not imposed on the material from without, but was rather generated in this force field, comprised by the relations between the weaver and the willow" (M 22-23). This force field is what Ingold refers to as the entanglements involved in *working with*: the resistance of the willow branches to being bent; the muscular movements of the weavers, each dependent on "such bodily dimensions as arm-reach and shoulder-height"; and the wind on the beach that was "bending all the verticals of the frame in one direction with an inclination that increased with height" (M 23)—all correspond in the formative process. The student basket makers might have struggled against the wind, as Detienne and Vernant's helmsman did, but it was a correspondence of forces that shaped the baskets and, as well, brought the ship safely to harbor. The students did not control the materials and forces they worked with any more than the helmsman defeated the wind. Indeed, the helmsman of a sailing ship does not "pit his cunning against the wind" since he needs the wind to make any progress at all, just as the skilled captain of a freighter takes account of the minds of the waves and the wind as well as of the boat.[6]

Aristotle's accounts of technē, both official and unofficial, are not as antagonistic as we see in accounts of mētis, but even the concept of phronetic technē fails to fully embrace form as always emerging from processes of reciprocal induction. When Dunne critiques the official concept for lacking a sense of "making that is itself intelligent, endowed with a know-how which is learned and actualized in the very process of making" (285), he begins by critiquing the hylomorphic model: it "throws no light on those cases in which we might want to say that the full-fledged form is simply not available at the outset to guide our thinking . . . but only emerges through a process that involves both thinking *and* making," and it also "gives no consideration to what is perhaps the most interesting aspect of production, namely, the devising of a *new* form" (284). Dunne argues that because for Aristotle "form *is* a disposition of matter," "the maker . . . is all the time immersed in the materials from which he must try to induce the form" (331). To support this position he offers Aristotle's abundant comparisons of technē to nature. Quoting James Joyce, Dunne argues that when Aristotle says art imitates nature, "he means that the artistic process is like a natural process" (461n65). Both the processes of technē and phusis produce form: Dunne says, "Both techne and nature are generative and work toward an end" (337). He quotes Aristotle's *Physics*: "If a house, e.g. had been a thing made by nature, it would have been made in the same way as it is now by techne; and if things made by nature were made not only by nature but also by techne, they would come to be in the same way as by nature" (ii.8). Dunne comments, "We would not be too far from the truth if we were to imagine the craftsman's activity itself as but a strategic detour through which nature goes," and he says that when Aristotle takes seriously the way that technē imitates phusis, he downplays the role of deliberation, as he does in the *Physics* where he says that "techne does not deliberate" (ii.8). Noting that this is a surprising statement, for it explicitly contradicts "the whole contemplative or theoretical side of techne—the working out of a form *in the mind of the technitēs*, prior to any engagement with the material," Dunne nevertheless suggests that perhaps emerging from Aristotle's work as a whole is a kind of technē in which "*noēsis* and poiesis are not separable ... but are, rather interwoven in one process which is at the same time intelligent *and* productive, and must be said to go on in the materials as much as in the mind of the *technitēs*" (338).[7]

I am persuaded by Dunne's argument for a phronetic technē that involves a process of becoming, but Aristotle's understanding of becoming still differs from that of enchantment ontology, as Dunne acknowledges. Dunne says that Aristotle's "preferred procedure was to analyze already-constituted beings and only through retrospective inferences from within this discourse of *being* to shed light on the process of becoming" (326). Aristotle writes, "For in house building too, these things come about because the form of the house is such and such, rather than its being the case that the house is such and such because it comes about thus" (*De Partibus Animalium* i.1). Here, as in Dunne's comment quoted above that "both techne and nature are generative and work toward an end," it is clear that the process of building is generative, but it is also, like nature in Aristotle's view, teleological. The form may be in the house as well as in the builder, but it precedes the process of making; the maker may be immersed in the material from which he induces the form, or the form may be revealed in the process, but this is different from saying, as Ingold does, that the form is generated in the force field of the entanglement of maker and material, or that the process of making brings the form into being.

The difference between Aristotle's focus on being and Ingold's on becoming is nicely illustrated in Ingold's discussion of architecture, which he begins by questioning whether there is "some determinate point at which the building is finished—when building yields *a* building—which means, in turn that its form must be judged as the realisation of a pre-existent design" (M 47). He takes issue with this statement on two points: first, that a building, like everything else in the world, never is completed but "ceaselessly unfolds along its innumerable paths of growth, decay and regeneration, regardless of the most concerted of human attempts to nail it down" (48), and second, that, directly opposite to what Aristotle says, a building takes the form it does because of the way it comes about: "There emerges an edifice of a kind . . . but it is rather a composite of many parts, imperfectly integrated, every part conditioned by ways of doing things peculiar to each of the teams that have contributed to its development, and patched together thanks to communicative exchanges between them" (57). A house neither begins nor ends with the architect's design, he argues, nor does the building elude the effects of unforeseen problems, incidents, and the vagaries of individual workers. A house's origin can be traced back as far as the growth of the trees that eventually became lumber, or to trees that were not planted expressly for this purpose; the designing continues into the building, as workers assemble and shape materials and use techniques that are never completely specified, and as they revise their work or the work of others; residents move in and use the house—Ingold says they perform the spaces of the house through their movements (M 85); residents call builders back to fix leaky roofs, add another room, update kitchens and bathrooms; residents sell the house and further performances and renovations ensue with new owners, or the house is repurposed into a bed-and-breakfast or a day-care center, or the house is abandoned, falls down or becomes a support for rampant vines; and on and on. Rather than revealing an essential form, making repeatedly brings forms into being.[8]

Nor do the "parts" of a house precede their function in the house: they become "parts" when they are brought into correspondence, as Ingold discusses in a later discussion of watchmaking: "Cogs and springs, among other minute pieces . . . become parts only as the assembly proceeds and tends increasingly to cohere. They gradually acquire a feel for each other, they *settle*, holding each other in place ever more tightly as the work advances asymptotically towards closure without ever absolutely reaching it" (M 69). On this point, Ingold, as he often does, compares human making with that of birds: "These pieces do not belong together, in preordained positions, by dint of some external necessity. They are no more parts of a watch than are twigs on the forest floor parts of a bird's nest" (M 69). His comment brought to my mind this description of a goldcrest building a nest at the top of a Norway spruce in Scotland:

> The nest [is] smaller than a tennis ball, built in layers of moss, fine twigs, and needles, then whiskery *Bryoria* and *Ramalaria* lichens, all stitched together with spider silk. . . . Two hours slid past and still she was beavering away, back and

forth, in and out, weaving, plucking, pulling and winding, drawing threads like a skilled seamstress, tucking in ends, twisting them off busying round and round the nest. She was a perfectionist, a precision purist, sometimes pleased with her work so that she could start afresh somewhere else, and sometimes clearly not, unpicking it and starting all over again. . . . Now both birds were at it . . . the male, unmistakable beneath his bright orange flash, was at least bringing in strands of sheep wool. . . . Off he went again. This time he returned with what I could clearly see were two long russet hairs from my Highland cattle . . . long and silky, perfect for goldcrests to weave into the lining of their nests. (Lister-Kaye 231–33)

Birds do have innate instincts for building nests, just as humans devise plans for building houses, but they also innovate with the materials at hand and they rework their nests as they weave, and the details of the location contribute as well to the ongoing form of the nest. It is the specific process of making that brings an actual form of a nest into being.

Nevertheless, makers and materials are not simply corresponding in an aimless activity: something—houses, watches, nests—is being made. Ingold quotes design theorist Lars Spuybroek who argues that a great designer/maker "not only sees the state of things, but senses where they are going" (240; qtd. in M 70). Ingold calls this crucial ability "anticipatory foresight: a foresight that does not so much connect a preconceived idea to a final object as *go between*, in a direction orthogonal to their connection, following and reconciling the inclinations of alternately pliable and recalcitrant materials" (70). Detienne and Vernant also include forethought as an intellectual quality necessary to mētis: "*Mētis* . . . takes the form of an ability to deal with whatever comes up, drawing on certain intellectual qualities: forethought, perspicacity, quickness and acuteness of understanding, trickery, and even deceit" (44). As an aspect of mētis, forethought seems similar to what the sociologist Richard Sennett, in his study of the work of the craftsman, calls "*anticipation:* being 'always one step ahead of the material'"(Sennett 175; qtd. in Ingold 69). But forethought or anticipation is more reactive than forward looking: it enables the maker to foresee what the material will do in order to "deal with it." In contrast, for Ingold, foresight is a matter "of opening up a path and improvising a passage"(69), a matter of bringing design and making into correspondence. He adduces the examples of composers trying to notate music that "flies ahead in his imagination" and of novelists "whose characters have a way of outrunning his capacity to write them down" (M 71). "The practical skill of painters, composers, and writers," he says, "lies in their practised ability to keep their distance whilst in the thick of the labours of proximity" (M 72), to have enough distance from their engagement with the materials to capture their dreams and at the same time, bring them back into their labors.

But doesn't this sound much like what Dunne is arguing for when he finds in Aristotle "a kind of technē in which "*noēsis* and poiesis are not separable . . . but are, rather interwoven in one process which is at the same time intelligent *and* productive" (284)? Especially where he discusses the way that technē imitates phusis, Dunne seems not to be just arguing that technai like medicine and navigation are phronetic, but arguing that this is true of all technai. He even suggests that Aristotle's distinction between technē and phronesis may not be very "significant or well-founded" (247). Though Dunne and Ingold seem in near agreement on this point, there is still a real difference between Aristotle's and Ingold's models of making that can be traced to Aristotle's prior distinction between kinēsis and energeia. How these two forms of activity differ turns on the question of where to locate the end or aim of the activity: "*kinēsis* is a process within a set limit [*peras*] toward an end [*telos*] and exists only as long as the limit has not yet been reached and the end does not yet exist . . . *energeia*, on the other hand, has no as yet unreached limit in that its end, or complete condition, already exists in it at any moment of its duration; it is an *entelecheia*" (Dunne 248, referencing *Metaphysics* ix.6). For Ingold, there is no set limit, no telos, no process that reaches an end. As Whitehead says, "There is no nature apart from transition" (MT 151–52). There is only entelechy, the actuality of becoming, what Whitehead calls concrescence—unities forming and reforming in continual intra-action—or what Ingold calls correspondence. He refers the notion to Alfred Schutz's characterization of social life as a process of "growing older together" (Schutz, *Problem*16–17; qtd. in M 106), and concludes, "To correspond with the world, in short, is not to describe it, or to represent it, but to *answer to it* . . . to mix the movements of one's own sentient awareness with the flows and currents of animate life." This process, he says, is "the essence of making" (108). Just as Dunne seems to want to efface the distinction between Aristotle's technē and phronesis, Ingold argues that all making, whether building houses or writing letters, is the interweaving of energies, the ongoing actualization of potentials. His preferred procedure, directly opposite to Aristotle's, is to analyze the process of becoming to shed light on the constitution of being.

A final useful point of comparison between Aristotle's technē and Ingold's making has to do with the role of experience, especially in the form of habituated movement, in how technē is acquired. Dunne argues that experience acquired over the years turns into expertise through being repeatedly applied in particular situations until it becomes habituated action. He derives this argument from examining how phronesis connects experience with present particulars: "Phronesis is a habit of *attentiveness* that makes the resources of one's past experience flexibly available to one and, at the same time, allows the present situation to 'unconceal' its own particular significance" (305–6). This significance is not the abstract knowledge of technē that refers to the particular only through general rules; instead it goes beyond simple experience through being "continually renewed in one's insightful dealings with particular situations [and becomes] a *hexis*, a formed disposition, only insofar as one is capable of such repeated renewals" (306). Thus, "Phronesis is not a completed state of knowledge that can be made the object of instruction" but instead is a continual learning process (306). Dunne argues that Aristotle's characterizations, in *Nicomachean Ethics*, of technē as a hexis and as an aretē suggest a technē that is "a fixed orientation to *act* (or *make*) in a determinate manner" (320). This leads him to the conclusion that teaching a technai does not depend on teaching rules but rather "must involve the apprentice *technitai* in a process where they work with their materials and have the teacher at hand to point out mistakes and to suggest ways forward toward mastery" (320). As I argued in chapter 1, habits do not become habits until they become habitual, become ingrained in bodily dispositions rather than residing in abstract rules.

The connection between technē and bodily disposition is echoed in discussions of mētis by Detienne and Vernant and by Hawhee. Detienne and Vernant list "agility, suppleness, swiftness, mobility" among the characteristics of mētis that enable hunters and fishers to capture their cunning prey (30). Hawhee, in her argument for connections between the arts of rhetoric and athletics, says that mētis becomes apparent in the body: it "cannot be thought separate from bodily state" (*Bodily Arts* 57). Noting that "the Greek word for bodily condition or bodily state, *hexis*, is indistinguishable from habits and practices" (58), she argues that "different thought trajectories are facilitated by different 'bodily conditions'" learned through repetition (57–58). Thus, like Dunne, she observes that learning through repetitive movement rather than learning rules is the way to acquire a skill: the sophists emphasized "corporeal acquisition of rhetorical movements" over the acquisition of "subject matter," a "manner of learning-doing [that] entails 'getting a feeling for' the work" (*Bodily Arts* 160). Dunne further observes that when Aristotle says that form is immanent in the soul of the artisan, he means that the soul is "present in the whole body and all its parts" (348). Thus he argues that "when Aristotle says that techne is in the soul, therefore, we can certainly interpret this to mean that it is in, e.g., the hand. . . . And when this raw potentiality is gradually disciplined into actual capacities for specific types of skilled activity, techne is present, we may say, as much in the hand as in the soul" (348). This is not a case of the soul directing the hands, but rather, as with the use of tools, the soul influences the motion that is habituated in the hands, for, as Aristotle says, "In [tools] lies in a certain sense the motion of the techne" (*De Generatione Animalium* i.22). Technē arises out of and consists in habituated instances of making by embodied technites.

Ingold agrees with Dunne in seeing habituated action as definitive of making: "Concentrated in skilled hands are capacities of movement and feeling that have been developed through life histories of past practice . . . put a pen in my hand and it knows how to write—how to shape the letters and allow them to run into each other" (M 115). He also agrees with seeing making, like phronetic technē, as founded in the experience of particulars rather than in general rules: it depends on an ability to recognize subtle cues in one's environment and to respond to them with judgment and precision, rather than on specification and articulation (M 109–10). He plays on a double meaning of the verb *to tell*, both the ability to "tell the whereabouts of animals from their tracks" and "to tell stories," to explain, in terms similar to Dunne's, how expertise is taught: "The telling of stories is an education of attention. Through it, things are pointed out to novices, so that they can discover for themselves what meanings the stories might hold in the situations of their current practice. . . . To tell, in short is not to explicate the world, to provide the information that would amount to a complete specification, obviating the need for would-be practitioners to inquire for themselves. It is rather to trace a path that others can follow" (M 110). Makers, like technites, pass on what they know by suggesting ways forward, tracing a path for others to follow. Ingold's telling is a way to teach the personal knowledge of makers that "both grows *from* and unfolds *in* the field of sentience comprised by the correspondence of practitioners' awareness and the materials with which they work" (M 111). Personal knowledge is not subconscious and it can be told to others, though it cannot, Ingold argues, be articulated as rules for making.

But, again, there is a difference between making and phronetic technē, and it lies in the conception of the interaction between the maker, tool, and material. While Aristotle, as interpreted by Dunne, sees technē residing in the motion of the soul and hands and tools of the technite, and also perhaps going on in the material, Ingold argues that it "is to be found neither in the brain nor in the hand, nor even in the tool it holds," but rather it "inheres in the technical act, the gesture, in which they are brought together" (M 115): "In the intelligent gesture, at once technically effective and perceptually attentive, hand and tool are not so much used as *brought into use*, through their incorporation into a regular pattern of rhythmic, dexterous movement. And the intelligence of this use . . . arises as an emergent property of the entire 'form-creating system' comprising the gestural synergy of human being, tool and material" (M 115–16; quoting Leroi-Gourhan 310). Indeed, Ingold argues that it is wrong to think of organisms, including human makers, as embodied; they are "not a thing that moves" but rather are "composed... in movement" (M 93). We experience ourselves "as moving and moved, in ongoing response—that is in *correspondence*—with the things around us" (M 94). Neither forms nor technē *reside* in makers or tools or even in their movement. They emerge in a "form-creating system" of corresponding beings, things, and materials.

Mētis and phronetic technē presage some of the aspects of Ingold's making: they are practical, grounded in experience and movement. In Greek thought they remained suspect and inferior kinds of intelligence, and they were considered to be teleological if not hylomorphic processes. But for Ingold, baskets and books are made in the everyday, entirely knowable "weather-world" of experience. Making is becoming, a continuous activity of forming and reforming, conditioned by habituated movements in which makers and tools correspond with materials and forces, thereby bringing forms and skills into being.

The Reanimation of Technē in Rhetoric and Composition

Kelly Pender details how technē experienced a surge of interest in the field of rhetoric and composition in response to Richard Young's 1980 introduction of the new classicist definition of art. As "a conscious rational ability to effect preconceived results," art contrasted with "knack, an unreflective and unteachable habit acquired through experience" (Pender 39). Unlike Pender, I am not trying derive a "better, more synthetic" version of technē from the debates over instrumentality and teachability that ensued (106), but rather to reanimate technē as a foil in order to define a sense of making that I see as essential to writing. I do see writing as a purposeful mode of bringing designing and making into correspondence, as Ingold says, and certainly as teachable, but teachable through inculcating habits, not through instilling strategies or rules. In this regard, I find in Janet Atwill's scrupulous reading of the ancient and classical accounts of technē some congruences with my account of writing as making.

Atwill discerns three stable characteristics of technē to ground her definition, all of which bear some relationship to my account. First, a technē "is never a static, normative body of knowledge... [it] is a *dynamis* (power) and a set of transferable strategies, both contingent on situation and purpose" (7). Like Byron Hawk, who says "*physis* can be seen as the very ground of *technê*" ("Toward" 381), Atwill identifies what I have argued is the process of intra-action as a power of (or in) nature rather than a body of knowledge residing in a maker or elsewhere, and although she also refers to a set of strategies, she insists that they are contingent on situation and purpose. Such strategies are learnable through habituation, as she argues elsewhere for kairos, which she notes is "the time 'associated with technē'" (57). She says, "'Knowing how' and 'knowing when' are at the heart of kairos, distinguishing technē from rule-governed activities that are less constrained by temporal conditions" (59). She quotes Isocrates on how an aspiring writer or speaker chooses good examples and by "habituating himself to contemplate and appraise such examples, he will feel their influence not only in the preparation of a given discourse but in all the actions of his life" (*Antidosus* 277; qtd. in Atwill 58). She also comments that "transmission of a technē has as much to do with constructing a subject as with transferring rhetorical strategies" and likens this "very complex kind of mimesis" to "what Bourdieu would call the 'embodiment' of an art" (Bourdieu 73; qtd. in Atwill 59). When strategies are learned through repetition and mentoring and become ingrained in bodily dispositions, they become habits. Hawk points out that Young's dismissal of habits "disregards the fact that habit can work for students who are not going to be teachers," and I would argue that turning technē "into a system via the knowledge of causes" (Hawk, *Counter-History* 27) doesn't work for teachers either.

Atwill's second characteristic of technē is that it "resists identification with a normative subject" (7). Atwill definitely retains a notion of a somewhat autonomous subject—both Hawk and Pender suggest that she "comes close to a reemphasis of a subject that implicitly preexists the situation and can will to intervene in it" (Hawk, "Toward" 381; and see Pender 159n37)—but she sees a hope for "a contingent, temporal subject that exists only in a situated, discursive exchange" (45), which begins to touch on the idea of a writer as maker entangled in the intra-actions of writing.

Atwill's third characteristic is that "technē marks a domain of human intervention and invention" (7). She retains the characterization of mētis as a struggle against opposing forces to align it with her project of disrupting the normative process of humanistic education that, she argues, turns rhetoric "into a discipline of representation" in which it "is far more prone to reproduce the given than to invent new possibilities" (207). In contrast, I follow Dunne in arguing for the unofficial concept of phronetic technē relieved of the moral deviousness associated with mētis in order to highlight technē's ethical and inventive facets. Given entanglement, technē has no need for intervening or transgressing boundaries. Hawk makes this point as he argues that "contexts can be altered just by being there, through our navigation, integration and coevolution. Such intervention is not necessarily consciously planned and achieved. It is not that decisions do not happen. Even when teachers, students, or workers consciously invent things such as techniques, the decisions to do so are products of complex ambient ecologies" ("Toward" 387). Barad observes this too, from the other direction, arguing that we cannot help intervening: "'Do I dare disturb the universe?' is not a meaningful question, let alone a starting point for ethical considerations. . . . There is no such exterior position where the contemplation of this possibility makes any sense" (396). Being there is enough, being there and being accountable for what happens.

Hawk comments that in his description of intervention as an enaction, it "becomes much closer to its neighboring concept: invention" ("Toward" 387). Even though Atwill links technē with mētis as a mode of intervention, she also sees it as a mode of invention and characterizes it as a movement on a path. Technē "intervenes when a boundary or limitation is recognized," but as it does so, "it creates a path that both transgresses and redefines that boundary. Fate and necessity may set temporary limits for invention, but their boundaries are perpetually redrawn by technē" (48). She comments that images of invention in ancient texts refer to paths, places, and roads; philosophical traditions of inquiry and invention emphasize places, while rhetorical traditions emphasize paths. "Some of these paths lead to familiar 'places'; other paths are themselves new trajectories" (66). Ingold, as I have noted, also sees invention in terms of movement, a matter "of opening up a path and improvising a passage" (M 69). And, like Atwill, who argues for "the appropriation of a habit of vigilance that is alert for indeterminacies and points of intervention" (210), Ingold argues that training makers involves "an education of attention," though for Ingold the goal is not to enable intervention but rather to suggest ways forward, tracing a path for others to follow.

Neither Atwill's nor Pender's reading of technē could be called posthumanist nor do they ascribe to the assumptions of enchantment ontology.[9] Rescuing vitalism from its "narrow, ahistorical" interpretation common in rhetoric and composition in the 1970s and connecting it with complexity theory, Hawk offers complex vitalism as an ecological approach to questions of invention.

Writing as Correspondence

"To correspond with the world, in short, is not to describe it, or to represent it, but to *answer to it* . . . to mix the movements of one's own sentient awareness with the flows and currents of animate life" (Ingold, M 108). This process, Ingold says, is "the essence of making" (108). Correspondence is an especially useful term in the context of my argument that writing is a kind of making because Ingold elaborates it with reference to the practice of carrying on an exchange of letters. A correspondence is an ongoing becoming: "Writing letters takes time, as does waiting for them and reading them when they arrive" (105). Correspondence has "no starting point or end point." A letter may turn into a correspondence, and "a lapsed correspondence may be rekindled" (105). Furthermore, a correspondence is about being present: "The lines of correspondence are lines of feeling, of sentience, evinced not—or not only—in the choice of words but in the manual gestures of the writing and their traces on the page. To read a letter is not just to read *about* one's respondent, but to read *with* him or her. It is as though the writer was speaking from the page, and you—the reader—were there, listening" (105). Ingold also cites the example of a string quartet as described by Schutz: the players are not interacting "but are rather moving along together, listening as they play, and playing as they listen, at every moment sharing each other's 'vivid present'" (M 106; quoting from Schutz, "Making").

Correspondence aligns well with Whitehead's concept of concrescence and with Barad's concept of intra-action, both of which also do not presume isolated entities but rather, as Barad says, "*the ontological inseparability/entanglement of intra-acting 'agencies'*" (139). As she says, "It is through specific agential intra-actions that the boundaries and properties of the components of phenomena become determinate and that particular concepts (that is, particular material articulations of the world) become meaningful" (139). Like Whitehead's concrescence, intra-action emphasizes the reciprocity involved in making, as entities are rewritten anew: humans become basket makers and kite flyers and writers as they intra-act with willow branches becoming a basket, the wind becoming a medium for kites, a set of observations becoming the material for a scientific paper. Not just letter-writing but all kinds of writing (and rhetoric) work in this way, it seems to me, entangling humans, language, and other entities and forces in the world in becoming.

An excellent example of writing as corresponding is provided by British plant biologist Nicholas Harberd whose book *Seed to Seed: The Secret Life of Plants* is an edited version of a notebook he kept for a year. It is a performative account of the emergence of two new research projects as they arose in the correspondences among the thinking feeling knowing being that is Harberd, a single thale-cress plant growing in nearby St Mary's cemetery, memories of his intra-actions with natural surroundings, visits to the nearby Wheatfen nature reserve, his knowledge of plant genetics, an account of the previous research of his group, and intra-actions with his children. Barad contrasts a performative account to a representative account, which positions itself outside the world and reflects on it: "A performative account insists on understanding thinking, observing, and theorizing as practices of engagement with, and as part of, the world in which we have our being" (133). In the preface to his book,

Harberd writes, "My intention was to try to capture a sense of the scientific process within a more general picture of a mind that is engaged with it" (2). In writing in his notebook, Harberd is fully intra-acting in the world, not only in his thinking and experimentation but also emotionally. Like the boat captain and the freighter, instead of describing or representing the world, he corresponds with it, mixing "the movements of [his] own sentient awareness with the flows and currents of animate life" (Ingold, M 108).

Dunne says that success in phronetic technē requires a "flexible kind of responsiveness to the dynamism of the material . . . sensitivity or attunement rather than mastery or domination" (256). The materials of writing are the subjects the writer is working with: in Harberd's notebook, the three principal subjects are the progress of his research, which consists of the results of past research, observations, hypotheses, experiments, and two research papers; the life cycle and adventures of the thale-cress plant; and Harberd's memories, activities, and thoughts and feelings. As we follow him through the year, three useful habits of writing as making become apparent:

> close observation of the subjects of the writing,
> connection of observations, experiences, memories, and feelings
>   through patterns, and
> wonder: speculating, and asking questions.

The habit of observation is a way of being attentive to the materials, to the subject matter of writing. Harberd is explicit about the importance of observation for a field naturalist—"Clear description of what is seen as the key. Illuminated by an account of the unseen events that drive those observed phenomena" (18)—but detailed observation is important in writing about almost any subject. It is a standard methodology in studies of cultures, central in news reporting and travel writing, a means of supporting project and policy proposals and arguments, and essential in offering testimony. The habit of connection derives from what Ingold sees as the essence of corresponding: mixing one's sentient awareness with the flows of everyday life. Harberd continually sees patterns and makes connections among observations, experiences, memories, and feelings. Thinking of things as structured as levels connects a range of experiences and memories: as a toddler, pulling parsnips with his father, he envisions "a plane, an extended flat surface, that divided all the other parsnips still in the garden into root and shoot" (10); after attending a concert, he comments that "the music exists simultaneously on different levels, on different scales of focus, is like life itself in this sense" (267); and of getting one of his papers to "form itself," he says, "It's a question of pace and level. For a paper to work it has to do so on several levels, from that of the overall to the detailed particular. ... And the pace has to work simultaneously at each of those levels" (291).

The habit of wonder is the one he seems most unconscious of, but it is essential to his work as a scientist. If, as Ingold says, to correspond is to answer to the world, natural scientists perhaps are more habituated to wonder. Harberd asks questions and speculates about every detail of plants he observes, and he wonders about many other things, such as why science seems so cut off from everyday life. Wonder might be thought of as the habit of critical thinking so popular in education, but as Harberd describes this feeling it aligns better with the felt recognition that something matters in a particular way, like Kimmerer's recognition of the plantain I described in chapter 1. He writes repeatedly of his excitement and awe at discovering something important. Near the end of his notebook, he comments on "the tendency for knowledge to become uninteresting once understood" and resolves to resist it: "I will see those thale-cress seedlings at St Mary's as the extraordinary things they are. ... When these things are clearly seen as being astonishing, their significance ... becomes more apparent" (286). As Barad might say, through Harberd's intra-action with the thale-cress plant, it has come to matter.

These three habits are already apparent in the beginning of his account of searching for a new direction in his research. After a brief introduction to his genetic work with thale-cress, "our own *Drosophila* (fruit-fly)" (5), he concludes his first entry in the notebook on January 8: "I've come up against a barrier. Where next?" (6). A few days later, chatting with his children Alice and Jack about what they did in school that day, he is startled into a memory by Jack's mention of growing beans in a jar: "A sparse classroom at my infant school . . . A beam of sunlight . . . falling on some twigs of horse chestnut standing in an old jam-jar of water" (7). The vividness of the memory gives him an idea: maybe he needs to get out of the lab, "get out into the real world more than I do. See something else" (8). He discovers a nearby nature reserve, Wheatfen, that he will visit repeatedly throughout the year; he looks at thale-cress seeds under a microscope with Alice and Jack; Jack's pride in the root and shoot growing from his bean sparks his memory of pulling parsnips with his father; he goes to a production of a play he saw as a child and muses how the phrases and actions he remembers are "re-formed now in the telling, making a new thing from the old," and he concludes: "This is the way to arrive at a new direction. By seeing things already seen in a new way, making predictions of unseen things, testing them. But how to do it in reality?" (12). Then, three weeks after thinking he needs to get out of the lab more, he bikes off to Wheatfen again and has an intense epiphany, sparked by noticing a leaf: "A momentary certainty that that blackberry leaf and I belonged to a single entity. And it was then that I thought of looking for the thale-cress" (17). He starts searching for thale-cress plants "in the wild," and when he doesn't find any, he checks out his guide to the *Flora of Norfolk*, where he finds a photo of thale-cress growing in a graveyard. He comments:

> I'm developing an idea. The seed planted in my mind by Jack's bean. That I should continue the search for a thale-cress plant growing in the wild. Then, when it is found, I'll record the growth and life-history of that plant in these pages. The same plant that I've studied so closely and for so long in the lab. Perhaps this will rekindle my sense of wonder, will help me to see the way forward for our stalled research. It will be a new natural history... I've been spending my life shaping a vision of hidden molecular events, invisible things that drive life. I think it's time to retell the old story in new terms. (18–9).

Five days later, in the graveyard at St. Mary's, he find the thale-cress he will study.

As a scientist, Harberd's habits of observation are well-practiced and quite specific. He has worked on them for his whole life so that he is always aware of the plants he sees in great detail. Later in the notebook, he comments on his habituation, comparing it to his sensitivity to music which he attributes to his forty-year experience of careful listening and playing: "I am aware of the growth and development of the thale-cress plant, of tiny changes in it, and I know that particular awareness helps me to see" (186). When he decides to record the growth and life history of the thale-cress plant, he reminds himself that "clear description is the key," and he continues to remind himself to look closer, describe in more detail, following William James's advice to pay attention and exert effort regularly in order to convert feelings and dispositions into action. The idea of seeing things in a new way as a way to find a new direction, followed by predictions (hypotheses) and testing, is of course his habitual scientific method, but it builds on observing closely—and is stimulated here by his reexperiencing of the play.

Connection is the most obvious habit in the notebook and is the one that sparks Harberd's new idea of getting out of the lab. Writing in his notebook reinforces this habit, enabling him to consciously attribute the new idea to Jack's bean and to repeat often the idea of making a new thing from the old. Making connections enacts entanglement as a crucial habit of writing, especially connecting past and present with the subject material through memories and experiences of daily life. It becomes explicit here because of the notebook (or diary) genre, but all writing emerges from the entanglements made more obvious here.

The habit of wonder is barely mentioned in the opening pages, though after he finds the thale-cress plant he immediately speculates about how it came to be growing where it is, especially since, besides the three plants he found (he chose just one to study), there were no others growing in the immediate vicinity. Wonder, though, is clearly identified in the notebook as the motive of science, and he discusses it more explicitly later. He observes that scientists don't write about feelings in their papers, but "wonder is what really drives us, and wonder is what we feel," and then he immediately turns to his "wonder at the present" about why the seedling growing in the shade is taller than the ones growing in the open (238). And again, later, "science too deals with a wonder in phenomena" (283).

Harberd's quest for a new direction in his research actually takes quite a long time to come to fruition, from January 8 through June 5, when he finally proclaims, "Thought at last of a way forward for our research. I feel no hesitancy in writing this . . . I know this new idea is the right one" (161). To someone reading (or rereading) his notebook carefully, his idea is amply forecast from the very beginning when he decides to get out of the lab into the real world. Not only is Harberd continually remembering incidents that connect with his present experiences and seeing patterns in what he observes, he continually, as Ingold says, mixes his sentient awareness with the flow of animate life, seeing himself and the world as a whole. The epiphany that came with seeing the blackberry leaf was accompanied with "a flash of recognition. That the life of the leaf, its cells, vessels, and hairs, was linked with my own" (16–17). Other examples of this feeling of connectedness are more elaborate.

As Harberd writes in his notebook, he corresponds with the world he is observing. He notes how the leaves of the thale-cress plant are angled to catch the sun's rays, and writes, "I had the strange feeling that they themselves were reminding me of their purpose" (59). Later in the day, he writes, "As I write, remembering what I saw this morning, it transiently seems to me that my writing about photosynthesis, pencil scratching across the pages of my notebook in the fading evening light, is photosynthesis writing about itself" (60). Again, returning from a visit to his thale-cress plant, he drinks some tea, and comments, "I've drunk and sat for a while, looking at the leaves clinging via a meniscus of dark tea to the bottom of the mug. I can see the veins and conduits that once carried water, salt, and energy, that fed the cells. These vessels part of the continuity of branch, stem, and leaf that connect me through the tea to the sun. I feel its light warming my mind" (140–41). Insights and ideas emerge from Harberd's juxtaposition and connection of observations of plants and the landscape and his emotions and memories with scientific explanations of plant growth, a process he experiences with "real excitement": "the widening of vision. When suddenly, one more piece of the world comes into view" (273–74). He comments explicitly on this process in many of his notes, often written while outside. In late April, he writes,

> And today the spring is so very lovely. . . . All over the garden there hangs this sense of excitement with the expanding juicy greenness.
>
> And there's delight in the knowing, the deep knowing that this expansion is a property of the protein we discovered. . . . That it is somehow a part of this beloved thing we call spring. The trick is to keep the spring's beauty and the knowledge of the protein together in the mind at one and the same time.[10] Not easy to do. I often lose it. But that trick enriches thought. (108–9)

In December, he returns to the importance of this trick, which he sees has preoccupied these notes: "A conceptual integration of scales, that somehow allows us to see life simultaneously at both the visible and invisible levels, would, I think, enrich our experience of the world" (298). He observes that "it's a shame that these ideas aren't more easily appreciated by non-specialists. . . . The writing of these notes has been, at least in part, an attempt to make a few of the images that science has generated more visible to others" (298–99). He concludes that achieving that purpose requires "a general adoption of the view that the world is a whole. That it is part of us and we are part of it" (299).

Harberd demonstrates the "responsiveness to the situation [which] is not fully specifiable in advance and which is experiential, charged with perceptiveness, and rooted in the sensory and emotional life" that Dunne says characterizes phronetic technē (355). The experience that led to what he knew was the right idea took place on holiday in Mallorca, an experience reminiscent of when Ingold took his students to the beach on a stormy day. Harberd stands in a churning surf:

> Feeling the backwards and forwards force around my legs as [the waves] surged up the beach and then back again. The salt spray in my nose, my shirt wet-cool and clinging to my back. Exhilarated by the energy of it all. Thrilled by a new experience: the sting of pebbles running back with the undertow and smashing into the backs of my calves.
>
> There was the flash thought that *this* is what science is about: the perception of things previously unknown or unfelt. And as the wave sucked back to the sea, its power almost unbalancing me, stones slamming again against my legs, so the idea came. A simple shining idea. That I should ask Why? (161)

Attuning to a new experience in which "bodily kinaesthesia interweaves contrapuntally with the flux of materials within an encompassing, morphogenetic field of forces" (Ingold, M 101) stimulates a new idea, a flash of insight. The idea that occurred to him here in the surf in Mallorca was indeed crucial, pivoting him away from the question he and his group had answered well—how certain proteins (DELLAs) restrain the growth of a plant—to a question they had not yet tried to answer: Why do they do so?

This incident also recalls Dunne's insistence that "phronesis is a habit of *attentiveness*," a habit "that makes the resources of one's past experience flexibly available to one and, at the same time, allows the present situation to 'unconceal' its own particular significance—which it may do comfortably within the terms of one's experience or else only by evincing an insight which, while it could not occur without one's past experience, still transcends, and so enriches it" (305–6). Harberd's attentiveness and responsiveness to his surroundings, whether here in Mallorca or in gazing at the veins in tea leaves in his mug, flexibly activates past experiences that situate and stimulate new insights or reveal the significance of observations.

Two weeks later, Harberd returns to thinking about the new research question, commenting that "why questions are always harder than how questions" (174). But he has found an answer that allows him to devise experiments: the restraint DELLAs impose on plant growth must confer benefits. Three days later, he elaborates this answer: "The idea is that DELLAs connect the plant with the world outside. That, I think, is the benefit that the DELLAs confer. They enable plants to grow at rates that are somehow appropriate to prevailing conditions" (176). And then on a trip to the seacoast with Alice and Jack two weeks later on July 4, he "suddenly" saw how he could test this idea: "Here in the salt-marsh, it was clear in an instant. The salt-marsh is a place of extremity. Thale-cress, I am sure, would not grow well in such adverse conditions. And that is the experiment. In essence, to recreate a salt-marsh in the lab. Then use it to test if DELLAs somehow regulate the growth of plants in response to adversity. If they do, then the evolution of DELLA-restraint is explained. It is so obviously the thing to do that I cannot for a moment understand why I couldn't see it before" (187). The "simple shining idea" that arose in the moment in the Mallorca surf had deep roots in Harberd's past experience. He had been studying thale-cress for years before he decided to study it in nature. Paying attention to the responses of the thale-cress in St Mary's graveyard to the seasons and weather, the loss of leaves and of the first flowering stem to predators, the taller growth of a seedling growing in the shadow of a dandelion leaf, made him more aware of how the plant's growth emerged from the force field of these environmental forces impinging on the DELLA proteins and the plant. In October he writes with excitement about how his decision to observe the thale-cress plant paid off: "What's the point of a mechanism to regulate growth if plants that lack it grow relatively normally? Now I think I have an answer to this question. DELLAs aren't essential to growth itself but provide the plant with a way of tuning their growth to environmental conditions. This was not obvious to me before, because, in the lab, plants are usually grown in 'ideal' conditions. Getting out into the world has opened my eyes, helped me to think of an experiment that shows that DELLAs have 'adaptive significance'" (265). He comments too on how writing in this notebook over the year has "served its purpose" of redirecting his research: "This telling of the tale of the thale-cress plant in St Mary's has helped me break through that barrier. . . . Studying one small plant and its place in the world has brought my science out of the confines of the lab, into reality" (191–92). What was not obvious to Harberd before was something he knew all along but hadn't quite connected with his research. Writing in his journal, connecting memories, feelings, experiences, with his effort to find a new direction, he came to see how the entanglement he felt when he was out in the world explained the purpose of DELLA restraint in plants.

In his accounts of designing experiments and writing papers, Harberd also reveals how he corresponds with the materials to bring about their form. Ingold argues that designers participate in bringing form into being by moving in correspondence with the direction in which the material is going. An important part of this process is anticipatory foresight, which he says operates not to connect a preconceived idea to a final object but by going "in a direction orthogonal to their connection, following and reconciling the inclinations of alternately pliable and recalcitrant materials" (Ingold, M 70). Harberd describes how he arrived at a complicated hypothesis in previous research as involving "logic and something more. . . . Taking it just a little beyond what is actually seen, so that what is seen is transformed in the mind" (106). He explains it as like looking at a reed-bed: "I cannot look at such a thing without making something out of what I see. Without seeing lines and shapes in it, connecting leaf to stem even when I cannot really see the junction. Penetrating the thicket of it with my vision" (106). He was trying to understand a result of a previous experiment: plants with a particular mutant gene grow dwarf rather than tall because the protein the gene encodes has an altered structure that changes the way it works. His hypothesis requires explaining why injecting a growth-promoting hormone into the plants containing the mutant gene does not restore their growth, as it normally would. The protein normally exhibits two states, one in which it restrains growth and one in which it permits growth, but the lack of the growth-promoting hormone causes an accumulation of the restraining state of the protein and the change in its structure must prevent the protein from converting into the permissive state. Following and reconciling the opposed actions of the proteins and hormones gets Harberd to his hypothesis.

Another way Ingold says that anticipatory foresight works in bringing form into being is by reconciling distance and immediacy: the imagination is "always inclined to shoot off into the distance" and needs to be brought "back into the immediacy of material engagement" (M 73). Harberd often contrasts the distancing necessary for objective science with his feelings of unity with the world. Near the end of the notebook, he muses about how both engagement and distance seem to be necessary. He says he feels "warmth from being part of the world, not a cool, detached observer," but adds, "there's another voice pushing me in the opposite direction. Saying that distance is necessary for focus, for perspective" (264). This is the trick that Harberd spoke of in April of keeping "the spring's beauty and the knowledge of the protein together in the mind at one and the same time," a trick that enriches thought (109).

Near the end of August, Harberd begins writing about the composition of the two papers that will report the results of the new research. Both papers are being composed while the research is ongoing, and though he says the structures for both are clear, being based on the results of the experiments, how everything fits together and the conclusions are not at all clear at the beginning and not for a while into the process of composing. He comments in most detail about the progress of the gravitropism paper. Ingold argues that the form of what is made does not reside in makers, tools, or material, or even in their movement but rather emerges in a "form-creating system" of corresponding entities. Harberd finds the process of writing papers frustrating, but he understands that the final form a paper achieves arises through the specifics of the process of writing—which has included the writing in the notebook. On October 27, he reports spending much of the day "writing the gravitropism paper. . . . It's getting to be pretty good" (279), and on November 2 he spent another whole day on it, saying, "I had great fun. . . . Still a long way to go before submission. . . . But more and more I have the feeling that it exists" (281–82). But it hasn't yet found a form: on November 5, he finds the paper "lacking in so many ways. Full of strands that don't connect, observations poorly described" (282). It seems, as Ingold says, that at this point the parts have not yet "become parts," have not acquired "a feel for each other," or settled (M 69). On November 7, he goes out into the woods with his daughter "to think more about the gravitropism paper" (283), and on November 9, he rewrites the whole thing, and still "it won't do. The writing lacks clarity" (285). On November 12, he says, "At last I think it's forming" (286), and finally, on November 20, he says, "Yesterday, I got the gravitropism paper to form itself. . . . Often it isn't obvious how to do it. One just has to keep on trying new things, and then suddenly you know you're there" (291). On December 10, he reports that he has "resumed work on the salt paper. It needs a lot of work.... Presumably I'll get there eventually" (297). The salt-growth paper was published in *Science* in January 2006. In the afterword, written in July 2004, he reports that the gravitropism paper was rejected and is in the process of revision, which includes further experiments. Despite the "forwardses and backwardses" in composing these papers, Harberd is clearly not trying to impose a form on the material or struggling with recalcitrant material. Nor is the form inherent in the material, even though he describes the structure of the papers in terms of the salient results of the experiments.

Harberd barely mentions language in his comments on his writing of these two papers, perhaps reflecting Heidegger's argument that when one uses tools, one is not aware of them. Though I find Ingold's theory of making quite useful in thinking about writing, I am troubled by his assumption that the tools of writing are pens or keyboards—which is a result of his equally troubling assumption that writing is inscription. Inspired by Whitehead's account of the sixth day, I instead argue that language is the tool of writing. In chapter 1, I said that language is not a tool in the sense of being an instrument, and Ingold agrees in that he says tools are "not so much used as *brought into use*" (M 115–16). Language is brought into use in writing, and, again as Ingold says, the intelligence of this use does not reside in language but arises as writer and language and material intra-act, as they are incorporated into a rhythmic flow, to borrow language from Harberd (276). Language is not a set of signs referring to the world, but rather participates in making meaningful entities.

The function of language, Whitehead argues is not to be "the vehicle of thoughts" but rather to link present experience to past experience both in terms of symbolic reference and causal efficacy, or affect (PR 182). He writes, "Language is handy as an instrument of communication along the successive occasions of the historic route forming the life of one individual. By an extension of these same principles of behaviour, it communicates from the occasions of one individual to the succeeding occasions of another individual" (PR 183). This is the same claim that Dunne makes about phronesis, that attentiveness to present occasions activates past experiences in a way that unconceals their significance.

Harberd recognizes the same relation when he talks of creating images of proteins that would speak to non-plant biologists. Seeing a flying heron, he "saw it momentarily as an image of the kind a painter might make—a few lines for a beak and flapping wings and a cylindrical blotch that in some way represented, or was an abstraction of, the idea of 'heron, flying'" (218). If we could do that with scientific images, he wonders, "Would there then be a familiar, at home sort of feeling about these things, which are as much a part of our landscape as flying herons?" (218). As Isabelle Stengers argues, saying "a tiger" when perceiving a patch of yellow and black is not an occasion of correctly labeling something but rather of an intensity of feeling that arises from entanglement in the world, and the work the word does is to link these feeling occasions allowing comparisons and elaborations (TW 213). Barad argues, "It is through specific intra-actions that phenomena come to matter—in both senses of the word" (140), and language (and other symbolic or abstract representations) enables an elaboration of how and why an occasion matters and whether it does indeed matter in the present circumstances.[11]

Scientific papers are meant to transform the messy processes of research into rational, representationalist accounts. Throughout his notebook, and increasingly as the year progresses, Harberd notices the limitations of representative accounts. He says that "the writing doesn't capture or restate shared experience" (283) and that science focuses "relentlessly on the subject in its view, to the exclusion of the rest of life" (222). Harberd's papers certainly fit this description, but in his observations in the notebook about working on the papers, he thinks of them in terms of the stories they tell. The stories Harberd is telling in these accounts are stories about how scientists work; they focus more on telling, in Ingold's sense, what he knows about doing science rather than on articulating the results of the research, which is what his papers do.

When he begins writing in August, he says he is sketching "a possible shape for a paper on the gravitropism story" (220–21), and on November 17, he announces "the conclusion of the gravitropism story": "So to the denouement. The final twist in the gravitropism tale" (290). He then describes how he was led to the conclusion through a series of experiments, explains what they observed in the plants' growth and how it all fits together, and says: "And so the case is made. Roots need DELLAs if they are to respond appropriately to gravity-induced auxin accumulations" (290). Earlier, when he said that the paper was "forming," he attributes this in part to the improvement in a section about "one of the sub-plots of the paper," which "wasn't properly realized" (286). Again, as he works on the salt-growth paper, he comments, "The story is complex, with many strands. Not a single line" (276).

Ingold says that makers pass on their knowledge by telling stories. His notion of telling is like Barad's performative account in that it does not represent the world. Telling is "a modality of performance that *abhors* articulation and specification (M 109). Instead it is "an education of attention"; it "offers guidance" (M 110). At the end of his first chapter, Ingold warns his readers, "Do not try to read [this book], as it will not inform you of what you need to know. You'll have to find that out for yourself. But do read *with* it. I hope, then, that it will guide you on your way" (15). Harberd's notebook works this way: in giving "a sense of the scientific process within a more general picture of a mind that is engaged with it" (2), he allows nonscientists to accompany him and learn from his stories how scientists correspond with the world. In this, Harberd's intentions for his book also align with Ingold's, who says it was his ambition to write a book that would "somehow resolve the opposition between the theoretical and the practical," a book in which "its lines would mingle with the writing of the world, and its pages with the world's surfaces" (M 15). A book, in short, that demonstrates what he calls knowing from the inside.

Beginning with his decision to do more observation of plants outside the lab, in the "real world," Harberd's writing is an essential and inextricable part of his answering to the world: it is an enactment of the interweaving of energies from which emerged the scientific conclusion that "growth is as much a property of the environment as it is of plants" (291) and the personal insight that because the world "is part of us and we are part of it," there is a message we need to learn from the plant, that when lacking restraint it becomes "insensitive, brash, a fast-liver that is unable to exercise appropriate restraint, and . . . dies young" (294). Harberd, the thale-cress plant, and all the rest of the entangled "progressions" he details in his notebook are changed by their entanglements. When a predator ate the thale-cress's original flowering stem, Harberd predicts that the plant will produce about 200 seeds instead of the 15,000 he originally predicted, and he comments, "That rabbit, or whatever it was, changed the world" (184). As Harberd enlisted the thale-cress in what Latour calls the mode of existence of research ("Textbook Case"), Harberd became a field naturalist and a believer in the "overwhelming importance" of "the world having inherent unity" (291).

Though the year has a beginning and end, his research and his thinking about the world, as well as the life of the thale-cress plant and even the notebook and the two scientific papers do not. Like any correspondence they continue indefinitely. The new projects grew out of previous research and will condition the research that follows; his thinking similarly, as recorded in the notebook, depends on past experiences and is only just emerging in sketchy form in December of the year. Near the end of the book, on November 17, he comments that "the story is already told. The purpose partially fulfilled. So this is the end, or at least part of the end, of these notes" (290). Only partially fulfilled and only part of the end: we read more about the life of the thale-cress and the progress of the two papers in an afterword written in July of the following year; and in its distribution, the published notebook continues to fulfill his purpose of helping lay readers to "think of the topological, the sculptural aspect of proteins with [the] same sense of comfortable familiarity" with which he views the landscape of his childhood (100). Waiting for a response after submitting one of the papers to a journal, Harberd wonders what weaknesses the reviewers might find in it and comments, "But every published scientific paper has holes in it, leaves questions unanswered. That's part of the process" (297). And the thale-cress plant continues from "seed to seed": "the cycle image is so accurate a representation. There's no defined point at which it stops or starts" (175). The beginnings and ends of conclusions, insights, writings, are arbitrary and often temporary pauses in the process of corresponding.

4

The Dynamics of Becoming

John Holland opens his book *Hidden Order* with the mystery of why Eleanor Petersson can go to her favorite specialty store in New York City to pick up a jar of pickled herring in full confidence that it will be there despite the fact that the city has no central planning commission to organize the purchasing and distributing of supplies. Adding to the mystery are the continual changes in the city—in people, buildings, administrations; he comments, "Like the standing wave in front of a rock in a fast-moving stream, a city is a pattern in time" (*Hidden Order* 1). He instances other patterns in time—the human immune system, the mammalian central nervous system, ecosystems—each of which maintain "coherence under change"(4) without benefit of a central organizing device or plan; instead, order arises in these complex systems out of nonlinear interactions in a continuous becoming. As Holland's example demonstrates, such interactions are not restricted to the natural world: "Nonlinearities clearly abound in social phenomena, where a yawn, a desire for an automobile with fins, or a life-style can spread contagiously throughout a population" (Prigogine and Allen 7).

Writing, too, creates patterns in time, as illustrated by my discussion of Nicholas Harberd's notebook in chapter 3. His memories, daily experiences, and research projects influence each other to create an interwoven pattern of meaning from which emerges not only his writing but also himself as a writer and researcher. Gunter Kress's definition of writing encapsulates the dynamic through which writers and the world transform in a constant becoming through their correspondence. He says that writing is a process of "transformative engagement in the world, [and] transformation constantly of the self in that engagement" ("Gains" 21). In this chapter, I look more closely at how this process of mutual and reciprocal becoming works.

The concept of becoming is probably most familiar from Gilles Deleuze and Félix Guattari's *A Thousand Plateaus*. They explain that becoming is not "a correspondence between relations . . . a resemblance, an imitation, or . . . an identification . . . neither dreams nor phantasies . . . not an evolution by descent and filiation" (237–38).[1] Instead, it is real; "it concerns alliance"; it is, they say, "a block" that "snaps up" beings like the wasp and the orchid or Ahab and Moby Dick (238, 243). It is a "contagion," an infection (241–42). The wasp and the orchid, Ahab and the whale are bound—snapped up—by affect. In terms I use, they become something different in their intra-action: the orchid, imitating the organs of a female wasp, becomes the subject of deluding and the wasp the object; Ahab becomes the subject of obsession and the whale the object. As Karen Barad says, their intra-action "enacts an *agential cut*" (333) between subject and object that did not precede their intra-action.[2] The orchid and Ahab were not these subjects before their intra-action, nor were the wasp and the whale these objects. Through concrescence they each become an actual entity, which Alfred North Whitehead says becomes by "infecting its environment with its own aspects" while at the same time "the aspects of all things enter into its very nature" (SMW 94). This is how a pattern in time is created, but it is also a pattern *in time*, as both Whitehead and Gilbert Simondon emphasize. Whitehead also refers to actual entities as actual occasions, which can be a single event in time or a "certain continuous limited stream of events" (CN 167); for example, Cleopatra's Needle on Charing Cross Embankment in London or an individual person. Simondon distinguishes between the more static individuation of a crystal and living beings, and describes the process of individuation as creating not only the individual but at the same time "the individual–milieu dyad" ("Genesis" 300). In the physical domain, as with the generation of a crystal, this process is produced "in an instantaneous fashion . . . leaving in its wake a duality of milieu and individual" (304), but in the living being this moment recurs in an ongoing becoming: "*the living being conserves in itself an activity of permanent individuation*" (305). Becoming is the dynamic of life. As Whitehead says, "It is nonsense to conceive of nature as a static fact, even for an instant devoid of duration. There is no nature apart from transition" (MT 151–52).

Emphasizing the dynamic of becoming over static being, along with the assumption of entanglement, requires significant shifts in how one conceives of change, and thus also of subjectivity and agency. I will address the latter two more fully in chapter 5. Here I focus on the principles of change and the process of the becoming of individual entities. Change is constant, but it isn't completely chaotic, for patterns in time form out of the intra-actions of multiple agencies (which include beings, things, institutions, forces). Because change is driven by complex and entangled intra-actions, it is also not predictable; causation is nonlinear, and the patterns that form are contingent. These patterns are omnipresent in organic domains and frequent enough in nonorganic ones. And they are remarkably diverse: from ecologies, cities, and economies to neural networks, genetic expression, epidemics, and individual beings and things. Individuals are not characterized by any essential qualities but rather continually become various kinds of subjects (or objects) depending on the intra-actions they enter into, though they do also endure as a "route of antecedent occasions" over time (Whitehead, PR 43). The origin of patterns in time is a mystery only from the point of view of Enlightenment thought with its focus on discrete entities in timeless moments, entities that do not interact or respond to each other in any meaningful way. From this point of view, the only source of coherence is rational thought mastering the chaos of the world—the central planning commission organizing the production and delivery of pickled herring, for example.

If we understand writing as a part of nature alive, a behavior of living entities, we understand not only how our world and we ourselves come to be but also what our role is in bringing this about. In writing, as in all behaviors, change is inescapable. We are accustomed to think of powerful individuals or significant writings as the engines of change—in the instance of the memo I discussed in chapter 2, the dean or the memo itself—and we overlook the long, convoluted processes by which writing comes into existence and influences us and by which individuals develop the commitments and happen into moments or positions that enable their writing to have substantial effects. Looking to particular individuals or texts to bring about change can lead one to conclude that change is difficult or impossible rather than an everyday occurrence, that if individuals are not smart enough or powerful enough, their ideas won't matter, or that, alternatively, since everything is determined by forces beyond anyone's control, no one can do anything that's really effective. In this resigned frame of mind, it could appear that only the dean or the department head can change hiring practices and that the situation of part-timers is deeply determined by the current economics of higher education. But what Steven Shaviro says about phenomena in general—"Each actual occasion is an endeavor to change the world, in the very process of constituting itself. And each actual occasion does in fact change the world" (*Without Criteria* 156)—is true of writing too.

Each of the participants in the writing event I discussed in chapter 2 brought to bear different experiences, perceptions, and commitments: each had something different to contribute and each had choices of what to bring into the discussions.[3] What each participant did inevitably had effects on the others and on the overall shape of the writing event. Multiple entities and forces in their surroundings also affected them and the outcome of their work. What happens results from such intra-actions—we bring forth worlds *together*—and thus each participant is in part responsible for the changes (both good and bad) that result, but no one individual is solely responsible. As Ilya Prigogine and Isabelle Stengers conclude: "We know now that societies are immensely complex systems involving a potentially enormous number of bifurcations exemplified by the variety of cultures that have evolved in the relatively short span of human history. We know that such systems are highly sensitive to fluctuations. This leads both to hope and a threat: hope, since even small fluctuations may grow and change the overall structure. As a result, individual activity is not doomed to insignificance. On the other hand, this is also a threat, since in our universe the security of stable, permanent rules seems gone forever" (312–13). Again, the loss of stable, permanent rules is a threat only from the point of view of Enlightenment thinking. Stability and permanence are not necessary to establishing or sustaining order; patterns in time result from intra-action. Enchantment ontology allows us to see that chaos is not the only alternative to an external agent imposing and maintaining order. Whitehead comments, "There is no reason . . . to conceive the actual world as purely orderly, or as purely chaotic" (PR 110).

Becoming Is Entangled and Contingent

The dynamics of becoming has been explicated most fully by process philosophers and complexity theorists, all of whom share an understanding of "the real [as] a product of nothing but the internal difference of its own self-realizing occurrence, bootstrapping itself or creatively advancing into ever new and more complex combinations" and who see "the processes of creativity and difference, immanence and temporality, relation and self-organization [as] fundamental in nature" (Robinson 159, 175). I have been discussing some of their work in previous chapters, especially that of the philosophers Alfred North Whitehead, Karen Barad, and Gilbert Simondon, and complexity theorists Stuart Kauffman and Humberto Maturana and Francisco Varela. Despite differences in their specific concerns, as Keith Robinson argues they share a commitment to becoming.[4]

Becoming is realized most obviously in the entangled systems of the everyday world. Unlike the isolated equilibrium systems of classical physics, complex systems are open systems that "form an integral part of the world from which they draw sustenance, and they cannot be separated from the fluxes that they incessantly transform" (Prigogine and Stengers 127). Consider again Holland's example. Eleanor Petersson's confidence that her favorite store will have pickled herring rests on the fact that New York City is an integral part of an economy that depends on distributing goods like pickled herring, of a social world in which people congregate to fulfill their purposes (including desiring, buying, and selling pickled herring), and of an ecosystem in which pickled herring is (for now at least) a possibility. People, products, and energy continuously flow into—and out of—the city, transforming and being transformed. Commenting on cities, Prigogine and Stengers note, "Not only are these systems open, but also they exist only because they are open" (127).

Complex systems also depend on multiple interactions. Eleanor's favorite store must have had enough customers to enable it to succeed, and enough of those customers must have desired pickled herring on a regular enough basis for the storekeeper to keep stocking pickled herring. Jane Jacobs, an early adopter of complexity theory, recognized the importance of enabling multiple interactions in her argument that the life of cities depended on sidewalks. With enough agents and intra-actions, the intra-actions become coupled and context-dependent: in mathematical terms, they become nonlinear and contingent (Holland, *Emergence* 121–22). What this means is that Eleanor may have been impelled to go to the store for pickled herring because she happened to be entertaining her cousin who loves pickled herring and because earlier in the day she encountered her neighbor who raved about the great pickled herring she had just bought at this store.

Holland explains that many predictions we encounter, such as the outcomes of elections or economic trends, rely on an assumption of linearity, though they do so imperfectly (*Hidden Order* 15). This assumption does not work well at all for complex systems. A linear function is one for which the value is obtained by summing the values of the variables: the fuel consumption of a plane in flight can be obtained by adding the weighted values of its velocity and altitude. In contrast, Holland offers as an example "one of the simplest" nonlinear models, the Lotka-Volterra model of predator-prey relations that predicts that "under most conditions, the predator population will go through a series of oscillations between feast and famine, as will the prey population" (18). Since there are separate variables for the various activities of predators and prey (encounters, birth and death rates, efficiency of turning prey capture into offspring) which must be multiplied instead of summed or averaged, predator-prey relations are nonlinear. Thus, even though the prediction of the model seemed to be borne out by an early study of lynx-hare interactions, subsequent studies, especially the long-term study of the wolf-moose relations on Isle Royale, have revealed how difficult it is to predict the outcomes of a complex system.

The longest running predator-prey study in the world, the wolf-moose study was begun in 1958 by Durward Allen and David Mech (Todd). The study's first twelve years of data showed up in textbooks as a perfect example of the Lotka-Volterra predator-prey model, but in 1970, when Rolf Peterson joined the study, the neat oscillations of predator and prey numbers went seriously awry and continued to do so. By the fiftieth anniversary of the study in 2008, Peterson commented, "It's like a big historical novel. Every five-year period looks completely unlike any of the previous five-year periods, and the dynamics are driven by external events that we cannot imagine, let alone predict" (qtd. in Todd). In 2010, when they finally got funding to study data on the genetic relationships of the wolves obtained from scats, they found out what some of the external events were: "The DNA tests uncovered the power of chance events (a tourist ignoring the rules and bringing his sick dog to the island) and individual personalities (the dominance of Old Gray Guy, the resilience of Ferocious Warrior) to shape populations. It undermined the notion of a natural balance" (Todd). Chance events, or contingencies, exacerbate the unpredictability of change in nonlinear systems, and the immigration of new wolves revealed that Isle Royale was a more open system than they had realized. The sick dog brought parvovirus to the island, which infected the wolves; a lone male (Old Gray Guy) emigrated across an ice bridge from Canada and bequeathed his genes to all wolves left on the island by 2010; a female (Ferocious Warrior) survived repeated attacks by another pack and produced many litters; and in the winter of 2012 three wolves fell into an abandoned mine shaft and drowned. Speaking of his hypotheses about the reasons for the decline of the wolf population made before the results of the DNA studies were found, Peterson said, "I was dead wrong" (Todd).[5]

Even though Holland says that "the interactions that form a city are typically more stable" than those between predators and prey (*Hidden Order* 18), a storekeeper in New York City similarly cannot figure out how much pickled herring to keep in stock by multiplying the number of customers times the average consumption of pickled herring by city inhabitants. If a lot of customers start raving about the store's pickled herring, or if the store happens to get listed in the *Village Voice* as having the best pickled herring around, the storekeeper will suddenly have to start stocking more pickled herring (or perhaps one day Eleanor's confidence will be misplaced). Given this dynamic, it's clear too that the existence of pickled herring in a store in this neighborhood does not depend on the particular store or building or location or storekeeper or customers staying the same, but rather on the contingencies and the nonlinear interactions of inhabitants of the neighborhood, as well as the contingencies of the economy, the society, and the environment.

To explain how nonlinear, contingent interactions drive the creation of diversity in the biosphere, Kauffman refers to the process Stephen Jay Gould calls exaptations, or, as Darwin calls them, preadaptations, the repurposing of existing organic structures to serve new functions. Kauffman recounts a variety of stories of exaptation: a squirrel named Gertude with seemingly useless folds of skin connecting her fore and hind limbs finds out she can fly when she spreads her legs and jumps from a tree to elude a predatory owl; tractor engineers solve the problem of how to mount the tractor's extremely heavy engine on a chassis by using the engine block as the chassis and attaching the wheels and seat and other parts to it; Sumerian traders who use clay tokens enclosed in little clay vessels to keep track of what was owed them begin marking the vessels with the number of tokens inside as a backup for when the vessels break, and soon, in about 3300 BC, the markings develop into Cuneiform writing. Kauffman asks, "Could we have said beforehand that Gertrude's ugly skin flaps would happen to be of use that day? ... Do you think you could finitely prestate all the context-dependent causal consequences of human artifacts that might turn out to be useful in some odd environment or for some odd purpose?" (I 131–32). Unlike the world of classical physics, the biosphere changes through "the expansion of the number of variables, that is, of the number of aspects of a situation that may come to matter, and that relevant description must take into account" (Stengers, TW 330). It is a world that can be described post hoc, as I described the writing of the memo, but not predicted or planned. It is a purposeful world, in the sense that agents in the world are interacting in terms of what matters to them, but not in the sense that what emerges results solely or even mostly from agents' intentions.

Change happens as individuating unities intra-act. A cloud moves in front of the sun and my mood changes; a gene mutates and a squirrel develops new folds of skin and one day soars from a branch to escape an owl; China's economy falters and the U.S. stock market falls; a reviewer comments on my manuscript and I make revisions. The events that bring about the changes are not efficient causes; however, events and changes are related. Tracing this idea of causation to Kant's Third Critique, Shaviro explains that "it is both the passive effect of preceding external causes, *and* something that is actively, immanently, self-caused and self-generating," an irreconcilable and generative antinomy of efficient and final causality (*Without Criteria* 84–85). For Kant, final causes are equated with purpose, but in the sense I discussed above. Shaviro says, "When we regard a given being as something that is alive, as an *organism*, we are rightly judging it to be an effectively purposive unity; but we do not thereby actually understand what impels it, or how it came to be" (84). Kauffman similarly notes that when we observe a bacterium swimming upstream in a glucose gradient, "without attributing consciousness or conscious purpose, we view the bacterium as acting on its own behalf in an environment"; we say, "It's going to get dinner" (I 7). Any organism or system that acts in this way is what he calls an autonomous agent, an organism that has "know-how . . . procedural knowledge about how to get on in the world"—"yuck" or "yum" (I 111). But know-how, he insists, is limited to what concerns the particular autonomous agent and thus cannot determine the outcome of its actions: "There is no autonomous agent, no one, who knows how the whole system works, any more than anyone at present knows how the global economic system works in its myriad interactions, deals, steals, hopes, and frustrations" (I 110). The autonomous agent acts with know-how, but the world is always risky, full of other autonomous agents acting on their own behalf. That bacterium seeking dinner may instead become dinner for a pursuing paramecium.

The self-organizing patterns that emerge in complex systems often appear to us as if they arose from a process of purposeful design. Selection pruning "an over-lush developing nature" leaves "a residual pattern of forms of life more or less well adapted to their environment [that] . . . assumes the appearance of universal purposiveness" (Wiener 37). Douglas Hofstadter, offering an analysis of communication in an ant colony, explains how what appears to be a purposeful response of the colony to a source of food, for example, is organized instead simply through the propagation of a signal through the colony until it reaches worker ants who respond to it instead of sending it on (320–21). And as Kauffman argues, the origin of life is neither unexpected nor miraculous, but the natural result of self-organizing processes.

That organization emerges in intra-action rather than being planned in advance was also the insight of ethnomethodology, as explained by Lucy Suchman: "The coherence of action is not adequately explained by either preconceived cognitive schema or institutionalized social norms. Rather, the organization of situated action is an emergent property of moment-by-moment interactions between actors, and between actors and the environments of their action. The emergent properties of action means that it is not predetermined, but neither is it random" (179). She argues that plans and intentions do play a role in social action, but they do not generate or control action: "Just as it would seem absurd to claim that a map in some strong sense controlled the traveler's movements through the world, it is wrong to imagine plans as controlling actions" (189). Instead, like maps, plans and intentions anticipate and reconstruct actions: "In our everyday action descriptions we do not normally distinguish between accounts of action provided before and after the fact, and action's actual course. As common-sense constructs, plans are a constituent of practical action, but they are constituent as an artifact of our *reasoning about* action, not as the generative *mechanism* of action. Our imagined projections and our retrospective reconstructions are the principal means by which we catch hold of situated action and reason about it, while situated action itself, in contrast, is essentially transparent to us as actors" (38–39). All action is situated—we act in an environment of other beings and physical forces—and in acting we respond to the situation without reasoning about what we are doing, unless something goes wrong. We have intentions in acting, we may change them in the course of acting, and we may formulate and reformulate plans before, during, and after acting, but these intentions and plans function as orienting devices (maps) not detailed instructions: "The foundation of actions ... is not plans, but local interactions with our environment, more or less informed by reference to abstract representations of situations and actions, and more or less available to representation themselves. The function of abstract representations is not to serve as specifications for the local interactions, but rather to orient or position us in a way that will allow us, through local interactions, to exploit some contingencies of our environment, and to avoid others" (188). Plans and intentions arise out of situated action: they are produced as shared understandings in intra-actions with others in particular situations.[6]

In writing, too, purposiveness arises out of the residual patterns of intra-actions of its agencies (which, as described in chapter 3, include writers, language, subject material, as well as other beings and forces) rather than being the cause of the patterns. Though we write for purposes we can describe—to change policies, to tell stories—those purposes result from our ongoing intra-actions, not from prior decisions to use writing in particular ways. Like writing, language itself "was never invented by anyone only to take in an outside world" (Maturana and Varela, *Tree* 234). Nor was it invented to describe an outside world, nor even was it invented to coordinate actions, for it was not invented at all. It takes only a little reflection on the history of changes in writing to realize that writing evolves out of the interactions of people in their writing, but observations of patterns in writing, as with any complex system, give an appearance of a system that was purposefully invented or planned, and the resulting metastable patterns in writing then can seem to be the basis of writing.

Even at the level of individual writers, the notion of purpose as separate from and prior to the activity of writing is an illusion. Maturana and Varela comment, "There are organisms that may even appear capable of specifying some purpose in advance (as the authors of this book) and conduct all their activities toward this attainment," but ascriptions of purpose as the origin or goal of activities "reflect our considering the ... system in some encompassing context" (*Autopoesis* 85). I may declare (as I have) in sabbatical proposals an intent to write a book; I may urge myself to write on a regular schedule; I may decline other commitments; I may explain what I hope to achieve in the book to others—but these are not the purposes of my writing, merely descriptions, relative to particular contexts, of promises, commitments, excuses, and predictions I have made about my activity. My activity of writing is purposeful, but the purposes arise in conjunction with the activity and are conditioned by the interactions I experience with others (colleagues, reviewers, publishers, other writers, reading, other experiences) throughout the activity. This is just what Ludwig Wittgenstein argued in his contention that the meaning of language is established in use; he says, "The intention *with which* one acts does not 'accompany' the action any more than the thought 'accompanies' speech" (217). Thus, the common directive in handbooks for writers to decide on their purpose before writing is nonsense if taken literally. As John Trimbur advises in his textbook *The Call to Write*, "Any plan a writer develops needs to be tested by writing a draft. Outlines, sketches, or other kinds of preliminary planning can tell you only so much. To see where your ideas are going, you must commit them to paper" (547). Writers do preliminary planning, but in writing they attend more to what is called for in the immediate situation and to how these demands constantly change in response to the interactions that their writing involves them in.

The two basic conditions for complex systems—an open system and multiple interactions—hold for writing. Patterns and innovations in vocabulary, sentence structure, argument structure, genres, politeness strategies, effective or expected personas for writers, theories and models, technologies for writing, page and type designs—all testify to an open system that feeds on the flux of variables and social energies flowing into it and that continually diversifies across time and space. The agents of writing, individual and collaborative, are multitude, and the density of interaction easily exceeds the critical level. And, as in other social phenomena, nonlinearities abound in writing as some innovations catch on and spread while others do not.

The Becoming of Entities

The processes from which patterns in time emerge in ecological and social systems like cities and predator-prey relationships also structure the ongoing becoming of individual entities, both living and nonliving. The jar of pickled herring waiting for Eleanor at her favorite specialty shop is an individuating or actual unity, an intra-action or coming together of other unities: not only her cousin's impending visit and the encounter with her neighbor but also perhaps her desire on this day for herring, her current preferences, the supply truck having arrived just the day before, the thriving state of the herring fishery, and so forth. She can count on it being there—usually—at least often enough that her confidence is warranted. But like all individuating unities it is continually in flux, maintained for awhile, but mutating into another form or expiring altogether as her desire or the herring fishery or other individuating unities change.

As mentioned above, Whitehead describes the becoming of actual entities as the process of concrescence.[7] As is true of complex systems, concrescence originates in "the multiplicity of data in the universe," which include actual entities, eternal objects (which are pure potentialities), and propositions (which are theories, "what might be") (PR 224). Each actual entity forms in an intra-action, "an act of experience . . . a process of 'feeling' the many data, so as to absorb them into the unity of one individual 'satisfaction'" (PR 40). An actual entity is the process by which "the many become one, and are increased by one" (PR 21), and it is also the (fleeting) result of that process. A conceptual feeling of "subjective aim" induced by God is progressively refined into a final decision as it interacts with feelings of and decisions about the multiplicity of data (PR 25). The actual entity becomes through this process of synthesizing its feelings of other actual entities, eternal objects, and propositions into a decision *for* itself made *by* itself (PR 43). It is a process of determination, an inclusion and an exclusion, as in Barad's agential cuts. Whitehead sums up: "'Actuality' is the decision amid 'potentiality.' It represents stubborn fact which cannot be evaded. The real internal constitution of an actual entity progressively constitutes a decision conditioning the creativity which transcends that actuality. The Castle Rock at Edinburgh exists from moment to moment, and from century to century, by reason of the decision effected by its own historic route of antecedent occasions" (PR 43). Actual entities are stubborn facts, real material entities that have decided for themselves. Actual entities are new particular entities: as Whitehead says, "The point to be emphasized is the insistent particularity of things experienced and of the act of experiencing" (PR 43). Conceiving actual entities also as actual occasions emphasizes concrescence as experiential and allows an understanding of entities we think of as stable, like the Castle Rock, as existing through successive decisions each of which transforms, however slightly, the previous actual entity. Experiencing is a process of becoming, and that process constitutes the multitude of data in the universe.

Propositions are a crucial aspect of concrescence, injecting the flash of novelty that characterizes the living occasion of concrescence (PR 184). Whitehead defines it as "a new kind of entity . . . the potentiality of an actual world including a definite set of actual entities in a nexus of reactions involving the hypothetical ingression of a definite set of eternal objects" (PR 185–86). Eternal objects are not actual, and only those that have "effective relevance" are felt and "have ingression in that subject" (PR 40, 41). The defeat of Napoleon in the Battle of Waterloo is a fact, a material event that significantly affected European history. The fact of the defeat is surrounded by "a penumbra of eternal objects," hypothetical alternative histories founded on the possibility of Napoleon's victory, that are entertained or denied, consciously or in daydreams, or simply as obscure influences on one's emotions (PR 185). Propositional prehensions are these feelings of possibility; they are theories, or lures for feeling, or "tales that might perhaps be told about particular actualities" (PR 184, 256). As I discussed in chapter 1, when propositions are entertained, admitted into feeling in the process of concrescence, "a novelty has emerged into creation" (PR 187), a novelty that makes a difference. Shaviro describes it: "As the result of 'entertaining' a lure, I have somehow been transformed—whether grandly or minutely. I have selected one definite outcome from among 'the penumbral welter of alternatives' (PR 187). As a result, I have become—however slightly or massively—a different entity from the one that I was before this happening. I am no longer the same as I might have been had I not been moved by this particular 'flash of novelty' (PR 184)" (Shaviro, *Universe* 56). This is the transformation, the moment of becoming, that Kimmerer experienced in entertaining the proposition produced by her encounter with the plantain.

Simondon, like Whitehead and like Barad, argues that understanding individuation requires not starting with the existence of the individual but rather with an attempt to understand the process of individuation.[8] He rejects both the hylomorphic and the substantialist procedures of searching for the principle of individuation "either before or after the individuation has taken place" ("Genesis" 299): either before, when the principle is thought to be contained either in the form or in the material, or after, when the principle is thought to be contained in the essence of the individual. Instead, he argues: "Individuation must . . . be thought of as a partial and relative resolution manifested in a system that contains latent potentials and harbors a certain incompatibility with itself, an incompatibility due at once to forces in tension as well as to the impossibility of interaction between terms of extremely disparate dimensions" (300). In this approach, he argues, ontogenesis "will be given its full weight," not in the sense of the genesis of the individual but rather as designating "the development of the being, or its becoming—in other words, that which makes the being develop or become, insofar as it is, as being" (300). The being is but one phase in the process of individuation, one of the results of the process and the only phase to which the characteristics of unity and identity apply. The "concrete being or the full being . . . [is] the preindividual being," which is "not a substance, or matter, or form, but . . . a tautly extended and supersaturated system, which exists at a higher level than the unit itself" (301). Individuation, then, is "a resolution taking place in the heart of a metastable system rich in potentials: *form, matter, and energy pre-exist in the system*" (304). As I mentioned earlier, in the case of living beings, the process of individuation is ongoing: the living individual is "a veritable theater of individuation," in which the individual maintains "a more complete regime of *internal resonance* requiring permanent communication and maintaining a metastability that is the precondition of life" (305).

Biologists Maturana and Varela also hold to the assumption that the becoming of an organism is a pattern in time. They focus on how organisms emerge as they interact with their environment, and, like Simondon who conceives of the individual-milieu dyad as a relation between two systems, they see the organism itself as an open system interacting with the open system of its environment. No system exists and can be considered in isolation; "every ontogeny occurs within an environment," insist Maturana and Varela (*Tree* 75). Every living being "is born in a particular place, in a medium that constitutes the ambience in which it emerges and in which it interacts" (95). Although they distinguish organisms and their environments as operationally independent, "between them there is a necessary structural congruence (or the unity [organism] disappears)" (95). Structural congruence—intra-action—is what drives the ongoing changes in living systems.

To explain how organisms respond to each other and to their environments Maturana and Varela introduced the paired concepts of structural determination and structural coupling. Structural determination recognizes that living systems have structural autonomy: how they respond to other systems is determined not by what acts on them but by their own structure: "The changes that result from the interaction between the living being and its environment are brought about by the disturbing agent but *determined by the structure of the disturbed system*" (*Tree* 96). Maturana and Varela emphasize that the interaction between systems "is not instructive, for it does not determine what its effects are going to be" (96). Another way to put it is to say that in the interaction between systems there are no inputs or outputs. Systems "can be perturbed by independent events and undergo internal structural changes which compensate these perturbations" (*Autopoesis* 81). As is clear in this statement, structural determination does not mean that systems do not change. Throughout their life their structure changes in response to their own internal dynamics and in response to other systems (*Tree* 74). It is the particular history of those changes that makes the structure of each system individual.

Structural determination may sound like a distinction that makes no difference, but as Maturana and Varela point out, it is a concept that we regularly apply in daily life, and not only to living systems. In our encounters with computers, for example, we understand them as structurally determined unities. Although we may say that "we 'instruct' the computer to give us the balance of our bank account" (*Tree* 97), we know that the connection between our clicking the balance button and the computer performing the process of calculating the balance in the account is determined by the computer's software, and if there is a breakdown and we don't get a balance when we click the button, we assume there is something wrong with the structure of the computer. Maturana says, "Nothing external to a living system can specify what happens in it" ("Autopoesis" 12). Complex systems are closed in this sense. Although they are open to energy flows and perturbations, the way they change is always determined by their structure: they change in the way their current structure allows and directs. As Whitehead says, they decide by themselves. Of course, one thing they change is their structure.

A very simple, yet striking, example of structural determination in writing is provided by Kress. He relates how his three-year-old daughter who was attempting to write a thank-you note to a friend asked him how to write "thank you." He printed out THANK YOU in capital letters on her piece of paper, and after a few minutes she came back and, showing him the paper on which she had written a single character that looked something like the Greek letter pi, said, "Look, I've done it" (*Literacy* 143; see the illustration on 144). He explains that she did not yet know the letters of the English alphabet though she was working out the idea of letters in her attempts to write. He rejects the oversimple and misleading assumptions that she copied or imitated what he wrote and argues that a better understanding of what she did in reading his THANK YOU and producing her sign, and a better understanding of the configuration of her sign, rests on "the assumption that she paid very close attention to the characteristics of the structure that she had read, that she read these in terms of principles which she already held, or 'had', so that the transformed sign was the product of the original sign transformed in line with the interested action of the child" (146). Kress's point here—and the point of the concept of structural determination—is that systems do not act on each other in the way that billiard balls do by mechanically picking up properties (momentum, traces of color) from each other but rather by responding to what we might call their affective evaluation of the action of the other: "yuck" or "yum."

The concept of structural determination cannot by itself capture the nuances of the relation between change and structure in individuating unities; it overstresses the relative permanence of unities, just as Deleuze and Guattari's concept of deterritorialization overstresses the evanescence of unities. Maturana and Varela thus pair structural determination with the concept of structural coupling in an attempt to account more fully for the role of other organisms and the environment in the process of individuation. They observe that two systems "can undergo coupled ontogenies when their interactions take on a *recurrent* or more stable nature" (*Tree* 75). This "history of mutual congruent structural changes" (75) is what they call structural coupling or structural congruence. Maturana offers the example of successful communication: "We keep meeting and, therefore, are not only in recurrent, constantly repeated interaction but also in recursive interaction. Our conversations form the basis for further conversations, the elements of our conversations refer to themselves and build on each other,—and that is recursion. Our meetings trigger structural changes inside each one of us, and they continue as long as we move in the dynamic congruence that leads to structural coupling. Structural coupling arises if the structures of two structurally plastic systems change through continual interaction without destroying the identity of the interacting systems" (Maturana and Poerksen 85).[9] Kress's daughter learns to write letters (and words) as she interacts with her father (and with others) over time. Her representations of language change in response to the interactions—but so do her father's and those of the whole system of writing.

The Endurance of Becoming

Recognizing that change is inevitable raises the question of how beings endure: William James famously puzzled over how things can change and still remain identifiably the same. Stengers explains that Whitehead's understanding of endurance relies on the English Romantic poets, especially Wordsworth, who "was haunted by the enormous permanences of nature" (SMW 86). Like Maturana and Varela, Whitehead allows for the relative autonomy of individuating unities that are intolerant of outside influence while at the same time insisting that they are not self-sufficient.

> The salvation of reality is its obstinate, irreducible, matter-of-fact entities, which are limited to be no other than themselves.... The endurance of things has its significance in the self-retention of that which imposes itself as a definite attainment for its own sake. That which endures is limited, obstructive, intolerant, infecting its environment with its own aspects. But it is not self-sufficient. The aspects of all things enter into its very nature. It is only itself as drawing together into its own limitation the larger whole in which it finds itself. Conversely, it is only itself by lending its aspects to this same environment in which it finds itself. (94)

Whitehead remarks that an "all-pervasive fact" of real things is their transitoriness, "the passage of one to another," but he argues that something else must not be omitted: "having value, . . . being an end in itself, . . . being something which is for its own sake" (93).

Whitehead argued that the interweaving of permanence and change "is a primary fact of experience" (MT 53): "We are in the present; the present is always shifting; it is derived from the past; it is shaping the future; it is passing into the future. This is process, and in the universe, it is an inexorable fact" (52–53). In chapter 1, in comparing Whitehead's and Ricoeur's approach to permanence and change, I explained that Whitehead saw it not as a tension or a dialectic of opposing forces but rather as two differing modes of participation in the process of ongoing becoming: permanence as the enjoyment of a completed unity and change as appetition for novelty. Entities endure by changing, as Maturana and Varela, Kauffman, and Simondon also recognize: all refer to the metastability of systems as enabling the conservation of attainment and the emergence of novelty. Maturana and Varela understand organisms as enduring through the complementary processes of structural determination and structural coupling; Kauffman envisions a creative tension between the subcritical regime of the individual cell and the supracritical regime of the diversifying biosphere; and Simondon describes a process of transduction within the individuating system, which maintains an inheritance of its preindividual reality that allows it to gradually extend itself into transductive individuation.

Maturana and Varela argue that the endurance of individuating unities also depends on the existence of a metastable boundary providing a measure of separation between organism and environment. They explain how the cellular membrane, which is produced by the network of cellular components and participates in that network, also limits the extension of that network, which would otherwise "disintegrate in a molecular mess that would spread out all over and would not constitute a discrete unity such as a cell" (*Tree* 46). The cell membrane does separate the unity, allowing it to constitute a network, but it also connects the cell to its environment, allowing particular elements to pass into and out of the cell. Niklas Luhmann, who recast his theory of social systems in line with Maturana and Varela's autopoetic theory, emphasizes how boundaries "have the double function of separating and connecting system and environment." He continues: "As soon as boundaries are defined sharply, elements must be attributed either to the system or to the environment. Yet relations between system and environment can exist. Thus a boundary separates elements, but not necessarily relations. It separates events, but lets causal effects pass through" (28–29). Couze Venn, also considering the question of boundaries in individuation, remarks that the idea of skin as a boundary or container for a living being makes sense as "all living things... are marked by actual physical containers," but adds that just like the cell membrane, skin connects the organism to its environment: "Skin is in fact one of the most complex of organisms, directly affecting the functioning of the rest of the body by regulating autopoesis in the organism and by acting as a kind of transductor between 'inside' and 'outside', thus doubling as the mechanism which modulates the co-poetic or symbiotic relation of the body to its 'environment'" (137). Metastable boundaries between systems reconceive causality in terms of the antinomy of efficient and final causes and, in turn, allow us to understand that agency and individuation are not in conflict with larger external systems but arise as part of the process of becoming.

Kauffman approaches the question of endurance as Simondon does individuation, beginning with the larger systems in which individuation takes place. He asks how we can understand "the diversity of organic molecules in the biosphere [which] is vastly greater than it was 4 billion years ago" (HU 113). His hypothesis is that the universe is a nonequilibrium complex system in which "cells interacting with one another and with the environment create new kinds of molecules that beget other kinds of molecules in a rush of creativity" similar to a nuclear chain reaction, which he calls supracritical behavior (114). Like Maturana and Varela, he notes that such behavior would be lethal to cells, so a new question arises: how do cells protect themselves from the supracriticality of the biosphere (122)? Kauffman rejects the idea that cells might develop an immune system or membranes that would exclude all foreign molecules; instead, he argues, the simplest defense would have been for cells to remain subcritical (126).[10] But then the question arises of how cells interact to form ecosystems that generate a supracritical world and universe. His answer is that these ecosystems—communities of cells such as gut bacteria or "communities crouched along the edges of hot springs in the far fields of Iceland" (127)—"evolve to the subcritical-supracritical boundary," a "delicate balance" between permanence and change (126). In a supracritical ecosystem, interactions that cause some species of bacteria to die off will move the system toward the subcritical by lowering species diversity, while in a subcritical ecosystem, bacteria mutating into new species or new bacteria migrating in will move it toward the supracritical by increasing species diversity. And "while each ecosystem is itself on the boundary between sub- and supracriticality, by trading their stuff they collectively produce a supracritical biosphere, one that inexorably becomes more complex" (129). The "creative tension" between sub- and supracriticality is, as Simondon says of individuation, "resolved but also preserved in the shape of the ensuing structure" of the biosphere, guided by the principle of *"the conservation of being through becoming"* ("Genesis" 301).

In his subsequent book *Investigations*, Kauffman revises the "rush of creativity" into a metastable process of "accumulated propagating organization" (I 85) in which, as Simondon says, the tension between permanence and change is both resolved and preserved: "Biospheres and the universe create novelty and diversity as fast as they can manage to do so without destroying the accumulated propagating organization that is the basis and nexus from which further novelty is discovered and incorporated into the propagating organization" (I 85). As an example of the necessity of both permanence and change in becoming, Kauffman offers British common law: when a judge makes a judgment that sets a precedent, "ripples of new interpretation pass to near and occasionally far reaches of the law." But if every new precedent altered the interpretations of all the old judgments, or if new precedents never sent out ripples, common law could not evolve or exist at all in a useful form. He argues, "Coevolutionary assembly must involve coevolving organizations flexible enough to change but firm enough to resist change" (I 20).

Arguing against the neglect of parole (language in use) in Saussurean-inspired structuralism, Mikhail Bakhtin also emphasized the interplay of permanence and change in the dialogical nature of living language. The centrifugal force of heteroglossia is complemented by the centripetal force of unitary language: "Everything means, is understood, as part of a greater whole—there is a constant interaction between meanings, all of which have the potential of conditioning others" (*Dialogic Imagination* 426).[11] Bakhtin argues that "stratification and the resulting heteroglossia of language are "what insures its dynamics: stratification and heteroglossia widen and deepen as long as language is alive and developing" (272). Heteroglossia is the centrifugal force that drives writing toward the supracritical regime of diversity of meanings and uses; it is complemented by the centripetal force of "unitary language" that drives writing toward the subcritical realm of "unification and centralization" (271). Both the stratification of language into different forms and unitary language arise from the responses—"yuck" or "yum"—of users. Meanings are material, they encounter each other, as Michael Holquist explains, in the utterances of "two actual people talking to each other in a specific dialogue at a particular time and in a particular place" (xx). He emphasizes that these actual people are not the "sovereign egos capable of sending messages to each other through the kind of uncluttered space" depicted in communication diagrams. Rather, each is "a consciousness at a specific point in the history of defining itself through the choice it has made . . . of a discourse to transcribe its intention *in this specific interchange*" (xx). Bakhtin insists that a unitary language is not simply an abstract system of forms that guarantee "a *minimum* level of comprehension in practical communication" but rather is "a world view ... insuring a *maximum* of mutual understanding in all spheres of ideological life. Thus," he concludes, "a unitary language gives expression to forces working toward concrete verbal and ideological unification and centralization, which develop in vital connection with the processes of sociopolitical and cultural centralization" (271). Languages exist in dynamic balance on the phase transition between diversity and unification, and like ecosystems, "by trading their stuff" they collectively produce a supracritical language system that inexorably becomes more stratified and heteroglossic.

This understanding of phase transition behavior in languages, where the tension between diversifying and unifying social forces produces a metastable balance, also underlies the New London Group's redefinition of writing conventions as resources and of writing as Design. Instead of seeing writers as users of a unitary language, they see writers as Designers who actively participate in the production of heteroglossia. In their designing, Designers transform Available Designs (resources) into The Redesigned (new resources) through creatively applying and combining them. What results is a dynamic system: "That which determines (Available Designs) and the active process of determining (Designing, which creates The Redesigned) are constantly in tension" (New London Group 20). Thus, as Kress explains, in any semiotic activity "individual action and agency" braid together "with the effect of social form and structure" ("Design" 158).

One process that maintains this dynamic balance in all complex systems is what Norbert Wiener called feedback loops, "a method of controlling a system by reinserting into it the results of its past performance" (26). Feedback loops spontaneously organize systems through both self-reinforcing and self-balancing feedback. The autocatalytic processes that drive the supracriticality of the biosphere are an example of self-reinforcing feedback, and homeostasis, the mechanism that keeps living organisms in balance, is an example of self-balancing feedback, as are control devices on machines, like the centrifugal governor of a steam engine. Wiener points out that many everyday actions like steering a car are accomplished through feedback—responses to other entities in the interaction: "If I find the car swerving too much to the right, that causes me to pull it to the left. This depends on the actual performance of the car, and not simply on the road; and it allows me to drive with nearly equal efficiency a light Austin or a heavy truck, without having formed separate habits for the driving of the two" (26). Fritjof Capra points out that both kinds of feedback were observed, and indeed used, in modulating social systems before Wiener described feedback as a general pattern: Adam Smith's "invisible hand" and the "checks and balances" of the U.S. Constitution are examples of self-balancing feedback, while phenomena called "vicious circles" or "self-fulfilling prophecies" are examples of self-reinforcing feedback (62–63).

Feedback loops in metastable systems also generate and regulate patterns and meanings in writing at all levels and account for its constantly changing, living character.[12] New meanings arise in individual writing events, and self-reinforcing feedback occurs if they are inserted into other writing events over and over until they spread into common usage. Or self-balancing feedback may occur as the writing system (writers) ignore or resist the meaning distinction that is attempting to enter the system.[13] A particularly vicious form of self-reinforcing feedback in language occurs in the development of hate speech, as Judith Butler explains. The power of hate speech to injure others arises through repetitions of expressions in socially traumatic language events. Expressions that are used over and over to subjugate others enact subjugation under cover of being "just words." Butler explains: "Social trauma takes the form, not of a structure that repeats mechanically, but rather of an ongoing subjugation, the restaging of injury through signs that both occlude and reenact the scene" (36–37). A history of being used to subjugate others distinguishes "nigger" as hate speech from "whitey." Though both expressions make a racial distinction, "whitey," lacking the force of a history of subjugation, cannot injure in the same way. Interestingly, as Butler points out, regulating hate speech by forbidding it only gives it more force. Instead, speakers (and writers) alter usage through repetition of the expressions in different kinds of events, a form of self-balancing feedback. She says, "The speaker renews the linguistic tokens of a community, reissuing and reinvigorating such speech. Responsibility is thus linked with speech as repetition, not as origination" (39). The altered usage of "nigger" in the United States is an example of a change in the writing system through the feedback loop that the citationality of writing provides.

Simondon recognizes the tension between attainment and novelty in the process of individuation, and concurs with Maturana and Varela in arguing that in living beings the tension is partially and relatively resolved by the being itself: "In the living being, *individuation is brought about by the individual itself*. . . . The living being resolves its problems not only by adapting itself—which is to say, by modifying its relation to its milieu (something a machine is equally able to do)—but by modifying itself through the invention of new internal structures and its complete self-insertion into the axiomatic of organic problems" ("Genesis" 305). The process by which the living being modifies itself is what Simondon calls internal resonance, a process in which the individual communicates with all other elements in the individuating system, especially the metastable system of the preindividual being: "The living being can be considered to be a node of information that is being transmitted inside itself—it is a system within a system, containing *within itself* a mediation between two different orders of magnitude" (306). In a footnote to this passage, Simondon says that the living being can be seen as "a node of interactive communication" (318n4). Venn explains that Simondon's understanding of information here is not that of clear transmission but rather Gregory Bateson's notion of a difference that makes a difference (146).[14] Thus, the living being, as a site of intra-action between the constituents of the individuating system, invents new internal structures, and as a site of intra-action between the system of the external milieu and its internal system, inserts itself into the "axiomatic of organic problems."

Simondon distinguishes transduction from the dialectic in that it does not rely on negation, but rather on the existence of potentials, "the most positive element in the preindividual being," that are the source of the incompatibilities and metastability of the system and allow it to move out of step with itself. "Individuation is not a synthesis, a return to unity, but rather the being passing out of step with itself, through the potentialization of the incompatibilities of its preindividual center" ("Genesis" 314). Unlike Graham Harman's and Thomas Rickert's understanding of the being of entities, in which potentials are properties that withdraw or can be disclosed, in Simondon's understanding the potentials harbored by the metastable system of the preindividual being are the source of incompatibilities that cause an individual to fall out of step with itself in its becoming. Venn comments that in Simondon, "the individual is never taken to be an isolated being or event but exists in relation to a dynamic mobile system: one must 'grasp the individual as an activity of the relation, not as the end-product of that relation'" (Venn 146).[15] Or, as Whitehead asserts, "*how* an actual entity *becomes* constitutes *what* that actual entity *is*. . . . Its 'being' is constituted by its 'becoming'" (PR 23).

The dynamics of becoming allow a new way to understand agency in writing. Neither the modernist autonomous subject nor the postmodern socially determined subject can serve as a model for an enchanted understanding of agents. Reconceiving the relation of permanence and change as complementary rather than dialectical and individuals as emergent within metastable complex systems suggests that agents are individuating entities. Subjects (like objects) emerge in transient fashion from the agential cuts enacted in intra-action, but subjects do still act. They are determinate but not determined. In chapter 5, I elaborate this suggestion and draw on an enactive approach to the study of mind to further illuminate how both nonconscious and conscious cognitive processes are involved in writing.

5
The Agency of Writing

[Casey Boyle] For my money, the most boring concept in rhetorical theory is "agency."

. . .

Here's my main issue . . . there are some (maybe many) exceptions here for sure but, for the most part, most want to argue for volition but they smuggle it through agency. Can agency be interesting? For sure. Has it? For sure, but not when it is actually an argument for volition.

. . .

[Scott Graham] My argument has always been that we've vastly exceeded the carrying capacity of a single term in "agency" theory. Shed of volition and intention, for me anyway, is when agency starts to get interesting.

Agency has been a problem—and not only in the field of rhetoric and composition—for a long time. If we accept that we live in a globalized world in which not only economies, cultures, and languages but also environmental crises are increasingly entangled in complex systems, and we accept the death of the autonomous conscious subject, the possibility of agency can seem increasingly impossible. An insistent question that arises, then, is whether we must simply resign ourselves to modernist lamenting or postmodern rejoicing at the loss of any responsibility for the way our world turns out, or whether some notion of agency in bringing about positive changes can be rescued. As you might expect from previous chapters, I'm for rescuing, rather than lamenting or rejoicing.

We have also for a long time understood an agent as a human autonomous subject who through conscious intention and free will causes effective changes in the world. This understanding lingers even though in the past half century, postmodern (and more recently posthuman) subjects have begun to usurp its position, causing some distress in the field of composition and rhetoric. Carolyn Miller notes that "the decentering of the subject . . . signals a crisis for agency, or perhaps more accurately, for rhetoric, since traditional rhetoric requires the possibility for influence that agency entails" ("What" 143). Thomas Rickert observes that subjectivity was a focus of attention in composition studies in the early 1990s, "especially the decentering or fragmentation of the subject, which was held to jeopardize political and rhetorical agency," but "the constructed nature of the subject" was also a concern for the same reasons (*Acts* 10). Carl Herndl and Adela Licona amplify the problem of the social construction of the subject, referring to John Clifford's opposition between the "autonomous, rational actors" assumed by composition handbooks and the "carceral model of subjectivity, as a nonporous, inflexible category into which subjects are interpellated by ideology and determined by discourse," and they assert that "neither of these formulations explains the rhetorical and social phenomena we experience" (136). As with other binary oppositions, the struggle over whether agency must be attributed to transcendental subjects or be denied to socially constructed subjects didn't get us very far in understanding what it means to be a writer or a rhetor, as Herndl and Licona observe. Agency became boring.

But as Boyle and Graham suggest, agency can be interesting, even crucial in understanding why we write and why we endeavor to help writers learn to write well. The phenomena of influence, inspiration, and creativity we associate with writing and rhetoric can be accounted for without recuperating traditional notions of volition and intention or acceding to determination. Replacing the antinomy of permanence and change by an understanding of their complementarity in the process of becoming, as I suggested in earlier chapters, reveals agency to be not "scarce, rare" or "nonexistent" but "radically and inexorably common" (Nealon 105, 103). Compositionists and rhetoricians have recognized everydayness of agency: Rickert says students are "productive agents already" and that "pedagogy does not so much instill productive agency as reshape, redirect, and redistribute what is already there" (*Acts* 119); Robert Brooke argues that students (and teachers) in writing classes actively resist the identities expected of them (though he characterizes students' actions as a form of "contained underlife"); and Christian Lundberg and Joshua Gunn aver that "none of these critics of a commonsense doctrine of agency [Derrida, Lacan, and Foucault] deny that the subject or representations of the subject exert significant effects, nor do they deny the subject a kind of social effectivity or agency" (87). Lundberg and Gunn argue that the real problem with the traditional account of agency is the assumption that "the agent or subject [is] the self-possessed seat of agency" (88). They conclude that what is required is "a decisive analytical cut between *agency*, understood as the production of effect or action, and the *agent* as the presumed origin of effect or action" (88). In other words, they argue, "the existence of agency-effects" does not entail "the necessary existence of an agent who initiates these effects" (88). I agree that assuming that the subject or agent is the origin of effects is indeed a problem, but I think that cutting agency off from any kind of actor is more mystifying than helpful. Rickert thinks so too, referring to Barbara Biesecker's "forward-reaching argument that a rhetorical situation is not given prior to the encounters that make up the situation, and that includes the relevant actants involved, for otherwise, change becomes difficult to understand and explain" (*Ambient Rhetoric* 105–6).[1]

Putting the agent back into agency raises three questions: What kind of entity is the agent? What must the agent do in order to be called an agent? And why is it important to once again include the agent in considering agency? Despite all the concern about the postmodern socially constructed subject, recent discussions of agency in composition and rhetoric have either retained some form of this subject, or tacitly assumed the transcendental subject by referring to volition and intention, or simply stopped talking about subjects or agents at all. Posthumanist broadening of the notion of agency to include nonhuman and material entities further undermined the transcendental subject—it's hard to argue for speed bumps as intentional subjects—but not necessarily the socially constructed subject, as discussions in rhetoric and composition have rarely if ever focused on the new nonhuman agents, whether living or material.[2] Outside of rhetoric and composition, discussions of nonhuman agents are more common. Alfred North Whitehead, Gilbert Simondon, Bruno Latour, and Karen Barad, among others, all consider human, nonhuman, and nonliving entities as agents or actants. Barad says, "Agency is not aligned with human intentionality or subjectivity" (177). Nor do they see agents as socially constructed; rather agents are entangled in intra-active constitutive becomings.

I propose that agents are individuating entities as described by Simondon. Individuating entities have a continuity of becoming that depends on the ongoing intra-activity of the world. They are not necessarily human, but there is a difference between living and some nonliving agents that derives from Simondon's observation that the individuation of physical entities such as crystals is "abrupt and definitive" ("Genesis" 304).[3] Agents are entities that act in the sense defined by Latour: "An actor is any entity that modifies another entity in a trial" (PN 237), or as Barad says, in an intra-action. Stuart Kauffman's autonomous agents are agents: any "physical system, such as a bacterium that can act on its own behalf in an environment" (I 8). Because agents are always intra-acting, they are always doing things that modify or influence other entities, like "the bacterium swimming upstream in a glucose gradient ... going to get 'dinner'" and "the paramecium, hot after the bacterium" (Kauffman, I 2). They are agents in their actions, which are, however, neither produced by their conscious intentions nor a matter of free will in the sense of being free from any influence, as agents are always entangled in the world and inherit influences from their past intra-actions. Their cognitive processes and neural dynamics are largely nonconscious nonlinear self-organizing systems;[4] Barad says, "'Minds' are themselves material phenomena that emerge through specific intra-actions" (361). Thus, their actions too emerge without conscious intent or volition. Further, individual agents don't directly cause what follows from intra-actions. It is the intra-actions that are the efficient and the formal causes of what follows: they enact agential cuts that divide what matters from what is excluded from mattering. As Barad says, "Cuts are agentially enacted not by willful individuals but by the larger material arrangement of which 'we' are a 'part.'" Still, "the cuts that we participate in enacting matter" (178). Agents' actions always make a difference; their actions, even though they are not consciously intended, are their own, and awareness of agents as agents is crucial to understanding what comes to matter.

It is on this basis that Barad derives an ethical imperative from her theory of agential realism: "Particular possibilities for (intra-)acting exist at every moment, and these changing possibilities entail an ethical obligation to intra-act responsibly in the world's becoming, to contest and rework what matters and what is excluded from mattering" (178). This is not, as Barad emphasizes, "about right response to a radically exterior/ized other, but about responsibility and accountability for the lively relationalities of becoming of which we are a part"—and by "we" she means "not only 'we humans'" (393). What individual agents do in their intra-actions matters: what they do helps determine "what materializes ... what comes to be" as well as "what will be possible" (Barad 361, 391). Whitehead also finds in his speculative philosophy an ethics that, like Barad's, emphasizes attention to possibilities although he largely restricts it to human agents. As I discussed in chapter 1, he argued for transforming contradictions into contrasts in order to realize the possibilities that lurk in their interstices (Whitehead, PR 348; Stengers, TW 333). Isabelle Stengers explains that for Whitehead, humans became souls when they became "able to entertain possibility as such, that is, also able to tell tales about what could have been but never will be" ("Whitehead's Account" 51).

Inspired by Barad, as well as by Whitehead, Latour, Kauffman, and my own life experience, I believe that an ethical imperative emerges from defining agents as essential participants in the world's becoming. It is a positive imperative, an invitation, based in the view of the ultimate creativity of the enchanted world, to dream of possibilities. It emerges, I say, because ethics does not define the agent as an agent; instead, it defines what makes an agent ethical. It is what makes a writer an ethical writer, a writer who adopts and holds to habits of ethical writing, good writing.

In my effort to make agency interesting again, I argue that agents are individuating entities who act and make a difference, but whose actions are not consciously intended and do not determine the difference they make. They are agents every day as they intra-act with other agents and agencies. Effective agency is a relation; it has effects. I illustrate these notions of agent and agency in an analysis of the speech Barack Obama gave on race in the course of his 2008 campaign. I conclude the chapter by considering in what sense productive agents—writers and rhetors—make decisions and choices and are responsible for them.

Why Does No One Speak of Agents?

The reason Lundberg and Gunn propose cutting the link between agents and agency is that presuming the necessary existence of an agent who initiates rhetorical effects results in an ontotheological humanist notion of rhetoric in which agency is considered to be a possession of the agent. Herndl and Licona also identify this as problematic: presuming a link between agency and "the concrete individual, whether she is figured as the *individual* or as the *subject*," and conceiving of agency as a possession, "a thing, something agents *have*, *possess*, or *gain*" (140) assumes agency is a substance or an attribute. They argue instead that, like Foucault's power, agency is a relation: "It does not reside in a set of objective rhetorical abilities of a rhetor, or even her past accomplishments. Rather, agency exists at the intersection of a network of semiotic, material, and, yes, intentional elements and relational practices" (137). And Lundberg and Gunn and Herndl and Licona offer the same, very postmodern, correction: focusing on agency as preceding and producing the agent. "It is the social phenomenon of agency that brings the agent into being" (Herndl and Licona 140); "The agency possesses the agent . . . the subject is an effect of structures, forces, and modes of enjoyment that *might* precede or produce it" (Lundberg and Gunn 97). In Herndl and Licona's proposal, agents languish as an agent function, an intersection that offers a potential for action that can be occupied temporarily (138, 141), and in Lundberg and Gunn's proposal as a Lacanian subject, a "fantasy" of an agent brought to life by the agency of tropes, the Symbolic, and enjoyment. The same downplaying of the agent occurs in Miller's account, in which "agency is an attribution made *by another agent*, . . . an entity to whom we are willing to attribute agency" ("What" 150), and in Diane Davis's account of the Levinasian subject, a subject "charged with acting: s/he is not a free agent but an assigned agent, an agent on assignment, infinitely responsible for responding to the call of the Other(s)" (*Inessential Solidarity* 113).

Both agency and agents disappear entirely from Nathan Stormer and Bridie McGreavy's ecological account of the ontology of rhetoric. Arguing for considering the struggle that characterizes rhetoric in ecological terms, "a striving pursued *with*, not contesting *against*, other things" (3), they propose replacing agency, which "identifies force by its application," with capacity, which, in contrast, "imagines force in its relations" (5). Their reasoning is posthumanist as well as ecological; they argue that capacity emphasizes "the ecology of entanglements between entities over the abilities that are inherent to humans" (5), and they align their shift from agency to capacity with "Rickert's 'stretched out' description of agency as '*material, affective, ecological, and emergent*'" (9; quoting Rickert, *Ambient Rhetoric* 129). They also agree with Davis in understanding the infinite responsibility of rhetorical subjects as a subjectification, an irremediable exposedness or vulnerability "in the sense of 'weakness,' 'frailty,' and 'destitution' . . . 'a not being able to not suffer'" (15; quoting Davis, *Inessential Solidarity* 156).

For the most part, these accounts neglect agents in order to focus on agency as emerging from a rhetorical environment from which individuals, whether agents or subjects or objects, cannot be disentangled, a project I too endorse. Herndl and Licona's network of semiotic, material, intentional elements and relational practices; Miller's kinetic energy of rhetorical performance; Davis's preoriginary presymbolic affectability; Stormer and McGreavy's ecological ontology of rhetoric; Rickert's ambiance—all are, in different ways, attempts to free the discussion of agency from the pall of the transcendental or socially determined subject and move toward Barad's focus on phenomena—intra-actions—rather than on individual entities. But I feel keenly the loss of agents who act, makers who make, writers who are not written but who write.

The Agent

Quoting from an interview of the painter Jasper Johns, Rickert offers a glimpse of such an agent. When Johns is asked "why he has just made a change in the handle of a spoon in a lithograph on which he is working," he answers, "Because I did." The interviewer then asks, "But what did you *see*?" And Johns says, "I saw that it should be changed" (123).[5] Rickert comments on Johns's answers: "When Johns tries out something new or makes a change in the lithograph, he is *doing so actively and materially.* Johns does not imagine or hypothesize the changes he makes; he simply makes them, and after making them, considers them." Rickert says that Johns's answers illustrate how creation "arises out of robust interaction with the environment" (*Ambient Rhetoric* 125). I entirely agree; this is what I argued in my discussion in chapter 3 of Tim Ingold's notion of the process of making as correspondence and of Nicholas Harberd's account of his year studying the thale-cress plant. But here I want to emphasize the equal importance of an agent's active doing and considering, which arise out of neural processes, in creating changes.

I find agents as well as agency in the enchanted world. They are not autonomous transcendental subjects or socially constructed subjectified subjects; they do not "have" agency as an attribute, a possession, a capacity; they are not occupying nodes or positions temporarily; agency is not attributed or assigned to them; they are not "an evolving situation-I that comes to will what will have taken shape" (Rickert, *Ambient Rhetoric* 125).[6] They are living individuating entities that are continually becoming through the dynamics of both internal and external correspondences,[7] a process described in detail in an enactive approach to the study of mind that proposes that neurological processes are nonlinear self-organizing systems intra-acting in and across individuating entities and other agencies in the world. Johns's acts of "simply" making changes and after making them considering them can be attributed to the process of neural systems creating meanings through nonconscious acting into the world followed by conscious perception of and considering of the consequent meanings. Johns markedly does not refer his action to a conscious intention but rather to a feeling—"I saw that it should be changed"—which is the initial step in the enactive account of action. When pushed by the interviewer to explain what he saw was wrong with spoon handle, he says, "Nothing," but the interviewer again pushes for an explanation of his intentions: "Then why change it?" Johns sighs and says, "Well, I may change it again." Again the interviewer asks for a reason, "Why?" and Johns says, "Well, I won't know until I do it." Johns considers what he has done consciously, but the reasons for the changes he makes are opaque, the result of feelings rather than conscious intentions, feelings created by the nonlinear dynamics of his neurological system intra-acting with the lithograph and integrating present and past experiences.[8]

Gunn argued that the debate over rhetorical agency was a fantasy that provided "simultaneously, a frame within which to exercise agency as well as a shield from the abject horror of contingency" and as "a shield from the investigation of "unconscious suasive processes as well."[9] As I envision them, agents like Jasper Johns are ignorant of postmodern theory. They thrive on contingency and feed on their nonconscious feelings. In addition, as I will argue further in chapters 6 and 7, ethical agents are not satisfied with dwelling; they seek Whitehead's adventures of ideas. They are eager to take up Barad's call to contest and rework what matters.

Seventy years before the debate over postmodern agency, and long before the distress over the postmodern subject as well, Whitehead, who was not horrified by contingency, emphasized the importance of affective experience in constituting a subject. Arguing against the translation of Descartes's cogito, Whitehead says:

> It is never bare thought or bare existence that we are aware of. I find myself as essentially a unity of emotions, enjoyments, hopes, fears, regrets, valuations of alternatives, decisions—all of them subjective reactions to the environment as active in my nature. My unity—which is Descartes' "I am"—is my process of shaping this welter of material into a consistent pattern of feelings. This individual enjoyment is what I am in my role as a natural activity, as I shape the activities of the environment into a new creation, which is myself at this moment; and yet, as being myself, it is a continuation of the antecedent world. (MT 166)

Whitehead is in this account emphasizing the presentness of the past and the future in becoming as well as the role of both agent and environment in creating an actual entity. But he also wants to focus on the fundamentally affective nature of thought, which, as he makes clear elsewhere, is not to be equated with consciousness.

Whitehead's account of the subject that emerges in concrescence, along with Simondon's account of the genesis of the individual, form the basis of my argument for individuating unities as agents. For Whitehead the subject emerges as an "actual occasion . . . a novel entity diverse from any entity in the 'many' which it unifies" (PR 21). He distinguishes his subject from Kant's: "For Kant, the world emerges from the subject; for the philosophy of organism, the subject emerges from the world" (88). Whitehead says he retains the term "subject" because it is familiar, but he comments that "it is misleading," for the subject cannot be abstracted from or opposed to its experience in the world. He thus also distinguishes his "philosophy of organism" from Descartes's "philosophy of substance": in the creation of an actual entity, "the operations of the organism are directed toward the organism as a 'superject,' and are not directed from the organism as a 'subject.' The operations are directed *from* antecedent organisms and *to* the immediate organism. They are 'vectors,' in that they convey the many things into the constitution of the single superject" (151). The superject is the undetermined aim of the process of concrescence, not its origin. Actual entities emerge as feelings—"objective data"—that pass into "subjective satisfaction": the superject is "the unity emergent from its own feelings; and feelings are the details of the process intermediary between this unity and its many data . . . [which] are the potentials for feeling; . . . they are objects" (88). Stengers explains that "to feel is 'to be affected by'" and that "if I feel something, this thing certainly enters into the definition of my experience: it belongs to my experience, and it is not forged by my experience. I sense it insofar as it testifies to something else. I produce myself *qua* feeling that which is not me" (TW 294–95). Whitehead's actual entities emerge in the same way that Barad's subject and object do in intra-action; they neither precede nor persist after the moment of concrescence. Whitehead says, "The actual entity 'perishes' in the passage of time, so that no actual entity changes" (PR 147). Instead, its completion in the process of concrescence is followed by the complementary fluency of transition "whereby the perishing of the process . . . constitutes that existent as an original element in the constitutions of other particular existents elicited by repetitions of process" (210). Steven Shaviro says that though the actual entity has a sense of continuity, "for the 'datum' of any new experience is largely composed of the remnants of immediately past experiences," it "does not outlive the feelings that animate it at any given moment" (*Without Criteria* 12). The actual entity is a product of its experiences, of how it is affected by what it encounters, but it is a fleeting moment in becoming, the momentary enjoyment of a completion that will be immediately followed by appetition in the complementary fluencies of becoming. As Johns says, he may change the spoon handle again.

Whitehead's actual entities are equivalent to Simondon's beings—the phase in individuation characterized by unity and identity—and like Simondon, Whitehead also emphasizes the mutual becoming—or reciprocal induction—that links the individual and its milieu. But he also insists on the importance of the individual action of the actual entity: the definite finite entity "is limited, obstructive, intolerant, infecting its environment with its own aspects." It is itself by "drawing together into its own limitation the larger whole in which it finds itself," but it is also "only itself by lending its aspects to this same environment" (SMW 94).

Latour's actors are derived from this understanding of actual entities as enduring, as "limited, obstructive, intolerant"—or as Latour says, recalcitrant—entities. Whitehead says they are defined as agents through their "self-retention of that which imposes itself as a definite attainment for its own sake" (SMW 94); Latour says, "Actors are defined above all as obstacles, scandals, as what suspends mastery, as what gets in the way of domination, as what interrupts the closure and the composition of the collective. To put it crudely, human and nonhuman actors appear first of all as troublemakers" (PN 81). His project in *Politics of Nature* is to displace a "bad distribution of powers" associated with the binary of society as subject and nature as object by a collective, which he defines not as "an already established unit" but "a procedure for *collecting* associations of humans and nonhumans" (PN 238), a process of concrescence and transition: "a movement of establishing provisional cohesion that will have to be started all over again every single day" (147). He argues that "humans no longer have to make this choice that is imposed on subjects" by Plato's myth of the Cave, the choice between a free disembodied interiority, cut off from other subjects and from objects, or an unfree social construction (51). He suggests instead that both humans and nonhumans are actors in the sense that their actions make a difference to other actors. He says, "An actor is any entity that modifies another entity in a trial," what Barad calls an intra-action. Actors are not free or determined subjects; they do not cause effects but make a difference by engaging with other actors in reciprocal induction: "Of actors it can only be said that they act; their competence is deduced from their performances" (237).

Accounts of individual agents in Whitehead, Simondon, Barad, and Latour do differ. Latour always writes of them as human and nonhuman actants. Simondon's process of individuation focuses on the meshing of the dynamic systems of the individual and its milieu in a way that is congruent with the enactive accounts of individual neural experience I will discuss shortly. Whitehead's actual entities arising in concresence are fleeting moments of becoming, entities he also calls actual events or actual occasions.[10] He does, however, allow that "personal unity is an inescapable fact" of human experience, which he articulates, as in the passage quoted above, as a coordination of physical occasions and "the immanence of the past energizing in the present" (AI 186–89). Of all of them, Barad is most intent on redirecting attention from individuals to the phenomenon of intra-action. She insists that "if we hold on to the belief that the world is made of individual entities, it is hard to see how even our best, most well-intentioned calculations for right action can avoid tearing holes in the delicate tissue structure of entanglements that the lifeblood of the world runs through" (396). We need never to forget the entanglement of all our actions, that we are not the only participants in intra-actions. But at the same time she also insists that "intra-acting responsibly as part of the world means taking account of the entangled phenomena that are intrinsic to the world's vitality and being responsive to the possibilities that might help us flourish" (396).[11] Agents are individualizing entities; they become in transitory phases, but still they act and they act creatively, in the sense that they make a difference.

Productive Agency

Puzzling about why so many people find a "problem of agency" in Michel Foucault's work, Jeffrey Nealon suggests that what they are looking for is "real" agency. For these critics, "agency, in short, is not simply action, or the emergence of something that wasn't there before, a happening; rather, agency is a code word for a subject performing an action that matters, something that changes one's own life or the lives of others. Agency is doing something freely, subversively, not as a mere effect programmed or sanctioned by constraining social norms" (102). I have been trying to upset the structure Nealon sets up here by refusing to separate the agent from the phenomenon of agency while not acceding to the socially constructed postmodern subject. I agree with Nealon (and Foucault) that there is "no such thing as unconstrained subjective action" (102). I agree that agency is simply action and the emergence of something new. But I also think that agency always has effects—it changes lives in ways that matter—it's just that it isn't either a free or determinate action of a conscious subject. With Herndl and Licona and Nealon, I conceive agency as like Foucault's power, as a relation (137). Nealon says, "Power is nothing other than what it does—power is an act or a situation, a *relation* among forces" (97–98; emphasis added); as Foucault says, it is "always a way of acting upon an acting subject or acting subjects by virtue of their acting or being capable of action. A set of actions upon other actions" ("Subject" 220). But Foucault insists that there are two indispensable elements of a power relationship, and the second is "that, faced with a relationship of power, a whole field of responses, reactions, results, and possible inventions may open up" ("Subject" 220).

Agency is a relation of agents, Foucault's "acting subjects," who are entangled in intra-actions, infecting each other with their own aspects (Whitehead, SMW 94). Thus, intra-actions always make a difference in lives, not by determining an outcome but by opening up "a whole field of responses, reactions, results, and possible inventions."

Nealon's gloss on Foucault's assertion that power "acts upon other actions" can be interpreted in line with Stormer and McGreavy's argument that "to persevere in being things must exist affectively in entanglement" and thus that agency "can ever and only be *acting with* the world, not simply *acting on* it" (13). Nealon says that power "is nothing other than a series of force relationships among bodies, human and otherwise," and using the example of gravity, he argues that "you can't fight gravity wholesale—you can't simply defeat it, because it defines the field of relations that comprises where we live. Though . . . you certainly can resist it; everything does so, by necessity, all the time. That's what getting up in the morning is, a drama of power and resistance: force on force" (124n15). Stormer and McGreavy reject "resistance" and "recalcitrance" as describing how things act with the world in favor of "resilience" with its connotations of responsiveness, adaptiveness, and persistence. Nealon's example of gravity can be read as a matter of acting with, just as I argue about making in chapter 3. Getting up in the morning is a matter of resistance only from one side of the relation; it is also a matter of working with gravity, which enables one not to fly up to the ceiling. It is a relation of forces: gravity and a skeletomuscular body together enable getting up in the morning. And walking. And skydiving. A relation that opens up a whole field of possibilities. As Foucault says, "We must cease once and for all to describe the effects of power in negative terms. . . . In fact, power produces" (*Discipline* 194).

Nealon also notes that for Foucault resistance is just the other side of power relations: "Where there is force deployed, there is also resistance" (104), which is why he argues that "agency is . . . everywhere, radically and inexorably common" (103): "This is crystal clear in Foucault: resistance or the possibility of resistance constitutes the cornerstone of the very definition of the 'power relation,' which is importantly *not* simply a relation of domination" (104). Nealon does admit that "the theme of 'resistance'"—especially in the sense of "authentic" resistance—"can often name a stopping point rather than a rallying cry—a moral condemnation or judgment rather than an ethical provocation or map" (110), and he argues for Foucault's "emphasis on irreducible experimental struggle" that recognizes the many forms resistance can take and does take every day, undertaken not by "heroic subjects," but by everyday people who "do tend to know their ways around the questions of power and resistance in their own contexts" (108). For me, referring to agency as resistance is too easily misread as a negative reaction rather than a productive action. I would rather say that people are agents in their everyday lives all the time, even if, and when, as Nealon says, they choose options that work against their best interests (109).

John Muckelbauer also emphasizes the productive nature of Foucault's understanding of power. He retains the term resistance, but he wants to turn it into "something quite different from a traditional understanding of resistance with its connection to 'agency,'" which invokes a binary opposition and a "programmatic" style of politics that attempts to mobilize collective opposition around a particular agenda ("Reading" 89). The style of engagement he offers as an alternative, "one that is more concerned with provoking responses to normalized concepts or practices," bears a striking resemblance to Whitehead's concern about the trick of evil and to Barad's ethical obligation to contest and rework what matters. Just as Muckelbauer articulates a productive form of resistance, they articulate a productive form of agency: all three look for the creation of possibilities rather than adherence to a "central concept," a "preexisting category" (Muckelbauer, "Reading" 89), or "what everyone knows to be true."

Muckelbauer says that his productive reading of Foucault is an example of this style of engagement: I "tried to make use of alleged failures, contradictions, or errors in his work in order to produce a different conceptualization of resistance, one that would move contemporary scholarship through a recurring impasse" ("Reading" 91). He argues that "the emphasis for productive reading . . . rests principally on the concept of invention, but not invention as it is usually conceived in rhetoric . . . Instead . . . invention is the *telos* of an encounter with a text—invention of both concepts and subjects. To read productively means not only the attempt to alter the question, but to alter oneself through the question, to encounter a text hoping to think differently through an engagement with it" (92). In Muckelbauer's understanding, invention is not only like agency in producing new concepts and subjects, but is also not to be attributed to an individual genius: instead it "occurs though the encounter of actual multiplicities, subjects, and texts" (92). He offers this style of engagement as an alternative to that of critique, which relies on dialectical argumentation (92). As Whitehead does when he converts contradictions into productive contrasts so that they do not resolve into a higher unity but instead participate in the creative advance into novelty, Muckelbauer in his productive reading of Foucault connects "failures, contradictions, and errors" in order to invent a new concept that resolves an impasse. He concludes thus that "it may be the case . . . that we shall have to rethink the very structure of argumentation, of scholarly writing as well as of rhetorical pedagogy, outside of its usual dialectical terms" (92). I couldn't agree more. As I argued along with Simondon in chapter 4, becoming—and agency—is not a dialectical process.

In productive reading, like the kind of agency I am arguing for, "success can never be guaranteed from the outset, nor can the trajectory of one's effects" (Muckelbauer, "Reading" 90). In an entangled world, agency is unavoidable: what one does always makes a difference, but as Jane Bennett suggests, one may not know quite what difference the doing makes (*Enchantment* 155). Even when "authorities" refuse to pay attention, even the doings of subalterns are influential. In discussions of rhetorical agency, the assumption that "real" agency produces consciously intended effects, that it can be successful only if it makes others change their beliefs or behavior in ways that the rhetor was arguing for, is particularly troublesome in discussions of arguments and persuasion. The assumptions of enchantment ontology suggest that agency is not dependent on this kind of uptake, and thus the understanding of agency I offer (and illustrate in the following section) also takes up Muckelbauer's suggestion to rethink argument outside of dialectics.

Obama's Speech on Race

Agency is a relation of intra-acting individuating agents that make a difference in lives and in the world. Agency is productive in the way that Foucaldian power is productive, and it is creative in the way Whitehead's concrescence is. Barack Obama's speech on race delivered in Philadelphia during the 2008 presidential campaign exemplifies the kind of difference rhetors and writers make and how, as individuating entities, they do so. Because the speech, its motivation, composition, and reception were much commented on, I can make reasonable hypotheses about why he and other agents and agencies involved in composing the speech acted as they did.[12] Obama is acknowledged—if not always applauded—across the political spectrum as an accomplished rhetor. The speech he gave in Philadelphia, entitled "A More Perfect Union," was widely hailed as a nuanced and powerful treatment of the question of race as well as a productive intervention in the media furor that had erupted in March 2008 over the circulation of what were labeled as incendiary remarks from the sermons of Reverend Jeremiah Wright, the minister of Trinity United Church of Christ, of which Obama was a member. Thomas Sugrue calls it "the defining speech of his political career" (92) and comments that Obama "turned what was a crisis of legitimacy into an extraordinary opportunity—and in the process offered a powerful, sophisticated, and wide-ranging address, surely the most learned disquisition on race from a major political figure ever" (118).

In my analysis of this speech, I supplement my conception of agents as individuating unities with an enactive approach to the study of mind that understands cognitive processes and neural dynamics as embodied, nonlinear self-organizing systems intra-acting in and across individuating entities and other agencies in the world. Evan Thompson explains that this approach views the nervous system as "an autonomous dynamic system . . . [which] does not process information in the computationalist sense, but creates meaning" and views experience not as "an epiphenomenal side issue, but central to any understanding of the mind" (13). My main source in discussing the neurodynamics that underlie agency as emergent in intra-actions of individuating entities is the work of neuroscientist Walter Freeman who uses the enactive approach to explain "how brains make up their minds." Freeman's concern is to account for the agency of individuals through explaining the nonlinear dynamics of self-organization that support the capacity to choose as "an essential and unalienable property of human life" (4–5). The enactive approach, combined with my consideration of agency as productive and creative, enables me to argue that agents have intentions and can and do make decisions and choices, though these are not free of influence, nor do they consciously direct actions.

In the first fourteen minutes of the speech, Obama stated his belief that we cannot solve our challenges unless we solve them together and suggested that he believes this because of his experience of being a member of a multiracial family and of the black community at Trinity United Church of Christ. Obama says, "It is a story that has seared into my genetic makeup the idea that this nation is more than the sum of its parts—that out of many, we are truly one." He then articulated his reason for addressing the issue of race: "The politically safe thing would be to move on from this episode and just hope that it fades into the woodwork. . . . But race is an issue that I believe this nation cannot afford to ignore right now. . . . If we walk away now, if we simply retreat into our respective corners, we will never be able to come together and solve challenges like health care, or education, or the need to find good jobs for every American." This is a clear example of productive agency. Obama's response was not determined by the rhetorical situation nor by his past experiences, but it was clearly also not a response that came out of nowhere; it was a choice he made, a choice that arose out of an intra-action among various agents and agencies and shaped by an individuating entity's current goals and past experiences. In his book *Dreams from My Father*, Obama explicitly recognized the dependence of his choices on the structure of his experiences and situation. He wrote about his choice to become a community organizer: "I can see that my choices were never truly mine alone—and that is how it should be, that to assert otherwise is to chase after a sorry sort of freedom" (*Dreams* 134). His choice of how to respond this time, to articulate what he believed and wanted to say about race at this moment, could, like his earlier choice, be traced to a "larger narrative," one he had been living and reflecting on and writing about for many years. Like all responses, it emerged from the moment-to-moment process of his becoming the person he is, as he responded to the world he encountered and the history he studied and as neural populations interacted within the complex system of his brain, creating emotions, intentions, moods, dispositions, meanings, memories, goals, and narratives.

An Enactive Approach to Productive Agency

Productive agency defines the possibility of individuals making a difference every day, in small and large ways, in the composition of what Latour calls a good common world.[13] The enactive approach explains the dynamic of productive agency as the process of reciprocal induction through which entities create meanings through acting into the world and changing their structure in response to the perceived consequences of their actions. Freeman refers to the process as assimilation, or intentionality; he translates Maurice Merleau-

Ponty's intentional arc into a diagram of brain function in terms of feedforward and feedback loops that initiate actions into the world and receive sensory stimulation from the world and from the body in response, forming and constraining spatial patterns of action potentials and shaping and biasing attractor landscapes in the brain (102). By this process, each individual nervous system is creatively and uniquely structured in an ongoing way.

Freeman and Humberto Maturana both say they came to understand entities as actively responding to rather than being determined by sensations through their study of perception. Freeman argues that instead of neurons passively "storing a memory," as earlier theories had proposed, neurons interact to create a pattern that is not a representation of an odor or color, for example, nor information about an odor or color, but rather a response unique to each sensing individual, shaped by each individual entity's history and shaped anew in every iteration. In response to recurrent stimuli, synapses between neurons are strengthened, forming neuron assemblies that respond as a whole to input coming from any of the neurons in the assemblies. Synaptic modifications from equivalent stimuli form a basin of attraction that leads to patterns of amplitude modification (AM). The structure of these patterns is determined by the structure of the assemblies as it has developed through past experiences. Freeman explains: "The form of the input from the world is assimilated by the form of the AM pattern in the brain through successive steps of creation by the brain . . . the form of the input is not transferred or injected as information into the meaning structure of a brain. Instead, the brain creates an individualized pattern that is compatible with the history and goals of the organism" (82). This pattern is what the odor or color means to the particular entity, a pattern and a meaning that is constantly changing with the everyday experiences of the entity.

This process of the creation of meaning is the basic property of intentionality, as Freeman explains: "Feedback loops of neural populations are responsible for this ability to create behavior freshly with each new moment. The state transition between attractors is the way in which itinerant trajectories of brain activity arise, governing what we experience as habitual behaviors, and it is the landscape of attractors formed by learning that is responsible for reliable sequences of goal-directed behaviors. These attractors and behaviors are constructions by brains, not merely readouts of fixed action patterns. No two replications are identical: like handwritten signatures, they are easily recognized but are never twice exactly the same" (62–63). He concludes, "This dynamic system is the self in each of us. It is the agency in charge, not our awareness, which is constantly trying to catch up with what we do. We perceive the world from inside our boundaries as we engage it and then change ourselves by assimilation" (139).

The process of assimilation defines an agent as an individual with its own intentions and goals; individual agents are determinate, but not determined, in an ongoing becoming driven by the intra-actions among the components of their nervous system and by their intra-actions with other entities. Agents are changed through these intra-actions as are the others they intra-act with. Intentional actions emerge in a continuous loop involving a number of interactive and largely nonconscious stages: emotions lead to intentions, then actions, then creation of meanings, then learning, in which "the consequences of a just completed action are being organized and integrated into meaning" (Freeman 135), and then the formation, based on the integrated meanings, of short- and long-term goals. Only the latter two stages, learning and the formation of goals, are conscious processes, which are shaped by global patterns in the brain, often in the form of narratives. Emotions, intentions, actions, and the creation of meanings are nonconscious processes involving AM patterns, basins of attraction, neuron assemblies, and neuromodulators producing memories, moods, narratives, and dispositions. Conscious processes are open to awareness as are some borderline nonconscious processes (prereflective awareness, skillful coping, and practical consciousness), and loss of circumspection can disrupt the intentional arc bringing nonconscious processes to awareness. Emotions precede intention, as Whitehead emphasizes in his definition of the subject as "the entity constituted by the process of feeling" (PR 88). Both nonconscious and conscious processes contribute to intentional action, and agents are aware of only some of the processes as they take place. Through these processes, the agent is provided with meaning for free.

Meaning provided for free—meanings built up nonconsciously through intra-acting in the world—accounts in large part for the ability to respond quickly to rhetorical (and other) situations, as Obama (and his speechwriter Jonathan Favreau and his aides) did in composing the speech. On the day after ABC broadcast the video clips from Reverend Wright's sermons, Obama told David Axelrod that he wanted to give a speech on race, and late at night on the next day, he called Favreau and dictated his thoughts in a stream of consciousness that Favreau called "pretty much a first draft . . . the logic of the speech was all there" (qtd. in Remnick 522). Favreau worked on the structure the next day, and Obama sent a final draft to him and other aides two days later, saying that he wanted no substantial changes in it.

Obama's immediate emotions in composing the speech are suggested by what he said when he talked by phone with Favreau: Favreau asked how Obama was and reports that he replied, "You know, I've had better days, but, this is what you deal with when you run for President. I should be able to tell people this and explain what happened and say what I believe. And if it goes right it could be a teaching moment" (qtd. in Remnick 522). He was distressed by the impression of Wright conveyed by the video clips but confident that he could and should respond to the situation in a productive way. Emotions are intentions to act in a certain way: "Actions well up from within the organism, and they are directed toward some future state, which is being determined by the animal in accordance with its perceptions of its evolving condition and history" (Freeman 92–93).[14] As mentioned above, emotions, intentions, actions, meanings, memories, dispositions, and narratives emerge from the complex system of the nervous system through processes of which the agent is mostly not aware. Experiments by Benjamin Libet and others show that the awareness of intent to perform an act *follows* the neural activity involved in planning and organizing an act. Neurologist Antonio Damasio also observes that we are often not conscious of our emotions (and thus of our intentions) and that although we can try to conceal them, we cannot control them: "We are about as effective at stopping an emotion as we are at preventing a sneeze" (*Feeling* 49). Emotions are, at base, preparations for action, and we become aware of them (as others do, often before we do) only when they are expressed in publicly observable, and internally felt, adaptations of the body that serve as signals of intent. Freeman argues, "Your awareness is one of your assets and tools, not the agency that initiates action" (124).

The habits that enable a skilled rhetor to realize possibilities for action are often so ingrained in the nervous system that their deployment is barely conscious; they dispose a person to act in a certain way in a given situation, and to do so instantly and seamlessly. Miller points to the development of such skills as a dimension of agency, referring to Jeff Walker's description of the purpose of rhetorical training, which, "in essence, is to develop an internalized knowledge, a habitude, a crafted intuition, a trained capacity for improvisational invention" (Walker, *Genuine Teachers* 37).[15] This skill can be cultivated consciously, but it also develops through everyday immersion in the surround. Anthony Giddens defines practical consciousness as skills developed in the process of everyday living that are enacted nonconsciously, though they can be brought to consciousness (xxiii). Hubert Dreyfus, following Merleau-Ponty, understands skillful coping as "experienced as a steady flow of skillful activity in response to one's sense of the situation" ("Intelligence" 378). He describes stages in the process of acquiring skills such as playing chess and driving a car as involving less and less conscious decision-making and more and more refined discriminations of situations that allow "the immediate situational response that is characteristic of expertise" ("Intelligence" 372).[16] In skillful coping, he argues, "we do not experience our intentions as causing our bodily movements," but nevertheless our actions can be attributed to us as agents if two conditions are fulfilled: if we can stop doing what we are doing if we want to, and if our actions are "*caused* by the gestalt formed by [us] and [our] situation" ("Intelligence" 380).[17] Thompson observes that Dreyfus sometimes seems to assume that skillful coping is unconscious, and he argues in contrast that "absorbed action in the world does involve the experience of acting . . . but this experience is usually lived in a prereflective way without becoming the focus of attentive awareness" (316). For example, in using well-worn phrases such as "this nation is more than the sum of its parts," Obama knew what he was saying, but he needed no deliberate attention to choose his words.

Obama had developed a lot of rhetorical moves tied to specific situations in previous speeches that he could access without focal awareness in composing this speech. He had positioned himself as a member of what he called the "Joshua generation" in the struggle for racial equality in a speech in Selma in March 2007 at an event commemorating "Bloody Sunday."[18] Even earlier, at an anti–Iraq War rally in Chicago in 2002, he spoke of the Civil War as the beginning of the effort "to perfect this union, and drive the scourge of slavery from our soil" (qtd. in Remnick 346). There is no doubt that deliberate crafting went into the construction of Obama's speech: for example, Favreau reported that they discussed whether to use the story of Ashley and the relish sandwiches at the ending (Remnick 522). But how to approach the topic of race, and a lot of the content emerged without focal awareness from the continuity of becoming that was Obama in intra-action with Favreau and his aides in March 2008.

Whether nonconscious or conscious, voluntary actions are clearly intentional and both the actor and observers "attribute the action correctly to the actor" (Freeman 137). In Freeman's account, both nonconscious and conscious processes are self-organizing. Consciousness arises out of the interactions of neural populations that create global patterns of shared activity that are integrated by awareness, which, in turn, acts as a constraint on local chaotic fluctuations, just as a thermostat samples and regulates temperature. Consciousness, then, he says, "is the process that makes a sequence of global states of awareness" (135). It comes into play as an action is being concluded and the consequences are being organized and integrated into meaning, the learning stage of the intentional arc in which goals are also being reformulated. Consciousness, says Freeman, "holds back premature action and, by giving time for maturation and closure, it increases the likelihood of the expression in considered behavior of the long-term promise of an intentional being" (135–36).

Obama's statements to Axelrod and Favreau show that he was eager to address the topic of race—according to David Remnick, he had been considering speaking about race "for months and had been talked out of it by the staff" (521). He was confident that he could explain why Wright made such comments and that he could turn the possible debacle into a teaching moment,[19] an opportunity to mediate seemingly irreconcilable racial tensions and misunderstandings. His emotions in response to the situation were shaped by his particular experiences with race and his study of the history and literature of the civil rights and black power movements as well as by his short-term goal of demonstrating presidential leadership abilities and his long-term goal of changing the public conversation on race. Explaining Obama's ability to address explosive racial issues confidently, Martha Minow, one of his mentors at Harvard said, "Obama is black, but without the torment . . . his life came largely—not completely, but largely—without the terrible oppression" (qtd. in Remnick 195). After the speech, civil rights–era activist Bob Moses observed, "People said he couldn't afford to be the angry black candidate, but the point is that he is not angry" (qtd. in Remnick 526). Responding to the immediate rhetorical situation, his impulse was to speak out on race and his emotions continued to condition the actions of composing and delivering the speech. Afterward, the reactions to the speech would be interpreted and fed back into his ongoing construction of meanings and goals in the learning stage of the intentional arc.

Emotional interpretations are the driving force of self-organization that takes place over repeated cycles of the intentional arc. In emotional interpretation, "cognitive and emotional processes modify each other continuously on a fast time-scale" resulting in "a global state of emotion-cognition coherence, comprising an appraisal of a situation, an affective tone, and an action plan . . . a global intention for acting on the world" (Thompson 371–73). Emotional interpretations are brief and not necessarily coherent, and they succeed each other rapidly. The action of neuromodulators such as histamine, dopamine, endorphins, vasopressin, and norepinephrine, which cause long-lasting changes in synaptic gains throughout the cerebral hemispheres, are, as Freeman notes, "essential for intentional action, including emotion, and for the construction of meaning, including remembering" (108). They are responsible as well for moods and dispositions, which develop over longer spans of time. Thompson explains the neurodynamics of these processes using a dynamic system model. In the immediate process of composing a speech or a piece of writing, many emotional interpretations (meanings) emerge and begin to cohere over hours or days in part through the development of moods, which alter the landscape of attractors within which transient emotional interpretations occur (Thompson 378). Finally, over a much longer span of time, personality emerges, "temporally extended, long-term patterns of habitual emotions linked with habitual appraisals, built up especially from moods" (Thompson 381). Considering agency as emergent from processes that take place largely without the agent's awareness may seem both commonsensical and trivial, but it is the way a person becomes who they are and it provides the motivation for taking responsibility for their actions. Personality is embodied, and, thus, to deny one's actions is to deny one's self. As Whitehead says, "We are in the world and the world is in us.... The body is ours, and we are an activity within our body" (MT 165).

Habits of Productive Agency

Personality is how we experience the neurodynamic structure of ourselves as individuating unities, and we can discern in Obama's speech three long-term patterns, or habits, of productive agency that are part of his personality:

> a centered flexibility that impels him to mediate differences,
> a recognition of the wider import of his personal narrative, and
> a mode of addressing others as agents acting out of their own subjective experiences.

Remember that for Aristotle a habit is "an active condition, a way in which we hold ourselves, having taken hold deliberately of the feelings and dispositions that are in us merely passively" (*Nicomachean* ix) and that even as habits become habitual, enacting them and holding to them is an ongoing project. These habits of productive agency differ from the more automatic habits that provide meaning for free that I discussed in the last section by being more, if not completely, consciously held. From what Obama has said and written, it's clear that he holds to these habits as important in how he understands himself and his actions.[20] I also argue that they are habits that lead to writing and speaking well.

Political scientist Bryan Garsten argues that people who are skilled at deliberative rhetoric, which Obama clearly is, have good judgment, which he traces to having "not only . . . the requisite intellectual quickness and cleverness but also . . . the right dispositions or habits of affective responses" (8). Garsten comments that these habits develop partly from nature (emotional self-construction) and partly by education, and that they "allow [rhetors] a measure of self-possession; from that relatively steady perspective they will be able to imagine accurately and empathetically what it would be like to take various courses of action" (8). Obama's self-possession is often commented on. Referring to the Philadelphia speech, Moses said of Obama, "His confidence in himself—and his peacefulness with himself—came through in a way that can't be faked" (qtd. in Remnick 526). Christopher Edley Jr., one of Obama's professors at Harvard said, "I claim to have been the first to use the phrase 'preternatural calmness' to describe him. That's what was so striking about him . . . he seemed so centered that, in combination with his evident intelligence, I just wanted to buy stock in him" (qtd. in Remnick 217). In assessing Obama's work in the U.S. Senate, Remnick, like Garsten, makes the connection between self-possession and skill in deliberation: "Obama felt it was essential to show that he possessed a distinctive equanimity and cool. Conciliation was his default mode, the dominant strain in his political personality. . . . This had been his way since Harvard when he extended a hand to conservatives even at the cost of disappointing some fellow liberals" (433). Obama's habitual self-possession, his "relatively steady perspective" is also what impels him to take up his role as a mediator. Robert Putnam, who led the Saguaro Seminars on civic engagement at the Kennedy School that Obama participated in, is one among many who comment on Obama's habit of seeing "common themes in the midst of an arguing bunch. It's a personal skill or a personality trait," says Putnam. "I don't think I have ever seen that same ability in anyone else" (qtd. in Remnick 306).

Obama's choice to respond to the furor over Reverend Wright's televised remarks as a "teachable moment" exemplifies this habit of centered flexibility. Instead of seeing it as a politically and personally difficult issue to somehow be finessed or deflected, or a chance to set the record straight on Reverend Wright's remarks, he seized it as an opportunity to offer a more nuanced approach to the crucial issue of race. Asserting that the American people were hungry for a message of unity, he argued that Wright's remarks not only "expressed a profoundly distorted view of this country" but also were divisive. Still, he refused to disown Wright or dismiss him "as a crank or a demagogue" because, he said, "race is an issue . . . this nation cannot afford to ignore right now . . . [or] simplify." He described sources of black anger and white anger, calling them "legitimate concerns" but arguing that dwelling on them was "unproductive." And he offered a way forward: "Working together, we can move beyond some of our old racial wounds."

Not everyone was happy with this approach. Some saw his remarks as a betrayal of his true beliefs, or at least as political posturing. About his assertion that "I could no more disown [Reverend Wright] than I could my white grandmother," conservatives acidly wondered how anybody could "throw his grandmother under the bus" in an attempt to win an election (Schultz 104). Though Cornel West held his fire in public as, he said, "it was a very delicate moment," he later criticized Obama for equating the oppression of blacks with white resentment, arguing, "I can understand that, the white moderates need that nice little massage and so on, but it has nothing to do with the truth, at all" (qtd. in Remnick 526). And Obery Hendricks, a professor at the New York Theological Seminary, was profoundly disappointed that Obama chose to respond to Reverend Wright's rhetorical style rather than defending "the substance of his social critiques" (176). He argued that Obama "soft-pedaled the full implications" (171) of his own similar descriptions of racial injustices, thereby reducing "the long and brutal history of systemic and institutionalized racism to mere moral lapses" (175).

Centered flexibility is a delicate posture: it demands both holding to one's central values and being open to other concerns that might make them more capacious, more productive in new situations. It is a habit that acknowledges how patterns in time shift in the becoming of an individuating entity. One of Aristotle's conditions on how good habits are to be enacted describes this posture as that of "being in a stable condition and not able to be moved all the way out of it" (*Nicomachean* 26). Sachs's illuminating note on this phrase offers an amusing image: "Aristotle's marvelous adverb *ametakinêtôs, akinêtôs* would mean in the manner of someone immovable or rigid, but the added prefix makes it convey the condition of those toys that can be knocked over but always come back upright on their own, a flexible stability or equilibrium" (*Nicomachean* 26n30). Equilibrium is the foundation for this habit, equilibrium as a response to the becoming of an individualizing entity. It is a habit of being open from a relatively steady perspective to the possibilities offered by other positions, willing to consider them and to nuance one's own position, but not to wildly swing from one alternative to another, forgetting the things that one believes are most important. It is a habit of what Stengers calls "the Whiteheadean dream of learning inside the cave": "this dream obliges the person it infects to address the dreams of others, for only dreamers can accept the modification of their dream. Only dreams and stories, because they are the enjoyment of living values, can receive the interstices without the panic effect of people who believe themselves to be in danger of losing hold" (TW 516–17). Centered flexibility, self-possession, is not a frightened clinging to values, but a trust in living values that can be modified without losing their personal value.

Obama's impulse toward mediation is also the source of what Remnick calls his "signature appeal, the use of the details of his own life as a reflection of a kind of multicultural ideal" (360). Erec Smith says that Obama's success in this speech was due to his seizing the kairotic moment of the furor over Reverend Wright's words to establish his *ethos* as a "living personification of the American melting pot" (5). Certainly it worked to establish his authority to speak of both black and white experience, as Denean Sharpley-Whiting argues. Suggesting that his approach was an embrace of W. E. B. Du Bois's second-sightedness, she argues that in "wrapping it around his biography" Obama is granted an authority that is based on "a bit deeper . . . more intimate" experience with whites than her own, and she argues: "So when Barack Obama speaks knowingly of white anger and the anxieties of working-and-middle-class white Americans, . . . we have to know that he may be voicing his own white grandfather's disappointments and failures, the sacrifices of his white grandmother" ("Chloro" 13). But his use of his life experiences goes beyond a matter of authority to speak. By recognizing and articulating the wider import of his personal narrative, Obama acknowledges his entanglement in history, how in his intra-actions he participates in creating both his own and his world's narratives.

Sugrue argues that it was through his experience of the complexities of race in late twentieth-century America that Obama "discovered his calling. It was to overcome the acrimonious history of racial polarization . . . to act on the understanding that such polarization was anathema to national unity" (54), and he comments that "Obama's power as an orator is his ability to seamlessly bring together . . . his personal story with a narrative of national redemption" (53). Damasio, among many others,[21] argues that nonconscious and conscious narrative processes provide individuals with a sense of themselves (*Self* 215–16). The construction of these narratives is an ongoing intra-action across individuating entities and the milieu, "derived from the past and aimed at the future" (Whitehead, MT 167). Self-narratives are always implicitly self-and-milieu narratives as Obama recognized in beginning his appeal for a new understanding of race by saying that his "is a story that has seared into my genetic makeup the idea that this nation is more than the sum of its parts—that out of many, we are truly one." He shaped a narrative that aligned his personal identity and disposition with strongly held cultural narratives of American optimism, belief in the inevitability of progress, and exceptionalism, and with a common understanding of Martin Luther King as a moderate conciliator and national healer. Sugrue says, "Our conventional histories of King and the Southern freedom struggle reinforce a broader and still deeply held vision of American exceptionalism, one that relates civil rights to a timeless American political tradition, dating back to the founding, of equality and opportunity" (51). Obama's shaping of this narrative, its intricate synthesis of emotions, dispositions, memories, cultural beliefs, and study of civil rights history, was not the work of couple of nights of focused thought. But his habit of articulating his narrative with American cultural narratives enabled him to create it anew in this important speech. Acknowledging his own entanglement, he can ask his listeners to do the same, suggesting that "working together," we can move forward beyond racial stalemates. Garsten argues that because deliberation is "a process of drawing upon citizens' capacity for judgment"(190),[22] it "requires the opportunity to change one's mind" (198), and this is what Obama offers at the end of his speech.

The flexibility Obama demonstrates in speeches and elsewhere is not a habit of compromise nor simply political pragmatism, but a principled response to other people as agents who act out of their own subjective experiences. This is the third habit of productive agency. It is based in one of Foucault's conditions for a power relationship, that the other "be thoroughly recognized and maintained to the very end as a person who acts" ("Subject" 220) augmented by Whitehead's understanding of actual entities as constituted by their subjective experiences and thus morally responsible for them: "The subject is responsible for being what it is in virtue of its feelings" (PR 222). All agents in an intra-action are responsible to the extent that they are able to be (Whitehead restricts it to "our own relatively high grade of human existence"). Together, Foucault's and Whitehead's understanding of agents implies a reciprocal responsibility for behaving toward others as people acting out of their own experiences. Maturana argues that responsible agency requires one to be aware that everyone acts out of their own space of meaning, that the isolation of perception and meaning in the body entails that no one can "claim to be rationally right through some explicit or implicit pretense of having a privileged access to an objective reality" ("Response" 96), and that to affirm one's own meanings as absolute truth is to negate the other person. Latour agrees, ascribing to "moralists" the skill of knowing that no one knows for certain and for all time what must be done (PN 156). It is the skill of moralists that enables the collective to resist the lure of certainty and of "matters of fact" and instead to embrace uncertainty and matters of concern by always being open to other voices, other opinions.[23] This is also a good habit of responsible writers, to be open to and responsive to the meanings of others, to not negate others by insisting that only they themselves own the truth.

Openness to other possibilities, to other opinions, to the voices of others, resonates with Foucault's second condition for a power relationship, "that, faced with a relationship of power, a whole field of responses, reactions, results, and possible inventions may open up" ("Subject" 220). It is also essential to the kind of deliberative rhetoric and persuasion Garsten argues for. He says that in real persuasion, "Speakers treat their listeners' existing opinions with a certain deference, and yet they do not cater to them. This respect for the actual opinions of one's audience serves to acknowledge the particular features of individuals—their histories, identities, commitments, and needs—in a way that respect for their autonomy does not. It is a respect for what Seyla Benhabib has called 'the concrete other' rather than the 'generalized other'" (198). Respect for listeners' opinions, being open even to "unreasonable" opinions, to "troublemakers," means being open to them as responsive beings who, like the speaker, will understand or assimilate meanings in their own way. It means to recognize both speakers and listeners as agents in persuasion, as people who are free to change their minds.

One aspect of Obama's speech that some reacted to negatively was his focus on emotions over empirical facts. The novelist Adam Mansbach wrote, "To place the experiences of white and black Americans on an equal footing, Obama had to abandon the empirical and speak the language of the emotional. Hence the focus on how people 'feel'—privileged or not, racist or not—rather than on the objective realities of what they have and do and say" (75). West had the same objection, arguing that instead of attending to the feelings of "white moderates," "You got to tell the truth, Barack" (qtd. in Remnick 526). Obama, in an interview three weeks after the speech, implied why he focused on emotions. He said, "My pastor said some very offensive things for a broad cross section of the American people, and I think any candidate for president would have had to deal with that on some level" (qtd. in Jackson 226). Despite the clear political motive, I also hear in Obama's concern about the offensive things Wright said a concern for "the particular features of individuals—their histories, identities, commitments, and needs" that Garsten calls for—and that Mansbach indirectly alludes to in his conclusion where he calls for "community forums" that could draw people into "genuine interaction" on racial questions (84). This is a habit that acknowledges the validity of listeners' experiences and thereby allows them the space and freedom to change their minds. It allows them their own agency enabling them to talk together as no litany of facts or critiques can do.

Obama concluded his speech by offering his audience a choice: "We have a choice in this country. . . . We can tackle race only as a spectacle . . . or in the wake of tragedy . . . or as fodder for the nightly news. . . . That is an option. Or, at this moment, in this election, we can come together and say, 'Not this time.'" Obama's statement that we had a choice, that we could say "Not this time," was an offer that made clear his respect for his listeners' opinions. It is a habit he is well-known for. Cass Sunstein, a close friend of Obama's in law school, when asked about Obama's legal ideology, said, "With Obama it's more like Learned Hand when he said, 'The spirit of liberty is the spirit which is not too sure that it is right.' Obama takes that really seriously. I think the reason that conservatives are O.K. with him is both that he might agree with them on some issues and that even if he comes down on a different side he knows he might be wrong" (qtd. in Remnick 266). Obama's offer was an invitation to responsible agency, an invitation to consider other alternatives to a politics of racial division. In concluding his speech in this way, Obama emerges as a productive—and responsible—agent. He strongly argues for the choice he would make, but as was clear in his actions as president subsequently, he is open to modifications of his dreams. He knows he might be wrong.

Syndicated columnist Connie Schultz also understood Obama's speech as offering his audience a choice of how to respond: "Would we, as white people, initiate the most painful of conversations with people we loved?" (107). She admits that his "eloquent speech" made "not so much" of an impact at the time on the listeners he was trying to reach (103). But over time, it did succeed "beyond what white people like me dared to hope for" as more of those white people "came to believe they knew him" (104). In July 2008, she published a column in which she recounted her regret that she never managed to confront her father's bigotry and "beseeched white readers to have the tough talk back home" (107). Some of her readers were outraged, but over time, readers began reporting on how their conversations went. One woman told Schultz that she finally told her father to stop saying he would never vote for a black man, and "after he got over the shock, we talked. And we're still talking. I don't know if he's going to vote for Obama, but at least he understands now why I will" (110). Schultz concludes, "It was hard to hear from so many readers ... and not think that Obama's entreaty had hit its mark" (111).

The question of how Obama caused people to believe that a politics that breeds divisiveness is bad for the country makes little sense. What happened is not the effect of a single action but rather a pattern that develops from the interanimating actions of a multitude of agents, of which the people mentioned by Schultz—and herself—are only a small sample. As Obama said in his speech at Howard University's convocation in 2007, "One man cannot make a movement" (qtd. in Sugrue 135). We attribute causes because of how we experience our intentions and their consequences, but as Freeman concludes, "causality is in the mind of humans" (133).

Free Will, Decision, and Choice

In the sense that our actions, ensuing from our emotions, are always our own, we act with free will; agency is grounded in the actions of individuating entities. Freeman argues that it is the misperception of the biological phenomenon of agency in terms of linear causality that leads to a belief in the impossibility of free will, and he comments, "No intentional action is free of its historical context, nor is it entirely constrained by genetic and environmental determinants. The nature-nurture deterministic dyad . . . fails to take into account the capacity for intentional beings to construct and pursue their individual goals within the contexts of their societies" (138).

As Obama tacitly understood in observing "my choices were never truly mine alone" (*Dreams* 134), the problem with linear causality is that it attributes effects to a single cause—either the agent free of any influence from history, social interactions, or genetics, or the body and the environment free of the influence of any current mind. Shaviro argues that Whitehead's rearticulation of Kant's antinomy of efficient and final causality offers a productive alternative to linear causality. As discussed earlier, Whitehead posits the coexistence of two kinds of "flux": concrescence, the flux "inherent in the constitution of the particular existent"; and transition, the flux "whereby the perishing of the process . . . constitutes that existent as an original element in the constitutions of other particular existents elicited by repetitions of process" (PR 210). Whitehead says, "Concrescence moves toward its final cause, which is its subjective aim; transition is the vehicle of the efficient cause, which is the immortal past" (PR 210). Shaviro explains, "Efficient causality refers to the naturalistic chain of causes and effects, or the way that an entity inherits conditions and orientations" from the past; it is "a passage, a transmission, an influence or a contagion" (*Without Criteria* 86–87). Final causality refers to the affective response of the entity that constitutes "its potential for change or novelty" (Shaviro 88) as the entity values the transmitted data according to the "qualities of joy and distaste, of adversion and of aversion, which attach integrally" to every experience (PR 234; cf. Kauffman, "yuck" and "yum"). Shaviro observes, "For Whitehead, the final cause is the 'decision' by means of which an actual entity becomes what it is" (*Without Criteria* 88).

Like Barad who says that intra-actions produce agential cuts, Whitehead uses "decision" in the "root sense of a 'cutting off'" (PR 43) of some potentialities while opening others. He says, "Just as 'potentiality for process' is the meaning of the more general term 'entity,' or 'thing'; so 'decision' is the additional meaning imported by the word 'actual' into the phrase 'actual entity.' 'Actuality' is the decision amid 'potentiality.' . . . The real internal constitution of an actual entity progressively constitutes a decision conditioning the creativity which transcends that actuality" (PR 43). And "'decided' conditions are never such as to banish freedom. They only qualify it. There is always a contingency left open for immediate decision" (PR 284). He adds that such decisions are not necessarily conscious, though in some decisions "consciousness will be a factor" (PR 43). Whitehead's actual entities include all entities, not just humans: entities like Kauffman's bacterium, an autonomous agent swimming upstream in a glucose gradient that decides for itself without conscious purpose. Shaviro says, "We don't make decisions because we are free and responsible; rather, we are free and responsible because—and precisely to the extent that—we make decisions" (94).

Stengers explains that decisions are the way that actual entities create their reasons: "A being becomes determined by determining its reasons . . . only in the process of constitution of the entity of which they will be reasons are reasons articulated, 'put together,' in a way that confers upon each of them its determinate power" (TW 263). Thus an agent's decision is conditioned by its context but still is not determined by it. Stengers offers the example of a judge's decision, which has itself assembled the multiple considerations on which it is based "and presented them in a way that makes the judgment their consequence." The decision "is 'conditioned,' but it is the judgment itself that determines the relation between the decision and what conditions it" (263).

When Obama writes that his choices were never his alone, he rejects the notion of freedom as freedom from determining conditions. Glen Mazis explains that the latter notion of freedom, the one most often assumed in American popular culture, is "the 'negative' moment of freedom . . . [which] does not address what freedom is to be used for—namely to pursue a meaning and purpose in life, which requires commitment and foreclosing one's options by making choices and seeing them through" (159). But he also argues that the ability to choose one way or another "is not the primary sense of freedom—it comes too late. Choosing between alternatives presupposes a human's ability to enter into a relationship with the surround in differing ways that give rise to differing senses and therefore differing choices" (159)—or, as Garsten said, an ability "to imagine accurately and empathetically what it would be like to take various courses of action" (8). Mazis traces that ability to the phenomenon of self-consciousness or metacognition, "the awareness of having an experience while in the midst of it—of tacitly recognizing the sense of the unfolding experience without halting it or distancing oneself from it" (158). He says that it is the interweaving of this "dual consciousness," a "feathered modulation of 'both and' or 'not one, not two'" (158) that he derives from Merleau-Ponty's notion of the interweaving of the subject and object, that opens a space for new possibilities. He explains: "The freedom here . . . is not the Cartesian will to order the mind in commanding itself to proceed in a certain predetermined line and corresponding behavior but is, rather, the letting emerge from a wider flow of meaning that can expand us in a different kind of direction toward a new relationship. The situation comes to have differing significances and therefore differing possible outcomes" (158). That differing significances and outcomes arise from shifts in consciousness is widely recognized: Heidegger argued that awareness of things as things in themselves, apart from our everyday interaction with them, arises from a loss of circumspection (*Being* 107), a breakdown of skillful coping that can interrupt the intentional arc. Psychologist Daniel Wegner recognizes this phenomenon, too, explaining that we experience conscious will more often when our thought processes are "inefficient." He says, "Controlled and conscious processes are simply those that lumber along so inefficiently that there is plenty of time for previews of their associated actions to come to mind and allow us to infer the operation of conscious will" (98).[24] Metacognition, loss of circumspection, and inefficient processes are all conscious—and consciousness-expanding—processes that are, as Mazis explains, at once focused and unfocused; they are a kind of concentrated attention on the beckonings of other possibilities in the brain and in the surround (135–36). The freedom in free will is this openness to different meanings, an openness to "the flow of fresh constructions within our brains and bodies" (Freeman 139) that arises in our interactions with each other and the surround and that, as Mazis says, creates choices, and as Whitehead says, requires decisions.

Intra-acting individualizing entities are ineluctably productive agents: their actions always produce new possibilities that they and others respond to unconsciously and consciously, and thus they participate in the ongoing reconfigurings of the world. Humans do so especially in their writing, and they do so ethically by developing and holding to habits such as the three I discern in Obama's rhetoric. Ethics is not just a matter of responding, but of responding in a way that acknowledges entanglement, becoming, and the creation of possibilities for being and becoming. Doing so means being accountable for the agential cuts made in intra-actions, by contesting and reworking what matters. This requires recognizing others not only as entities that act but also as individualizing entities, concrete others who have opinions and beliefs grounded in their own experiences and perceptions and meanings constructed in their bodies.

6

The Creativity of Writing

"I can't write; I'm not creative. I can't think of anything to say." Complaints I often heard at the beginning of writing courses I was teaching. A similar query from a student to a colleague in an advanced subject course: "I am having trouble even finding a starting point. I know the topic has to be environmental but do you have any recommendations for topics to choose from or a resource where I could get started?"

Writing assignments given to students are often not particularly salubrious places from which to start writing. Students have no exigency to write, no experience of "this is important," just a duty to perform. Michael Carter comments on how the high value placed on "creative writing" (fiction, poetry) implies that what we teach in writing classes is "not-good" writing (120), but my students seemed to think that all writing required creativity beyond their abilities. I think they are partly right. All writing is creative—but it is not beyond anyone's ability. Creativity isn't a matter of thinking of something original to say—creating something out of one's head with no reference to anything else. The student in the advanced course knows that but still needs the experience of finding something that is important to him in order to get started. Everyone has those experiences, and everyone creates whenever they write. This project started with my belief that writing is important. The question, though, is always not why something is important, but how it is important. At this point in the book, you should have guessed my answer: writing is important as the way humans participate in creating our worlds. There are, of course, other answers, but that's the answer that emerged in my experience of reading and connecting ideas and teaching writing over several decades.

Creativity is the pulse of the cosmos that beats in every moment of life as entangled beings intra-act. It is not a power belonging to beings but the basis of their existence, the process through which they become what they are through affecting and being affected by other beings and entities: as Kimmerer meets her "old friend" plantain on a trail on the Pacific coast, as Eigler and a scanning tunneling microscope move atoms of gadolinium, as my dog Scout teaches me to retrieve inaccessible toys, as Archanthropians chip flint, as Ingold's students correspond with willow branches to make baskets, as Harberd observes the thale-cress plant in St Mary's cemetery, as Obama remembers racist remarks made by his white grandmother, and in chapter 7 as I encounter a dragonfly, and geochemist Bill Green tracks cobalt in the lakes in Antarctica's Dry Valleys. And, importantly, in writing and rhetoric as humans (mostly) intra-act, face-to-face and textually, creating phenomena of meanings that matter, that move people to action or reflection that materially change the world and that induce speculative adventures of ideas.

Alfred North Whitehead proposes that "'creativity' is the universal of universals, characterizing ultimate matter of fact" (PR 21). "The creative advance into novelty" is "the ultimate metaphysical ground" (PR 349), a fundamental appetition "involving realization of what is not and may be" (PR 32). Like Whitehead, Gilles Deleuze and Félix Guattari see the creative process as fundamental: "The plane of composition, the plane of Nature, is precisely for participations of this kind, and continually makes and unmakes their assemblages" (258). And, again, Whitehead echoes Deleuze and Guattari: "The world expands through recurrent unifications of itself, each by the addition of itself, automatically recreating the multiplicity anew" (PR 286).

Though the creative process is fundamental to everything that exists, Whitehead observes that it is more significant in living systems: "'Life' means novelty. . . . What has to be explained is originality in response to stimulus" (PR 104). Response is characteristic of inorganic systems as well, "but as soon as individual experience is not negligible, the autonomy of the subject in the modification of its initial subjective aim must be taken into account" (PR 245). Ilya Prigogine similarly observes that complex systems that give rise to a "wealth of possible new structures and organizations" are more common among living systems than among inorganic ones (Prigogine and Allen 9). There are inorganic complex systems (chemical clocks are a good example), but among living systems complex systems are "virtually the rule" (Prigogine and Stengers 153). It is in living systems that the feedback loops of autocatalysis, autoinhibition, and cross-catalysis lead systems to bifurcation points that enable the processes of morphogenesis, metabolism, growth, and organismic and ecosystem complexity that are necessary to life on earth.

In what follows, I explore how seeing creativity as an intra-active process helps us conceive writing as what Whitehead calls an adventure of ideas "in which one does not feel oneself to be the master of what one writes, but where writing forces one to think, to feel, and to create" (Stengers, TW 354). I continue my discussion, begun in chapter 4, of Whitehead's concrescence, a concept that embodies "the production of novel togetherness" (PR 21), by focusing on the interplay of determination and indetermination, novelty and loss. In this interplay, two questions demand answers that must in turn answer to each other: how does determination arise out of indetermination? and how does what is determined endure? In more familiar terms, how do writers create meaning out of the overwhelming babble (Babel) of past meanings? and how do their meanings hold together at all? Whitehead refers both questions to the "miracle of creation" described in Ezekiel: "So I prophesied as he commanded me, and the breath came into them, and they lived, and stood up upon their feet, an exceeding great army" (xxxvii:10; qtd. in PR 85). How does Ezekiel's prophesy bring about the reassembling of those scattered dry bones, not even skeletons, into a living, breathing army? Whitehead's answer can be understood by considering the cosmology he constructs in the final chapter of *Process and Reality* and by considering in more detail his concept of propositions. Along with these somewhat lofty excursions, I engage with Michael Carter's similar appropriation of Whitehead's understanding of creativity as I explore more fully the possibilities that arise from saying that writing is essentially creative. I conclude by looking at three examples of the creativity of writing that forces one to think, to feel, and to create.

Creativity Is an Intra-Active Process

Creativity is the process of reciprocal self and world creation. Novelty arises from processes of intra-action, many of which I discussed in chapter 4. Humberto Maturana and Francisco Varela call the process autopoesis and refer it to the dynamic of "structural coupling," a history of mutually congruent structural changes resulting from reciprocal perturbations between an organism and its environment (or another being) (*Tree* 75). Donna Haraway calls it "becoming with": "To be one is always to *become with* many" (*When* 4).[1] Describing her intra-action with her dog Cayenne in the sport of agility, she says: "Who are you, and so who are we? Here we are, and so what are we to become?" (221) She also refers to it as reciprocal induction, a concept she was familiar with from her graduate studies in developmental biology and that she uses to describe how behaviors are created in the process of training. "A behavior is not something just out there in the world waiting for discovery; a behavior is an inventive construction, a generative fact–fiction, put together by an intra-acting crowd of players" (211). In the case of agility, the players are the dog and the trainer creating behaviors conditioned by a course of various obstacles. Creating these behaviors requires attunement between the two players and the agility course, very specific modes of responding that are not natural to either dog or trainer. Each must respond to the authority of the other in becoming a cross-species team: trainers set the acceptable criteria for navigating each obstacle and dogs run the course, and each must respond appropriately to the other's performance until coherence is attained.[2] It is not so much a matter of teaching the dog a behavior as it is each suggesting actions to and responding to the other, responses that may or may not be what was expected—a reciprocal induction. Haraway comments: "The coming into being of something unexpected, something new and free, something outside the rules of function and calculation, something not ruled by the logic of the reproduction of the same, *is* what training with each other is about" (223). Quoting Whitehead's description of concrescence—"The many have become one, and are increased by one" (PR 21)—she comments, "This is ordinary reciprocal induction" (*When* 244).

"There is a rhythm of process whereby creation produces natural pulsation, each pulsation forming a natural unit of historic fact" (MT 88), says Whitehead. Each pulsation is an actual entity forming in concrescence, "but no actuality is a static fact. . . . The completed fact is only to be understood as taking its place among the active data forming the future" (MT 90). He defines concrescence as "the production of novel togetherness" (PR 21), but it needs to be understood as a reciprocal process, the becoming of actual entities that in turn constitute the world in an unending, eternal creation: "The world is self-creative; and the actual entity as self-creating creature passes into its immortal function of part-creator of the transcendent world" (PR 85). At the moment in which an actual entity attains absolute determination of itself through its own decisions, it perishes and becomes one of the many data that participate in the concrescence of new actual entities: "The 'perishing' of absoluteness is the attainment of 'objective immortality'" (PR 60). As past actual occasions, "objective immortalities" become objects in new concrescences, either in the trajectory of an enduring entity, an individual person, for example, or in other actual entities. In this perishing, however, they lose their power to decide; as Isabelle Stengers says, "having acceded to 'objective immortality,'" they are "categorically incapable of appealing against the use other occasions will make of [their] decision" (TW 469). The attainment of objective immortality is equally the loss of finite actuality.

In the penultimate chapter of *Process and Reality*, Whitehead raises the question of the primordial tragedy reflected in the process of concrescence: "The world is thus faced by the paradox that, at least in its higher actualities, it craves for novelty and yet is haunted by terror at the loss of the past, with its familiarities and loved ones" (PR 340). To rethink such paradoxes in a way that they become productive rather than remaining at impasse as universal ideals requires more complex treatment of opposing concepts like permanence and flux, order and novelty. Whitehead says, "What is required . . . is order entering upon novelty; so that the massiveness of order does not degenerate into mere repetition; and so that the novelty is always reflected upon a background of system" (339). In the following final chapter of *Process and Reality*, "God and the World," he explores on the cosmic level the interanimation of permanence and flux in the process of creativity—the reciprocal creation of God and the World—focusing this time more on loss than on the thirst for novelty.[3]

A whole set of ideal opposites are lined up as traditionally characterizing God and the World—God as mental (conceptual), infinite, and permanent (eternal); the World as physical, finite, and fluent (passing)—as Whitehead despairs of "the vicious separation of the flux from the permanence" that leads to "the concept of an entirely static God, with eminent reality, in relation to an entirely fluent world, with deficient reality" (346). This cosmology, which characterizes Greek, Hebrew, and Christian thought, "involves contradiction at every step" especially with regard to the world, which "is *either* thoroughly fluent, *or* accidentally static, but finally fluent" with some exceptions described by a new set of ideal opposites: happiness for the good; torture for the evil (347). Whitehead's cosmology will instead turn all the ideal opposites into contrasts necessary to the creativity of a universe in which nothing will be lost—except fixed ideals.

In Whitehead's cosmology, God and the World are in a relation of reciprocal induction, becoming together by inducing in each other their contrasting primordial natures. In each actuality, God and the World,[4] "there are two concrescent poles of realization" (PR 348): the conceptual pole of appetition—infinite, potential, unconscious, and permanent (eternal); and the physical pole of enjoyment—finite, actual, conscious, and fluent (passing). God's primordial nature is conceptual, "the unlimited conceptual realization of the absolute wealth of potentiality" (343), and he induces in the World the appetition for potentiality. The World's primordial nature is physical, "the multiple solidarity of free physical realizations in the temporal world" (346), and it induces in God the enjoyment of actuality. Through these inductions God and the World acquire consequent natures. Thus God enjoys the actual, conscious, completion of the physical world, and the World thirsts for the unconscious, infinite potentialities of God. Stengers says that "by means of the correlated twofold definition of God and the actual occasions," Whitehead affirms "the equal dignity of both poles, the physical pole that affirms that what has occurred has occurred, and the conceptual pole, by which nothing of what has occurred constitutes the last word" (TW 458).

Although we might say that the World, at least in the sense of the Universe, is eternal, the multitude of actual entities that constitute the primordial nature of the World are not: in affirming that what has occurred has occurred, they still perish. And God enjoys the physical completion of actual entities but still retains his primordial eternal nature: he ensures that nothing of what has occurred constitutes the last word. The paradox is not yet resolved. In what sense can we say that God enjoys the finitude of each actual entity such that it is saved in his unlimited realization of the wealth of potentiality? How do actual entities satisfy their thirst for potentiality without losing the satisfaction of completion? Essentially, how do the contradictions of the finite and the infinite condition each other in a process of genuine creation, a becoming not determined by the other? An answer lies in an investigation of the efficacy of the cry of the actual entity that it not be lost and in an interrogation of the words "perish" and "completion." Whitehead suggests an outline of this answer: "This discordant multiplicity of actual things, requiring each other and neglecting each other, utilizing and discarding, perishing and yet claiming life as obstinate matter of fact, requires an enlargement of the understanding to the comprehension of another phase in the nature of things. In this later phase, the many actualities are one actuality, and the one actuality is many actualities. Each actuality has its present life and its immediate passage into novelty; but its passage is not its death. The final stage of passage in God's nature is ever enlarging itself" (PR 349). In constructing his cosmology, Whitehead modulates his description of the process of concrescence—"the many become one, and are increased by one." Now both the World and God are both one and many. If actual entities perish in their completion and God completes himself in the enjoyment of their completion this is not, as Stengers says in a slightly different context, the end of the story (TW 470).

The cry of the actual occasion that it be not lost is an appeal to the future in which, as an objective immortality it will take its role as the past. Its appeal, its prayer to God, will be answered, but not as a demand to be heard "for itself": its final determination as an actuality perishes. Still, it does not die, in the sense of sinking into oblivion; it becomes the object of God's feeling of an actual, physical fact. "The completion of God's nature into a fulness of physical feeling is derived from the objectification of the world in God" (345). Stengers explains that "objectified" here means "'being felt' by something other than oneself" but felt according to the nature of the other doing the feeling, and "God is he for whom every occasion, even the most tenuous, 'matters,' insofar as it is new" (TW 472). What in the actual occasion matters to God is the very specifics of its concrescence: what was felt and what was excluded as well as included in its decision. Thus, as Whitehead says, continuing the statement just quoted, "the concrescent creature is objectified in God as a novel element in God's objectification of that actual world" (PR 345). "Divine experience," says Stengers, "is the experience of limitation *qua* completion, not of completion *qua* limited" (TW 475).

> The wisdom of [God's] subjective aim prehends every actuality for what it can be in such a perfected system—its sufferings, its sorrows, its failures, its triumphs, its immediacies of joy—woven by rightness of feeling into the harmony of the universal feeling. . . . The revolts of destructive evil, purely self-regarding, are diminished into their triviality of merely individual facts; and yet the good they did achieve in individual joy, in individual sorrow, in the introduction of needed contrast, is yet saved by its relation to the completed whole. The image . . . of God's nature is best conceived [as] that of a tender care that nothing be lost. (PR 474)

What needs to be emphasized here is the absoluteness of God's embrace of actuality, of not only what was included but what was excluded. He saves each actual occasion in all its specific detail, and if the details are not felt as the actuality would wish them to be, they are felt in a way that prolongs their role in the creativity of the world. The experiences of objective immortalities are saved as contrasts thus constituting possibilities, all part of the divine vision, all "woven into the 'eternal ordering'" that is neither a transcendent knowledge nor a determinate anticipation (TW 476). Thus neither the actualities in the form of objective immortalities nor the "harmony of the universal feeling" are limited in their completion. Whitehead says, in the passage I omitted from the quote above, "The harmony of the universal feeling . . . is always immediate, always many, always one, always with novel advance, moving onward and never perishing" (PR 474).

God, Stengers says, is "a unique concrescence, without a past, in perpetual becoming, in unison with a world that transcends him as much as he transcends it" (TW 477). Actual occasions enjoy a full determination of actuality, submerging for the moment the appetition for potentiality; they endure in the form of objective immortalities that induce new possibilities. But "the divine feeling 'never' perishes'; it is experience 'together,' perpetually increasing, of contrasts, each of which implies the feeling of an individual completion in its living immediacy. . . . Each new contrast, as it is added, will be integrated into harmony in the form of what it has made possible, the feeling of what was 'best' for that impasse" (TW 476). Whitehead defines God's role: "In his overpowering rationality of his conceptual harmonization[,] He does not create the world, he saves it" (PR 346), patiently collecting in his actuality all actual occasions without exception as contrasts that initiate the emergence of new entities (350). For Whitehead, God is neither creator nor the principle of creativity: "The ultimate creativity of the universe is [not] to be ascribed to God's volition . . . [for]

there is no meaning to 'creativity' apart from its 'creatures,' and no meaning to 'God' apart from the 'creativity' and the 'temporal creatures,' and no meaning to the 'temporal creatures' apart from 'creativity' and 'God'" (225). Neither God nor objective immortalities determine the outcome of the possibilities they induce; they are, as I said, in a relation of reciprocal induction.

Both Stuart Kauffman and Gilbert Simondon explain the creativity of the universe in ways strikingly parallel to Whitehead's cosmology. Kauffman describes the "vastly nonergodic" nature of the universe as a process of propagating organization (I 151). Propagating organization arises from "the mathematical concept of an 'adjacent possible,' persistently explored in a universe that can never, in the vastly many lifetimes of the universe, have made all possible protein sequences even once" (I 22). The actual is a multiplicity, for example, all the species of organic molecules in, on, or around the Earth out to twice the radius of the moon. The adjacent possible, then, "comprises just those molecular species that are not present . . . but can be synthesized from the actual molecular species in a single reaction step from the substrates in the actual to products in the adjacent possible" (I 142). The process is indefinitely expandable, as the addition of more molecular species to the actual leads to an ever larger adjacent possible.

For Simondon, transduction is "a process—be it physical, biological, mental, or social—in which an activity gradually sets itself in motion, propagating within a given area, through a structuration of the different zones of the area over which it operates. . . . Its dynamism derives from the primitive tension of the heterogeneous being's system, which moves out of step with itself and develops further dimensions upon which it bases its structure" ("Genesis" 313). The continuous expansion of possibilities with each intra-action in these processes captures as well the evolution of new forms of life when evolution is seen not as a simple matter of adaptation to a particular environment but as a "virtual creativity that allows it to respond to life not mechanically but as a problem. This means that the outcome of these creative responses will also create new problems. . . . What is possible, therefore, is never given once and for all, but expands with each development of potential" (Colebrook 169).[5] The intra-active processes of reciprocal induction that create individuating unities, their worlds, and the cosmos lead to persistently greater diversity in all complex systems—societies, biospheres, economies, and languages.[6]

Beginnings and Becoming

In his book *Where Writing Begins*, Carter, also working from complexity theory and Whitehead's process philosophy,[7] posits, as I do, that "writing . . . is, by its very nature ... creative" (122). From an analysis of competing creation myths, he defines an "archelogical" vision of creativity as "beginnings," the plural form intended to convey an "ongoing and continuous potential for newness ... a creative potential ... [that] is perpetual and unlimited" (59) as opposed to a singular creation that occurred only once. He refers to Whitehead's final chapter of *Process and Reality* as "the most radically archelogical vision of the universe I have found" (95) and describes Whitehead's concrescence as "the process of beginnings" (97): in the moment of concrescence "both God and the World may be made new. Each completes and thus creates the other. Thus creation is a shared process, continuous, occurring moment by moment" (98). There are clearly strong resemblances between Carter's understanding of creativity as the process of beginnings and my understanding of it as the process of becoming, the process of reciprocal self and world creation. And yet there are several significant divergences.

Carter describes his project as a reconstruction of postmodernism, an attempt to construct "a positive worldview within postmodern indeterminacy" (151). Reacting against the problematic separation of reality from human consciousness (Whitehead's bifurcation of nature) that underlies all the incarnations of modernist and postmodernist theories, he avers that humans share the essence of the experience of the world with all other beings, a "panexperientialism" (158). He suggests that the essence of experience is creativity, and that the value inherent in creativity is enjoyment (132). All beings enjoy the experience of creativity, but, he argues, humans do so more intensely thanks to their possession of consciousness and of language, language being one of the main ways humans experience the world (160). Consciousness—"the capacity of the *awareness* of enjoyment, the ability to participate in enjoyment more fully"—as well as consciousness of language intensify the enjoyment of being while at the same time allowing "a certain authority concerning language ... that is represented in our ability to play with language, to construct it, mold it, enjoy it, talk about it, learn about it, and teach it" (168). Thus he argues that writing has value in itself: writing is "an experience of being ... [that] orders and shapes being, rendering being more complex and creative and thus enhancing the enjoyment of being" (161).

Carter's version of reconstructive postmodernism derives in part from that of David Ray Griffin who with others elaborated a process theology on the ground of Whitehead's philosophy. It is from Griffin that Carter takes his emphasis on enjoyment as "intrinsic to that moment in each actual occasion when the indeterminate forces of the past are brought into conjunction with the conceptual force of the future to become, in an instant of creative freedom, a concrete existence in the present" (132).[8] This is the phase of final determination or completion of the actual entity. Carter says that "there is a sense of delight at work in Whitehead's term, but not a hedonistic delight. Rather, it is the pleasure that comes from participating in the creative event of concrescence" (132).

My project of enchantment ontology began with much the same goal of turning postmodern indeterminacy to productive ends, in my case by reconnecting writing and reality as a fluid, creative process. Inspired by ecological principles I learned from my father at home and the sociolinguistics I studied in graduate school, I proposed rethinking writing and writers more interactively, as entangled with others and their worlds. I posited writers as neither the essentialist, autonomous authors envisioned in modernist theories nor the fragmented, determined writers-written-by-writing envisioned in postmodernist theories but as conditioned individuals in the process of becoming and making their worlds in interaction.[9] I came upon Whitehead later than Carter did, and not through the American interpretations in process theology but through readings by continental scholars, especially Bruno Latour and Stengers,[10] both of whom emphasize the interactive nature of the creative process, "a movement of establishing provisional cohesion that will have to be started all over again every single day" (Latour, PN 147). Thus, even though working very closely with the "same" concept of Whiteheadean creativity, Carter and I ended up in rather different places. Carter celebrates the creativity of writing as the writer's aesthetic enjoyment of being, "a way of participating in more complex and creative ways in the shared essence of being" (168). I instead conceive of the creativity of writing more pragmatically as the intra-active process of making meanings that matter.

Whitehead, I believe, would be pleased with the divergence in what we have each made of his suggestions. And though I find Stengers's reading more interesting than that of the process theologians[11]—and certainly more useful to my project—I have found myself inexorably lured to the possibilities in the interstices of the contradictions between our readings that at the very least lead to broader understandings of the possibilities that arise in defining writing as creative.

Two significant contradictions are worth exploring. First, is creativity a dialectical or reciprocal process? Second, does the creativity of writing have the intrinsic value of the enjoyment of being or the pragmatic value of creating meanings that matter? Dialectical and reciprocal processes may not actually be completely contradictory: they do both involve at least two things that are thought of as opposites interacting in some way. In Carter's archelogical dialectic (as in Ricoeur's, discussed in chapter 1), the opposites do not resolve but exist in a "living tension" that enables creation; in reciprocal processes, too, the opposites do not resolve but instead create new entities. There is enjoyment in the sense of pleasure involved in both processes as is clear in Haraway's training with Cayenne. And both processes certainly seem to originate in a similar feeling, a feeling of difference, dissonance.

Carter began looking for an answer to his original question—where does writing begin?—by surveying what seventy-five composition textbooks had to say about it. He found only two texts that suggested recognizing dissonance as a starting point, which he called "an important pedagogical departure"(16). *Rhetoric: Discovery and Change* by Richard Young, Alton Becker, and Kenneth Pike is the prototype; the other text, explicitly derived from it, is *Four Worlds of Writing*, by Janice Lauer, Gene Montague, Andrea Lunsford, and Janet Emig.[12] In the chapter on "the process of inquiry," Young, Becker, and Pike describe the feeling of dissonance as a "tension" within the writer, "being puzzled or disturbed by our experiences," and they go on to observe that if the experiences "seem sufficiently important to us we try to find out what bothers us." They promise that in the following pages, they "will discuss in detail what a person can do when he is confronted with problematic experiences" (71). For them, dissonances arise in experience, and not all dissonances are worthy of thinking about further, suggesting that where writing begins might be more complex. Another of Carter's groups of textbooks suggest beginning with observation. Carter quotes Donald Murray on how writing can begin in perception: the writer "finds significance in what the writer observes or overhears or reads or thinks or remembers" ("Write" 376; qtd. in Carter 20). For Whitehead, philosophical thinking—and concrescence—begins with a feeling of importance. He describes how prehending particular entities involves linking them to relevant generalities: "One characteristic of the primary mode of conscious experience is its fusion of a large generality with an insistent particularity. . . . For example, characteristic modes of thought, as we first recall ourselves to civilized experience, are—'This is important,' 'That is difficult,' 'This is lovely.' In such ways of thinking there is an insistent particularity, symbolized above by the words *this* and *that*; and there is a large, vague characterization indicative of some form of excitement arising from the particular fact in the world without" (MT 4–5). In an epigraph to their chapter on the process of inquiry, Young, Becker, and Pike quote a similar statement of Whitehead's suggesting that they might think of inquiry as Whitehead does, as discovery: "The true method of discovery is like the flight of an aeroplane. It starts from the ground of particular observation; it makes a flight in the thin air of imaginative generalization; and it again lands for renewed observation rendered acute by rational interpretation" (PR 5). Perhaps, then, writing begins not just with dissonance but more generally with some form of importance arising from a particular experience or observation, something marked out as significant or different in some way. An astute fourth-grade teacher, for example, once introduced a writing assignment by asking her students to list three things that interested them (one student listed Doritos, North Korea, and life).[13] An alternate way of understanding the difference between dialectic and reciprocal induction could be to say that they are based on opposing kinds of difference—difference needing a solution (dialectic) versus difference needing elaboration (reciprocal). Considered as contrasts, these opposites lead to an open question of how particular differences are to be further thought about beyond the simple opposition of solution and elaboration.

Another group of textbooks that Carter found suggested that writing begins by finding a purpose. Though Young, Becker, and Pike focus on problematic experiences as a starting point, Carter notes that they do not characterize problems in terms of purposes, "what the writer hopes to accomplish," but rather focus on "the problem as an initiating state . . . an incongruity that sparks inquiry" (16). The pedagogical departure that Young, Becker, Pike helped initiate was more generally concerned with moving the beginning of the "process" of writing back into what was then called the "pre-writing" stage of inquiry. They introduce dissonance in their fourth chapter, "The Process of Inquiry," which follows two chapters on experience. The first of these discusses "the writer as interpreter of experience," stating that "constantly changing, bafflingly complex, the external world is . . . an enigma requiring interpretation" (25), again aligning themselves with Whitehead in seeing writing as beginning on the ground of particular observation and needing a flight of imaginative generalization. Like the linking of particularities and generalities, interpretation is a type of interactive process, "a result of a transaction between events in the external world and the mind of the individual" (Young et al. 25). Problems arise because "people are seldom aware of their uniqueness," that "the same event may have strikingly different meanings" for others than it does for them. But then Young, Becker, and Pike assert that resolving "such differences of interpretation" and eliminating "the misunderstandings they can create" is the goal of rhetoric (26). Here they part company with Whitehead's conception of inquiry, as actual entities do not understand or misunderstand, but rather prehend each other as whole feeling entities not just interpreting minds. Nor does Whitehead want differences to be eliminated; for him they serve as lures for feelings that produce possibilities. Nevertheless, considering both dialectical and reciprocal processes as concerned with ways of discovering and inquiring into differences in experience brings them closer together while also suggesting a value in the creativity of writing beyond that of intrinsic enjoyment. But before moving on to the question of the value in creative writing, I will consider the time and space of Whitehead's creativity as it is configured differently in dialectical beginnings and in reciprocal becoming.

An important characteristic of concrescence is that it starts over again each time, a characteristic that Carter recognizes in his notion of beginnings: "an ongoing and continuous potential for newness in beginnings ... a relationship between opposing forces that could occur at any point in time, the disjunctive event of new beginnings" (59). I feel a disjunction if not exactly a contradiction between Carter's "beginnings" and my "becoming" that raises the question of when and where creativity occurs. Carter addresses the when question as he explores why John began his gospel with the words εν ἀρχή. He says John chose a particular form of the Greek word "archē" in the context of a mixed audience of Greeks and Jewish and Christian Gnostics to negotiate the "theologically delicate issue" of whether Jesus could be both human and divine (54). In contemporary Greek philosophy, the universe had no single origin in time. Using archē adverbally would convey to Greeks a different perspective on beginning—"the point where the infinite enters the finite, and the eternal the temporal" (Ehrhardt 20; qtd. in Carter 55)—thus shifting the temporal concept of beginning to the ontological concept of incarnation, the potential intersection of opposing worlds. The notion of a productive relation between infinite and finite, divine and human, and spiritual and material would also have been attractive to the Gnostics, as well as achieving "a special messianic emphasis on newness, a new beginning, a new order, a new creation" (59; cf. Ehrhardt). For Carter, then, archē offers "an alternative paradigm for beginning as a new creation that is not encumbered by time" (55). Shifting from temporal to ontological time fits better with the notion of beginnings Carter is furthering, and it responds to the clear sense that time in Whitehead's notion of concrescence has no extension.

To answer the where question, Carter links beginnings to the notion of thresholds through the image of Janus, the two-faced god of beginnings and thresholds: "On a threshold, you are neither in nor out but at once in and out, at once facing the past and the future, the known and unknown" (9). Carter says, "Writing ... engages the writer in the threshold experience of beginnings" (122). He explains: "Process philosophy envisions time not as a smooth and seamless flow but as a succession of distinct actual occasions, each of which is an act of creation, a coming-to-be in the present.... This creation is formed not in the beginning but in beginnings, each pulse of the universe a creative event on the threshold of past and future, definiteness and indefiniteness, what is given and what is possible" (129–30). The threshold between definiteness and indefiniteness seems to locate the "creative event" at the phase of final determination in concrescence, the phase in which one could say that the infinite enters the finite, the eternal, the temporal. Carter is right to emphasize how Whitehead "atomizes time" into a succession of occasions in which actual entities determine themselves, for Whitehead was quite insistent on the primacy of actual entities in his scheme: "The actual world is a process, and . . . the process is the becoming of actual entities" (PR 22). Occasions are distinct in the sense of providing an enclave in which elements are separated out of the overwhelming multiplicity in the world: it gives the actual entity enough "*elbow room* for self-determination" (Stengers, TW 191). The notion of a threshold also rightly emphasizes concrescence as a place of change involving the intersection of ontological opposites.

Beginnings, especially new beginnings, suggest endings, which may be why Carter focuses on the "end" of concrescence, calling it the "primary creative event in the process" (97). He describes this event as the moment of enjoyment, "an instant of creative freedom, a concrete existence in the present" (132). He comments, "In that moment, the universe is opened as the conceptual principle frees the occasion from the deterministic tendencies located in the physical, the accumulation of past occasions" (97–98). On this threshold, a point of intersection of finite and infinite, actual and potential, completed actual entities that are conscious become "fully creative," "aware of their enjoyment of the intensity and harmony in the marked contrast between the actual and the possible" (133). Carter's is a credible attempt to account for the atomized time and the interaction of opposing forces in concrescence. But the time and space he allots to concrescence seems too small. The creative event shrinks to an instant and halts on the threshold of the archelogical dialectic where the opposing forces are held in tension. Is there enough room for process? The archelogical dialectic moment of creativity seems to be more of a stasis, a completed incarnation to be enjoyed, "a new creation that is not encumbered by time."[14]

There are two aspects of Whitehead's notion of creativity that Carter does not account for that help explain the difference between dialectal beginnings and reciprocal becoming. First, though the process of concrescence does not have a temporal extension, it is still a process: it progresses through phases all of which constitute the creative event. Whitehead says, "Each new phase in the concrescence means the retreat of mere propositional unity before the growing grasp of real unity of feeling" (PR 224). Second, there are two entangled processes of creativity in Whitehead's scheme: the process of the becoming of actual entities (concrescence) and the process "in which the universe accomplishes its actuality" (350). The shorthand description of creativity—"the many become one and are increased by one" (21)—gestures at the two processes, and Whitehead sometimes distinguishes transition, in which the one increases the many, from concrescence. But in the final chapter, as I discussed above, he also describes the becoming of the universe as a reciprocal double concrescence of God and the multiplicity of actual entities that constitute the World. Creativity is a becoming together that "starts all over again," and it does create new entities in each pulse of time, but each pulse is not a new beginning for either the actual entities or the universe. Whitehead's ontological principle forbids creation de novo: "There is nothing that floats into the world from nowhere. Everything in the actual world is referable to some actual entity" (244). The one (a singularity) and the many (disjunctive diversity) are always becoming together in the world, mixing it up in multiple and overlapping events that start all over again only in the sense of never coming to any final end.

How Whitehead conceives of the time and space of creativity is not easy to understand because he articulates the atomistic, or "epochal," time of concrescence with the creative advance of the universe. Referring to Zeno's paradox, he asserts that "there is a becoming of continuity, but no continuity of becoming. The actual occasions are the creatures which become, and they constitute a continuously extensive world" (PR 35). The continuity of the extensive world becomes through the intra-action of actual entities in concrescence; actual entities become in the "pulses" of concrescence, each of which is a separate occasion, but not one that begins or ends in the commonsense notion of time as a "unique seriality" of moments. Whitehead instead adopts the notion of space-time as developed in quantum physics (35).

Whitehead notes that reducing a process to a point in time or space is problematic: "The concept of a point in process is fallacious. . . . For example . . . the notion of a moment of time devoid of any temporal spread . . . [or] a point in space" (MT 96). Instead, "the unit of process is the 'specious present' of the actuality in question" (MT 89). Specious present is William James's concept, similar to Henri Bergson's duration. It is the subjective "time" of an experience conceived also as a "space" that encloses whatever in the world is relevant to an individual experience. Like a quantum leap, what happens in a reciprocal process "does not 'take any time' in the physical, continuous sense of the term. As an 'atomic individual event,' it is indivisible, unanalyzable in terms of a succession of instants" (TW 371). Whitehead says, "The actual entity is the enjoyment of a certain quantum of physical time. But the genetic process is not the temporal succession. . . . Each phase in the genetic process presupposes the entire quantum, and so does each feeling in each phase" (PR 283). There are no "moments" in concrescence, no beginnings and endings or sequential stages. The "phases" discriminated as constituting a concrescence are characterizations of aspects of the experience; each phase presupposes the experience in which the actual entity determines itself. Thus the subjective aim is not located at the "beginning" or "end" of concrescence and does not determine what it aims at: "Concrescence ... as long as it is not completed, as long as it has not produced its own position, corresponds to an 'elsewhere'" (TW 372). The "creative event" is the concrescence, which has no temporal beginnings or endings; it is a process of becoming, of reciprocal induction, which also "continues" in a trajectory of inheritance as long as the entities involved are still intra-acting. Where does Haraway and Cayenne's creation of a behavior begin and end in their training together? New behaviors always derive from previous ones and they condition those that follow.

Carter also recognizes that the beginning of writing is difficult to locate in time, citing Murray's comment that "writing begins with all that we have known since we were born" (Write 3; qtd. in Carter 22). He refers, too, to Einstein's concept of space-time, observing that "events exist in a complex relationship, each having its existence in the other" (24). He concludes that "there is no point at which we can say writing begins that is not entirely arbitrary" (25). It is at this point that he shifts course to determining the ontological origin of writing, which he finds in the archeological dialectic: "Beginnings as a state of being marked by the intersection of contradictory forces and the potential for newness generated in that contradiction"(75). Having given up on beginnings, he still remains focused on a particular moment—a state of being, in fact—an awareness of contradiction that creates a "potential for newness." Concrescence does have a result. Rather than hovering on the threshold between actuality and potentiality, the actual entity determines itself in its final decision. This is a significant difference between the archeological dialectic and the reciprocal process of becoming: as a living tension of opposing forces, the dialectic has no way of explaining the mystery of creation, how something new arises from the tension, while reciprocal induction explains the "mystery" as resulting from the ongoing intra-action of actual entities. It may be an unfamiliar or slightly suspect process, but it is no longer a mystery, as I will explain in the next section.

Carter recognizes this ongoing process when he refers to Epicurus's concept of the clinamen, which "sets up a turbulence ... that leads to other turbulences and eventually accounts for the infinite variety of the universe" (129). He explains that the clinamen "is an argument for the creative power of disorder, a mode of creativity founded not in order and oneness but in chaos and the potential for novelty that lies in multiplicity" (129), but in his discussion he focuses on disorder, ignoring the potential for novelty: he says, God is the "emblem of both the reality of contradiction and the contradiction in reality" (97). Whitehead agrees that disorder is an important aspect of creativity, saying that "the essence of life is to be found in the frustrations of established order" (MT 87). But he emphasizes the role of the many, central in complexity theory, and crucial for concrescence.

I turn now to the second contradiction between Carter's and my conception of the creativity of writing: does writing offer enjoyment or does it produce meanings that matter? Framed in that way, the question implies a difference in agency: writers receiving enjoyment versus writers creating something new that matters. Recalling my earlier discussion of Young, Becker, and Pike's convergence with Whitehead, and turning the contradiction into a contrast, I can propose a new statement: writers enjoy creating new meanings that matter in a process of inquiry. My statement requires a shift in the meaning of "enjoyment": enjoyment is a matter of experience rather than of receiving pleasure, which is what Whitehead means in saying that the actual entity is the *enjoyment* of a certain quantum of physical time (PR 283). To explore to what extent I can produce this convergence between Carter and myself on the question of "the good of writing" (Carter 142), I need to think further about the meanings of enjoyment and mattering.

In attributing enjoyment in the sense of "the value inherent in coming-to-be" to Whitehead (132), Carter says, "It is the pleasure that comes from participating in the creative event of concrescence" (132), and, later, that it is an awareness "of being in the state of being creative" (142). What pleases writers as creators is participating in the creative process and being aware of that process as creative. The value inherent in coming-to-be sounds somewhat like what Whitehead calls satisfaction, although satisfaction implies having achieved something, giving creativity and writing an extrinsic goal that Carter wishes to avoid: "In its phase of satisfaction, the entity has attained its individual separation from other things; it has absorbed the datum, and it has not yet lost itself in the swing back to the 'decision' whereby its appetition becomes an element in the data of other entities superseding it" (PR 154). Also unlike Carter's enjoyment, this satisfaction is not a conscious feeling: "No actual entity can be conscious of its own satisfaction; for such knowledge would be a component in the process, and would thereby alter the satisfaction" (85).

When Whitehead uses the term "enjoyment," it is associated with the physical pole in contrast with the appetition of the mental pole. Thus, God *enjoys* the actual, conscious, completion of the physical world, and the World *thirsts* for the unconscious, infinite potentialities of God. Explaining how the actual entity "feels" or "prehends" the data it is unifying, he says his use of enjoyment is closely analogous to Samuel Alexander's (PR 41). Alexander says: "Cognition is . . . the delivery of direct experience . . . in every act of cognition there are two separate entities or finites in compresence with each other, the one an enjoyment, the other what in relation to that enjoyment is a contemplated object. The enjoyment of the mind's self is at the same time the contemplation of an object distinct from it and non-mental. To know anything is to be along with it in Space-Time" (87). For Whitehead as for Alexander, enjoyment is subjective prehension of the physical world, as in "the 'experience' of the actual world enjoyed by that actual entity" (PR 166), "the subjective enjoyment of experience" (159). The closest he comes to implying a value for enjoyment is when he says, "The sense of worth beyond itself is immediately enjoyed as an overpowering element in the individual self-attainment" (350). He is discussing here how the desire that what has been attained not be merely "a transient enjoyment, transiently useful" (340). As discussed earlier, God answers to this desire by saving all the details of an actuality's experience—"the complete adjustment of the immediacy of joy and suffering"—as contrasts that enable the attainment of the multiplicity of individual entities in the universe (349)—admittedly a rather barren sort of enjoyment.

Still, there are echoes of Whitehead's enjoyment in Carter's description of the three values inherent in the enjoyment of individual self-attainment: "One is the 'receptive' value that comes of simply being associated with conditions that stimulate creativity. The second is the 'achievement' value that comes from taking an active role in the self-creation of each occasion. And the third is 'contributory' value that comes from the anticipation of the creative effect that occasions can have on future occasions, the further enjoyment that occasion can have on future occasions, the further enjoyment that may be experienced later by self and others" (132–33).[15] Though I don't find any reference to a receptive value in Whitehead's discussion of concrescence, his understanding of satisfaction is somewhat similar to Carter's achievement value, especially in assigning an active role to the actual entity (although in everyday life I'd say it is tied less to the feeling of being active than to final completion, as in the final completion of this book manuscript that I am intensely looking forward to enjoying). In describing her training with Cayenne, Haraway talks about the "taste of copresence," the "sense that inside this other body, there is 'someone home,'" (Smuts 308; qtd. in Haraway, *When* 236) and "joy" in "the inventive potency of play [that] redoes beings" (*When* 237), which are certainly pleasures that come from participating in a creative event, although again they gesture toward attainment in the sense of outcomes—copresence and the redoing of beings. The contributory value is sort of what Whitehead is talking about in referring to "the sense of worth beyond itself," but as I said, his sense of worth is a rather attenuated enjoyment that does not look forward to future enjoyments of the actual entity itself. I am not trying to argue that the forms of enjoyment Carter describes here are not experienced by writers, though. (I definitely hope that others enjoy reading my book eventually.) It's just that they seem ancillary to a more intense and fundamental emotion that I am positing as essential to creativity and to writing. I discussed it earlier: it is the feeling of importance that leads to inquiry and discovery, both in the concrescence of the individual actual entity and in its desire for a sense of worth beyond itself. Whitehead says, "The generic aim of process is the attainment of importance" (MT 12).

Importance is what I am thinking about in saying that writing creates meanings that matter. Meanings that matter are simply meanings that are important to someones or somethings. They do not inspire questions of why they matter; they simply do matter. It is the question of *how* they matter that inspires inquiry, for they will matter in an immense variety of ways: fear and joy, curiosity and repulsion—anything except indifference. They inspire further creation of things that matter and are only evaluated with reference to whether they create this intense emotion of importance. Meanings that matter are Whiteheadean propositions, lures for feeling, the feeling of possibilities. This is the kind of "creative effect that occasions can have on other occasions" (Carter 132–33), prolonging a sense of self-worth beyond attainment by creating new possibilities, new lures for feeling, in a speculative adventure that rejects nothing except fixed ideals.

The Miracle of Creation

Now, finally, I can attempt to answer the question raised by the miracle of Ezekiel and the dry bones. Gilles Deleuze says, "Actualisation or differenciation is always a genuine creation. It does not result from any limitation of a pre-existing possibility" (*Difference* 212). How genuine creation arises without being predetermined or limited by what went before is the question to which enchantment ontology responds: creativity is an interactive process. The processes of concrescence, intra-action, reciprocal induction, breaking symmetries, phase transition behavior, and structural coupling all describe undetermined determination, what complexity theorists call "order for free."[16] And yet, what remains underexplained, at least in the instance of sentient beings, is the miracle of creation: how *exactly* does Ezekiel's prophesy bring about the reassembling of those scattered dry bones? Simondon alludes to it as "a capacity beings possess of falling out of step with themselves, of resolving themselves by the very act of falling out of step" ("Genesis" 300–301). So, also, how *do* beings fall out of step with themselves? And how are actual entities induced to prehend possibilities in a way that enables them to decide what they will become?

The answer lies in the concept of propositions, "one of the major inventions of Whitehead's philosophy" (Stengers, TW 396). I outlined the basic concept of propositions in chapter 1: they are the entities that inject novelty into concrescence, "tales that might be told"; they are "entertained"—admitted to feeling—by humans but also by other sentient beings; and they are not verbal, although language enables humans to entertain propositions more complexly. In chapter 4, I described how propositions integrate actual entities and eternal objects as a lure for feelings that when entertained create new entities. What still needs to be explained is the mode in which propositions are entertained, how they effect the becoming of the novel actual entity. The proposition is a lure, not a determination, and God, lurking in the background as the initiator of concrescence, also functions analogously as a lure. Stengers comments that propositions "are curiously absent from most Whiteheadean studies," possibly because as "theories" they "seem quite particularly enigmatic" entities (TW 397). They are especially important to my project because how they operate underpins my proposal that writing is an adventure of ideas, a truly creative route of discovery and wonder. The role that language plays in entertaining propositions also illuminates how language augments the creativity of writing.

Whitehead begins his first chapter on propositions: "A living occasion is characterized by a flash of novelty among the appetitions of its mental pole" (PR 184). To be exact, propositions prehend impure conceptual prehensions (those that integrate actual entities and eternal objects) and propose possibilities in the form of a question: Is that a tiger? Or, What if that's a tiger? (TW 476). Though propositional feelings can be either conscious or not, those that cause a flash of novelty are conscious, an awareness of a contrast between what was prehended (that tiger) and the possibility that it might or might not be true—what if? (PR 261). Propositions are felt by a subject, located in space and time in the world, and aimed at objects, also so located. Whitehead says, "A proposition presupposes the actual world as exhibiting some systematic aspect" (PR 195). He instances the proposition "Caesar has crossed the Rubicon." The prehending subject of the proposition feels what Caesar and the Rubicon are and feels that the proposition refers to some time in the past, but as Whitehead says, there are a number of propositions that can arise from these words because of the variations in how the prehending subject is located vis-à-vis this event: a modern subject prehending a proposition about a past event known to her only indirectly as opposed to "the proposition which might have been in the mind of one in the crowd who listened to Antony's speech, a man who had seen Caesar and not the Rubicon" (PR 196). One could say that a proposition is a version of the feeling "this is important" with variable specifications of *how* it is felt to be important.[17] "The role that propositional feeling will play, the meaning that will be associated with it, the decision concerning the 'might be' . . . depends on the prehending subject of the proposition"

(Stengers, TW 413). Everything in the experience bounded by the concrescence conditions the subject's decision, but nothing determines it.

Whitehead defines a proposition as "a new kind of entity. It is a hybrid between pure potentialities and actualities. A 'singular' proposition is the potentiality of an actual world including a definite set of actual entities in a nexus of reactions involving the hypothetical ingression of a definite set of eternal objects" (PR 185–86). What is felt in entertaining a proposition begins with the awareness of "the marked contrast between the actual and the possible that Carter says characterizes the enjoyment of creativity (133). But entertaining a proposition doesn't stop with awareness; it is first of all a specific feeling of importance of some kind followed by a conscious activity directed to a real, specific possibility, something that might matter quite insistently: what if that's a tiger? Propositions are realized when they are admitted into feeling and cause a novelty to emerge, "a new type of individual, and not merely a new intensity of feeling" (PR 187). When Ezekiel prophesizes to the dry bones, he isn't merely aware of them as a possibility, he subjectively feels them, clothing them "with the flesh of a real being, emotional, purposive, appreciative" (PR 85).

The new actual entity arises as an answer to the "what if?" question posed by the proposition. As the question merely poses a possibility, it doesn't determine the answer; that is up to the subject, the entity entertaining the proposition. A slightly fantastical example occurs in Muriel Barbery's novel *The Life of Elves*: Clara is a talented young pianist whose coach gives her pieces to play that bore her to tears. She asks him why he does this; he never answers, but "she had learned to discern the elements of an answer in the question he asked her the second she finished. Thus, one morning when she was asking him about a piece that made her yawn continuously, he frowned and asked her what it was that made a tree look beautiful in the light. She changed tempo, and the piece took on an elegance that, initially, she would never have suspected" (96). Clara sees landscapes as she plays, so the question is relevant to her experience in a way she can interpret, and it induces her to feel the music differently. Stengers comments on such experiences: "If I ask you a question at the right moment, in the right terms, with the right intonation, so that you suddenly see a way out where the situation was blocked, my question will have proved its relevance by its effects, by the way that your experience is transformed . . . your transformation is an answer, but it is by no means an answer 'to my question': it answers for the relevance of the question as a lure that has initiated the process of which your experience is the truth" (TW 384). The answer is conditioned by the question—it *is* a response—but it is not determined by it. Stengers is discussing here the analogous role of God as the "'instigator,' operating as a 'lure for feeling' for the nascent concrescence" (TW 383).

Whitehead describes God's role in this phase: the entity "derives from God its basic conceptual aim, relevant to its actual world, yet with indeterminations awaiting its own decisions" (PR 224).

How an actual entity entertains a proposition echoes Mikhail Bakhtin's comments on understanding: "Every concrete act of understanding is active: it assimilates the word to be understood into its own conceptual system filled with specific objects and emotional expressions.... Understanding comes to fruition only in the response.... An active understanding ... establishes a series of complex interrelationships, consonances and dissonances with the word and enriches it with new elements" (*Dialogic Imagination* 282). Stengers calls this intra-active understanding induction, deriving it not from the reciprocal induction of developmental biology but from hypnotic suggestion.[18] The hypnotist, she says, does not command a subject, but suggests a possibility: "The order corresponds to a 'making felt,' whence the subject of this feeling emerges, initiating ... the raising of the hand 'as ordered'" (TW 462). The "order" is rather a "path" that gives rise to an entity that is able to do what is suggested.[19] Stengers says, "This is a path suggested to the new 'you' made to emerge by the addressing, by which the corresponding 'I' will verify its own existence" (TW 462). Hypnotic suggestion induces the same feeling of reciprocal induction as Haraway describes in her training with Cayenne: "Here we are, and so what are we to become?" (*When* 221)—a feeling of "what if?"

Like hypnotic suggestion, God's commandment to Ezekiel and Ezekiel's prophesizing to the dry bones seems miraculous largely because we neglect the fact that suggestions and commandments require an active respondent. When Ezekiel was set down in the valley full of bones, God suggested a possibility in the form of a question: "Son of man, can these bones live?" (xxxvii.3). God did get more specific, though still indirect; he told Ezekiel to "Prophesy upon these bones, and say unto them, O ye dry bones, hear the word of the Lord," although he did go on to say to the bones that "I will lay sinews upon you, and will bring up flesh upon you, and cover you with skin, and put breath in you, and ye shall live; and ye shall know that I *am* the Lord" (xxxvii.5–6). As Stengers explains, between God and Ezekiel and between Ezekiel and the bones, "There is a relation of reciprocal presupposition between a germ of subjectivity and what answers to it, a multiplicity henceforth correlated, the shudder of the dispersed bones becoming data for physical feelings aiming at their subject" (TW 459). The feelings elicited by God's suggestions to Ezekiel and Ezekiel's suggestion to the bones (presumably similar to what God told him) aim at a presumed subject, a subject that does not yet exist but is elicited by the feelings to become able to do what was suggested. And since we know that Ezekiel is a prophet (who began his book with a fantastical vision of four living creatures each with four faces and four wings) and that God has ordered him to prophesy to the Israelites, we know not to take those dry bones literally.

If we look back at Kimmerer's encounter with the plantain, we can now understand more fully how she entertained the proposition it offered. Propositions are often more complicated than "what if that's a tiger?" and that's the case here. Kimmerer was surprised by her encounter with the plantain and felt "this is important," but in her actual experience her feeling was probably less focused than it appears in her recounting of it. The proposition could be framed as "what if this is an immigrant?" Her feeling of the plantain as kin, as an "old friend," connected with her feeling at that moment of herself as an immigrant in this place and initiated a speculative adventure that language helped her elaborate. Language helps to provide the "social environment" enabling one to amplify the impact of the proposition "into many divergent, entangled consequences" (Stengers, "Whitehead's Account" 53). Kimmerer recalls the plantain's Latin name, its Potowatomi name, and Nanabozho's footprints that Kimmerer has been following; remembers what she has learned of the history and habits and human uses of plantain as a species; and recalls Nanabozho's instructions to learn from the plants and animals he encountered—all in the context of her musings on the difference between being an immigrant and being indigenous. The response to the possibility that arises with the question "What if this is an immigrant?" is a speculative idea: "Maybe an immigrant becomes indigenous by being a good neighbor."

Propositions are not essentially linguistic, and thus they are not exclusive to humans. But language does affect how humans entertain propositions. Its role is somewhat different from what Carter envisions, that of ordering and shaping being, thus enhancing the enjoyment of being (161). Stengers explains that to understand what Whitehead is suggesting when he says "the account of the sixth day should be written, He gave them speech, and they became souls" (MT 41; cf. Genesis ii.7), requires focusing on "what we became when we were given speech, not what was given to us by speech" (Stengers, "Whitehead's Account" 50). We became souls, that is, beings who receive their worth, their importance "from the way in which unrealized ideals shape [our] purposes and tinge [our] actions" (MT 27). Stengers says, "For Whitehead, the experiences which came to matter on the sixth day are those which may be associated with the intense feeling of alternative, unrealized possibilities" ("Whitehead's Account" 49). Becoming souls was becoming creatures who "no longer know ... closed facts" but instead "require to understand": creatures who "require the capacity never to reduce anything to a mere matter of fact, or matter of proof, to become able to feel its relevance to unrealized potentialities" (42–43). Language, however, does not create this feeling, "even if this feeling came to crucially matter on the sixth day, when we were given speech"; it rather presupposes "the feeling of those tales that may be told" (51). It presupposes the entertainment of propositions, whose efficacy is, she says, quoting Whitehead, "a tremendous mode of excitement. Like a stone thrown into a pond it disturbs the whole surface of our being" (MT 36). This is important! Stengers cautions, "If, on the sixth day, being given speech, we became souls, it is thus not because we entertain propositions: so does a rabbit or an oyster, or a living cell" ("Whitehead's Account" 53). She concludes: "We became souls because of the difference language makes in the rippling consequences of a proposition's impact. Being given language means that when a proposition is entertained it is given a social environment such that its impact may be amplified into many divergent, entangled consequences, activating that mode of functioning which is the soul" (53). As she explains, language induces "not the reaction of a rabbit becoming aware that this grey shade is what we call a wolf, that is, a convinced 'it matters!' but a speculative adventure entailing questions such as 'how does it matter?' 'does it really matter?' 'what if I accepted that it does not matter?' 'how did it come to matter?'—unrealized ideals then shaping our experiences" (54). Kimmerer asks herself, how does it matter that the plantain is an immigrant? It's the way the plantain behaved: "It arrived with the first settlers and followed them everywhere they went. It trotted along . . . like a faithful dog so as to be near them." It offered gifts: a pot of greens in the spring; first aid for cuts, burns, and insect bites; good medicine for digestion. Unlike other immigrant plants like loosestrife, kudzu, and cheat grass, "its strategy was to be useful, to fit into small places, to coexist with others around the dooryard." And in this description, another link provided by language pops up: "It has earned the name bestowed by botanists for plants that have become our own. Plantain is not indigenous but 'naturalized'" like the foreign-born when they become citizens and pledge to uphold the laws (Kimmerer 214). So, she concludes, maybe an immigrant cannot become indigenous, but it can become naturalized: a good citizen.

Entertaining propositions requires conscious thought: the rabbit becoming aware of the gray shade as a wolf is thinking, and its action, freezing in place, expresses that thought. Whitehead says that for humans language is one of the most important ways of expressing thought, but it "is not the essence of thought." Still, he adds, "Apart from language, the retention of thought, the easy recall of thought, the interweaving of thought into higher complexity, the communication of thought, are all gravely limited. . . . Freedom of thought is made possible by language: we are thereby released from complete bondage to the immediacies of mood and circumstance" (MT 35). Language allows us to integrate the past and future into present experience, thus amplifying the impact of propositions and extending our exploration of the possibilities they open up. Other sentient animals integrate past and future into the present in limited ways: my dog Scout will run off to the site of an important odor she suddenly remembers and will put up a big fuss when I reach for my boots to go out, but novelty doesn't inspire much more than curiosity in her. In contrast, for the human animal, life "receives its worth, its importance" from novelty, "from the way in which unrealized ideals shape its purposes and tinge its actions" (MT 27). That's what we became when we were given language: not a being with a mere capacity to enjoy the contrast between the actual and the possible but a being with the capacity to enjoy it in the sense of speculation, elaborating propositions into meanings that matter.

How Writing Is Creative

Carolyn Miller attributes her persistent revising of her "Genre as Social Action" article to the "intuition that there was something here, and maybe this is the experience of every writer: the fact that I could write about it made me think it was real" (Dryer). Writing is a creative process of reciprocal induction that creates both meanings that matter and the writer, both the concept of genre as social action and Miller as the writer who believes in it. What both Carter and I are trying to save from postmodernist theories is this sense of language and writing as processes that create possibilities rather than communicating information or submitting to authoritative regulation. If I see writing as more thoroughly embedded in and responding to feelings of the living experience of the world, as discovering and making meanings that really matter to others as well as to the writer, it is perhaps because fifteen years after the publication of Carter's book, I acutely feel the need for all of us—not just teachers of writing—to understand how writing creates not just texts and not only our society but the actual world we inhabit. Writing—not only writing, but writing too—makes reality, whether it is in scholarly books like this, or in reports of scientific research, or in business prospectuses, or in instruction manuals, or in Facebook posts, or in tweets—or in student papers. All writing is creative, even the scribing that Carter deplores as "the kind of literate composition that is characterized [by] . . . the generation of text without questioning, challenging, without upsetting, without interpretation, at best only ornamenting what is already there" (115). I deplore this kind of writing too, but it is still writing; it creates meanings that matter in both good and seriously not good ways. I will address what good writing is in the conclusion where I suggest that it is writing that is well made, writing that results from habits of intra-acting ethically in the world. But now, to demonstrate how writing is an adventure "in which one does not feel oneself to be the master of what one writes, but where writing forces one to think, to feel, and to create" (Stengers, TW 354), I describe Whitehead's and Stengers's processes of composing, John Muckelbauer's "productive reading," and Kay Halasek's "pedagogy of possibility."

Whitehead's composing process is not one I would recommend on the whole to students, nor is it one that publishers would approve of, but it exemplifies the mode of thought he hopes his speculative philosophy inspires. Lewis Ford, who traced and analyzed the stages of Whitehead's composing and revising of *Process and Reality*, comments, "Most philosophers, in endeavoring to present their ideas in the most systematic and rigorous form possible, eliminate all traces which would suggest how they arrived at them. Whitehead has left his scaffolding standing. It may obscure the systematic presentation but it certainly aids the study of his creativity" (xii). When Whitehead approached the final revisions, despite having a nearly complete draft of the book, he found that "unexpected breakthroughs" required "massive interpolation, to reorient the reader from the start to his newest vision" (Ford 231). Ford suggests that perhaps because he wanted to get the book done, he did not undertake to eliminate or revise passages that were inconsistent with his current positions. Instead, he opted for inserting passages that "amplified" his understandings of important concepts.[20] Commenting on Whitehead's treatment of conceptual reversion, Ford says, "He first shows the reader the train of reasoning leading him to espouse reversion, and then abolishes it. An author who could stipulate part way through that henceforth 'actual entity' shall ordinarily mean 'actual occasion' could also stipulate the abolition of reversion" (237). Other passages testify to Whitehead's commitment to ongoing speculation. Ford, referring to a passage in the final chapter on God and the World, says "In this particular case (V.2.7), his intuitions seem to have outrun any means he was later able to devise, so the problem has been bequeathed to his followers" (229). Stengers approaches Whitehead's work differently than does Ford, endeavoring not to narrate a "final philosophy" (Ford xii) but to pursue a movement of coherence, "even when, on several occasions, this pursuit will imply a 'tale' of what has caused a mutation in a meaning or an articulation, a tale that will be my interpretation" (TW 242). She tackles the problem Ford says Whitehead bequeathed to his followers, for example, commenting "What I have just proposed does not appear anywhere in *Process and Reality*, but the proposition is technically acceptable" (TW 471). Whether for reasons of finishing or for revealing his mode of thought, Whitehead's insertions result in writing that demands of the reader what Whitehead espouses throughout his book, the necessity to think.

Stengers says that in *Process and Reality*, "to the perplexity of his readers, Whitehead put his own doctrine into action." His "raw, continuous interventions" were "the work of successive rereadings that wager on the possibility that a given insertion, here, in the middle of this paragraph, will suffice to make the text's meaning slide for the reader as it 'slid' for the author when he reread: '*Yes, I agree, but* . . . '" (TW 241). Stengers describes it as a method of rereading and writing in the mode of "yes, but" that aims at a "back-and-forth between concepts, and between concepts and empirical experience, the movements of thought entangled in one another, one of which never becomes apparent without appealing to others that have not yet been deployed" (TW 242). This is Whitehead's answer to the problem of explaining—Stengers says he never explains himself (TW 243)—which would imply a final understanding of concepts that are instead continually becoming in relation to other concepts and experiences, concepts whose function have to be understood always in terms of their relevance for other concepts (TW 241).

Stengers suggests that Whitehead's insertions may be attributable to nonconscious feelings as well as conscious consideration:[21] "When Whitehead went back to his work in the mode of '*yes, but*' that authorized him to carry out insertions without rewriting, he probably would often not been able to 'tell' what had made him 'change his mind.' He had become capable of 'feeling' a new aspect of the indefinable, that is, just as much, by contrast and retroactively, to feel the definition of a notion as too 'isolated' from the others, or too slanted, unduly privileging certain types of existence" (TW 242–43). The point is that Whitehead not only is not correcting his text; he also didn't really change his mind. He had a new thought as he intra-acted with what he had written and now agreed with *(yes), but* found something more to say about. As Stengers comments, Whitehead "considered it boring to 'start all over again,' to write in order to say more clearly what he had already understood" (243).

Treatments of *Process and Reality* by some other scholars change the nature of the text and of the writer, Stengers argues. In his "key" to *Process and Reality*, Donald Sherburne selected and rearranged passages, turning the text into "a book with which one could 'become acquainted'" and in which "an author endowed with a well-defined thought, his own, sets forth his ideas" (TW 242). Stengers says this is the boredom that Whitehead rejected, a "mendacious fiction, which wants authors to establish the portrait of a world they claim to have understood once and for all" (TW 243–44). Whitehead refused to simplify or omit questions to "spare his reader" (TW 243), instead calling on readers "to leave behind the status of an ignoramus, faced by an author who says what it is appropriate to think. They have to head, in their turn, 'down the road,' a road on which thought stumbles at every step, and must invent itself all over again" (TW 244). In his composing process, Whitehead blurs the distinction between writer and reader suggesting that what is required of both is not "scribing," reeling off ready-made thought, but thinking and feeling, creating both concepts and subjects in the reciprocal process of becoming. Of Whitehead, "We must speak of the author in the process of becoming.... The hand that writes the insertion is not that of the author correcting himself, but that of the reader fashioned by reading, or else that of the author-reader undergoing the series of thought-events that happen to him more than he produces them" (TW 242). Perhaps not all writers enact this mode of writing as spectacularly as Whitehead does, but it certainly resonates with my experience and with that of Miller revising "Genre as Social Action" and that of many others, and especially teachers of writing for whom the slogans of "writing is thinking," "writing comes from experience," have long been familiar.

Whitehead's mode of *yes, but* writing produces a text that refuses definitive interpretation, instead transforming "its readers into coauthors, accepting the adventure of the imagination to which the text calls us" (TW 242). It calls—perhaps more directly so than most texts—for Muckelbauer's productive style of reading, a style that "rests principally on the concept of invention . . . [as] the *telos* of an encounter with a text—invention of both concepts and subjects. To read productively means not only the attempt to alter the question, but to alter oneself through the question, to encounter a text hoping to think differently through an engagement with it" ("Reading" 92). This seems a good description of what Whitehead was doing in revising *Process and Reality*, though Whitehead perhaps was more expecting than hoping to think differently. Muckelbauer also comments on the blurring of the activities of writing and reading, observing how the ambiguity in academic uses of "reading" and "writing" productively emphasize "the inventive and disciplining character of both terms" ("Reading" 93n).

Muckelbauer proposes that styles of reading are "styles of engagement . . . fundamentally different ways of encountering texts" and producing "different effects" ("Reading" 74). While the programmatic style "emphasizes reproduction," the productive style inclines "toward invention and novelty" (74); "productive reading demonstrates a greater concern for producing different concepts than for reproducing a preexisting program" (73). The difference between these two styles seems much like Stengers's distinction between writing that makes the text's meaning slide for the reader and boring writing that strives to establish the portrait of a world that has been understood once and for all.

Muckelbauer's reading-writing of Foucault focuses on a critical impasse in Foucault scholarship: "Foucault's apparent dismissal of the concept of 'resistance'" (71). Rather than attempting to correct errors in the many critiques of Foucault's resistance, Muckelbauer elects to question the commonly accepted "programmatic" concept of resistance in order to offer an alternative, not necessarily better, but different concept. "Concepts," he says, "are not necessarily single, unified entities—they are not necessarily programs—[instead] they may indicate multiple and divergent trajectories, or 'swarms' in Gilles Deleuze's and Felix Guattari's idiom" (73). He notes that "Foucault spoke longingly" of this kind of reading, one that "rather than judging his concepts or texts, forces them to 'land in unexpected places and form shapes that [he] had never thought of'" (*Politics* 324; qtd. in Muckelbauer, "Reading" 74). This is the kind of reading that *Process and Reality* invites—and that Stengers's reading provides. The whole tenor of Whitehead's philosophy invites the kind of reading that Foucault longed for. Indeed, Whitehead lamented the scientific thought of the nineteenth century for the way it undermined the creative character of knowledge: "It criticized and exploded, where it should have striven to understand" (MT 44–46).

In *The Future of Invention*, Muckelbauer elaborates his concept of a productive style of reading into an affirmative style of reading and writing carried out through the "extraction of singular rhythms," affirmative repetitions "both irreducible to and inseparable from the movement of dialectical negation" (12).²² Based in Deleuze and Guattari's concept of flights of intensity, the extraction of singular rhythms from dialectical repetition refers to what is commonly called "'moments of insight,' 'inspiration,' or, more generally, . . . creativity" (*Future* 34)—or what Whitehead called the entertainment of propositions. Using this style of reading and writing, Muckelbauer explores a number of rhetorical concepts in an "attempt to redirect the modality of scholarly critique as argumentation toward an experimentation with *what particular concepts can do*" (43–44). To guide him, he distilled five "stylistic" principles: generosity, neglect of intentions, selective reading, connectivity, and non-recognition. Neglecting intentions and selective reading both involve not attempting to get it right, not delivering a correct reading, but also "doing so in a fashion that can't simply be dismissed as wrong" (45). Stengers strives to get it right in this sense; she is interested in explaining how to experiment on, but not misread, Whitehead's philosophy as presented in the last several of his books. I have also tried mightily in my treatment of concepts to get them right in a fashion that can't be dismissed as wrong, but I have also connected them widely to disciplines outside of those of their origin. Making connections is one of the habits I discerned in Harberd's writing in his journal discussed in chapter 3: his habit of seeing patterns and making connections among observations, experiences, memories, and feelings. Such connections, Muckelbauer says, "function more as relays in whatever movement is developing itself," not as representations or misrepresentations. Reading concepts for what they can do and connecting them elsewhere add more ways in which to engage "past" meanings through experimentation thereby prolonging their effects.

Muckelbauer concludes that the opposition of "tradition (the same) and innovation (the different)" (4) can be dissolved when we realize that "tradition itself may be nothing but the constant overcoming of any particular tradition, the movement of constant innovation" (148). This movement is what Whitehead is referring to when he says educators must trust the creative character of what they are charged with transmitting. Positing change—becoming—as fundamental, and constant innovation—creativity—as affirmative suggests a shift of focus in writing pedagogy toward teaching interactive reading and writing, encountering "a text hoping to think differently through an engagement with it" (Muckelbauer, "Reading" 92). This is what Kay Halasek, drawing on Bakhtin's interactive theory of discourse, argues in *A Pedagogy of Possibility*.

Halasek suggests that "an academic discourse of proficiency, productivity, and possibility . . . [that] encourages creativity from students" (174) will help students actively engage texts in their writing, to understand them, in Bakhtin's sense, to respond to them rather than simply reproducing them in the kind of writing Carter calls scribing. Her thinking about creativity in student writing began with the same observation I made in the opening to this chapter: "Students keep telling me that they 'can't find topics to write about'; they 'have nothing to say'" (121). Her insight was to think with Bakhtin and ask how these students relate to discourse; in particular, how they perceive the texts they are asked to write about. She turned to Bakhtin's concepts of authoritative and internally persuasive discourse to help her explore what might be going on.

Bakhtin focuses on how dialogic interaction structures the "ideological becoming of a human being," which he sees as "the process of selectively assimilating the words of others" and characterizes as the development of internally persuasive discourse (*Dialogic Imagination* 341). Internally persuasive discourse originates in a struggle between authoritative discourse ("the word of a father, of adults, and of teachers") and purely internally persuasive discourse ("backed up by no authority at all") (342). Halasek observes how in college courses, the power of authoritative discourse overwhelms students' purely internally persuasive discourse: "Students very often view the subjects about which they write, the people who have written about those subjects, and the instructors delivering the lecture or evaluating the essay as authoritative and unquestionable" (124). As she says, "An authoritative text insists on only one reality—its own" (122). Authoritative texts are what Whitehead tacitly rejected as boring, ones in which authors "establish the portrait of a world they claim to have understood once and for all" (TW 243–44). As Halasek points out, authoritative texts gain their authority not so much from how they are written but from assumptions, derived from social and cultural traditions, about how they should be read. Students, "conditioned to receive knowledge and discourse passively" (121) are not likely to engage texts as Stengers and Muckelbauer do. But that kind of active reading is exactly what they need to be doing in order to find "something to say." Bakhtin says, "When someone else's ideological discourse [becomes] internally persuasive for us and acknowledged by us, entirely different possibilities open up" (345). He explains that "alien discourses" become "tightly interwoven with 'one's own word'": "a word awakens new and independent words, . . . it organizes masses of our words from within, and does not remain in an isolated and static condition. It is not so much interpreted by us as it is further, that is, freely, developed, applied to new material, new conditions; it enters into interanimating relationships with new contexts" (*Dialogic Imagination* 345–46). Whitehead rereads his concepts this way in the context of his current thinking, just as Stengers reads Whitehead and Muckelbauer reads Foucault. Halasek, rightly, emphasizes the difficulties students face in understanding discourse dialogically: unequal power relations in the classroom and an overemphasis on proficiency in writing pedagogy. She describes her own difficulties with engaging Bakhtin's writing as internally persuasive—I have struggled with this too, especially in engaging Whitehead's writing. She discusses at length a number of dialogic approaches to teaching writing that focus mostly on rhetorical analyses of texts and on assignments that require students to write to real audiences, but I was most interested in a suggestion that she dismisses. Citing Bakhtin on how encountering an "alien" meaning is like entering a foreign culture, a matter of open dialogic questioning, she comments, "The task this sets out for the student is formidable, for it requires that she encounter the subject of her study . . . with questions already in mind" (126). But as Whitehead and Stengers suggest, questions that induce thinking do not require deep knowledge of a subject, just an intense feeling of importance.

Bakhtin's analogy with entering foreign culture suggests this too. He is arguing against the idea that in order to understand another culture one needs to "enter into it, forgetting one's own"; he says, yes, but "if this were the only aspect of this understanding, it would merely be duplication and would not entail anything new or enriching." He states, "*Cultural understanding* does not renounce itself, its own place in time, its own culture; and it forgets nothing" (*Speech Genres* 7). Dialogism is like Whitehead's approach to turning contradictions into contrasts. All it requires is attentiveness to the contrasts as revealing possibilities. All students need to do to read dialogically is to not forget their own experiences but bring them to bear on what they are reading and to actively feel the contrasts: "that is important," "that is ridiculous," "that is wrong." And then to entertain the propositions that arise and ask those questions that elaborate propositions into inquiry: "how is that important?" "what if I accept that it is not ridiculous?" "how did it come to be wrong?"

Both Whitehead and Bakhtin see understanding as an important aspect of creativity, and both understand it in the same way. Whitehead says, "Understanding is never a completed static state of mind. It always bears the character of a process of penetration, incomplete and partial" (MT 43). Bakhtin says: "To understand a given text as the author himself understood it. But our understanding can and should be better. Powerful and profound creativity is largely unconscious and polysemic. Through understanding it is supplemented by consciousness, and the multiplicity of its meanings is revealed. Thus, understanding supplements the text: it is active and also creative by nature. Creative understanding continues creativity, and multiplies the artistic wealth of humanity. The co-creativity of those who understand" (*Speech Genres* 142). The creativity of writing (and reading) lies in writing in the mode of "yes, but," "but then," and "what if?" It is writing that forces concepts to land in unexpected places, that doesn't try to get it right while trying not to get it wrong. It is finding what to say in response. For students as well as philosophers.

A while back, in outlining what I would accomplish in this chapter, I suggested that understanding the interplay of determination and indetermination would enable answers to the questions of how writers create meaning out of past meanings, and how meanings hold together. I think I have answered these questions. Some aspects of what has turned up are familiar: the "death of the author" (who perishes but does not die) and intertextuality, the abandonment of meanings to future appropriation. More significant aspects include feelings of experience as fundamental and prior to conscious thought: the prehending of objective immortalities and the limiting of what is relevant to what is being experienced helps answer the question of how the writer "selects" out of the wealth of meanings what to say. Felt novelty arising out of intra-action as in dialogic questioning and all forms of reciprocal induction with all kinds of other entities explain why meanings are not predetermined by language, ideologies, social beliefs, or cultural traditions. How entertaining propositions induces responses and how language elaborates them into adventures of ideas explains the inexhaustibility of writing—the wealth of humanity, as Bakhtin says. Decisions by the writers for themselves, by themselves, that are the only reasons explain how meanings hold together but are never final. Writers create meanings out of their entanglements; they are never the sole creators, never the masters of the meanings they create, but they do create meanings that matter in a process that at the same time creates themselves anew.

7

Ethical Persuasion

I talk with skunks ("please don't have your babies under my porch"), and just-hatched snapping turtles ("let's get you across the road"), and stranded earthworms ("let's get you off the sidewalk before you dry out or get stepped on"). I talk with eagles, and loons, and especially chickadees, who talk with me too, in their own way. I try to learn to listen to them and heed what they propose. I am inspired by Isabelle Stengers who emphasizes that "we need propositions that would . . . activate the importance of new modes of thinking and feeling the togetherness of our lives" with creaturely others ("Whitehead's Account" 55), and by Karen Barad who proposes that "ethicality is part of the fabric of the world; the call to respond and be responsible is part of what is" (182). They suggest that intra-action is not just about beliefs but about action too, and not just a human matter but an intra-action with all kinds of other creatures. Other creatures are not the Others of diversity studies, human others who may be recognizably "interlocutor[s] . . . presumed to possess at least as much discursive or cultural human sameness as we," though "if [these others are] found to be so unlike us as to be unable to find a language or feature they hold in common with us" our conversation "cannot proceed, and this leads to silence or, at the very least, misunderstanding" (Bernard-Donals, "Against Publics" 37–38).[1] Finding a language or feature in common is not necessary to converse with or persuade others; neither is understanding. Other creatures share only their creaturelyness; like each of us, they are all created and re-created anew in their intra-actions.[2] They do not all have a "face" nor are they necessarily biotic. (I talk with my vacuum cleaner, too, and with the big Lake Superior.) But all are capable of persuading each other, as much recent work in animal studies and new materialism has demonstrated.[3]

In this chapter, I focus on the ethics of persuasive intra-actions among creaturely interlocutors of all kinds. Like Michael Bernard-Donals, I see persuasion as inherently ethical. He says, "The moment in which we engage another in a speech situation is the ethical moment *par excellence*. . . . This is a radically open moment . . . in which the question of how one ought to act has not been definitively decided. It resists the temptation to name the other, to foreclose courses of action, or to describe the situation or context (the public) in which the speaker finds herself" ("Against Publics" 40). He argues that the dominant approach to persuasion that has depended on finding common ground "in which our differences can be hashed out and solved through [rational] argument" risks "eliminating the odd case, the preposterous, or the altogether other" (45). Like Bruno Latour arguing for a new collective of humans and nonhumans (PN 38), Bernard-Donals concludes, "We urgently need to find a way to argue that doesn't eliminate that surplus, and leaves room for it to trouble us and make us feel very much out of place" (45). In what follows, I interrogate a variety of persuasive encounters, some just involving human creatures and some between human and other creatures who are indeed "odd cases" or "strange strangers" (Morton 15). I begin with an encounter I had that persuaded me of something.

I was driving down a gravel road near my summer cottage when something buzzed in through the open passenger-side window and landed on my thigh. Glancing down, I saw a bright blue spangled dragonfly about three inches long with crawly looking legs. Fortunately, before I panicked about what to do, it buzzed out the window on my side of the car. I was startled, and the encounter left a lasting impression. It drew me out of myself, as Bryan Garsten says of the effort that persuasion requires (210). I was still thinking about it hours later.

My encounter was an intra-action in the material world, an encounter in which the dragonfly and I affected—prehended—each other. Barad emphasizes that this intra-active taking into account is fundamentally material: it consists in material-discursive practices, a concept she derives from Foucault's discursive practices and Niels Bohr's apparatuses. They are "not speech acts" but "specific material configurings of the world through which determinations of boundaries, properties, and meanings are differentially enacted" (335). The specific material configuration of me driving a car with open windows when a dragonfly flew in and out enacted "an *agential cut* . . . effecting a separation between 'subject' and 'object'" (333–34). The articulated unit of me and my car was defined in that moment as "object" and the dragonfly as "subject." Barad argues that "insistence on the materiality of meaning making . . . entails a much more intimate relationship between concepts and materiality, matter and mattering" (147). In an intra-action, "part of the world," in this case the dragonfly on my thigh, is "making itself intelligible to another part," me and my car (Barad 185).

In what way did it make itself intelligible? Dragonflies are not entirely strange to me: I don't believe they will harm me, and many are beautiful, including this one. This slight bit of familiarity accounts in part for the particular impression the dragonfly made on me, but prehension has less to do with familiarity than with divergence. As Stengers observes, divergence is a more productive focus for thinking about encounters with all kinds of creatures. She contrasts "argumentation, interaction, and rational conversation [which] bet everything on homogeneity, that is, the possibility of putting oneself in the other's place" (TW 514) with Whitehead's brand of speculative thought, which involves "presence rather than argument, a presence whose efficacy is to infect every justificatory argument with the adventurous questions of what is demanded by the position whose legitimacy it expresses, of what it recruits to endure or propagate, and of the ways it is liable to be affected by the encounter with another position" (TW 512–13). The actual moment of this encounter was radically open: the dragonfly affected me through its presence, its sudden arrival and nimble departure. Later, as I thought about the encounter, I considered how its actions affected me and questioned why I thought I had to be the one to evacuate it from my car—or, as I thought further, why I was also impelled to move newly hatched turtles and earthworms out of harm's way.

Much attention to persuasion in rhetoric and composition in the twenty-first century has focused on the ethics of addressing what Iris Marion Young memorably called "unassimilated otherness." She proposed that city life offered an ideal public, "a being together of strangers, diverse and overlapping neighbors" whose interactions create a public that is "heterogeneous, plural, and playful, a place where people witness and appreciate diverse cultural expressions that they do not share and do not fully understand" (240–41). Ethical persuasion crucially depends on considering other creatures as strangers, paying attention to the specific presence of other creatures in a reciprocal intra-action. It means not putting oneself in the other's place, not naming the other, not assuming that one can understand nor attempting to understand the other. It means taking account of what material configurings were enacted in the encounter with the other, what meanings were created. Stengers refers to it as a test: "One may call 'ethical' the habits that concern a social identity such that it accepts, or does not accept, the test constituted by the encounter with other, divergent identities" (TW 515). Ethical persuasion shifts the focus from how to produce consciously intended changes to how changes arise in intra-action. Donna Haraway observes that intra-action opens up "what is not known to be possible, but might be for all the intra-acting partners" (*When* 223). Instead of critiquing positions deeply held by others, instead of compromising between them, instead of tolerating them and thereby dismissing their importance, ethical persuasion can turn contradictory positions into contrasts that "can be celebrated in the manner of a new existent, adding a new dimension to the cosmos" (Stengers, TW 513). Ethical persuasion invents new possibilities that lead to change.

Following Whitehead, Stengers refers to it as a polite modification of dreams. She explains that "the Whiteheadean adventure does not aim at awakening, leaving the cave. It is itself a dream, a storytelling: to learn 'inside' the Platonic cave, together with those who live and argue within it. Not in the hope that the false appearances will gradually yield their secrets, but in the hope that these 'appearances,' if they are appreciated in their affirmative importance, might be articulated into fabulous contrasts" (TW 516). Storytelling in the cave, offering dreams in the hope that they will be appreciated, is a polite invitation to further adventures, the invention of which is the measure of successful ethical persuasion. Like stories, dreams persuade through suggestion; as Garsten says, the orator "merely puts words into the air," and listeners engage in "an active process of evaluation and assimilation" (7). Stengers also emphasizes that it does not concern interlocutors' identities but their responses, both affective and cognitive: "if one dream may induce the modification of another or evoke another, it is insofar as their point of junction is always a tangent point: neither a frontal clash between rival powers nor being swallowed up in the other's dream, not confusion in a banal dream of power but a local resonance, designating past tenses of divergent accomplishments and future tenses responding to distinct tests" (TW 518). It is a behavior that neither forgets diverse histories nor dictates future behavior but accepts the test posed by the encounter with a strange stranger by considering what is demanded by the commitments, beliefs, attachments that you hold to.

Ethical persuasion takes place in the everyday world of the cave, of which we are only one part, as Barad reminds us. John Muckelbauer also suggests considering everyday instances of persuasion as paradigmatic, replacing Aristotle's "highly specialized and idealized" forensic, deliberative, and epideictic rhetorics, which "present a dramatically oversimplified and reductive image of how persuasion actually happens in the world" ("Implicit Paradigms" 35). As a new image of persuasion, he offers "heliotropism," the behavior of plants turning to follow the sun, remarking that "this sense of simply 'turning' is a more adequate rendering of an earlier, pre-Platonic sense of persuasion, one that only mutated into the consciousness-driven sense through Aristotle and his teacher" (39–40).

Muckelbauer's image of turning is very much what Alfred North Whitehead conceives of as a prehension, a general term for the activity of concrescence (PR 52). It has "a 'vector character'; it involves emotion, and purpose, and valuation, and causation" (PR 19)—but not necessarily conscious intention. As Nicholas Harberd, whose book I discussed in chapter 3, explains, the intra-actions of plants with their environments are not simple responses. Seedlings, for example, control the growth of their hypocotyls (stems) in intra-action with the qualities of light they receive—its intensity, direction, and wave length. Harberd comments, "It is an active, regulated rather than a passive-response thing. . . . Like me, these seedlings see and respond" (197, 239). Stengers describes prehension as "a 'taking into account'"; it refers to "all situations in which something makes a difference for something else," including not only living beings—"for instance, the earth's trajectory 'takes account' of the sun" (TW 147). Muckelbauer instances the difference made by the first full-color image of the earth published in 1967: "As a result of the distribution of this image, a great many more people began to think of the earth as a living thing and even potentially as fragile and in need of care . . . this image produced persuasive effects (even if only a slight change in perception or attitude) without an argument and without the necessity of a conscious intention" ("Implicit Paradigms" 38). He notes that as in this example, "People are frequently persuaded by things that most of us would not readily call arguments—images, or sounds, or even by physical structures" (36). Turning, like prehension, is an active and purposeful intra-action—a good general term for persuasion.

Broadening our understanding of persuasion to recognize the multitude of ways we are persuaded by creaturely others has many advantages. Not being blind and deaf to what our emotions and senses tell us and to creatures who communicate in different modes and in different languages doesn't just enrich our lives but may save us from damaged relationships, violence, or environmental catastrophe. Ethical persuasion enacts the respect for specific differences that has not often been extended to nonhumans even as it has also been denied to other humans deemed not worth listening to. Humans have for far too long assumed that nonhumans are automatons or generic others—the Animal, as Jacques Derrida says (*Animal* 31)—or mute things, having nothing to teach us. Gemma Fiumara observes: "There must be some problem of listening if we only hear from earth when it is so seriously endangered that we cannot help paying heed" (6).

Eros and Agonism

The question of how to ethically argue with strange strangers has proved to be somewhat fraught. The answer depends on assumptions about identity and agency and the purpose(s) of persuasion. Most current answers offered by scholars in rhetoric and composition agree with Bernard-Donals in rejecting stable individual identities and the "traditional" understanding of persuasion as resolving differences through rational argument and finding common ground. Most concern discursive interactions among conscious human agents. But besides agreement on issues, the assumed purposes include making decisions and policies, refining positions, raising questions, drawing attention to injustices and to unarticulated or otherwise ignored perspectives—and perhaps others—all of which could be considered purposes of deliberation.[4] In chapter 5 I detailed my understanding of agents as dominantly unconscious individuating entities that act in reciprocal intra-actions with other agents. Above, I offered a general definition of persuasion as a taking account of other creatures and argued briefly for ethical persuasion as an inventive, polite modification of dreams. In order to elaborate these positions, I look next at a few other theories of persuasion and argument.

One way to think about the persuasive intra-actions of diverse creatures is through the entangled affects of eros and agonism. In their most opposed forms, these affects create two often-mentioned dangers: blind eros (consensus) and steadfast agonism (wrangling). Whitehead refers to the danger of consensus as the trick of evil, the inhibition, whether intentional or not, of anything that would make someone doubt (Stengers, TW 333). Blind eros is what Stengers refers to as "being swallowed up in the other's dream" (TW 518). It can take the form of not listening or not hearing, not thinking, avoiding trouble, following orders. The danger of consensus is also a central theme in Hannah Arendt's work: "It keeps people from thinking, and it keeps them behaving" (Roberts-Miller, "Fighting" 598) Arendt's understanding of Adolph Eichmann's behavior was that "he was able to engage in mass murder because he was able not to think about it, especially not from the perspective of the victims, . . . he was just following orders" (Roberts-Miller, "Fighting" 591). Patricia Roberts-Miller comments, "The public discourse surrounding the Final Solution was designed to ensure that people like Hoess and Eichmann never heard the Jewish arguments against it" (*Deliberate Conflict* 185). Bernard-Donals also refers to the Third Reich as exemplifying the danger of consensus: "National Socialist Germany was the culmination of the politics of identity . . . in which difference itself became a threat . . . a triumph of rationality and identification" ("Against Publics" 39–40). Steadfast agonism also involves refusing to listen but takes the form of an attack, the action of sworn enemies with a desire (or need) to win at any cost. Stengers refers to wrangling as "a frontal clash between rival powers" (TW 518). It is the eristic discourse attributed by Plato and Aristotle to the Sophists. Jim Corder describes it as the "hopelessness of steadfast arguments opposing each other" (23) brought about, he proposes, by a failure to love the other. Between these poles, there is room for reconciling eros and agonism, as Roberts-Miller suggests in her description of the "best discourse for a diverse and inclusive public sphere": "If people think for themselves, they will resist dogma; if people think of themselves as one of many, they will empathize; if people can do both, they will resist totalitarianism" ("Fighting" 598). The problem is how to achieve this reconciliation.

Persuasion's involvement with both eros and agonism goes way back, as revealed not only the ancient Greek philosophers' denunciation of eristic discourse but also in Michele Kennerly and Carly Woods's recent analysis of the images of the classical goddesses Rhetorica and Peithō. One of the repeated elements in images of Rhetorica is a caduceus, "a herald's staff, about which intertwine two antagonistic-loving serpents, a symbol of mediation" (10).[5] The caduceus traditionally belonged to Hermes, "the god best known for his boundary crossing" (10), and the idea of persuasion as a mediation between or alliance of eros and agonism adheres to representations of both Rhetorica and Peithō. Though the use of Rhetorica to represent the discipline of rhetoric has persisted up to the present day, in 1996 the Coalition of Women Scholars in the History of Rhetoric and Composition chose instead to name their newsletter after Peithō, the Greek goddess of persuasion, and in 2003 they replaced the image of Rhetorica on the newsletter with one of Peithō. The image they chose, from a mid-fourth-century BCE Apulian nuptial vase, depicts Peithō fleeing the scene of Zeus's rape of Leda. Peithō "stretches one hand toward the incipient violence," and a dove, a symbol of Aphrodite, flies over her head (Kennerly and Woods 22). The link between the goddesses of persuasion and love was also anchored in their paired statues on the Acropolis symbolizing both the union of "the demes of fractious Attica" (19) and the link between the persuasive power of erotics and "the amicable coming together of deliberative bodies" (22). Persuasion and love are joined in opposition to violence as indicated by the rape of Leda, for "when erotic encounters degrade into demonstrations of force, persuasion is no longer present" (23), an opposition that also applies to the political realm. Kennerly and Woods comment, "Peithō's tale provides a different possibility for persuasion, one that does not abandon power but recognizes its limitations and encourages its capacity to pull together the disparate and the separate" (23). Persuasion still involves a form of agonism as represented by the two antagonistic-loving serpents, but it's an agonism that is distinguished from violence.

As a demonstration of how "love and persuasion scale up from partner relations to political ones" (20), Kennerly and Woods instance Pericles's funeral oration for the heroes of the first battles of the Peloponnesian wars. Speaking after a disappointing first year of war and to an audience that included many who opposed his strategic decisions, Pericles chose to praise not the men who had fought but rather the citizens of Athens. He admonished them not to listen to "words of the advantages" of defending Athens; instead, he said, "you must yourselves realize the power of Athens, and feed your eyes upon her from day to day, till love of her fills your hearts" (Thucydides). He proceeded to spend most of the speech detailing qualities he attributed to the actions of its citizens: laws that "afford equal justice to all in their private differences"; the affordance of freedom of action—"we do not feel called upon to be angry with our neighbour for doing what he likes"; the openness to outsiders—"we throw open our city to the world, and never by alien acts exclude foreigners . . . trusting less in system and policy than to the native spirit of our citizens"; and the valuing of discussion—"instead of looking on discussion as a stumbling-block in the way of action, we think it an indispensable preliminary to any wise action at all." Commentators observe that Pericles was "speaking less as an epideictic orator than as a politician" (Sicking 411). Because the results of the war had been disappointing, it was necessary for Pericles "to silence . . . the demoralizing grievances of the opponents . . . and at the same time to restore his supporters' confidence and readiness to fight to the best of their ability" (Sicking 413). He attempted to persuade his listeners to unify in defense of Athens through a love of what they had achieved together, which included respect for differences. Although achieving consubstantiality was easier for Pericles—the freedoms he lauded were extended only to citizens—and despite the undoubted idealization of the accomplishments of Athens's citizens, appealing to their ability to "realize the power of Athens" through their love of her was a strategy that gestures at the politeness Stengers advocates for persuasion.

Making "the case for conflict" against feminist and expressivist compositionists in the 1980s who argued that "any attempt to persuade is an act of violence" (106), Susan Jarratt reached back to the Sophists to revive a nonviolent notion of agonistic persuasion. She argued that the resistance to persuasive discourse arose from equating it with wrangling, "competitive contentiousness . . . engaged in for its own sake" (114). Twentieth-century compositionists similarly complained of students' wrangling as clinging to "positions as if [they] were sacred to home, country, and spiritual identity . . . a pointless argument among people who do not care very much about the outcome . . . except that it is always better to be on the winning rather than the losing side" (Lynch et al. 61). Though valuing conflict, the Sophists rejected wrangling. The "amicable coming together of deliberative bodies" that Kennerly and Woods associate with Peithō is evident in *Protagoras* when Prodicus asks the interlocutors to argue more amicably: "I would beg you . . . Protagoras and Socrates,

... that you will dispute (*amphisbetein*) with one another and not wrangle (*erizein*), for friends dispute with friends out of good will, but only adversaries and enemies wrangle" (337b; qtd. in Jarratt 117). Jarratt points out that the word "amphisbetein" means, loosely, to "go both ways," "an ability to move into different positions" (117), another ability Kennerly and Woods identify with Peithō. By conceptualizing persuasion as amicable dispute rather than discord and violence, Sophistic rhetoric, like Peithō, draws together the positive characteristics of love and conflict. Pointing out that Sophistic rhetoric was denounced because its valuing of *dissoi logoi* encouraged a democratic politics that threatened the oligarchy Plato supported, Jarratt argues that a Sophistic brand of agonistic argument will similarly be politically efficacious in addressing issues of gender, race, and class in composition classrooms. Jarratt advocates classrooms in which students learn "to see how differences emerging from their texts and discussions have more to do with" their location in specific personal historical and social experiences "than they do with an essential and unarguable individuality" (121), an understanding that will enable them to deliberate about both private and public issues.

Roberts-Miller also sees agonism as essential to democratic politics: "Because deliberative democracy assumes that people are different, that no viewpoint is universal, then conflict among viewpoints is necessary" (*Deliberate Conflict* 201). Referring to Jarratt's account of composition pedagogies that resist argumentation, she suggests that it arises from "assuming that conflict must be resolved, and it must be resolved through some kind of exertion of power" (201). She finds both assumptions—or fears—to be unfounded. Distinguishing between irenic deliberations (in which there is little conflict) and agonistic deliberations, she states that unlike irenic deliberations, agonistic deliberations do not aim at reaching agreement on a correct position, though "one does need to come to communal decisions" (201). But, she notes, "such decisions are always necessarily contingent and cannot be seen as ending the process, or permanently answering the question" (201). As in the debate between the Federalists and the Anti-Federalists, which continued in some form throughout American political history without ever reaching agreement, agonistic deliberation leads to appropriate policies and interesting questions (12). It also draws attention to injustices and silenced positions and promotes good thinking in public discourse, the latter as exemplified by Hannah Arendt who, Roberts-Miller says, advocates the most adversarial of conflictual argument. Arendt is not interested in persuasive agonism, in which "one plays down conflict and moves through reasons to try to persuade one's audience," but instead engages in polemical agonism, the aim of which is "to make public one's thought in order to test it," to "provoke critique and counterargument," to engage "interlocutors, not acolytes" (Roberts-Miller, "Fighting" 595–96).[6] Arendt thinks of it as "fighting without hatred, and 'without the spirit of revenge'" (qtd. in Roberts-Miller, "Fighting" 596). Describing Arendt's take on public discourse, Roberts-Miller says, "Good thinking requires that one *hear* the arguments of other people . . . it is not a discourse in which one announces one's stance; participants are interlocutors and not just speakers; they must listen . . . it must be a world into which one enters and by which one might be changed" ("Fighting" 593). Persuasion as requiring interaction and listening is what Jarratt emphasizes too in her discussion of the centrality of conflict in Sophistic rhetoric: "Only through recognition of and argument over differences can conflict be resolved into *homonoia*, like-mindedness" (114). However, Roberts-Miller worries that an agonistic public sphere may be elitist and antidemocratic, open only to a few because of the demands it places on interlocutors: one must "simultaneously trust and doubt one's own perceptions, rely on one's own judgment and consider the judgments of others, think for oneself and imagine how others think" ("Fighting" 597), a concern for deliberation in college classrooms too.

While Jarratt and Roberts-Miller emphasize how agonistic deliberation in classroom discussions and in the public sphere can enable amicable decision making and good thinking about issues and viewpoints, Jim Corder emphasizes eros as essential in avoiding wrangling. He says, "Rhetoric is love, and it must speak a commodious language, creating a world full of space and time that will hold our diversities" (31). Corder was not explicitly addressing Young's concern about openness to unassimilated otherness (her book was not published until five years after his article appeared); he was concerned about how individuals could avoid conflict and reach out to others. For Corder, there is a lot at stake in persuasion, as an argument "is not something we *make* outside ourselves; argument is what we are" (18). And thus an argument "of genuine consequence," one that "confronts one life with another" (19), "threatens one's identity" (23). Because Corder sees the conflict in argument as a clash of identities and not just of issues or ideas as in Arendt's polemical agonism, it is thus more dangerous. It requires

> a readiness to testify to an identity that is always emerging . . . it calls for an untiring stretch toward the other, a reach toward enfolding the other. It is a risky revelation of the self, for the arguer is asking for an acknowledgment of his or her identity, is asking for a witness from the other. . . . In argument, the arguer must, with no assurance, go out, inviting the other to enter a world that the arguer tries to make commodious, inviting the other to emerge as well, but with no assurance of kind or even thoughtful response. (26)

The risk can be taken, he says, "if we learn to love before we disagree" (26). "If there is to be hope," he says, "we have to see each other, to know each other, to be present to each other, to embrace each other" (25).

Because identities are diverse, the persuasive burden falls on the maker of the argument: "The arguer must go alone ... unassisted by the other because the other is over in a different place" (30). Corder suggests that the arguer is capable of reaching the other by developing "a genuinely provocative and evocative *ethos*" that "issues an invitation into a commodious universe" (31). The arguer makes his invitation more inviting by pursuing "the reality of things only partially knowable," abandoning "authoritative positions," and holding "the audience wholly in mind," "viewing matters both as the arguer sees them and as others see them" (28–31). And, most important, by learning "the lessons that rhetoric itself wants to teach us" (29). Just as Roberts-Miller allows that decisions are always contingent and never settle the matter, Corder notes that argument, like identity, is "always emerging." Speaking requires closing off some possibilities, but invention "asks us to open ourselves to the richness of creation" (29). This cycle of closing to speak and opening to invent enables the arguer to "nurture and replenish [his or her] inventive world and enable[s] him or her to reach out around the other" so that his or her argument "may grow to hold both arguer and other" (29).

Seeing identity as a narrative enables Corder to envision identity as open to change and accepting of other realities but still providing a grounding. Roberts-Miller takes a similar, but slightly different position, stating, "One is expected to move beyond one's own subjectivity, but not to free oneself of it entirely.... These are real people with compelling commitments that are different from one's own" (*Deliberate Conflict* 183). Corder's commodious universe is like Roberts-Miller's deliberative public sphere in its emphasis on contingency and the possibility of change—at least he says that "sometimes ... we [may] encounter another narrative and learn to change our own" (19). But unlike Roberts-Miller's vision of argumentative encounters, Corder's is not reciprocal. While she insists that "participants are interlocutors and not just speakers; they must listen" ("Fighting" 593), Corder's arguer only reaches out to the other and tries to hold them in mind and see things from their perspective. Corder's suggestion that arguers learn to love also seems similar to what Haraway refers to as the "regard and respect" necessary in an encounter "where *who and what are* is precisely what is at stake" (*When* 19), but in Corder's world, the participants are not looking back reciprocally and becoming a "we" (*When* 19, 164); they are not paying attention to each other, or corresponding, as Tim Ingold says. Corder's argument for loving and open-ended argument is thoughtful and heartfelt, but the commodious universe he envisions is created by the actions of a single speaker instead of in interaction.

Corder—as well as Roberts-Miller—views arguers as autonomous agents. In contrast, Bernard-Donals explicitly rejects the assumption that interlocutors are "individuals that exist prior to their engagement with others, and who, by dint of their more or less individual agency, choose to engage with one another" (Bernard-Donals, "No" 655). He argues that "subjects only become subjects *in* these acts of engagement" ("No" 655). He lauds Young's approach for conceiving of the encounter as "a radically particular intersubjective engagement" in which "individuals are thrown together and are forced, by dint of their pressed-together location, to 'meet and interact'" ("Against Publics" 35). For Bernard-Donals, though, discursive encounters are not just radically particular but singular; interlocutors do not meet and interact in like-minded groups, "clusters of people with affinities" as Young proposes (237), but as "a proximity among individuals" a "*between*" that forms as Jean-Luc Nancy says, "each time according to determined modes that are themselves multiple and simultaneous" (65; qtd. in "Against Publics" 43–44), modes that also form the individuals as subjects, as in Barad's intra-action. This line of thought, he argues, lends to Young's notion of unassimilated otherness "an added dimension of complexity" ("Against Publics" 43). A speaker doesn't represent "a self, a community, or a prospective position in discourse or politics or argument" that can be known, even imperfectly, "but speaks only 'the infinite singularity of meaning' that is, nonetheless, uttered in the presence of others" ("Against Publics" 48; quoting Nancy, *Being* 15). Bernard-Donals says, "When the individual enters into a discursive relation with the other, she resides in a kind of no-man's land, in which she is both at home and in exile, neither completely apart from, nor completely a part of, the community or the location in which she speaks" ("Against Publics" 42). Like Young's city dwellers, the individuals in Bernard-Donals's discursive relation "are always close by and proximate," but instead of thereby coming to some knowledge of each other, their complex differences are highlighted: "Otherness cannot be overcome through discourse but is made radically evident *through* discourse" ("Against Publics" 39). Interlocutors are never fully known to each other (or themselves) nor do they identify with the others: they are "troubled" by them. The difference between others "is a space that, as often as not, can't be traversed" ("Against Publics" 48).[7] For Bernard-Donals, the ultimate danger in discursive relations lies in the belief that the other can be known, that otherness can be overcome. Fences are needed, he says, "not only to keep out . . . neighbors but also to ensure that even our kinsmen are recognized as necessarily distinct from us, lest we create a name for ourselves, a "we" that becomes insurmountable" ("Against Publics"

49). Like Corder, he says that engaging in discourse requires "a willingness for the speaker to approach the other and to become vulnerable, exposing the speaker to the possibility that she will be rebuffed, in some cases violently" ("Against Publics" 46). But unlike Corder, Bernard-Donals does not envision encounters as achieving an amicable and mutual understanding, rather "a radically singular ethics of engagement" that "doesn't anticipate concepts in which alterity is denied" ("Against Publics" 47, 46).

Bernard-Donals adopts Emmanuel Levinas's understanding of individuals as ethically bound by their face-to-face discursive encounters and by the presence of witnesses. Levinas says they are "freedoms who neither limit nor deny one another, but reciprocally affirm one another" (35). They affirm each other as singular beings who are thus responsible for one another's being, but they are in no way open to one another. All they know is that they have "a palpable (and potentially disruptive) effect upon that other" as well as upon the unseen witness (Bernard-Donals, "Against Publics" 45). Bernard-Donals's individuals do affirm each other and become subjects, but they do not become a "we" in Haraway's sense nor are they corresponding in Ingold's sense. In correspondence, entities affect each other in a "dance of animacy," an "ongoing response" (Ingold, M 100, 94) from which some new entity emerges. Keenly aware of the evil of consensus, Bernard-Donals imagines a truly open public where differences interact and mingle, as in Nancy's description of Sarajevo as a *mêlée*—"a fight, but also a mingling of a more sexual nature" implying also "the ideas of mixture, mixing, motley, and variegation."[8] It is a public very much like Young's ideal public: "heterogeneous, plural, and playful, a place where people witness and appreciate diverse cultural expressions that they do not share and do not fully understand" (240–41).

My vision of persuasion as a taking account of other creatures and of ethical persuasion as an inventive, polite modification of dreams accords at many points with those offered by Roberts-Miller, Corder, and Bernard-Donals. Like Roberts-Miller, I see persuasion as embracing an impulse broader than reaching agreement, as including all forms of deliberation as well as Muckelbauer's more general impulse of turning. Like Corder, I see it as inventive, as an opening to "the richness of creation." Like Bernard-Donals, I see it as an inherently ethical encounter in which subjects emerge; like him, and unlike Roberts-Miller and Corder, I do not see interlocutors as fully autonomous agents. Like all of them, I see persuasion as contingent, never finally resolving anything, and as in various ways reconciling the affects of eros and agonism. Unlike all of them, I see it as not restricted to linguistic encounters between human creatures.

The shift in understanding persuasion I am proposing, however, is a major shift in the style of engagement persuasion involves. Among the implicit attributes of Aristotle's rhetoric that Muckelbauer identifies as still orienting the field's image of rhetoric is the presumption of the "importance of intentional argument and, in most cases, the immediacy of a recognizable decision (on the part of those being persuaded)" ("Implicit Paradigms" 35). Instead of focusing on rhetors' intentions, I focus on all participants' actions in persuasive encounters, how they affect each other unconsciously and consciously in intra-action and what new possibilities emerge. Ethical persuasion takes seriously the otherness of all other creatures (as in Bernard-Donals's vision). Polite interlocutors respect the importance of others' narratives, commitments, attachments, beliefs, and habits that provide not identity but a hold on experience that might change, or become modified, but that cannot "be explained away, for instance through the appeal to something in common" (Stengers, "Ecology" 189).

Dreams are attachments like the habits of experience I discussed in chapter 1: they "evoke a style of experience or adventure that is endowed with a certain stability" (Stengers, TW 26). Kimmerer recognized the plantain on the trail as an immigrant because of her habits as a botanist and an indigenous woman. Stengers also refers to the hold on experience as a practice, a set of habits that enable a hold in a specific environment: a practice enables botanists to think about plants and ecologists to "accept that a wolf is a wolf and a lamb is a lamb" and not try to manipulate them into a peaceful cohabitation; "that is, they do not dream of submitting them to their own human ideas about what would be a better world" ("Ecology" 191). Practices and the habits associated with them do not constitute an identity, nor do the narratives Corder equates with identity; they enable "a situation . . . to matter in its particular way" (192). Such a "cosmic event" is "not something that can be produced at will"; it "does not depend on humans only, but on humans as belonging, which means they are obliged and exposed by their obligations" (192). Narratives, commitments, attachments, beliefs and habits are experiments, adventures: just as ecologists "do not know how wolves and lambs may become able, as wolves and lambs, to behave in different circumstances," Kimmerer does not know how the plantain will come to matter as she recognizes it as an immigrant. Practices are technologies that provide holds, ways to "think for the world" (192) that also impose responsibilities: "What you are responsible for is paying attention as best you can, to be as discerning, as discriminating as you can about the particular situation. That is, you need to decide in this particular case and not obey the power of some more general reason" (188). Polite persuasion is inventive, offering an invitation, not to a "more commodious universe," but for a situation to matter in a particular way. As Stengers says of the related practice of diplomacy, "It is not a matter of negotiation among free humans who must be ready to change as the situation changes, but of constructions among humans as constrained by diverging attachments, such as belonging" ("Ecology" 193).

Polite persuaders do not try to understand or identify with others, but instead offer and entertain possibilities, and they do so, as did Kimmerer, in the form of propositions, tales that might be told, that may suggest new paths. And in turn, polite persuaders accept the test posed by encounters with others by considering what is demanded by their own hold. Stengers says that a dream may induce a modification or invoke another dream tangentially through "a local resonance." A proposition inspires change by resonance, or reciprocal induction, and it requires of interlocutors reciprocity and trust in what others can do.

Whitehead was a great fan of Pericles's oration. He cites it as "the first explicit defence of social tolerance": "It puts forth the conception of the organized society successfully preserving freedom of behaviour for its individual members" (AI 50–51). He notes that Pericles focuses on the actions of individual citizens as a model of persuasion opposed to the actions of the "Barbarian" who "speaks in terms of power" and persuades by his "will imposing itself upon other wills" (51). In contrast, "The Periclean ideal is action weaving itself into a texture of persuasive beauty analogous to the delicate splendor of nature" (51). The actions of the citizens in realizing the power of Athens are seen as the finite analogue of the divine vision that weaves all actualities without exception into an eternal ordering, God's "tender care that nothing be lost" (PR 474).[9] Whitehead refers to it here as "the aesthetic end of all action" (51) and concludes, "The duty of tolerance is our finite homage to the abundance of inexhaustible novelty which is awaiting the future, and to the complexity of accomplished fact which exceeds our stretch of insight" (AI 52).

Later in *Adventures of Ideas* Whitehead envisions a new Protestant Reformation that could arise from inserting Pericles's oration in the Bible as a replacement for the book of Revelation, "which illustrates the barbaric elements which have been retained to the undoing of Christian intuition" (AI 170–71). He argues that Protestant theology should be founded on the recognition of "the Universe which grasps its unity amid its many diversities" and on an understanding of "the tenderness of mere life itself, in a world which is superficially founded upon the clashings of senseless compulsion" (AI 170). Stengers's reading of this suggestion illuminates what is required by ethical persuasion: "Pericles addressed the Athenians as free citizens, that is, animated by divergent priorities, values, goals, all without asking them to strip themselves of these attachments in the name of what transcends them. At the same time, however, he addressed them as Athenians, on whose action the life of the city depends. Athens will only be saved by its citizens. . . . He interpreted them as attached but not defined by, or subject to, what attaches them, and therefore susceptible of a new type of unity that would be Athens" (TW 497). Pericles recognizes "the multiplicity of individual enjoyments that constitute the primordial truth of the world"—individuating unities becoming through their intra-actions and decisions for themselves—"but he trusts in what 'his' world is capable of, that is in 'his' fellow citizens *qua* able to feel, each in their own way, the need for common action" (TW 498). Whitehead's admiration for Pericles does not focus on Pericles's admonition that Athenians come to love their country; rather he is concerned about how they are persuaded, that they do not need to submit to coercion, to "barbarians" imposing their will on them, requiring them to give up their priorities, values, and goals. But he also sees them as open to change: susceptible to the lure of "a new type of unity." The proposition Pericles offers in saying "you must yourselves realize the power of Athens" is, What if Athens might only be saved by its citizens?—a real, specific possibility, something that might matter quite insistently, whether for good or ill.

Though Garsten's theory of persuasion is firmly fixed in humanistic assumptions of self-contained human entities, beset by what Barad calls "the sticky problem of humanity's own captivity within language" (137), it also emphasizes reciprocity and trust in others. Garsten says that true persuasion, "persuasion that lies between manipulation and pandering," preserves the "active independence" of the listener: the orator "merely puts words into the air," and listeners engage in "an active process of evaluation and assimilation" (7). He argues, thus, that the project of persuasion requires that "we once again look directly at one another and speak directly to one another," that it requires that "we pay attention to our fellow citizens and to their opinions" (210). He sees persuasion as a matter of influence, rather than proof: "In addressing our fellow citizens directly, we make an effort to influence them . . . with articulated thoughts that appeal to their distinctly human capacity for judgment" (211). And he notes that engaging listeners' capacity for judgment allows them to consider new positions: "We judge best when we are situated within [our] structures of value, able to draw upon their complexity and able to feel, emotionally, the moral and practical relevance of different considerations in as subtle a way as experience has equipped us to do. And . . . because much of the art of rhetoric consists in drawing new pathways between hitherto weakly related parts of these structures, we need not view ourselves as trapped in our situation but simply grounded there" (192). Like Whitehead, he sees emotion as important in persuasion, and he trusts that listeners are able to consider new possibilities without losing their hold.

Understanding persuadability as affective and not dependent on language begins to explain how I can say that the dragonfly persuaded me: I was persuaded by its presence, startled by its unexpected actions that caused me to question my assumptions about dragonflies. I do not claim that the dragonfly consciously intended to persuade me of something. As I discussed in chapter 5, even in humans, conscious intentions do not precede actions and are intentional only in retrospect. Instead, I was persuaded in the material intra-action: persuasion was the result of the prehensive unity that emerged in the encounter.

Whitehead also uses the terms actual entity and actual occasion to refer to prehensive unities, emphasizing not only the relative impermanence of entities that "stay for a while" in the process of passage into another actual entity but also that in its formation, an actual entity expresses something. Expression in Whitehead's usage, is the activity of the finite actual entity "impressing itself on its environment," diffusing "in the environment . . . something initially entertained in the experience of" the actual entity (MT 20, 23). Stengers explains that expression is "that which will make itself felt," the novelty that "in one way or another, will have to be taken into account" (TW 423). In the moment of my intra-action with the dragonfly something was expressed that had to be taken into account, and what we experienced at that moment was a unity of prehension, an occasion of mutual influence.

Whitehead says that expression is "more than interpretable. It is creative. It elicits the intuition which interprets it . . . the existent intuition which would not otherwise emerge" (RM 132–33). While Oscar Wilde famously criticized Wordsworth's communion with nature saying, "He found in stones the sermons he had already hidden there" (301), Whitehead, instead, argues that Wordsworth "always grasps the whole of nature as involved in the tonality of the particular instance" (SMW 83). Whitehead especially praises the first book of *The Prelude*: "It would hardly be possible to express more clearly a feeling for nature, as exhibiting entwined prehensive unities, each suffused with modal presences of others" (SMW 84). Thus, what the dragonfly persuaded me of is not simply my interpretation. As Garsten argues, being persuaded involves action by both the rhetor and the listener. The dragonfly's action was creative: it impressed itself on me; the proposition it proffered elicited an intuition that would not have otherwise emerged.

Being persuaded is not something that rhetors do to listeners; it is something listeners do—or experience—in a specific material intra-action. And because persuasion involves multiple agents (at least two), it is an iffy business. Garsten says, "Even the most attentive and skillful efforts at persuasion often fail for reasons unconnected with the merits of the cause" (211). Stengers offers the analogy of an infection that runs its course differently in each individual and that cannot foresee "what causes, resources, and what consequences it will invent for itself" (TW 515). The polite introduction of a new possibility "invokes particular and personal forms of knowledge" (Garsten 192), and, juxtaposed to the structures of a listener's beliefs, a new proposition that can lead to a transformation of habits arises. Whitehead attributes such a transformation to imagination, which "deliberately suspends 'what we know well'" and allows us to become aware not of its falseness, but of its partiality (Stengers, TW 351).

My encounter with the dragonfly persuaded me not because I identified with it, but because it infected me with a new tale that might be told, a proposition that shook my certainties about the importance of my role and that of humans in general in saving individual animals and species. The advantage of listening to others like dragonflies—or people from unfamiliar cultures—is that they have divergent interests and abilities, and their actions refuse our simple assumption that we can put ourselves in their place. They thus can seem more difficult or even impossible to listen to than other humans. But adopting and practicing habits that increase our capacity to respond to them enables us to creatively contribute to a society that demands sensitive attunement to the complex becoming of an increasingly diverse world.

Habits of Listening

I propose three habits of listening to add to the habits of good writers. They are not meant to be definitive or exclusive, nor as a repudiation of other habits. They testify, I believe, to values associated with enchantment ontology, primarily the values placed on difference and on becoming. Again, habits are ways of behaving in specific circumstances—"the satisfactory way in which the mind will function when it is poked up into activity" (Whitehead, AE 27); they are capacities, not abilities or character traits. The habits of listening I propose are:

> assuming there are creatures to listen to;
> letting creatures be in themselves in our relations to them;
> exploring new styles of listening.

All are ways of paying due attention to creaturely others, as Stengers suggests, to be as discerning, as discriminating as possible about the particular encounter.

First, I have to assume I *can* listen to the other, that the other is capable of and often desirous of addressing me. This is a matter of attention, of acknowledging the presence of another creature and how it is affecting me. Krista Ratcliffe points out that a creature's desire to be heard—as well as the hearer's opposing desires not to listen—may include unconscious as well as conscious desires.[10] Refusing to listen by "pretending the 'desire to be heard' does not exist, hoping it will disappear, or waiting for someone else to handle it" needs to be transposed, she says, "into a self-conscious desire for receptivity" (29). Fiumara, who like Garsten argues that listening is of equal importance to speaking in promoting thought, says that it is a mistake to think of listening as passive; instead, listening requires "laborious involvement . . . and some degree of commitment" (189–91). Rosina Lippi-Green observes that mainstream language speakers who claim they can't understand those who speak with an accent are rejecting their "fair share of the communicative burden" (70). In the same way, sometimes humans who, like Wittgenstein, aver that even if a lion could talk we could not understand him (223) are simply refusing to make the effort to listen.[11] We can and often need to listen as well to creatures that do not seem to have a desire to be heard, as in the case of the dragonfly and of nonliving creatures—technologies, for example, or the willows that Ingold's students were making baskets with that "did not want to be bent into shape" (M 22). Listening is not done just with ears.

Second, I have to attend to the other as a specific instance of a specific individual in a specific time and place. Heidegger says that when we do not let something be in itself, "the nature of a thing never comes to light, that is, it never gets a hearing" ("Thing" 168). For Heidegger, things come to presence through gathering aspects of the world "into something that stays for a while: into this thing, that thing" (172). The dragonfly, for example, gathers the currents of air produced by the car's passage, the open window, my thigh, into what Whitehead calls an actual entity, something "that 'decides for itself': thus, and not otherwise" (Stengers, TM 263). Whitehead says, "The point to be emphasized is the insistent particularity of things experienced and of the act of experiencing. . . . *That* wolf [ate] *that* lamb at *that* spot at *that* time" (PR 43). Letting creatures be in themselves is not a matter of grasping their "true identity" but rather refusing any general notion of who or what they are or could be. Ratcliffe addresses this problem when considering the trouble caused by disidentification, the disavowing of an identification with what one imagines a creature to be: "Imagination alone is not enough when trying to understand a person from a different tradition. Imagination must be grounded in material reality via a kind of cultural/historical archaeological/ethnographic work that the subject doing the conscious identifying must be willing to perform" (62). Such "faulty identifications" are certainly one of the behaviors that prevent letting a creature be in intra-actions. Trying to come to understand the creature through research can be a useful aid in listening better, certainly better than imagination, but it does not allow one to pay attention to the particular creature one is intra-acting with nor does it allow the creature to become what it can be. Paraphrasing Stengers, you need to listen in this particular case and not obey the power of some more general observation ("Ecology" 188). I can turn to my guide to dragonflies of the north woods, as I have, and discover that the one I encountered was a blue darner, probably a Canada darner or a Lake darner, but in doing so I am not listening to that dragonfly that flew into my car on that day.

Finally, I have to be open to new styles of listening, approaches that, as Latour and Despret have said, allow the other to become interesting (Latour, "Well-Articulated"; Despret, "Sheep"). Stengers suggests that successful scientists learn "to discern what matters to what is being interrogated" (TW 440), and Latour and Despret suggest that experimental apparatuses function as speech prostheses enabling nonhumans to participate in discussions with humans (Latour, PN 67; Despret, "Becomings"). Inadvertently, my leaving the car windows open set up an experiment in which this particular blue darner's actions could express a proposition about its concerns and my relation to them. Turning to or doing research can function as a speech prosthesis as one entertains propositions: as I remembered what I had read about dragonflies—that they are fast and agile fliers due to their nearly 360-degree field of vision and ability to move their four wings independently—I realized that dragonflies didn't always need my help.

The three encounters I turn to next demonstrate in more detail how the three habits of listening play out in encounters between humans and nonhuman others. In each, the humans assume that there are particular creatures they can listen to through emotional, physical, and cognitive attunement; various speech prostheses; and carefully designed experiments. The encounters also demonstrate that listening to others requires nonconscious attunement as much as conscious intention and that persuasion occurs through entertaining new possibilities that arise in the prehensive unity of the encounter.

First, an encounter with a thing, a technology.[12] In discussing how Michael Chorost became attuned to his cochlear implant, Glen Mazis notes that a breakthrough came when Chorost was talking on the phone to his mother, which he had been avoiding because he hadn't been able to understand what he was hearing. Chorost reports, "I was understanding her. Believing that I could do it seemed to be half the battle. That let me extend myself into the sound and let it sink into me" (99; qtd. in Mazis 66). Mazis attributes the change not primarily to the way Chorost's brain was restructuring itself in response to the implant but to his changed attitude: "As he started to have positive experiences with his new implant, Chorost made the call to his mother ... believing there was something for him to hear" (66).

Mazis draws on Merleau-Ponty's ideas about attuned perception to explain Chorost's growing ability to attend to his implant. Like Fiumara, he emphasizes the active nature of human listening, but also the activity of the ecology in which all are entangled. "When we 'pay attention' . . . we are not throwing an inert, indifferent 'searchlight' onto the scene about us. We are actively looking at something that promises to mean something for us. . . . In some way, whatever we perceive 'beckons' to us and is therefore an invitation to enter a dialogue with the promise of further meaning" (64–65). The data coming from a cochlear implant are as much an invitation as a rhetor's words to which we may pay attention or not.

But Mazis goes on to explain that fully conscious, intentful consciousness is not what is needed. Chorost discovered that while listening to the radio as he drove, he could understand what was being said only when he wasn't explicitly focused on trying to make sense of it. Mazis refers this phenomenon to Merleau-Ponty's concept of embodied understanding, in which the body attunes itself to its environment as a gestalt "which reflects our felt and habitual relationships" (67) and which dissipates when it is focused on. He says that in addition to believing in the promise of meaning in perception, "we have to let our attention be captured, not willed. We have to open to the world as a partner in dialogue that has to be given space to form." Its meaning cannot be "wrestled into our grasp" (67). Being open to the world—or things or beings in it—as a partner in dialogue and giving that dialogue space to form meaning is part of what I am getting at in saying we need to pay attention to the specific being, letting it be in itself, as Heidegger says. Mazis alludes to Heidegger in saying "this 'letting be' of the surround is . . . a matter of modifying the will or ego" (68). It is also what a good teacher I know is doing with her students when she says to them, "Can you say more about that?" The difference lies in being open to the world, as Mazis says, rather than listening from one's own space of meaning.

Attunement leads to openness to possibilities largely through emotional attachment to aspects of the environment, feelings "that make us oriented and connected to phenomena in different ways that will enable us to know them in different ways" (Mazis 68). Mazis notes that through Chorost's earlier experience with hearing aids and with the implant, he realized that "to become able to hear with the potential that the machine provide[s] him, 'I would have to become emotionally open to what I heard'" (78; qtd. in Mazis 69). Mazis comments, "To experience the way machines can open parts of the world to humanity and become more kin to us will require an emotional relatedness to things of which they can become a part" (69). But I also argue that paying attention to the machines we interact with in ways that allow us to grasp the possibilities they offer depends on our feeling a connection with them and respecting them as specific things in themselves. Chorost not only became emotionally open to the people he interacted with but also more open to the implant. His initial fear of how his body and life would be changed by the implant was replaced by a more positive attitude toward the different reality it offered (Mazis 61–62).

Donna Haraway also argues that attunement is a matter of respect and "becoming with": "To knot companion and species together in encounter, in regard and respect, is to enter the world of becoming with, where *who and what are* is precisely what is at stake" (*When* 19). She uses the term *respecere* to convey the many aspects of this relationship, which she contrasts with the "gaze" that is the focus of much cultural theory: "to have regard for, to see differently, to esteem, to look back, to hold in regard, to hold in seeing, to be touched by another's regard, to heed, to take care of. This kind of regard aims to release and be released in oxymoronic, necessary, autonomy-in-relation" (164). Haraway notes that companion species "is a permanently undecidable category, a category-in-question that insists on the relation as the smallest unit of being and of analysis" (165). The relation, the encounter, is the focus of attention both in Haraway's notion and in Whitehead's related notion of the unity of a prehension. As Whitehead says, "Our whole experience is composed out of our relationships to the rest of things, and of the formation of new relationships constitutive of things to come" (MT 31).

Respect and regard are not only essential to the habit of paying attention to the specific individual but also, as Haraway argues, to how entities are changed in the unity of prehension, how they "become with," transform and become persuaded in the encounter. Her example is her experience of agility training with her dog Cayenne, which she says depends on a dialogue of response between the real, specific human and the real, specific dog. She observes, "Training is for opening up what is not known to be possible, but might be for all the intra-acting partners" (*When* 223). Respect and regard open up possibilities through paying attention to the specific other emotionally and physically as well as cognitively.

Haraway says she learned about *respecere* from her relationship with her father. Not surprisingly, families are one place habits are acquired, and the encounter I turn to next also begins in a daughter-father relationship. Julie Zickefoose, a bird artist and wild bird rehabilitator, acknowledges her father in the preface to *The Bluebird Effect* by remembering him encouraging her to pat a tom turkey's head: "I still remember the jolt of pure empathy that coursed through me upon laying my hand on the bird's bare head. . . . The warmth of his skin awakened something deep and primal, a realization that, despite his bizarre appearance and feathered armor, there was someone in there, someone I could understand" (ix). Zickefoose's assumption that there is someone in there when she intra-acts with animals underpins all her writing. Her description of raising orphaned hummingbirds illustrates not only the importance of the habit of assuming that creaturely others may desire to be listened to and the habit of emotional connection with specific individuals but also of finding new styles of listening.

Presented one July day with two sets of unfledged hummingbirds whose nests had been blown down in a storm, Zickefoose quickly learned to identify each of them by their behavior and subsequently named them. "Naming them honors their distinct personalities, proclivities, and idiosyncrasies," she says (79). She is often surprised by the way their behavior contradicts her beliefs about what hummingbirds can do. When she releases them from the aviary, they return and importune her for feedings for ten days, though the literature suggests that they should be independent at this stage. She is also happily surprised that, despite her earlier fears, she doesn't have to climb up to their high perches to feed them. She comments, "There is so much more going on in their tiny heads than I give them credit for" (71) and concludes:

> They know me, know my voice, my names for them. They have observed that I can't fly up to them as their own mother would, and they have the sense to come down to eye level to be fed.... They listen for my voice in the house and come to the window where they can watch me. They peep and I call back; they beg and I feed them. They regard me as their mother, a strange, huge, earthbound, flightless mother, but a source of sustenance and even comfort.... It is knowing what they know that utterly beguiles me, that has me humming with joy along the invisible lines that connect us. (84)

How does Zickefoose come to know what "her" hummingbirds know? She assumes that listening to them is possible. She understands them by responding to them as specific individuals in a specific situation. And in addition, she also has the habit of finding ways to let them become interesting.

She employs a variety of "speech prostheses" that enable her to listen to them and that enable them to become interesting. She reads the scientific literature about them, but instead of being blinded by what she has read and by her assumptions—focusing on what everyone knows hummingbirds are—she pays attention to what these particular hummingbirds are capable of, what propositions they offer. Her intra-actions with the hummingbirds fit with Despret's understanding of polite experiments as a practice of domestication that proposes new ways to behave that transform both entities involved. Despret notes that "an intelligent animal may provide an opportunity for the 'becoming' intelligent of the ethologist who observes it" ("Body" 132n8). Zickefoose's joy at knowing what they know demonstrates how allowing nonhumans to become interesting leads not only to new possibilities but also to wonder. At the end of *Modes of Thought*, Whitehead says, "When philosophic thought has done its best, the wonder remains. There have been added, however, some grasp of the immensity of things, some purification of emotion by understanding" (168–69). Like Whitehead, Zickefoose believes that by due attention more can be found in nature than that which has been observed at first sight: "Whatever is going on, I know that I will never be through learning about how birds' minds work" (88).

Polite scientific experiments are one way of listening to others, functioning as speech prostheses enabling humans to understand others on their own terms. Latour asks, "Who is better able than scientists to make the world speak, write, hold forth?" (PN 137). As he describes further skills of listening that scientists use—making it possible "to shift viewpoints constantly by means of experiments, instruments, models, and theories"; "imagining possibilities"; and composing and sheltering knowledge "in forms of life, instruments, paradigms, teachings, bodily skills, black boxes" (PN 138–40)—it becomes clear that these are practices that researchers in all disciplines use. He explicitly connects them with the discipline of sociology, for instance, in *Reassembling the Social*, where he explains to a graduate student that experimental description requires "very specific texts" and "very specific protocols" (RS 155). These ways of listening, whether in an actual laboratory, in the field, or in a written text, are also ways of engaging in persuasion.[13]

The third encounter I offer is of the geochemist Bill Green who combines wonder with very specific protocols of investigation in his study of Antarctic lakes. There are humans like Green who do pay due attention to the material world: many natural scientists are fascinated and persuaded by nonhuman others. In this case, Green was persuaded by the element of cobalt.[14] He encountered cobalt in one of the lakes in the Dry Valleys, and it presented him with a proposition: "In Vanda, something seems to be removing the metals from the oxygen-rich shallow waters and releasing them to the oxygen-poor deep waters" (149–50).

Green attends to cobalt by engaging it in a procedure that allows it to become interesting.[15] One of his colleagues suggests that manganese might be involved in the behavior of cobalt, so Green collects water samples at different depths in the lake and transports them back to his lab in Ohio where he uses an automatic sampler and a graphite furnace to analyze the amount of cobalt and manganese present in the different water samples. His handling of the samples, both in their collecting and analysis, evinces respect: he describes his obsession with the purity of the samples, his exactitude in setting up the autosampler and its interface with the computer that translated the analyses into a graph relating the depth of the water to the concentration of cobalt and manganese. He comments on how the instruments repeated the analysis of each sample in triplicate: "It was working, but I couldn't watch. I was too nervous" (163). When at last he looked at the graph, he found that "point for point, the curve for cobalt analysis matched the curve for manganese. Matched it to a T. Where the dissolved manganese was low, so too was the cobalt. Where the manganese rose, in response to the disappearance of oxygen, so too did the cobalt. . . . The story was beginning to write itself" (163). Green's intra-action with the cobalt allows it to tell this story: In the spring, with water rushing in rising rivers, cobalt is set free into the lake where it is captured by manganese oxide adhering to a piece of clay. "The cobalt transferred from water to stone, perhaps oxidized even, an electron transferred in the wink of an eye . . . from the cobalt to the manganese," it sinks, "and in the oxygen-poor waters the manganese is reduced, falls away, unravels like a thread. The atom of cobalt is free again, waterbound." If it encounters a few organic cells, it is captured again through the process of chelation and sinks into the sediments at the bottom of the lake. The intra-action also allows Green to listen intelligently: "But even buried you can hear it, you can hear the cobalt. Like the salt plains, you can hear it sing" (159–60).

As I said earlier, propositions are not essentially linguistic. Latour says, "Propositions . . . do not pertain to language but to the world" ("Well-Intentioned" 373). But unlike statements, he says, "the notion of propositions allows things to be loaded into words. Whereas a statement implies the existence of a talkative human surrounded by mute things, a proposition implies that we are made to speak in this way *by what* is talked about" ('Well-Articulated" 374). The respectful attention Green paid to cobalt warrants his response to the proposition the cobalt expresses. As he says, in the analysis, the story writes itself.

The dragonfly I encountered expressed a proposition: it offered me a relationship, a perspective, that I became attentive to as something that mattered. The impact of the proposition was amplified by the social environment made up of my articulated memories of past experiences of dragonflies and of reading about them. It induced me to speculate about how it mattered, which brought to mind memories of my helping newly hatched snapping turtles across the road and into the slough, and of how my help was sometimes not helpful. This is how the dragonfly persuaded me—offered me a new possibility—that humans are not always the best means of securing the survival of others. And this is also how cobalt persuaded Green of something similar, that "in every lake and ocean, in every parcel of atmosphere, there is a cleansing that tempers the Earth. . . . Metals pour into the lake, but the lake removes them" (256). The cobalt in Lake Vanda offered Green a proposition. Its disappearance mattered to him; it changed his perspective on lakes, disrupting his beliefs. The impact of the proposition was amplified by his memory of reading about chemical bonds in Linus Pauling's book that his mother gave him in high school; by reading a related study concerning the Laurentian shield in Canada; by discussions with colleagues over the ten years he was working in Antarctica; by Pablo Neruda's poem "Ode to Salt" that he alludes to at the end of the story. He was struck with the intense feeling of unrealized possibilities, and of the entangled consequences that follow. In his musing on what he learned in the Dry Valleys, Green echoes Whitehead's claim that the feeling of unrealized possibilities is what's important in human life. Green says, "What is beyond is all, but what is beyond is hinted at, is eternally present, in what is here—in the swift river and the fierce wind, in the glass, in the ice. It is as though we were destined to wonderment and to praise" (270).

Successful Persuasion

All the encounters I have discussed so far, including the one between me and the dragonfly, have focused on a dyad of human and nonhuman entities, though each was also entangled in a wider ecology. The next encounter I will discuss is more complicated, involving an intra-action among three disparate groups of humans in Indonesia, entangled in the social and political and natural environments that amplify the effects of the propositions they entertained. The encounter exhibits the same habits of listening: the groups believe they can listen to each other, they attend to each other as specific individuals in specific times and places, and they employ a variety of ways of listening. But this encounter also highlights how conflicts can be resolved through respecting different commitments rather than striving for consensus. Anna Lowenhaupt Tsing, from whom I draw this example, notes that the encounter suggests "other political avenues" for bringing about change than those of progressive activists, who "spend most of their time either searching for seamless consensus or making a point of their irreconcilable differences" (*Friction* 262). She argues that the "friction" of differences is often what produces productive collaborations among disparate groups in this global world. Ethical persuasion, too, as a matter of politely modifying dreams, is more often successful in bringing about changes than seamless consensus or steadfast agonism.

I have argued that creatures are agents in their actions, but they are not the subjects of persuasion. Instead subjects (and objects) emerge in events of persuasion, specific phenomena of novel becoming arising from the entanglement of some "parts" of the material world. Brian Massumi says that the fundamental assumption of the "activist philosophy" of William James and Whitehead is "something's happening," and that something is an event that makes a difference (1). Difference and becoming are at the heart of the understanding of persuasion I am arguing for here, and they are exemplified in Tsing's account of the intra-actions of three groups in the Meratus Mountains of South Kalimantan: nature lovers, environmental activists, and village leaders. Tsing observes that despite each group's "rather different kind of commitment to nature," the project was successful, "at least for a while, in establishing a landscape removed from corporate destruction because it could be considered a community-managed forest" (*Friction* 246). Tsing describes their work as a "collaboration with friction at its heart" (246).[16]

The nature lovers were students at the provincial university who became interested in the culture and life of the Dayak people who lived in the forests the students regularly went hiking in. When they heard that a timbering company had begun operations in the Manggur village lands, their organization, Kompas Borneo, took the issue to the national environmental advocacy group, Wahana Lingkungan Hidup Indonesia (WALHI), at a meeting in the provincial capital. They brought men from Manggur to the meeting to speak, and members of WALHI subsequently went to Manggur and met with employees of the timber company. After this meeting, the regional government did not renew the timber concession and the forest returned to local management. Kompas Borneo emerged as able defenders of the villagers' rights to their traditional lands, which helped the organization get a grant from the Ford Foundation to support their further research in the village. Their presentation of the village in their grant proposal reflected their stance as intermediaries between the villagers and national policies, characterizing the Manggur alternatively as a "wise community that lives with and manages nature" and a primitive people in need of modernization.

WALHI also saw Manggur as a traditional community, but focused instead on its "long-established land and resource rights," which were being abrogated by the loggers. Unlike Kompas Borneo, WALHI was not particularly concerned with what happened in Manggur but rather with how the conflict contributed to their efforts to develop policies and strategies in line with their view of the conflict as a struggle between grassroots communities and corporate foresters in Indonesia. They saw the resolution of the conflict between the timber company and the villagers simply as evidence of how grassroots advocacy can work.

The Dayak people had a sharply contrasting understanding of their community and its relation to the forest. They saw themselves neither as WALHI's community "united by rational resource planning" nor as Kompas Borneo's "community united by traditional ritual" (256). In fact, they did not experience themselves as united by much of anything, interacting rather in a fluid network of family groups "continually reshuffling their social ties and geographical locations" (257) in response to ecological cycles of growth, harvesting, and regeneration and interrelational histories. Tsing says, "The forest landscape is not just managed by social networks or a model for them; it is simultaneously the shaper of social networks and the material through which they are shaped" (257).

Stories told about the encounter by two of the village leaders, a brother and a sister, demonstrate how they understood the conflict not as about saving the forest but rather as a struggle over resources. The sister relates that the timber company was complaining that the villagers were clearing swiddens in the timber concession causing the forest to revert to grasslands. She remarks, "If [the timber company] had not complained, we would never have gotten involved; they could have kept cutting for ten years" (259). She went to the District Office and the governor and finally to Forestry Department officials, whom she asked for a map of the concession. The map showed that the company was logging in the wrong place; the logging moved to an adjoining district; and, with her village's regained ability to cut swiddens where they chose, she declared the conflict resolved. In a different account of the resolution, the brother complained that the timber company was cutting fruit and honey trees and rattan that his village relied on. He describes going to President Suharto who, he says, backed him up, returning the land to the village. A document issued in the brother's name offers an interpretation of the victory in "a serious mimicry of authoritative rhetoric": "We, the people of Manggur, are indigenous people who protect the environment with our traditional culture. We will consider any offense against the environment to be an offense against our human rights" (260).

The varied stories of the success of the project reflect the different commitments of the groups and individuals. Tsing notes that such collaborative efforts "draw groups into common projects at the same time as they allow them to maintain separate agendas" (246). Collaborations, she says, "bring misunderstandings into the core of an alliance," making "new objects and agents possible" (247). The community-managed forest emerged as a new object. The students through their engagement in the issue became agents of environmentalism. A number of propositions arose in this encounter, eliciting varying responses and, elaborated by the specifics of the sociopolitical situation in Indonesia, sending ripples up to national and global levels. The Dayak people's regaining access to important resources offered a proposition elaborated in the brother's statement, supported by governmental rhetoric, that his people's control of their environment was a question of human rights, which in turn caused Manggur to become "a real village, . . . the kind of village other people imagine" (260). The proposition rippled up to the national level where WALHI elaborated it into an argument that grassroots advocacy is necessary to combat corporate foresters, and to the international level where it became allied with the Ford Foundation's community-based natural resource management program.

Tsing says that "one of the most striking things about the [community-managed forest] campaign is the fact that the varied, and equally satisfied, protagonists never came to any agreement about what happened" (246), and she argues that "it succeeded in part because no one stopped to realize the depth of their disagreements" (247). If one understands persuasion as a matter of changing individual hearts and minds, one would conclude that there is no persuasion in this situation. But persuasion in the everyday world, as Stengers says, more often takes the form of "constructions among humans as constrained by diverging attachments" ("Ecology" 193). Tsing argues that collaborations like these are more successful in bringing about changes than efforts to reach agreement. I suggest that persuasion that respects commitments and invites interlocutors to consider what is required by the commitments and beliefs they hold are also more successful.

As discussed earlier, Stengers believes that polite modification of dreams "cannot be produced by discursive argumentation [which] . . . is ruled by the fiction of the everybody or the anyone—'everybody should agree that . . . ,' 'anyone should accept this or that consequence . . .'" ("Ecology" 194). Offering diplomacy as a figure of persuasion that acknowledges and respects difference, she argues, "Diplomacy does not refer to good will, togetherness, a common language or an intersubjective understanding" (193) but rather to belonging that imposes obligations that must be addressed "as [they] diverge . . . rather than posing insulting questions" (184). The insulting questions framed by the fiction of the everybody or anyone are based in an understanding of truth rejected by diplomatic intra-action, as Stengers explains: "What is true [instead] is what succeeds in producing a communication between diverging parties, without anything in common being discovered or advanced. Each party will indeed keep its own version of the agreement; just as in the famous example given by Deleuze of a 'noce contre nature' (unnatural coupling) of the wasp and the orchid, we get no wasp-orchid unity. Wasps and orchids give each quite other meanings to the relation which was produced between them" (194).

In the same way, the diverse groups in Indonesia each gave quite different meanings to the resolution of their conflict. Stengers says that this "diplomatic achievement" is "the production of a new proposition, articulating what was a contradiction." "Such an achievement," she says, "the slight modification in the formulation of some obligations derived from an attachment, does not result in any final convergence overcoming a preceding divergence. The articulation is always a local one. There is no general opening of the border" (193). Polite persuasion does not aim to change attachments, for when differences in attachments are respected new meanings as well as new agents and objects and behaviors can emerge.

I will conclude by offering one last example of polite persuasion. Highly successful in persuading a grieving and angry crowd not to riot, Robert Kennedy's speech to a largely black crowd in Indianapolis on the night of Martin Luther King's assassination exemplifies the effectiveness of ethical persuasion. The *New York Times*, on the fiftieth anniversary of the speech, noted that it has been "hailed as one of the great political orations of the late 20th century" and that it "has been credited with diffusing tensions in Indianapolis," which escaped the riots that erupted in Washington, Chicago, and Baltimore and a hundred other cities around the country (Stack). Its success has been attributed to Kennedy's ethos, a credibility with black people derived from his "progressive politics and history of personal tragedy" (Stack). But I see it as a habit that he exercised in the speech, not something that he simply possessed. As did Pericles in his oration and Barack Obama in his speech on race in Philadelphia in 2008, Kennedy believed his audience was capable of considering a new possible response.

Kennedy heard of King's assassination as he was boarding a plane to Indianapolis where he was scheduled to speak at a campaign rally in what was considered one of the city's worst neighborhoods. The mayor, Richard Lugar, and the chief of police as well as his campaign aides recommended he cancel his appearance, that it would be too dangerous: many in the crowd knew King had been killed and were taunting whites, and gang members were bent on violence. One gang member later said, "They kill Martin Luther, and we was ready to move" (qtd. in Margolick). On the way to the rally, Kennedy scribbled notes on a pad, but he spoke extemporaneously, the notes held crumpled in his hand. He began by asking those holding campaign signs to put them away, and he said, "I have some very sad news for all of you and I think sad news for all of our fellow citizens and people who love peace all over the world, and that is that Martin Luther King was shot and was killed tonight in Memphis." After the gasps and wails died down, he continued, saying that King "dedicated his life to love and to justice between fellow human beings. He died in the cause of that effort." But then he offered a choice, very much like the choice Obama offered in Philadelphia: Kennedy said:

> In this difficult day, in this difficult time for the United States, it's perhaps well to ask what kind of a nation we are and what direction we want to move in. For those of you who are black—considering the evidence evidently is that there were white people who were responsible—you can be filled with bitterness and with hatred and a desire for revenge. We can move in that direction as a country, in greater polarization—black people amongst blacks, and white amongst whites, filled with hatred toward one another. Or we can make an effort, as Martin Luther King did, to understand and to comprehend, and replace that violence, that stain of bloodshed that has spread across our land, with an effort to understand and compassion and love.

Offering a choice is an invitation, an act that allows the audience to decide for themselves, even if the reference to King's effort urges them to choose what King would do. But then Kennedy added a statement that startled and silenced his audience: "For those of you who are black and are tempted to be filled with hatred and distrust of the injustice of such an act, against all white people, I would only say that I can also feel in my own heart the same kind of feeling. I had a member of my family killed, but he was killed by a white man." It was the first time Kennedy had mentioned in public the assassination of his brother five years earlier. Civil rights leader and U.S. congressman John Lewis, who was present at the speech, said of Kennedy's statement, "To do it that night was an incredibly powerful and connective and emotionally honest gesture" (qtd. in Tye 411). Kennedy's expression of his own pain, emphasized by the quote from Aeschylus that followed—"Even in our sleep, pain which cannot forget falls drop by drop upon the heart until, in our own despair, against our will, comes wisdom through the awful grace of God"—resonated with the pain of those grieving King, especially in light of the deep affection and respect in which they held both Kennedy brothers. It was not an attempt at empathy and more than a pathetic appeal; as Davis says about Freud's "suggestive influence," it recovers a new version of pathos, "except that this version involves not an emotional appeal but an immediate affection, a kind of 'mimetico-affective contagion'" (*Inessential Solidarity* 33; quoting Borch-Jacobson 67). It was a proposition, a lure for feeling that can be entertained by the listeners in their own various ways. Bobby Kennedy speaking of his feelings at his brother's assassination invited his audience to consider what they too might be capable of. A gang member was quoted as saying, "After he spoke we couldn't get nowhere" (Margolick).

Like Obama, Kennedy framed the choice he offered as a choice for all of us, and he returned to it at the end of his brief speech adding, as Pericles did, a comment that evinced his trust in what the people of the United States are capable of: "We can do well in this country. We will have difficult times. . . . But the vast majority of white people and the vast majority of black people in this country want to live together, want to improve the quality of our life, and want justice for all human beings that abide in our land." These remarks were followed by applause and cheers. What was so persuasive in Kennedy's speech was his respect for and trust in his audience, a trust in their capability and their desire to live together in peace and justice—not that necessarily they would do it, but he believed that they could. It's not good manners or tolerance or empathy or understanding that makes ethical persuasion polite, but reciprocity, respect, and trust.

Persuasion is successful when interlocutors are themselves changed, unconsciously and consciously. In the intra-action that night in Indianapolis, both Kennedy and the people listening and responding to him changed, and in various ways. Not all persuasion is successful, though when interlocutors won't or don't or can't listen, persuasion usually fails. Ethical persuasion works as Michel Foucault's power relationship does, when the other is addressed as a person who acts and when a whole field of responses and possibilities opens up ("Subject" 220). Persuasion requires reciprocity: all interlocutors act; all speak and listen and respond. And persuasion requires respect for and trust in interlocutors' responses, reactions, and inventions so that deliberations will be continuously renewed, not ending in silence, frustration, or resistance.

Conclusion

Good Writing Is Well Made

At the beginning of this book, I said that writing matters because it is the way we make things that are meaningful to and have important effects on ourselves and others and on the world as a whole. It is because writing always has real effects on others, because it always changes the world by creating new possibilities, that writing is essentially ethical. Inspired by my understanding of enchantment ontology, especially its "worldly ethics" as enunciated by Karen Barad, Donna Haraway, Stuart Kauffman, Isabelle Stengers, and Alfred North Whitehead, I have proposed that writing ethically entails developing habits of paying attention to the relationalities of becoming and always entertaining the possibility that "what everyone knows"—and what you believe—might be wrong. Barad says, "Intra-acting responsibly as part of the world means taking account of the entangled phenomena that are intrinsic to the world's vitality and being responsive to the possibilities that might help us flourish" (Barad 396). Writing well requires developing habits as active dispositions to pay due attention to all the creatures in the world, reaching out to grasp the world in a way that still lets creatures become through their own decisions. Habits are ethical ways of acting. They are practices of *hexis*, an active having-and-holding that depends on paying attention to differences and embracing them as engendering propositions that can lead to new possibilities. Making and persuasion are also ethical actions. Defined with reference to Joseph Dunne's phronetic technē, making is a determinate shaping through intra-action that confers value and meaning. Ethical persuasion depends on paying attention to the specific presences of others, not putting oneself in the other's place, not naming the other, not assuming that one can understand the other.

Here in the conclusion, I address more directly—but still briefly—how the concepts of enchanted writing might be enacted in the design and teaching of writing courses.¹ Because writing that is well made is writing that matters, the primary goals of writing courses are to help students find something that is important to them, that offers propositions they are impelled to explore, and to encourage them in ethical habits of well-made writing. I also address here how my theory of enchanted writing intra-acts with my practice of teaching. The persuasive strategies in the speeches of Pericles, Barack Obama, and Bobby Kennedy that I analyzed in chapters 6 and 7 made me think about teaching also as a practice of ethical persuasion, of polite invitations that do not require students to relinquish their holds on their experience, beliefs, and values but invite them to become writers. This idea, augmented by my recent encounter with Rasha Diab's analysis of Muḥammad Anwar al-Sādāt's speech to the Israeli Knesset, led me to explore further the educative function of epideictic rhetoric. As Chaim Perelman observed in considering how to distinguish between education and propaganda, "In this respect, the speaker engaged in epidictic discourse is very close to being an educator" (Perelman and Olbrechts-Tyteca 52). Jeffrey Walker observes that "epideictic is definable, in larger terms, as argument directed toward the establishment, reconfirmation, or revision of general values and beliefs" ("Aristotle's Lyric" 7)—and in my teaching of writing, as well as in this book, I am interested in revising beliefs about the value of writing. Walker also suggests that epideictic discourse operates as an invitation: "Epideictic argument *invites* its listener/'spectator' . . . to an act of contemplation, evaluation, and judgment" (8; emphasis added).² I strive to teach writing in a way that invites students to become writers who make meanings that matter, meanings that have real effects, and I trust them to develop habits that will enable them to do that well.

Writing well is not just making texts but making meaningful things like facts and inquiries. Like all makers, writers work with materials (experiential perceptions and feelings) and with tools (language, images, sounds). They never work alone, but always in intra-action with materials and tools and with other creatures (which include all kinds of creations, like dragonflies and environmental organizations and Antarctic lakes). Writing—making an inquiry, for example—is very much like making a table. On the home renovation series *Fixer Upper*, the interior designer Joanna Gaines often elicits the help of a furniture maker to supply an important piece she wants to add to the design. Clint has made a lot of tables for her. The tables have been important in a variety of ways: one was for a children's playroom that was a priority for the grandparent homeowners; one was to be made from wood from an old table that belonged to the father of the homeowner; several were made with wood that Clint found important so had reclaimed from various local sources. Jo and Clint work together with these materials (designs, feelings, and wood) in elaborating how they are important: they decide it is a table they want to make and what kind of table while taking into account their own feelings about the design of the house and the features of the wood and their responses to the homeowners' desires and experiences and the projected uses of the table and many other things. As Tim Ingold says, they correspond in answering to the materials, mixing "the movements of [their] sentient awareness with the flows and currents of animate life" (M 108). Ingold calls this the essence of making. This is also the essence of writing, a making inspired by a feeling arising in intra-action that something is important and carried out though finding out how and to whom it is important.

Krista Ratcliffe describes a student's work in her class that is a good example of well-made writing. She says that Rachel "put rhetorical listening into action" by noticing a connection between a discussion of parole in her criminology class and a discussion of Toni Morrison's *Beloved* in her literature class. "By laying [them] in front of her and letting them lie there," [she] was attempting to invent topics and arguments for her second essay; hence . . . employing rhetorical listening as a *trope for interpretive invention*" (Ratcliffe 43). Connecting experiences through patterns is one of the habits of making I have proposed, but I understand the effect of that habit not as leading automatically to the invention of topics and arguments but as inspiring a feeling of importance and offering a proposition. Rachel begins her email to Ratcliffe: "Hi! Something 'strange' just occurred, and I was wondering if I could bounce it off you because the oddity of the situation just intrigues me" (Ratcliffe 41). She describes how the guest speaker in her criminology class talked about paroling prisoners who have been kept in high security/maximum prisons using the metaphor of letting a dog off a chain, which she says "shares a striking similarity with the words that the schoolteacher says to his nephew [in *Beloved*] about breaking Sethe, as well as having a connection to the idea of people as animals" (42). She says that she had planned on writing about something else, but that "now this just seems completely interesting. . . . I just find this similarity too shocking to let it go" (42). Rachel clearly found the similarity between the guest speaker's talk about prisoners and the passage in *Beloved* to be very important—strange, intriguing, striking, completely interesting, shocking—especially so to her since she was hoping for a career in the penal system.

Rachel's writing, just like Jo and Clint's table making, starts in a feeling of importance. Importance is a decision to focus on something against the backdrop of the matter-of-fact, mere existence. It is "a value experience . . . here is something that matters" (Whitehead, MT 116). But though it is an affective experience, importance is not merely individual, not just what matters to the writer. It is an apprehension of holistic value, value to self, others, and the future (117–18), for "importance, limited to a finite individual occasion, ceases to be important" (20). Encouraged by Ratcliffe to continue with her idea, Rachel considered *how* the connection she saw was important, thus elaborating its importance. The experience of the two classes offered her a proposition: what if we have been treating prisoners like slaves, like animals? Entertaining this proposition, asking how it matters, is what leads her to look for answers, to making an inquiry. She notes that despite his metaphor, the guest speaker clearly does not believe in dehumanization, and she observes that "a practice often lasts for a long time after the theory which inspired it has lost its hold" (44). She observes that the practice of slavery contradicts the founding principles of our country and still lingers in the present. And she concludes that "the dehumanization of any person . . . and large groups of people over long periods of time is wrong" (45). But still a question lingers. She ends the paper by musing: "It seems that white 'rule-abiding' society could be suffering from fear. They could be worried that both criminals and blacks are inherently no different from themselves, and with that as a fact, how do they make themselves feel superior? . . . The question is: why do we need to feel superior? What does this say about us? What have we become?" (45). Rachel told Ratcliffe when she handed the paper in that she had wanted to answer these questions but she could not because they were too new to her. But as an inquiry, her paper is still successful. The questions she asks, generated as she entertained the proposition that we have been treating prisoners and slaves like animals for a long time, articulate a new possibility that matters to her and potentially to others. The questions are specific: if people fear there is no difference between slaves and prisoners and themselves, how have they made themselves feel superior? And why do we (all of us) need to feel superior? Many other possible questions could have arisen from this "what if" proposition. Writing comes from someplace, but it also takes you places. Well-made writing is an adventure of ideas, and it doesn't often end with a firm conclusion. There is always more to know. As Ratcliffe says, "Rhetorical listening maps new possibilities for interpretive invention" (46).

Deciding that something is important is a good place to start writing. As I began designing and teaching first-year writing classes as a graduate student, I very quickly focused on what was then called prewriting, "the initial and crucial stage of the writing process," "the stage of discovery in the writing process when a person transforms a 'subject' into his own categories" (Rohman and Wlecke 12, 13). I also quickly abandoned the methods associated with prewriting (brainstorming, heuristics), and though I still believe in some sense that prewriting is the "crucial stage of the writing process," I don't believe it is a stage, nor would I call it *prewriting*. It's just writing, the crucial part of which is the intra-action with other creatures, tools, and materials, an activity that goes on throughout any writing experience. It's an activity that could possibly be called discovery, but I think of it as making. Writing in this sense, if done ethically, through the habits of I have proposed, is well-made. So then, how does one teach writing with this focus? Though this is the back of the book, I caution that The Answers are not here—just some examples of what I have done.

In an essay entitled "The Answers Are Not in the Back of the Book," I described a first-year writing course that I taught at Michigan Technological University that exemplifies my approach. The course was grounded in Herbert Marcuse's *One-Dimensional Man*, a critique of the technological society. As the majority of the students at Michigan Tech are planning to be engineers, I thought that reading and discussing and writing about this book would engage them, that in responding to it they would find something important that they felt they had to write about. Marcuse's ideas were certainly important to them: they were outraged. Why are we reading a book by a Marxist who hates technology? they asked. (Michigan Tech students also tend to be conservative in their political views.) I told them that Marcuse presents a theory in his book and that theories help us think about things in new ways. I told them that when you encounter a theory, the most useful response is not to ask whether it is true or correct but rather to ask questions like, How does this work? And, If this is true, what follows? I said these were the kind of questions I would be asking them to ask and answer in their reading and writing for the course. They were not happy about this either. Early on, one student wrote in a response, "The answers to this class are not in the back of the book. Or for that matter within the text either. This makes it very hard to get a firm concept to write about" (65).

Finding a firm concept to write about is definitely not what I had in mind for them to do in the course. Their outrage and unhappiness was cheering to me: they recognized that they were being challenged to write differently. And, as with Ratcliffe's student Rachel, my students' prospective careers were at stake in engaging with Marcuse's argument that technology, rather than enhancing life, perverts social values and denies to individuals the freedom to choose their own goals. It challenged their vision of themselves as society's problem solvers. As the term progressed, instead of finding a firm concept to write about, they struggled with their feeling that some of Marcuse's Marxist ideas made sense to them. "Jim" wrote in the computer conference: "The material base for domination, as Marcuse speaks of, I feel is the profit motive. . . . Cutting production costs, marketing a variety of products, and selling goods actually needed or not needed, all seem to play into the hands of making money." "Phil" responded, "I like what [Jim] wrote a lot. I've been trying to defend everything that you have been cutting down. But now I guess I see whats wrong. . . . American society always wants more, and more and more" (86–87).³ ("Phil" had been most outspoken in his rejection of all of Marcuse's ideas.) Another student found Marcuse's argument that competition isn't always good useful in explaining what he had found in his research on genetic engineering: "Competition makes transplants and other highly technical operations only available to those who can afford them. . . . Competition for these rare organs and for the highly trained doctors makes it extremely difficult, expensive, and requires a substantial amount of time to wait for an organ" (88). What pleased me in these responses is not that the students were adopting Marcuse's ideas. Instead, I saw them developing a habit of centered flexibility,⁴ modifying beliefs they valued without being afraid of losing hold, willing to consider Marcuse's ideas and use them to modify and support their own.

Helping students find something that is important to them to write about has been the primary goal of my designs for writing courses, but I also have been committed to enabling them to learn habits of writing well. Teaching writing is about guiding individual behavior, not about transmitting information either about the "subject" addressed in the course or about the principles of writing. As Joseph Dunne said, teaching a technai "must involve the apprentice *technitai* in a process where they work with their materials and have the teacher at hand to point out mistakes and to suggest ways forward toward mastery" (320). Because habits do not become habits until they become habitual, become ingrained in bodily dispositions rather than residing in abstract rules, I don't try to directly teach habits. I design courses so that students will be engaged in activities in which habits of writing well will become useful, I draw their attention to habits they are developing, and I make occasional suggestions.

I told students in the Marcuse course that writers depend on discussing ideas with colleagues and friends, and so to learn how to do this they would get a lot of practice in discussing Marcuse's ideas with each other. They were required to write weekly on a computer conference discussing Marcuse's ideas and their research projects. In the classroom, they also discussed Marcuse's ideas and their research projects in groups in which I did not participate. Other than what I said on the first day about what questions to ask when responding to a theory, I did not tell them how to discuss Marcuse's ideas. Nor did I lecture on Marcuse or even explain any of his ideas in any detail. They found this "frustrating": one student commented, "She would not always give you an answer to your Quesitons. She would more often than not answer your question with another question" (85). In truly peer discussions, where the teacher's participation is minimized, students are more likely to see themselves as responsible for the ideas that are discussed and the way the discussion proceeds and they come to see how other people's ideas can help them. Confronted with difficult ideas that their instructor would not explain, they learned to ask questions and hazard answers and to make and criticize hypotheses because these practices helped them make their writing better.

I did occasionally offer suggestions in class and on the computer conference designed to encourage particular habits. On the computer conference, I directed their attention to particular passages in *One-Dimensional Man* as a means of getting them to pay close attention to the specifics of what Marcuse was saying, encouraging the habit of close observation of the materials of making writing. I also suggested that trying to understand things from Marcuse's perspective could be useful, encouraging the habit of centered flexibility. I did not belabor these suggestions or try to enforce them. Nor did I remind them of the questions to ask about theories I mentioned at the beginning of the course (at least not very often or very directly). Both in class discussions and in "bull sessions" with friends (face-to-face and in tweets), students get a lot of experience of talking to one another about things that are important to them, trying to figure out what they believe, connecting what they read and what they are taught with their lives, and I trust that with just a little direction and encouragement they will develop many of the habits they need.

In other first-year writing courses, I tried to position students to find something that was important to them to write about by setting a startlingly general topic: water resources, for instance. The students in this course were reasonably nonplussed at first, but after reading a few articles, one commented, "What amazes me most about water resource management is its complexity" (Lynch et al. 76). The questions of who owns the water in North America and how it should be used concern agribusinesses, golfers, small farmers, white-water rafters, mining companies, American Indians, fishers, electrical companies, environmentalists, operators of ski resorts, urban residents, and many others, and the conflicting demands of these interests result in strange and shifting alliances. For their first paper, I asked students to find aspects of the issue of water resources that interested them; I asked them to write about what aspects related to their career plans, what experiences they had had with water resource issues and how these experiences had affected them, and what else they might want to find out about water resources. Students had little trouble in finding a way in which it mattered to them: one student whose dairy-farming stepfather had committed suicide when the price of milk declined and he couldn't repay his bank loans was especially concerned when he read about the plight of a small rancher in Nevada who lost his water to the newly irrigated large farms down the valley; another student with a passion for golf looked into water-conserving designs for the abundant golf courses in western deserts. Some were moved by questions of fairness; others were interested in technological problems. Not all students were equally engaged. Given all the complexity of the issues, I told them they needed to consider the perspectives of all the stakeholders in the particular issue they addressed—an attempt to encourage the habit of addressing others as agents acting out of their own subjective experiences. One student handed in an early draft of a paper in which he argued that since irrigated farming in the West made no economic sense, the government should buy out western agricultural concerns and subsidize the development of more agriculture in the Midwest and East. This was a "skilled" writer who had developed an effective way of doing writing classes: quickly take stock of an issue and offer a novel and definitive solution.[5] I suggested to him that people who had lived and farmed in the West for generations might not appreciate having their livelihood eliminated and that the federal government certainly didn't have the funds needed to finance his plan. He did some further reading and discovered strategies that took into account the needs and responsibilities of the people experiencing water shortages in the West and the increasing pressure of development on the availability of agricultural land in the Midwest (Lynch et al. 78–79). The habit of paying attention to the diverse experiences of others, like many of the other habits I have described, can turn routinized and alienated student making of texts into making meanings that matter—or at least into solutions that could work in the real world.

The explicit purpose of writing courses is to intra-act with students in ways that bring about changes in their understanding of and behavior in writing. Recognizing the ethical import of changing students in this way has been a recurrent problem for teachers of writing and rhetoric; it is the problem that impelled Perelman to connect education to epideictic rhetoric. How can valuable practices of writing be instilled in students without indoctrinating them—or, as he says, without engaging in propaganda? In 1969 Perelman offered epideictic rhetoric as a solution: he argued that because educators, like speakers of epideictic discourse, address issues in which "no immediate practical interest is ever involved" and have been "commissioned by a community to be the spokesman for the values it recognizes," thus "there is no question of attacking or defending, but simply of promoting values that are shared in the community" (Perelman and Olbrechts-Tyteca 52). In the 1990s this problem became acute as teachers began to pay attention to the diversity present in their classrooms and thus to the improbability of shared values, and they consequently began to address the way practices of teaching writing imposed the values of the dominant culture (cf. Sullivan 71). Writing teachers arguing that classrooms were not apolitical spaces advocated avoiding practices that constrained the subjectivities of students, teaching methods of cultural critique, and negotiating race, class, and gender issues in the classroom. In response, Maxine Hairston complained about this new model for freshman writing programs for putting "dogma before diversity, politics before craft, ideology before critical thinking, and the social goals of the teacher before the educational needs of the student" (180). Many practices of critical pedagogy, as I mentioned in chapter 1, often did focus more on politics than on writing. Byron Hawk later echoed Hairston's critique, pointing out that James Berlin structured his teaching "around emphasizing, if not imposing, his politics," which derived from "a more progressive Marxist-Hegelian version of dialectics" (*Counter-History* 211–12). But, as Don McCloskey argued on the H-Rhetor listserve in 1993, writing teachers *must* teach values: "We teach virtue in the classroom, and should. . . . My Lord, if we don't teach intellectual virtues, which have some connection with other virtues . . . we are doing bad by the world" (qtd. in Sullivan 70).

In 1996, Cynthia Sheard took up Perelman's suggestion, noting that "value rather than reason has long been seen as the special province of epideictic rhetoric" and adding that "it invokes shared values as a basis for promoting a vision of what could be" (766); it instills "a sense of responsibility for and possibility of change for the better" (786). Thus, though epideictic rhetoric does not address situations in which immediate decisions must be made, it does prepare the ground for future change, as Walker also suggested in 1989 when he defined epideictic as "argument directed toward the establishment, reconfirmation, or revision of general values and beliefs" ("Aristotle's Lyric" 7). Arguing that "epideictic speaks to the recurring, or experientially 'permanent' or chronic issues in a society's pattern of existence," he posits that "the *kairos* of epideictic is a moment or juncture within the pattern . . . about which something must or can be said" ("Aristotle's Lyric" 8). Thus, "epideictic is philosophically, rhetorically, and formally prior to pragmatic discourse" (9); it "belongs, in sum, to the domain of theory and it invites its listener/'spectator' (or *theoros*, as Aristotle says) to an act of contemplation, evaluation, and judgment" (8).Inviting students to think seriously about experientially permanent patterns in their society, to embrace the possibilities of change, and to take responsibility for their part in bringing about changes for the better is very much what Barad calls for in defining responsible intra-acting in the world: "being responsive to the possibilities that might help us flourish" (Barad 396).

Walker says his definition of epideictic is derived from Perelman's later article "Rhetoric and Politics," published in 1984, in which Perelman emphasizes that the goal of the epideictic rhetor is "to contribute to the enhancement of values, to create a spiritual communion around common values . . . to exalt publicly the values around which the community is formed and through which it communes" (131). Perelman argues that it is devotion to such values that unites a community and permits it "to surmount the passing crises," and he offers as examples of eloquence in epideictic discourse Pericles, Lincoln, and Churchill, "who sought to exalt the community values before facing a dangerous test" (131). Common values that "are not put into question" and that command unconditional fidelity (Perelman 132) but at the same time do not contradict the diverse values of individual citizens can function as the intellectual values McCloskey says we must teach even now.

This was what attracted Whitehead to Pericles's speech. Stengers says that Pericles addresses the citizens of Athens "as free citizens . . . as attached but not defined by, or subject to, what attaches them (TW 497), and thus the common value he exalts, their love of Athens, is not meant to replace "those [individual values] which tend to separate" community members (Perelman, "Rhetoric" 131)—but it does make them "susceptible of a new type of unity that would be Athens" (TW 497). The goal of epideictic discourse to create a new unity by exalting a common value was also the goal of Barack Obama, Bobby Kennedy, and Anwar al-Sādāt in their speeches. Obama invited his audience to unite around the founding value of the United States: "This nation is more than the sum of its parts—that out of many, we are truly one." Kennedy invited his audience to unite around the values King espoused, "love and wisdom and compassion toward one another." And al-Sādāt invited his audience to unite around God's commandments: "We all love this land, the land of God, we all, Muslims, Christians and Jews, all worship God . . . God's teachings and commandments are: love, sincerity, security and peace" (qtd. in Diab 131). Such values, though people may often not observe them, are also values that few would question.

Like Pericles, Obama, Kennedy, and al-Sādāt were speaking at a dangerous time: racial sentiments were inflamed by the airing of Reverend Wright's comments, violence was immanent in the neighborhood where Kennedy was speaking, and al-Sādāt was addressing the Israeli Knesset in the midst of a prolonged diplomatic stalemate in peace initiatives in the Arab-Israeli wars. al-Sādāt was arguing more directly for a decision—the resumption of peace talks—but Diab's analysis of the speech in terms of the practices of the Arab-Islamic peacemaking process of ṣulḥ, epideictic rhetoric, and Ratcliffe's rhetorical listening bring it close to the speeches of Obama and Kennedy as examples of ethical persuasion. All are attempting to create a spiritual communion around common values by inviting their audiences to an act of contemplation, evaluation, and judgment. All used personal narratives to foreground their ethos in addressing the value they were promoting: Obama through the accounts of his interracial family, Kennedy in his brief mention of his brother's assassination, and al-Sādāt through an extended account of his past efforts at peacemaking. Diab notes that in invoking the value to all of peace in the middle east, al-Sādāt "invites others' accountability," and he reciprocates by establishing his own accountability through these narratives (132). In the same way, Kennedy invites his audience to make an effort to go beyond hatred and distrust and reciprocates by alluding to his own efforts to listen to Aeschylus and overcome pain and despair. All are demonstrating that they have listened to and are open to others and address them as acting out of their own subjective experiences. al-Sādāt acknowledges the Arabs' role in stalling the peacemaking process "by representing and responding affirmatively to Israeli grievances: . . . *We refused to meet with you, anywhere, yes*" (136). Obama similarly responded affirmatively to complaints about Reverend Wright: "Did I ever hear him make remarks that could be considered controversial while I sat in church? Yes. Did I strongly disagree with many of his political views? Absolutely."

All "indirectly call for reciprocity"; they invite their audiences to be like those whom they have been praising. As Aristotle says, "To praise a man is in one respect akin to urging a course of action" (*Rhetoric* I.ix). Creating a new unity, a community of people devoted to the value of peace by interpellating audience members is one of the main features of ṣulḥ (Diab 112), and Diab points out how "using proximal deictic terms like *we* and *us* is a viable way to deescalate and resolve conflict" (139). al-Sādāt says, "Let us be frank with each other . . . as we answer this important question: How can we achieve permanent peace based on justice?" Kennedy and Obama use this strategy too. Shifting from addressing his audience as "you who are black" and himself as an I who feels in his own heart the same kind of feeling, Kennedy says, "We have to make an effort to understand." And Obama says, "We have a choice in this country." As Diab says, "Rather than being just observers, they are invited/mobilized to pursue peace" (139), or to forgo violence and hatred and pursue compassion toward others, or to forgo divisive racism and pursue community. Grievances and feelings of hatred are not dismissed or diminished, but audience members are invited in addition to try other ways of responding, ways that enact values that they do or could believe in.

To the epideictic practices of exalting common values and inviting contemplation and judgment, rhetorical listening and ṣulḥ add practices of paying attention to the concerns of audience members and interpellating them as pursuing the goals of the speaker. Enchantment ontology adds practices based on understanding the intimate entanglement of creatures in the world and their responsibility to the well-being of all and practices based on understanding intra-action as the undetermined determination of individual creatures who decide for themselves. Whitehead and Stengers add the practices of polite modification of dreams: the acceptance of the importance of all experiences and habits as "woven by rightness of feeling into the harmony of the universal feeling" (PR 474) and the entertainment of propositions as a lure for feelings from which new possibilities emerge. The concept of ethical persuasion resulting from the interweaving of these practices underlies my approach to teaching writing.

Ethical persuasion suggests how teachers can enhance the values of writing in their courses and how they can intra-act with students in ways that do not impose values on them. The central values of enchanted writing and of my approach to teaching writing are the same: writing matters because it makes the world what it is, and differences matter because they enable writers to create possibilities that change the world. In the courses I have described, my goal was to invite students to a community of writers who write things that are important to them and others and who pay attention to how they intra-act with the creatures with whom they share the world. Because writing always changes the world, students need to take it seriously, even in writing classes. When students do writing that has little importance to them, they do not learn how to write well. When teachers tell them what to write about and how to write, they do not learn how to write well. I design courses to be lures for feeling, with readings that challenge or outrage them or with topics so multifaceted and complex that they cannot fail to find something in them that they feel strongly about. I do not teach about these readings or topics; I make them grapple with them on their own.[6] I "exalt" the value of writing by taking their writing seriously: when they create solutions or recommendations that won't work in the real world because stakeholders' concerns have not been taken into account or because needed information about the situation has been omitted, I respond by pointing out these problems. In classroom and virtual discussions, I enact habits of paying attention to differences by listening carefully to their ideas, not dismissing any of them out of hand, and asking questions and directing attention to the differences that are arising—an indirect call for reciprocity. I suggest habits like centered flexibility, explaining what they are useful for, but leaving it up to the students how and when to adopt them, thus enacting another habit of good writing (and good writing teaching) of letting creatures be in themselves in our relations to them. I praise writers by telling students that these are the things that writers do: they listen to others, they make connections between ideas. Rather than being just observers, students are interpellated as writers (cf. Diab 139). Through these intra-actions I am trying to create not a spiritual but an ethical community based on shared values of well-made writing.

Writing is intra-active behavior, and writers always change in writing. Cynthia Haynes complained about my desires for students in the water resources course I described: the "goals seem less motivated by a desire to teach students strategies for writing than a desire for them to change" (198n16). The passage that drew her attention was about asking students to consider the perspectives of the stakeholders in the issue they were writing about. Students were asked, more specifically, to discuss what they might learn from this position: what beliefs and feelings they could sympathize with, what experiences they found out about that enabled them to see new aspects of their issue, how the concerns of stakeholders related to their concerns. Haynes quoted us (the article was coauthored): "We reminded ourselves that the risk in argument is not that you may lose but rather that you may change.... We also knew full well the rhetorical force of the questions we asked: thoughtfully pursued, these questions could and did prompt change in our students" (Lynch et al. 80). The student whom I used as an example in this section of the article was the student whose stepfather committed suicide on losing his farm: he was opposed to corporate agriculture because they put small farmers out of business and he thought that was unfair. In working his way through the linked writing assignments, he found out more about corporate farming and found a statement from René Dubos about farming being a "symbiotic relationship between man and earth" that captured his feelings about small farmers. He wrote in a statement at the end of the course:

> My position on the topic of water at first was corporate farms are no good and we shut them down completely.... I didn't realize all the jobs that would be lost and how it would affect California's economic system.... The corporate farms that should be kept after and taxed super high are conglomerates like Prudential [which] would possibly force them to sell their land to people who care and respect the land and soil. These are the corporate farms that don't care for the land and if the land becomes worthless they just buy land somewhere else.... I guess I'm still against corporate farms but mostly only them being owned by conglomerates. (80–81)

The purpose of writing courses is to change students, as I said earlier, but I aim to achieve this goal by encouraging students to modify their attitudes toward writing, to add to their understanding of writing that it makes meaningful changes in the world. This farmer's stepson has had the experience of making a recommendation about something that matters to him, and matters enough that he wants to make it a good recommendation. He desires to understand better why he feels that corporate farms driving small farms out of business is unfair. I also try to change students by encouraging them to develop more habits that will make their writing well-made, habits that enable them to work better with the material and tools of writing, for instance by making connections between Dubos's statement and one's feelings about corporate and small farms and by finding other ways of listening to the perspectives of corporate farmers. Writing and teaching writing is all about possibilities for what could be.

Notes

Introduction

1. A "camp" up north is a cabin in the woods and/or on a lake, often used as a fishing or hunting camp, but now also as a summer home.

2. In my usage, "writing" is meant as a general term to refer to the practices of writing and rhetoric. It is not restricted to composing inscribed texts in language but also includes, at the least, spoken, visual, and multimodal compositions.

3. "Intra-action" is Karen Barad's term for interaction that through mutual influence creates the entities that result rather than being an encounter between already existing, bounded entities; "trading their stuff" is Stuart Kauffman's description of how organisms collectively produce ever more complex biospheres (HU 129). I will have more to say about both of these concepts later.

4. Cf. Rickert: "Humans have a role, but not an unconditioned one" ("Towards Ecosophy" 74). Rickert draws on Empedocles and Heidegger to sketch a cosmology in which "all of human doing is interwoven within the world, and made possible through it, not only materially but meaningfully, and not only meaningfully but sacredly" (75).

5. As Barad makes clear, her use of first-person plural pronouns is not meant to refer exclusively to humans: "We (but not only 'we humans') are already always responsible to the others with whom and which we are entangled" (393).

6. Alluding to Morris Berman's 1981 book *The Reenchantment of the World*, which similarly argues for a revisioning of humans' place in the world, and not to Bernard Stiegler's more recent (2014) book of the same title which instead argues for reenchanting the world as a progressive project (although one may lead to the other). Jane Bennett (*Enchantment*) also uses "enchantment" to signify the vibrant agency of things.

7. The focus on emergence and becoming in this vision answers to Sidney Dobrin's call for "a more dynamic systems approach to writing" than the more conservative versions of complex systems theory (*Postcomposition* 150).

8. One memorable adventure: spending a whole summer puzzling through Ilya Prigogine and Isabelle Stengers's *Order out of Chaos* handicapped by a total lack of background in physics.

9. You can read more about the dragonfly encounter in chapter 7.

10. Like Carolyn Miller, I do not consider these things as fixed genres, but rather as actions that have effects, not merely social effects but real material effects in the world.

11. And as the watercolorist Tom Lynch says, what distinguishes making art from making a representation of a tree.

12. "Cosmos" is Isabelle Stengers's as well as Alexander von Humboldt's, term for the entangled world.

13. Arca draws on enchantment ontology, which she describes as "a view of the world and society that sees all biological, psychological, social, and environmental phenomena as interdependent" (133). She cites the quirky but well-informed film *Mindwalk* as one of her prime sources, a film I have also shown in graduate classes as an accessible introduction to enchantment ontology.

14. Cf. Welch.

15. See chapter 5.

1. Enchanted Writing

1. Kimmerer notes that this traditional teaching has been published in Benton-Banai.

2. "Reciprocal induction" is a term from developmental biology (see Oyama 35).

3. Cf. Latour's similar disavowal of social constructionism and phenomenology in the first chapter of *Pandora's Hope*, "Do You Believe in Reality?" He suggests: "Why not let the 'outside world' invade the scene . . . and turn the mind into a brain, into a neuronal machine sitting inside a Darwinian animal struggling for its life?" (PH 9).

4. For more complete histories, see Capra; Connolly, *World*; Harrington; Hayles, *How*; Taylor; and Waldrop.

5. Buchanan provides a comprehensive account of Uexküll's influences on Heidegger, Merleau-Ponty, and Deleuze, and Harrington notes his influence on Heidegger, 53–54.

6. See Barnett and Boyle, Davis, Hawk, Phelps, Rickert, Syverson, and others.

7. Barad's book, published in 2007, was not available to Phelps.

8. See Hawk, *Counter-History* 211–15.

9. See Davis, *Inessential Solidarity*.

10. I discuss concrescence more completely in chapters 4 and 6.

11. I discuss propositions in more detail below and in chapter 6.

12. In this description of Kimmerer's perception of the plantain, I am drawing on Whitehead's explanation of how the constituents of a perceptual event are related (CN 152).

2. Writing as Entangled

1. It is difficult to capture the intimacy of our entanglement in the universe. Barad says, "Bodies are not situated in the world. They are part of the world" (376). Ingold argues that it is wrong to describe organisms as embodied: "We have bodies—indeed we *are* our bodies. But we are not wrapped up in them. The body is not a package. . . . It is rather a tumult of unfolding activity" (M 94)—an animacy.

2. Sticks have a lot of lively entanglements around my camp: as kindling, chase objects for Scout, components of eagle nests.

3. Barad's source is a segment on NPR's *Morning Edition* in summer 1996.

4. I researched this event through collecting notes and drafts of the memo and interviewing the principals involved (which included myself), and I reported the results in a paper presented at the Penn State Conference on Rhetoric in 1989.

5. In saying that these individuals intra-acted, I mean that they acquired some different "properties" through their participation in the event.

6. I discuss enaction more fully in chapter 5.

7. "Structural coupling" is Maturana and Varela's term for recurrent interactions with other entities; for further discussion, see chapter 4.

8. Lawrence Shapiro badly misunderstands this approach in his description of the related discussion in Varela, Thompson, and Rosch (VTR); he says, "VTR believe that color does not exist in the world, but is rather like what John Locke long ago described as a secondary quality: a power to produce an experience that does not resemble any quality in the world" (55). Unlike Shapiro, Maturana, Varela, Thompson, and Rosch are operating with enchanted ontology. For them, color is not a quality or a power, but an experience that emerges from the interaction of perceptual structures and wavelengths of light, all of which exist in the world and are not pre-given.

9. For discussions of scientific resistance to seeing "human" cognitive abilities in animals see Beckoff 122–31, Donald Griffin 24, Haraway, *When* 375n55, and Goodall xiv–xv.

10. They cite other studies that have also shown that dogs use gaze to communicate with humans: following directional gestures and indicating desired objects, for example.

11. As the *CCC Poster Page* on language says, "Language is understood to be a distinguishing feature of human beings."

12. A more recent study of Campbell's monkeys concluded that they exhibit "the most complex example of 'proto-syntax' in animal communication known to date," combining six different calls into various sequences in context-specific ways (Ouattara et al. 22026).

13. See especially the forum edited by Erik Doxtader and the special issue of *Rhetoric Society Quarterly* edited by Jeremy Gordon and others.

14. To learn about more remarkable bird behaviors, such as pigeons who can tell a Picasso from a Monet, see Ackerman.

15. Latour's project in these accounts differs from Hutchins's, as he is concerned more with the question of "how . . . we pack the world into words" (PH 24). I will return to this question of how writing brings forth worlds in chapter 4.

16. For exceptions, see Prior and Shipka, and Wertsch.

17. In the area of vocal behavior, for example, some songbirds (especially thrushes) can produce two notes at once, singing in harmony with themselves, due to the structure of their syrinx, and humpback whales can be heard over much greater distances than humans (and both songbirds and humpbacks produce music the complexity of which rivals that of humans).

18. In the introduction to the English edition of Leroi-Gourhan's *Gesture and Speech* published in 1993, Randall White reminds readers that the discovery of new fossil remains since the original publication of the French edition in 1964 makes Leroi-Gourhan's taxonomy of early humans "somewhat outdated, even obsolete" (xxi). Despite the explosion of new discoveries in paleoanthropology recently, Leroi-Gourhan's basic argument that human evolution was led by structural rather than cognitive changes may still hold. Klein argues that *Zinjanthropus* was not an ancestor of *Homo* and that the tools found by Leakey with *Zinjanthropus* were very probably made by *Homo habilis*. *Homo habilis* had a bigger brain than *Zinjanthropus*, but it was still half the size of that of *Homo sapiens*, so it's still difficult to see the original toolmaker as a genius inventing tools. Further, the reason the tools are attributed to *Homo habilis* is not because of its larger brain but because it had a longer thumb and thus a more precise grip for making tools and because its ancestors, *Homo ergaster/erectus*, survived throughout the period of the Acheulean tool kit, whereas *Zinjanthropus* went extinct near the beginning of the period (235–37). Leakey, who fervently believed that toolmaking is definitive of the human, agrees with this attribution (Johanson and Edgar 162). Steven Mithen adds the correction that *Homo habilis* might have been any of a number of human ancestral species. In contrast to Leroi-Gourhan, Mithen equates the advent of the modern human with the advent of symbolization and language, which he argues the static nature of Neanderthal technicity and the lack of any aesthetic artifacts prior to those produced by *Homo sapiens* testify against.

19. See Clark: "Our brains just don't bother to create rich inner models. Why should they? The world itself is still there, a complex and perfect store of all that data" (*Natural-Born Cyborgs* 66).

20. Cf. Simondon: "Individuation, moreover, not only brings the individual to light but also the individual-milieu dyad" ("Genesis" 300).

21. Protention and retention are terms used by Husserl who argues that both are

necessary accompaniments to primal impression in the perception of any temporal object (145, 175).

22. Recent evidence of cultural traditions in nonhuman animals qualifies Gould's claim that cultural evolution is specific to humans; see Donald Griffin 41; Hauser 115–39.

3. Writing as Making

1. On epistemic rhetoric, see Berlin, *Rhetoric* 165–79.

2. In their argument for embodied cognition, Varela, Thompson, and Rosch similarly characterize Western thought as dependent on what they call the either-or Cartesian anxiety: "There is the enchanting land of truth where everything is clear and ultimately grounded. But beyond that small island there is the wide and stormy ocean of darkness and confusion, the native home of illusion" (141). They turn instead to the "middle way" school of the Buddhist tradition in India and Asia that embraces "groundlessness," which consists "in knowing how to negotiate our way through a world that is not fixed and pregiven but that is continually shaped by the type of actions in which we engage" (144). I discuss their enactive approach to mind in chapter 5.

3. Atwill defines humanist values as centered on universalist conceptions of the human, knowledge, and value. But as both Byron Hawk and Kelly Pender suggest, she "comes close to a reemphasis of a subject that implicitly preexists the situation and can will to intervene in it" (Hawk, "Toward" 381; see also Pender, 159n37).

4. All quotations from Aristotle in this discussion are from *The Complete Works of Aristotle: Revised Oxford Translation*.

5. In *Perception of the Environment* (2000), *Being Alive* (2011), and *Making* (2013).

6. Hawk speaks of co-responsibility, which he derives from Heidegger, as characterizing how the maker works with other forces: "The navigator does not have mastery over *physis* but is carried along with it, works in relationship with it" ("Toward" 380, 381–82).

7. Pender draws a somewhat different conclusion from Dunne's comment that the craftsman's activity might be a strategic detour through which nature goes, arguing that it implies a passivity on the part of the maker, a passivity she aligns with kairos as waiting for the opportune moment. She further argues that "that passivity exists alongside the artist's rational activity, not as an alternative to it" (131). My interest is rather in how Aristotle holds to the notion of a preexistent form, contrasting with Ingold (and my) argument that the form arises in the intra-action of the maker, material, and other forces.

8. See Hawk's "more complex notion of entelechy": "A seed, for example, might be in the process of becoming a tree but it also carries the potential to become a house, a chair, or home to a bird's nest" (*Counter-History* 125).

240   Notes

9. Pender's approach to defining technē is explicitly dialectical and so is at odds with mine in predictable ways (104). As Hawk comments, "ecological complexity ... is post-dialectical" (*Counter-History* 223).

10. This trick is a good example of Whitehead's remedy for the bifurcation of nature. As he says, "For us the red glow of the sunset should be as much a part of nature as are the molecules and electric waves by which men of science would explain the phenomenon" (CN 29).

11. I will have more to say about the account of the sixth day and how language contributes to making meaning in chapter 6.

4. The Dynamics of Becoming

1. Deleuze and Guattari are using "correspondence" in the sense of a one-to-one matching, not in the sense of the ongoing interaction that Ingold uses it to mean.

2. Cf. Haraway's description of her work with Cayenne as reciprocal induction in chapter 1, and Stiegler's description of the coupling of flint and cortex as an exteriorization in chapter 2.

3. As I will discuss in chapter 5, choices may be nonconscious as well as conscious.

4. Despite their varying disciplinary fields, these scholars, as well as others I draw on in this book, are entangled through direct and indirect intra-actions, each developing in their own way the assumptions of enchantment ontology. Whitehead's process philosophy, especially his concept of concrescence as an innovating becoming, was recognized as influential by complexity theorists Ilya Prigogine and Isabelle Stengers. Along with jointly authoring *Order out of Chaos*, Stengers more recently authored the incisive commentary on Whitehead's work, *Thinking with Whitehead*, to which I am much indebted in my reading of his work. Whitehead is also a major influence on Bruno Latour, Donna Haraway, and Vinciane Despret. Karen Barad, like Whitehead, was influenced by quantum physics and especially Niels Bohr (her doctorate is in theoretical particle physics) in developing her concept of intra-action and she is Haraway's colleague at University of California, Santa Cruz. Biologists Maturana and Varela developed their theory of autopoiesis together; Varela also developed an enactive theory of cognition, which I discuss in chapter 5. Maturana and Stuart Kauffman were both associated with Warren McCulloch, chair of the Macy Cybernetics Conferences, which were an early source of complex systems theory, Maturana as a colleague at MIT, Kauffman as a protégé. John Holland and Kauffman were both associated with the Santa Fe Institute, a main birthplace of complex systems theory. Gilbert Simondon was a student of Maurice Merleau-Ponty and a major influence on Gilles Deleuze, Bruno Latour, and Bernard Stiegler.

5. In 2017 the wolf population succumbed to inbreeding. With only two wolves left on the island, the National Park Service at last announced a plan to import twenty to thirty wolves from Canada to control the burgeoning moose herd.

Notes

6. This understanding of the relation between intentions, plans, and action is further developed in the enactive account of neural functioning discussed in chapter 5.

7. In the process of composing and revising the manuscript of *Process and Reality*, Whitehead inserted many passages without, for the most part, revising sections of the book that represented his earlier thinking. I puzzled a great deal over the contradictions in the concept of concrescence as discussed in various sections until I discovered Lewis Ford's study of the order of composition of *Process and Reality* and two previous books, *Science and the Modern World* and *Religion in the Making*. The description of concrescence here is based for the most part on pages 224–25 and related changes and insertions, and not on pages 244–45. The concepts of God and of subjective aim were also changed significantly in later insertions.

8. Barad argues that "the primary ontological unit is not independent objects with inherent boundaries and properties but rather *phenomena*" (139). Also note Ingold's rejection of Aristotle's procedure of beginning with analyzing already-constituted beings to shed light on the process of becoming discussed in chapter 3.

9. Cf. Ingold's concept of correspondence in chapter 3.

10. As he explains at the end of this discussion, Kauffman doesn't completely reject the notion of cell membranes as helping cells remain subcritical: "Cell membranes block many molecular interactions and hence block a supracritical explosion, just as carbon rods in a nuclear reactor absorb neutrons and hence block collisions of those neutrons with nuclei, which would lead to a supracritical chain reaction" (HU 130).

11. The quote is from the glossary compiled by the translators.

12. For example, one of the first popular American comic strips, "The Yellow Kid," by Richard Outcault, published in the *New York Journal* starting in 1896, printed dialogue on the characters' clothes. By the 1900s, in comics like Lionel Feininger's "The Kin-der-Kids," text appeared only in word-balloons, but comics that followed the convention in British comics by running text in captions below the drawings also appeared at least until 1914 (see Blackbeard and Williams, 41, 42, 54). In an interesting transition, many American comics in the 1900s, including Winsor McCay's very popular "Little Nemo in Slumberland," used both captions and word-balloons. The combination continued through some time in 1906, but gradually more of the content of the story was shifted to the dialogue in the word-balloons, until the captions finally vanished (see Marschall). As a popular genre, comics competed fiercely for readers; the conventions used in those comics that happened to be more successful thus fed back into the system and influenced the shape of the genre.

13. For example, in English, many new gender-neutral third-person singular pronouns were proposed around the end of the twentieth century, but none succeeded in persisting. Instead, use of the third-person plural as a singular is finally becoming accepted (as it has been, off and on, since at least the sixteenth century).

14. Cf. Deleuze: "A metastable system thus implies a fundamental *difference*, like a

state of dissymmetry. It is nonetheless a system insofar as the difference therein is like *potential energy*, like a *difference of potential* distributed within certain limits" ("On Gilbert Simondon" 87).

15. Quoting Simondon, *L'Individuation à la lumière des notions de forme et d'information*, Millon, 2005, 63 (qtd. in Venn).

5. The Agency of Writing

Epigraph: An excerpt from a Facebook conversation, September 16, 2017. Used with permission from Casey Boyle and Scott Graham.

1. Rickert is arguing that they don't preexist the situation, with which I also agree, but at least he includes actants in the situation.

2. See Ehren Helmut Pflugfelder: "There is very little discussion of nonhuman agents as rhetors, aside from indirect discussions on the sometimes powerful positions occupied by various technologies that affect our thoughts and actions" (120). Further, Miller argues that "most of us agree that we do not" owe attribution of rhetorical agency "to automated assessment systems" ("What" 153), nor does she seem inclined more recently to grant it to a snake or a potted fern ("Appeal(s)" 458). For exceptions, see Davis, "Autozoography"; Gries, "Defense" and *Still Life;* Rickert, "Tuning."

3. Other physical entities may have a "perpetual individuation" that Simondon identifies as "life itself" ("Genesis" 305), entities such as artificial intelligence systems or other entities that change through repurposing. The line between living and nonliving is as blurry in technology as it is in biology.

4. As elaborated by neurologists and neurophenomenologists in what is called an enactive approach to the study of mind.

5. Johns was interviewed by Michael Crichton for his book *Jasper Johns* (Harry N. Abrams, 1994). Rickert quotes this excerpt from Mandell, who is quoting from Marvin Bell's column in *American Poetry Review*, Summer 1978.

6. Though later I will suggest that agents become responsible when they see themselves as owning, or willing, their actions.

7. In the sense that Tim Ingold uses the term to refer to the intra-actions among agents and other entities involved in making. See chapter 3.

8. Mandell makes a similar point about Johns: "Johns sees that a work of art happens and that an artist creates it—out of no prior knowledge, thought, plan, or expectations. Not that there aren't prior thoughts and plans, but that the work of art does not arise from them; they did not cause the work of art to materialize" (370). Mandell concludes: "Writing does not emanate from the conscious mind" (371).

9. Quotes from Gunn's position paper for the 2003 Alliance of Rhetorical Societies conference, reprinted in Lundberg and Gunn, 100–101n10.

10. But he also refers to them as "creatures," explaining that the "business of phi-

losophy is to explain the emergence of the more abstract things from the more concrete things," and that "the individual fact is a creature, and creativity is the ultimate behind all forms, inexplicable by forms, and conditioned by its creatures" (PR 20).

11. As mentioned above, Barad uses the first-person plural to refer to all entities, not just humans.

12. I focus on Obama's agency as there is more information about the influences on his actions, but he is clearly not solely responsible for the rhetorical effects that arise from the speech. I also emphasize that my description of the processes involved in composing the speech is not meant to be definitive. An exhaustive analysis of the influences on Obama and of his nonconscious and conscious intentions is probably impossible, nor is it my project here.

13. Latour uses "the good common world" to signify the bringing together of the moral question of the common good and the epistemological question of the common world by ensuring that all propositions, entities, voices, stakeholders are heard in the deliberations that compose the "collective" (PN 93, 106–7). The good common world is "the *best* of all *possible* worlds" (146).

14. When I use the words "intention" and "intentions," I mean them in this sense, as emotions impelling action (as Kauffman says, "yuck" and "yum"), not in the phenomenological sense of directedness at an object or in the sense of socially constructed intentions such as those connected with speech acts.

15. Miller quotes a similar passage from Walker's response to the 2003 Alliance of Rhetorical Societies conference plenary on rhetorical traditions: "The purpose of declamation is . . . to develop a capacity, a *dunamis* of thought and speech, a deeply habituated skill" (qtd. in Miller, "What" 149). Elsewhere, Walker describes habitude with reference to *Nicomachean Ethics*: "Aristotle considers the process to operate quickly and below the level of conscious awareness, and thus to have the effect of instantaneous nonlogical 'feeling' or intuition" (*Genuine Teachers* 227).

16. Chess is more often used as an example of rule-governed activity, but Dreyfus is focusing on the acquisition of the strategic skills that make one into an expert player.

17. Dreyfus draws on Freeman to explain the neurodynamic processes underlying skillful coping; see also his similar argument in "Overcoming."

18. Obama likened the leaders of the civil rights struggle as Moseses, who challenged the Pharaoh, and his generation, who stood on the shoulders of those giants, as Joshuas, who would "lead them into a multiracial Canaan" (Sugrue 15).

19. Remnick notes that "a teachable [or teaching] moment" is a favorite phrase of Obama's (437).

20. In late fall 2017, Obama sent an email from his foundation listing four "rules" for productive civic work. The first two match up with the habits I observe in his speech: "Listen to the people around you. Share your stories with one another and try to make a connection. If possible, find someone who's not like you—who doesn't look

like you, think the way you do, or share the same experiences as you—at least on the surface." And, "When you disagree, don't be disagreeable. Real change comes through persuasion and openness to others. Have a point of view, be rooted in your experience, and don't be afraid to share, but listen and be open, don't be partisan. This isn't about politics; it's about our civic culture."

21. See Benson, Bruner, Dennett.

22. As opposed to defining deliberation as ensuring universally acceptable practices of argumentation as do Hobbes, Rousseau, Kant, and Habermas, a definition that he argues is based in "a deep suspicion of individuals' ordinary private judgments and opinions" (Garsten 191).

23. Matters of concern is a concept that depends on Latour's reading of Whitehead, who says, "Each occasion is an activity of concern, in the Quaker sense of that term" (MT 167).

24. See Freeman, who observes that such awareness can arise from a strong reaction to something amiss in the situation of action (91): for example, an odd expression on the face of a companion interrupts what a person was about to say; and Deleuze and Guattari, who see new lines of flight emerging from destratification, in which the assemblage is gently tipped, revealing "connection of desires, conjunction of flows, continuum of intensities" (161).

6. The Creativity of Writing

1. She credits the term to Vinciane Despret, "Body" (Haraway, *When* 308n19).

2. As Haraway points out and I know from my own experience, dogs are much better at responding coherently to the actions of their trainers than trainers are to the actions of their dogs: she notes several instances in which Cayenne was performing precisely right but she tried to correct her.

3. Whitehead's God is not the Christian God or any religious god, but rather an element required by Whitehead's metaphysical system. He says, "We must provide a ground for limitation which stands among the attributes of the substantial activity. This attribute provides the limitation for which no reason can be given: for all reason flows from it. God is the ultimate limitation, and His existence is the ultimate irrationality. For no reason can be given for just that limitation which it stands in His nature to impose" (SMW 178). Stengers adds, "The God Whitehead has just introduced . . . has nothing to do with the despotic God toward whom all explanatory chains go back. . . . [God] answers to a need produced by metaphysics" (TW 225).

4. The idea that God is an actual entity (not quite) like all other actual entities was added to the text late (see Ford 227–29 and Stengers, TW 265–66).

5. Colebrook is commenting here on Bergson's notion of creative evolution, which influenced both Whitehead and Deleuze.

6. Cf. Bakhtin's heteroglossia, discussed further below.

7. For "complexity theory," Carter uses the alternate, earlier term "chaos theory."

8. This is Carter's paraphrase of David Ray Griffin, 81–82.

9. In 1986, I concluded "The Ecology of Writing" with statements I find that I have repeated, almost word for word, in this book: "Writing is one of the activities by which we locate ourselves in the enmeshed systems that make up the social world . . . an activity through which we become most truly human. By looking at writing ecologically we understand better how important writing is—and just how hard it is to teach" (373). Just replace "enmeshed" with "entangled," take out "social," and replace "ecologically" with "enchantment ontology," and this is an accurate representation of my proposal now, some thirty years later.

10. Latour's *Politics of Nature* (2004) and Stengers's *Thinking with Whitehead* (2011), both of which were published after Carter's book came out.

11. Stengers comments briefly on the "improbable survival of [Whitehead's work] through the intermediary of American theology" (TW 5), and takes exception with Charles Hartshorne's suggestion of making God "a lineage of occasions that has inherited from themselves and from the world . . . according to a new 'worldly' satisfaction" (TW 457).

12. I first encountered this work at Janice Lauer's Rhetoric Seminar at the University of Detroit in 1978. *Rhetoric: Discovery and Change* is (nearly) the only composition textbook I still own (the others are written by friends).

13. Posted on Facebook by Saralinda Blanning. The student, her son, went on to write about Doritos, which one commenter remarked was a great topic.

14. Carter's position is actually somewhat difficult to reconcile with Whitehead's, partly because he has conflated the process "in which the universe accomplishes its actuality" through the reciprocal concrescences of God and the World (PR 350) with the process of the concrescence of actual entities (PR 224). He is referring to the former on pages 97–98 and the latter on page 132. With regard to the creation of the universe, Whitehead says it is the fourth phase, not the third, in which "the creative action completes itself" (PR 351), although he intends all four phases to comprise creation. In the third phase of the creation of the universe, Whitehead says that "immediateness is reconciled with objective immortality" (PR 351), in other words, the present is reconciled with the past, the actual with the possible, the determinate with the indeterminate, not that the actual occasion is freed from the deterministic tendencies of the past. With regard to the concrescence of actual entities, what Carter refers to as the conjunction of the indeterminate past with the conceptual force of the future roughly describes the process of the determination of the finite actual entity, which is creative and could be considered "free" in the sense that the entity decides for itself, by itself, but not in the sense of being freed from deterministic tendencies of the past as Carter describes Whitehead's process on pages 97–98.

15. Cf. David Ray Griffin, 81–82.

16. Kauffman offers an example of breaking symmetries: "a pole standing vertically on a horizontal plane" will eventually fall over" (I 84). Prior to falling, it is in a symmetrical relation: it could fall in any direction. When it falls, its position is determinate, a result of interacting forces: gravity, wind, decay, insect infestation, being struck by a vehicle or cut down with a chainsaw. On phase transition behavior and structural coupling, see chapter 4. Readers who feel a disjunction between Whitehead's metaphysics and physics here may wish to read Stengers's discussion of the relation (TW 364–91).

17. Ford says that "an actuality is singled out merely in terms of its individuality, not in terms of any quality or characteristic it might possess" (225).

18. In arguing for "an affectability or persuadability . . . that precedes and exceeds symbolic intervention," Davis refers to Freud's interest in hypnosis (*Inessential* 36) adducing Mikkel Borch-Jacobsen's analysis of Freud's related notion of transference: "'Transference reveals that the influence of the hypnotist' is grounded . . . in 'an a priori affectability (a 'spontaneous receptivity') in the patient" (71; qtd. in Davis 31). Spontaneous receptivity seems much like what Stengers is referring to here, though her basis is philosophical, not psychological.

19. Cf. Ingold's definition of foresight as a matter "of opening up a path and improvising a passage" in chapter 3.

20. See, for example, Whitehead's insertion that begins, "With this amplification the doctrine, that the primary phase of a temporal actual entity is physical, is recovered" (PR 225). The "amplification" contradicts a statement earlier in the same paragraph: "Each temporal entity, in one sense, originates from its mental pole" (PR 224).

21. Like Jasper Johns's "correction" of the handle of a spoon in his lithograph (chapter 5), or more like Michelango's drawings as exhibited at the Metropolitan Museum of Art (November 2017–February 2018) in that Whitehead does not erase what went before.

22. Though Muckelbauer's dissatisfactions with dialectic are similar to mine, he opts for locating his affirmative style of reading within the dialectic rather than offering an alternative movement as I do in proposing reciprocal induction.

7. Ethical Persuasion

1. Bernard-Donals is paraphrasing Alain Badiou's critique of other-oriented models of the public sphere that Bernard-Donals observes "founder *because* they remain wedded to a notion of 'publicity'—a common location, a communitarian 'we,' a polis—that takes rationality (even in the 'agonistic' model of argument) as argument's stock in trade, and the establishment of common ground (if not agreement) as its ultimate end" ("Against Publics" 31).

2. I am following Whitehead here: "The individual fact is a creature, and creativity is the ultimate behind all forms, inexplicable by forms, and conditioned by its creatures" (PR 20).

3. Cf. Barnett and Boyle, *Rhetoric through Everyday Things*; Bjørkdahl and Parrish, *Rhetorical Animals*; Davis, *Inessential Solidarity;* Derrida, *The Animal That Therefore I Am*; Gordon, Lind, and Kutnicki, "Special Issue: A Rhetorical Bestiary"; Muckelbauer, *The Future of Invention*; Parrish, *Adaptive Rhetoric*; Rickert, *Ambient Rhetoric*.

4. Cf. Roberts-Miller, *Deliberate Conflict* 12.

5. Kennerly and Woods are quoting Kerényi, 77.

6. "Arendt describes Kant's 'hope' for his writings not that the number of people who agree with him might increase but 'that the circle of his examiners would gradually be enlarged'" (39; qtd. in Roberts-Miller, "Fighting" 596). Kant's hope for his writings is the same as what Stengers says Whitehead hoped for and what Muckelbauer says Foucault hoped for; see chapter 6.

7. Lyotard makes the same argument in *The Differend*, observing encounters where the language in which an individual's complaint must be phrased does not allow the complaint to be heard.

8. Translators' note in Nancy, 205n2.

9. See the discussion of divine experience in chapter 6.

10. Ratcliffe focuses on conscious listening to human discourses, but she does also acknowledge how discourses "permeate bodies and become embodied . . . [and] affect my attitudes and daily interactions" with others (69). I see such affects as also important forms of persuasion, as does Diane Davis, who refers to it as "originary . . . affect*ability* or persuad*ability*" (*Inessential Solidarity* 2).

11. Though, I think he is mostly trying to say here that a common language is not enough for understanding, that beings talking with one another must first share a way of life.

12. For the full account, see Chorost.

13. Jenny Rice argues for using Latour's method of tracing networks as a more effective form of public debate: "By encouraging subjects who relate to the world through questions, wonder, inquiry, investigation, archive, we are disallowing subjects who write themselves out of the scene of rhetoric" (196). In so doing, she shifts the notion of public subjectivity toward the kind of engagement with others on their own terms that is characteristic of politeness in persuasion.

14. You can find cobalt, if you want to see it, in cobalt blue watercolor paint. Cobalt is a heavy metal, so this paint is toxic—but it's also a lovely paint to work with.

15. Green says this about analyzing samples: "To dip a spatula into a powdered reagent, to probe its texture and graininess, to draw it slowly out of its confines, and to watch it lump and plate and roll about in the cavity of a porcelain spoon is to be invited to imagine it in other settings and in other times, to conjure up its possible lives, to

cast off the notion that anything, even this inert powder imprisoned on a spatula's tip, could be dull or anything other than shocking in its very being" (67).

16. The encounter had many more complexities than I can adequately address here; see *Friction*, ch. 7.

Conclusion: Good Writing Is Well Made

1. At the explicit request of the rhetoric reading group at Michigan Tech, with whom I shared a draft of chapter 1.

2. Walker, admittedly, is referring to the inviting nature of lyric poetry and prose, while I am thinking of the politeness of invitations as opposed to commands.

3. All quotations from students are reproduced without changes or correction of mistakes.

4. I hadn't yet defined this habit in precisely this way, but it does capture what they were doing.

5. I developed a similar strategy when I was an undergraduate, which eventually made me quite cynical about writing papers.

6. Their struggle with reading Hegel's master-slave discussion was perhaps a bit too intense, although it did lead one student to talk with a friend at another university to help her figure it out—a very good habit of writing.

Works Cited

Ackerman, Jennifer. *The Genius of Birds*. Penguin, 2016.
Adler-Kassner, Robert Crooks, and Ann Watters. "Introduction to This Volume." Adler-Kassner et al., pp. 1–17.
Adler-Kassner, Robert Crooks, and Ann Watters, editors. *Writing the Community: Concepts and Models for Service-Learning in Composition*. American Association for Higher Education/National Council of Teachers of English, 1997.
Alexander, Samuel. *Space, Time, and Deity*. Vol. 2, Macmillan, 1920.
Arca, Rosemary L. "Systems Thinking, Symbiosis and Service: The Road to Authority for Basic Writers." Adler-Kassner et al., pp. 133–41.
Arendt, Hannah. *Lectures on Kant's Political Philosophy*. Edited by Ronald Beiner, U of Chicago P, 1982.
Aristotle. *Complete Works of Aristotle: Revised Oxford Translation*. Edited by Jonathan Barnes, Princeton UP, 1984. 2 vols.
Aristotle. *Nicomachean Ethics*. Translated by Joe Sachs, Focus/Hackett, 2002.
Atwill, Janet M. *Rhetoric Reclaimed: Aristotle and the Liberal Arts Tradition*. Cornell UP, 1998.
Austin, J. L. *How to Do Things with Words*. 1962. 2nd ed., edited by J. O. Urmson and Marina Sbisà, Harvard UP, 1975.
Bacon, Nora. "Community Service Writing: Problems, Challenges, Questions." Adler-Kassner et al., pp. 39–55.
Badiou, Alain. *Ethics: An Essay on the Understanding of Evil*. Translated by Peter Hallward, Verso, 2001.
Bakhtin, M. M. *The Dialogic Imagination: Four Essays*. Edited by Michael Holquist, translated by Caryl Emerson and Michael Holquist, U of Texas P, 1981.
Bakhtin, M. M. *Speech Genres and Other Late Essays*. Translated by Vern W. McGee, edited by Caryl Emerson and Michael Holquist, U of Texas P, 1986.

Barad, Karen. *Meeting the Universe Halfway: Quantum Physics and the Entanglement of Matter and Meaning.* Duke UP, 2007.

Barbery, Muriel. *The Life of Elves.* Translated by Alison Anderson, Europa Editions, 2016.

Barnett, Scot, and Casey Boyle. "Introduction: Rhetorical Ontology, or, How To Do Things with Things." Barnett and Boyle, pp. 1–14.

Barnett, Scot, and Casey Boyle, editors. *Rhetoric through Everyday Things.* U of Alabama P, 2016.

Basso, Keith H. *Wisdom Sits in Places: Landscape and Language among the Western Apache.* U of New Mexico P, 1996.

Bateson, Gregory. *Steps to an Ecology of Mind: A Revolutionary Approach to Man's Understanding of Himself.* Ballantine, 1972.

Beckoff, Marc. *The Emotional Lives of Animals.* New World Library, 2007.

Benhabib, Seyla. *Situating the Self: Gender, Community, and Postmodernism in Contemporary Ethics.* Routledge, 1992.

Bennett, Jane. *The Enchantment of Modern Life: Attachments, Crossings, and Ethics.* Princeton UP, 2001.

Bennett, Jane. *Vibrant Matter: A Political Ecology of Things.* Duke UP, 2010.

Benson, Ciarán. *The Cultural Psychology of Self: Place, Morality and Art in Human Worlds.* Routledge, 2001.

Benton-Banai, Edward. *The Mishomis Book: The Voice of the Ojibway.* Red School House, 1988.

Bergson, Henri. *Creative Evolution.* 1911. Translated by Arthur Mitchell, Dover, 1998.

Berlin, James A. *Rhetoric and Reality: Writing Instruction in American Colleges, 1900–1985.* Southern Illinois UP, 1987.

Berlin, James A. *Rhetorics, Poetics, and Cultures: Refiguring College English Studies.* National Council of Teachers of English, 1996.

Berman, Morris. *The Reenchantment of the World.* Cornell UP, 1981.

Bernard-Donals, Michael. "Against Publics (Exilic Writing)." *JAC*, vol. 28, nos. 1–2, 2008, pp. 29–54.

Bernard-Donals, Michael. "No, Not Really: A Reply to Stephen Yarbrough." *JAC*, vol. 28, nos. 3–4, 2008, pp. 653–62.

Bjørkdahl, Kristian, and Alex C. Parrish, editors. *Rhetorical Animals: Boundaries of the Human in the Study of Persuasion.* Lexington Books, 2018.

Blackbeard, Bill, and Martin Williams, editors. *The Smithsonian Collection of Newspaper Comics.* Smithsonian Institution Press / Harry N. Abrams, 1977.

Bohr, Niels Henrik David. *The Philosophical Writings of Niels Bohr.* Vol. 1: *Atomic Theory and the Description of Nature.* Ox Bow Press, 1963.

Bok, Gordon. "Introduction to 'Do Something.'" *In Concert,* Timberhead, 2006.

Borch-Jacobsen, Mikkel. *The Emotional Tie: Psychoanalysis, Mimesis, and Affect.* Translated by Douglas Brick, Stanford UP, 1992.

Bordieu, Pierre. *The Logic of Practice*. Translated by Richard Nice, Polity Press, 1990.
Boyle, Casey. "Writing and Rhetoric and/as Posthuman Practice." *College English*, vol. 78, no. 6, July 2016, pp. 532–54.
Bradshaw, John. *Dog Sense: How the New Science of Dog Behavior Can Make You a Better Friend to Your Pet*. Basic Books, 2011.
Braidotti, Rosi. *The Posthuman*. Polity Press, 2013.
Brodkey, Linda. *Academic Writing as Social Practice*. Temple UP, 1987.
Brooke, Collin, and Thomas Rickert. "Being Delicious: Materialities of Research in a Web 2.0 Application." Dobrin et al., pp. 163–79.
Brooke, Robert. "Underlife and Writing Instruction." *College Composition and Communication*, vol. 38, no. 2, May 1987, pp. 141–53.
Bruner, Jerome. *The Culture of Education*. Harvard UP, 1996.
Buchanan, Brett. *Onto-Ethologies: The Animal Environments of Uexküll, Heidegger, Merleau-Ponty, and Deleuze*. State U of New York P, 2008.
Burke, Kenneth. *Language as Symbolic Action: Essays on Life, Literature, and Method*. U of California P, 1966.
Burke, Kenneth. *A Rhetoric of Motives*. 1950. U of California P, 1969.
Butler, Judith. *Excitable Speech: A Politics of the Performative*. Routledge, 1997.
Capra, Fritjof. *The Web of Life: A New Scientific Understanding of Living Systems*. Anchor Books, 1996.
Carroll, Sean B. *Endless Forms Most Beautiful: The New Science of Evo Devo*. Norton, 2005.
Carter, Michael. *Where Writing Begins: A Postmodern Reconstruction*. Southern Illinois UP, 2003.
CCC Poster Page 7: Language. *College Composition and Communication*, vol. 63, no. 1, Sept. 2011, p. 162.
de Certeau, Michel. *The Practice of Everyday Life*. Translated by Steven Rendall, U of California P, 1984.
Chorost, Michael. *Rebuilt: How Becoming Part Computer Made Me More Human*. Houghton Mifflin, 2005.
Clark, Andy. *Natural-Born Cyborgs: Minds, Technologies, and the Future of Human Intelligence*. Oxford UP, 2003.
Clark, Andy. *Supersizing the Mind: Embodiment, Action, and Cognitive Extension*. Oxford UP, 2011.
Clark, Katerina, and Michael Holquist. *Mikhail Bakhtin*. Harvard UP, 1984.
Colebrook, Claire. *Understanding Deleuze*. Allen and Unwin, 2003.
Connolly, William E. *The Fragility of Things: Self-Organizing Processes, Neoliberal Fantasies, and Democratic Activism*. Duke UP, 2013.
Connolly, William E. *A World of Becoming*. Duke UP, 2011.
Coole, Diana, and Samantha Frost. "Introducing the New Materialisms." *New Materi-

alisms: Ontology, Agency, and Politics, edited by Diana Coole and Samantha Frost, Duke UP, 2010, pp. 1–43.

Cooper, Marilyn M. "The Answers Are Not in the Back of the Book: Developing Discourse Practices in First-Year English." *Developing Discourse Practices in Adolescence and Adulthood*, edited by Richard Beach and Susan Hynds, Ablex Publishing,1990, pp. 65–90.

Cooper, Marilyn M. "The Ecology of Writing." *College English*, vol. 48, no. 4, Apr. 1986, pp. 364–75.

Cope, Bill, and Mary Kalantzis, editors. *Multiliteracies: Literacy Learning and the Design of Social Futures*. Routledge, 2000.

Corder, Jim. "Argument as Emergence, Rhetoric as Love." *Rhetoric Review*, vol. 4, no. 1, Sept. 1985, pp. 16–32.

Csányi, Vilmos. *If Dogs Could Talk: Exploring the Canine Mind*. Translated by Richard E. Quandt, North Point Press, 2000.

Damasio, Antonio. *Descartes' Error: Emotion, Reason, and the Human Brain*. Penguin, 1994.

Damasio, Antonio. *The Feeling of What Happens: Body and Emotion in the Making of Consciousness*. Harcourt, 1999.

Damasio, Antonio. *Self Comes to Mind: Constructing the Conscious Brain*. Vintage, 2012.

Darwin, Charles. *The Origin of Species*. 1859. New American Library, 1958.

Davis, Diane. "Autozoography: Notes Toward a Rhetoricity of the Living." *Philosophy and Rhetoric*, vol. 47, no. 4, 2014, pp. 533–53.

Davis, Diane. *Inessential Solidarity: Rhetoric and Foreigner Relations*. U of Pittsburgh P, 2010.

Davis, Diane. "Some Reflections on the Limit." *Rhetoric Society Quarterly*, vol. 47, no. 3, 2017, pp. 275–84.

Deleuze, Gilles. *Difference and Repetition*. Rev. ed., translated by Paul Patton, Columbia UP, 1995.

Deleuze, Gilles. "On Gilbert Simondon." *Desert Islands and Other Texts*, edited by David Lapoujade, translated by Michael Taormina, Semiotext(se), 2004, pp. 86–89.

Deleuze, Gilles, and Félix Guattari. *A Thousand Plateaus: Capitalism and Schizophrenia*. Translated by Brian Massumi, U of Minnesota P, 1987.

Dennett, Daniel C. *Consciousness Explained*. Little, Brown, 1991.

Derrida, Jacques. *The Animal That Therefore I Am*. Edited by Marie-Louise Mallet, translated by David Wills, Fordham UP, 2008.

Derrida, Jacques. "'Eating Well,' or the Calculation of the Subject." *Who Comes After the Subject?* edited by Eduardo Cadava, Peter Connor, and Jean-Luc Nancy, translated by Peter Connor and Avital Ronell, Routledge, 1991, pp. 96–119.

Derrida, Jacques. *Of Grammatology*. Translated by Gayatri Chakravorty Spivak, Johns Hopkins UP, 1974.

Derrida, Jacques. "Signature Event Context." *Limited Inc.*, translated by Samuel Weber and Jeffrey Mehlman, Northwestern UP, 1988, pp. 1–23.
Despret, Vinciane. "The Becomings of Subjectivity in Animal Worlds." *Subjectivity*, vol. 23, iss. 1, July 2008, pp. 123–39.
Despret, Vinciane. "The Body We Care For: Figures of Anthropo-zoo-genesis." *Body & Society*, vol. 10, iss. 2–3, 2004, pp. 111–34.
Despret, Vinciane. "Sheep Do Have Opinions." *Making Things Public: Atmospheres of Democracy*, edited by Bruno Latour and Peter Weibel, MIT P, 2005, pp. 360–68.
Detienne, Marcel, and Jean-Pierre Vernant. *Cunning Intelligence in Greek Culture and Society*. Translated by Janet Lloyd, U of Chicago P, 1978.
de Waal, Frans. *Are We Smart Enough to Know How Smart Animals Are?* Norton, 2016.
Diab, Rasha. *Shades of Ṣulḥ: The Rhetorics of Arab-Islamic Reconciliation*. U of Pittsburgh P, 2016.
Dobrin, Sidney I. *Postcomposition*. Southern Illinois UP, 2011.
Dobrin, Sidney I., J. A. Rice, and Michael Vastola, editors. *Beyond Postprocess*. Utah State UP, 2011.
Dolmage, Jay. "Metis, Metis, Mestiza, Medusa: Rhetorical Bodies across Rhetorical Traditions." *Rhetoric Review*, vol. 28, no.1, 2009, pp. 1–28.
Doxtader, Erik, editor. "Forum: Addressing Animals." *Philosophy and Rhetoric*, vol. 44, no. 1, 2011, pp. 79–100.
Dreyfus, Hubert L. "Intelligence without Representation—Merleau-Ponty's Critique of Mental Representation: The Relevance of Phenomenology to Scientific Explanation." *Phenomenology and the Cognitive Sciences*, vol. 1, iss. 4, Dec. 2002, pp. 367–83.
Dreyfus, Hubert L. "Overcoming the Myth of the Mental: How Philosophers Can Profit from the Phenomenology of Everyday Expertise." *Proceedings and Addresses of the American Philosophical Association*, vol. 79, no. 2, Nov. 2005, pp. 47–65.
Dryer, Dylan B. "'The Fact That I Could Write about It Made Me Think It Was Real': An Interview with Carolyn R. Miller." *Composition Forum*, vol. 31, Spring 2015. http://compositionforum.com/issue/31/carolyn-miller-interview.php.
Dunne, Joseph. *Back to the Rough Ground: Practical Judgment and the Lure of Technique*. Notre Dame UP, 1993.
Ehrhardt, Arnold. *The Beginning*. Barnes, 1968.
Fiumara, Gemma Corradi. *The Other Side of Language: A Philosophy of Listening*. Rev. ed., Routledge, 1995.
Ford, Lewis S. *The Emergence of Whitehead's Metaphysics, 1925–29*. State U of New York P, 1984.
Foucault, Michel. *Discipline and Punish: The Birth of the Prison*. Translated by Alan Sheridan, Vintage Books, 1979.
Foucault, Michel. *Politics Philosophy Culture: Interviews and Other Writings 1977–*

1984. Edited by Lawrence Kritzman, translated by Alan Sheridan, Routledge, 1988.

Foucault, Michel. "The Subject and Power." *Michel Foucault: Beyond Structuralism and Hermeneutics*, 2nd ed., edited by Hubert L. Dreyfus and Paul Rabinow, U of Chicago P, 1983, pp. 208–26.

Framework for Success in Postsecondary Writing. Developed by Council of Writing Program Administrators, National Council of Teachers of English, and National Writing Project, 2011. www.wpacouncil.org/files/framework-for-success-postsecondary-writing.pdf.

Freeman, Walter J. *How Brains Make Up Their Minds*. Columbia UP, 2000.

Garsten, Bryan. *Saving Persuasion: A Defense of Rhetoric and Judgment*. Harvard UP, 2006.

Gee, James Paul. "Literacy, Discourse, and Linguistics: Introduction and What Is Literacy?" *Literacy: A Critical Sourcebook*, edited by Ellen Cushman, Eugene R. Kintgen, Barry M. Kroll, and Mike Rose, St. Martin's Press, 2001, pp. 525–44.

Gibson, Kathleen R. "General Introduction: Animal Minds, Human Minds." Gibson and Ingold, pp. 3–19.

Gibson, Kathleen R., and Tim Ingold, editors. *Tools, Language and Cognition in Human Evolution*. Cambridge UP, 1993.

Giddens, Anthony. *The Constitution of Society: Outline of the Theory of Structuration*. U of California P, 1984.

Godfrey-Smith, Peter. *Other Minds: The Octopus, the Sea, and the Deep Origins of Consciousness*. Farrar, Straus and Giroux, 2016.

Goodall, Jane. "Foreword." Beckoff, pp. xi–xv.

Gordon, Jeremy G., Katherine D. Lind, and Saul Kutnicki, editors. "Special Issue: A Rhetorical Bestiary." *Rhetoric Society Quarterly*, vol. 41, no. 3, 2017.

Gould, Stephen Jay. *The Mismeasure of Man*. Norton, 1981.

Green, Bill. *Water, Ice, and Stone: Science and Memory on the Antarctic Lakes*. Harmony, 1995.

Gries, Laurie E. "In Defense of Rhetoric, Plants, and New Materialism." *Rhetoric Society Quarterly*, vol. 47, no. 5, 2017, pp. 437–42.

Gries, Laurie E. *Still Life with Rhetoric: A New Materialism Approach for Visual Rhetorics*. Utah State UP, 2015.

Griffin, David Ray. "Creativity in Postmodern Religion." *Creativity in Art, Religion, and Culture*, edited by Michael H. Mitias, Rodopi, 1985, pp. 64–85.

Griffin, Donald R. *Animal Minds*. U of Chicago P, 1992.

Hairston, Maxine. "Diversity, Ideology, and Teaching Writing." *College Composition and Communication*, vol. 43, no. 2, May 1992, pp. 179–93.

Halasek, Kay. *A Pedagogy of Possibility: Bakhtinian Perspectives on Composition Studies*. Southern Illinois UP, 1999.

Haraway, Donna J. *Simians, Cyborgs, and Women: The Reinvention of Nature.* Routledge, 1991.
Haraway, Donna J. *When Species Meet.* U of Minnesota P, 2008.
Harberd, Nicholas. *Seed to Seed: The Secret Life of Plants.* Bloomsbury. 2006.
Harman, Graham. *Tool-Being: Heidegger and the Metaphysics of Objects.* Open Court, 2002.
Harrington, Anne. *Reenchanted Science: Holism in German Culture from Wilhelm II to Hitler.* Princeton UP, 1996.
Hauser, Marc D. *Wild Minds: What Animals Really Think.* Henry Holt, 2000.
Hauser, Marc D., Noam Chomsky, and W. Tecumseh Fitch. "The Faculty of Language: What Is It, Who Has It, and How Did It Evolve?" *Science*, vol. 298, Nov. 2002, pp. 1569-79.
Hawhee, Debra. *Bodily Arts: Rhetoric and Athletics in Ancient Greece.* U of Texas P, 2004.
Hawhee, Debra. *Rhetoric in Tooth and Claw: Animals, Language, Sensation.* U of Chicago P, 2017.
Hawhee, Debra. "Toward a Bestial Rhetoric." *Philosophy and Rhetoric*, vol. 44, no. 1, 2011, pp. 82-87.
Hawk, Byron. *A Counter-History of Composition: Toward Methodologies of Complexity.* U of Pittsburgh P, 2007.
Hawk, Byron. "Reassembling Postprocess: Toward a Posthuman Theory of Public Rhetoric." Dobrin et al., pp. 75-93.
Hawk, Byron. "Toward a Post-*Technê*—Or, Inventing Pedagogies for Professional Writing." *Technical Communication Quarterly*, vol. 13, no. 4, 2004, pp. 371-92.
Hayles, N. Katherine. *How We Became Posthuman: Virtual Bodies in Cybernetics, Literature, and Informatics.* U of Chicago P, 1999.
Hayles, N. Katherine. *Unthought: The Power of the Cognitive Nonconscious.* U of Chicago P, 2017.
Haynes, Cynthia. *The Homesick Phone Book: Addressing Rhetorics in the Age of Perpetual Conflict.* Southern Illinois UP, 2016.
Heidegger, Martin. *Being and Time.* Translated by John Macquarrie and Edward Robinson, HarperCollins, 1962.
Heidegger, Martin. "Building Dwelling Thinking." *Poetry, Language, Thought*, translated by Albert Hofstadter, HarperCollins, 2001, pp. 143-59.
Heidegger, Martin. *Parmenides.* Translated by André Schuwer and Richard Rojcewicz, Indiana UP, 1992.
Heidegger, Martin. "The Question Concerning Technology." *The Question Concerning Technology and Other Essays*, translated by William Lovitt, Harper, 1977, pp. 3-35.
Heidegger, Martin. "The Thing." *Poetry, Language, Thought*, translated by Albert Hofstadter, HarperCollins, 2001, pp. 163-80.

Hendricks, Obery M. Jr. "A More Perfect (High-Tech) Lynching." Sharpley-Whiting, pp.155–83.
Herndl, Carl G., and Adela C. Licona. "Shifting Agency: Agency, *Kairos*, and the Possibilities of Social Action." *Communicative Practices in Workplaces and the Professions*, edited by Mark Zachry and Charlotte Thralls, Baywood, 2007, pp. 133–53.
Hoagland, Edward. "Small Silences: Listening for the Lessons of Nature." *Harper's Magazine*, July 2004, pp. 45–58.
Hofstadter, Douglas R. *Gödel, Escher, Bach: An Eternal Golden Braid*. Basic Books, 1979.
Holland, John H. *Emergence: From Chaos to Order*. Basic Books, 1998.
Holland, John H. *Hidden Order: How Adaptation Builds Complexity*. Basic Books, 1995.
Holquist, Michael. "Introduction," Bakhtin, *Dialogic Imagination*, pp. xv–xxxiv.
Horkheimer, Max, and Theodor W. Adorno. *Dialectic of Enlightenment*. Translated by John Cumming, Continuum, 1989.
Husserl, Edmund. *Ideas Pertaining to a Pure Phenomenology and to a Phenomenological Philosophy, First Book: General Introduction to a Pure Phenomenology*. Translated by F. Kersten, Martinus Nijhoff, 1983.
Hutchins, Edwin. *Cognition in the Wild*. MIT P, 1995.
Ingold, Tim. *Being Alive: Essays on Movement, Knowledge and Description*. Routledge, 2011.
Ingold, Tim. *Making: Anthropology, Archaeology, Art and Architecture*. Routledge, 2013.
Ingold, Tim. *The Perception of the Environment: Essays in Livelihood, Dwelling and Skill*. Routledge, 2000.
Ingold, Tim. "Tool-use, Sociality and Intelligence." Gibson and Ingold, pp. 429–45.
Jackendoff, Ray, and Steven Pinker. "The Nature of the Language Faculty and Its Implications for Evolution of Language." *Cognition*, vol. 97, no. 2005, pp. 211–25.
Jackson, Derrick Z. "Mutt on CP Time, Discipline of Macolm." Sharpley-Whiting, pp. 224–34.
Jacobs, Jane. *The Death and Life of Great American Cities*. Random House, 1961.
James, William. *The Principles of Psychology*. Vol. 1. 1890. Cosimo Classics, 2007.
Jarratt, Susan C. "Feminism and Composition: The Case for Conflict." *Contending with Words: Composition and Rhetoric in a Postmodern Age*, edited by Patricia Harkin and John Schilb, Modern Language Association, 1991, pp. 105–23.
Jegstrup, Elsebet. "Letter to the Editor." *Daily Mining Gazette* [Houghton, MI], 11 Jan. 2012, p. 4.
Johanson, Donald, and Blake Edgar. *From Lucy to Language*. A Peter N. Nevramont Book/Simon and Schuster, 1996.
Johnson, Steven. "Tool for Thought." *New York Times*, 30 Jan. 2005.
Kant, Immanuel. *Critique of Judgment*. Translated by Werner Pluhar, Hackett, 1987.
Kauffman, Stuart. *At Home in the Universe: The Search for the Laws of Self-Organization and Complexity*. Oxford UP, 1995.

Kauffman, Stuart. *Investigations*. Oxford UP, 2000.
Kelly, Kevin. "The Hacker Historian." *Wired*, March 2012, pp. 94-97, 122.
Kennedy, George. "A Hoot in the Dark: The Evolution of General Rhetoric." *Philosophy and Rhetoric*, vol. 25, no. 1, 1992, pp. 1-21.
Kennedy, Robert F. "Statement on the Death of Martin Luther King, Jr., April 4, 1968." John F. Kennedy Presidential Library and Museum. Accession Number RFK309. (Video.)
Kennerly, Michele, and Carly S. Woods. "Moving Rhetorica." *Rhetoric Society Quarterly*, vol. 48, no. 1, 2018, pp. 3-27.
Kent, Thomas. "Preface: Righting Writing." Dobrin et al., pp. xi-xxii.
Kerényi, Karl. *Hermes, Guide of Souls*. Translated by Murray Stein, Spring, 1987.
Kimmerer, Robin Wall. *Braiding Sweetgrass: Indigenous Wisdom, Scientific Knowledge, and the Teaching of Plants*. Milkweed Editions, 2013.
Klein, Richard G. *The Human Career: Human Biological and Cultural Origins*. 2nd ed., U of Chicago P, 1999.
Kress, Gunter. "Design and Transformation: New Theories of Meaning." Cope and Kalantzis, pp. 153-61.
Kress, Gunter. "Gains and Losses: New Forms of Texts, Knowledge, and Learning." *Computers and Composition*, vol. 22, iss. 1, 2005, pp. 5-22.
Kress, Gunter. *Literacy in the New Media Age*. Routledge, 2003.
Latour, Bruno. "Cogito Ergo Sumus! Or Psychology Swept Outside by the Fresh Air of the Upper Deck . . ." *Mind, Culture, and Activity*, vol. 3, no. 1, 1995, pp. 54-63.
Latour, Bruno. *On the Modern Cult of the Factish Gods*. Duke UP, 2010.
Latour, Bruno. *Pandora's Hope: Essays on the Reality of Science Studies*. Harvard UP, 1999.
Latour, Bruno. *Politics of Nature: How To Bring the Sciences into Democracy*. Translated by Catherine Porter, Harvard UP, 2004.
Latour, Bruno. *Reassembling the Social*. Oxford UP, 2005.
Latour, Bruno. "A Textbook Case Revisited: Knowledge as a Mode of Experience." *The Handbook of Science and Technology Studies*. 3rd ed., edited by Edward J. Hackett et al., MIT P, 2007, pp. 83-112.
Latour, Bruno. *We Have Never Been Modern*. Translated by Catherine Porter, Harvard UP, 1993.
Latour, Bruno. "A Well-Articulated Primatology: Reflections of a Fellow Traveler." *Primate Encounters: Models of Science, Gender, and Society*, edited by Shirley C. Strum and Linda Marie Fedigan, U of Chicago P, 2000, pp. 358-81.
Latour, Bruno. "Why Has Critique Run Out of Steam? From Matters of Fact to Matters of Concern." *Critical Inquiry*, vol. 30, no. 2, 2004, pp. 225-48.
Latour, Bruno, Graham Harman, and Peter Erdélyi. *The Prince and the Wolf: Latour and Harman at the LSE*. Zero Books, 2011.

Lauer, Janice M., Gene Montague, Andrea Lunsford, and Janet Emig. *Four Worlds of Writing*. 2nd ed., HarperCollins, 1985.

Leroi-Gourhan, André. *Gesture and Speech*. 1964. Translated by Anna Bostock Berger, MIT P, 1993.

Levinas, Emmanuel. *Entre Nous: On Thinking-of-the-Other*. Translated by Michael B. Smith and Barbara Harshav, Columbia UP, 1998.

Levy, Steven. "Loitering on the Dark Side." *Time*, 3 May 1999, p. 39.

Libet, Benjamin. "Do We Have Free Will?" *Journal of Consciousness Studies*, vol. 6, no. 8–9, Aug. 1999, pp. 47–57.

Lippi-Green, Rosina. *English with an Accent: Language, Ideology, and Discrimination in the United States*. Routledge, 1997.

Lister-Kaye, John. *Gods of the Morning: A Bird's-Eye View of a Changing World*. Pegasus Books, 2016.

Lundberg, Christian, and Joshua Gunn. "'Ouija Board, Are There Any Communications?' Agency, Ontotheology, and the Death of the Humanist Subject, or, Continuing the ARS Conversation." *Rhetoric Society Quarterly*, vol. 35, no. 4, Fall 2005, pp. 83–106.

Lynch, Dennis A., Diana George, and Marilyn M. Cooper. "Moments of Argument: Agonistic Inquiry and Confrontational Cooperation." *College Composition and Communication*, vol. 48, no. 1, Feb. 1997, pp. 61–85.

Lynch, Tom. *150 Charts*. Available at www.tomlynch.com.

Luhmann, Niklas. *Social Systems*. Translated by John Bednarz Jr., with Dirk Baecker, Stanford UP, 1995.

Lyotard, Jean-François. *The Differend: Phrases in Dispute*. Translated by Georges Van Den Abbeele, U of Minnesota P, 1988.

Mandel, Barrett J. "The Writer Writing Is Not at Home." *College Composition and Communication*, vol. 31, no. 4, Dec. 1980, pp. 370–77.

Mansbach, Adam. "The Audacity of Post-Racism." Sharpley-Whiting, pp. 69–84.

Marcuse, Herbert. *One-Dimensional Man: Studies in the Ideology of Advanced Industrial Society*. Beacon Press, 1964.

Margolick, David. "The Power of Bobby Kennedy's Eulogy for Martin Luther King." *New York Times*, 4 April 2018.

Marschall, Richard, editor. *The Best of Little Nemo in Slumberland*. Stewart, Tabori & Chang, 1997.

Massumi, Brian. *Semblance and Event: Activist Philosophy and the Occurrent Arts*. MIT P, 2013.

Maturana, Humberto R. "Autopoesis, Structural Coupling and Cognition: A History of These and Other Notions in the Biology of Cognition." *Cybernetics and Human Knowing*, vol. 9, no. 3–4, 2002, pp. 5–34.

Maturana, Humberto R. "Biology of Language: The Epistemology of Reality." *Psychol-*

ogy and Biology of Language and Thought: Essays in Honor of Eric Lenneberg, edited by George A. Miller and Elizabeth Lenneberg, Academic Press, 1978, pp. 27–63.

Maturana, Humberto R. "The Nature of the Laws of Nature." *Systems Research and Behavioral Science*, vol. 17, iss. 5, Sept.–Oct. 2000, pp. 459–68.

Maturana, Humberto R. "Reality: The Search for Objectivity or the Quest for a Compelling Argument." *Irish Journal of Psychology*, vol. 9, no. 1, 1988, pp. 25–82.

Maturana, Humberto R. "Response to Berman's Critique of *The Tree of Knowledge*." *Journal of Humanistic Psychology*, vol. 31, no.2, Spring 1991, pp. 88–97.

Maturana, Humberto R., and Bernhard Poerksen. *From Being to Doing: The Origins of the Biology of Cognition*. Translated by Wolfram Karl Koeck and Alison Rosemary Koeck, Carl-Auer, 2004.

Maturana, Humberto R., and Francisco J. Varela. *Autopoesis and Cognition: The Realization of the Living*. D. Reidel, 1980.

Maturana, Humberto R., and Francisco J. Varela. *The Tree of Knowledge: The Biological Roots of Human Understanding*. Rev. ed., Shambhala Press, 1998.

Mazis, Glen A. *Humans, Animals, Machines: Blurring Boundaries*. State U of New York P, 2008.

Merleau-Ponty, Maurice. *Phenomenology of Perception*. Translated by Colin Smith, Routledge, 1962.

Miklósi, Ádám, Enikö Kubinyi, József Topál, Márta Gácsi, Zsófia Virányi, and Vilmos Csányi. "A Simple Reason for a Big Difference: Wolves Do Not Look Back at Humans, but Dogs Do." *Current Biology*, vol. 13, no. 9, 2003, pp. 763–66.

Milius, Susan, "In Tests of Planning, Ravens Act Like Apes." *Science News*, 19 Aug. 2017, p. 9.

Miller, Carolyn R. "The Appeal(s) of Latour." *Rhetoric Society Quarterly*, vol. 47, no. 5, 2017, pp. 454–59.

Miller, Carolyn R. "Genre as Social Action." *Quarterly Journal of Speech*, vol. 70, 1984, pp. 151–67.

Miller, Carolyn R. "What Can Automation Tell Us about Agency?" *Rhetoric Society Quarterly* vol. 37, no. 2, 2007, pp. 137–57.

Mindwalk. Directed by Bernt Amadeus Capra, produced by Klaus Lintschinger, screenplay by Floyd Byars and Fritjof Capra, 1990.

Mithen, Steven. "Creations of Pre-Modern Human Minds: Stone Tool Manufacture and Use by *Homo habilis, heidelbergensis,* and *neanderthalensis*." *Creations of the Mind: Theories of Artifacts and Their Representation*, edited by Eric Margolis and Stephen Laurence, Oxford UP, pp. 289–311.

Morton, Timothy. *The Ecological Thought*. Harvard UP, 2010.

Muckelbauer, John. *The Future of Invention: Rhetoric, Postmodernism, and the Problem of Change*. State U of New York P, 2008.

Muckelbauer, John. "Implicit Paradigms of Rhetoric." Barnett and Boyle, pp. 30–41.

Muckelbauer, John. "On Reading Differently: Through Foucault's Resistance." *College English*, vol. 63, no. 1, Sept. 2000, pp. 71-94.

Murray, Donald M. "Write before Writing." *College Composition and Communication*, vol. 29, no. 4, Dec. 1978, pp. 375-82.

Murray, Donald M. *Write to Learn*. Holt, 1984.

Nancy, Jean-Luc. *Being Singular Plural*. Translated by Robert D. Richardson and Anne E. O'Byrne, Stanford UP, 2000.

National Commission on Writing in America's Schools and Colleges. *The Neglected "R": The Need for a Writing Revolution*. College Entrance Examination Board, 2003.

Nealon, Jeffrey T. *Foucault beyond Foucault: Power and Its Intensifications since 1984*. Stanford UP, 2008.

New London Group. "A Pedagogy of Multiliteracies: Designing Social Futures." Cope and Kalantzis, pp. 9-37.

Obama, Barack. *Dreams from My Father: A Story of Race and Inheritance*. 1995. Three Rivers P, 2004.

Obama, Barack. "A More Perfect Union." Constitution Center. Philadelphia, 18 Mar. 2008. (Address.)

Obery, M. Hendricks Jr. "A More Perfect (High-Tech) Lynching." Sharpley-Whiting, pp. 155-83.

Ouattara, Karim, Alban Lemasson, and Klaus Zuberbühler. "Campbell's Monkeys Concatenate Vocalizations into Context-specific Call Sequences." *Proceedings of the National Academy of Sciences*, vol. 106, no. 61, Dec. 2009, pp. 22026-31. www.pnas.org/content/early/2009/12/08/0908118106.abstract?sid=/.

Oyama, Susan. *The Ontogeny of Information: Developmental Systems and Evolution*. 2nd ed., Duke UP, 2000.

Parrish, Alex C. *Adaptive Rhetoric: Evolution, Culture, and the Art of Persuasion*. Routledge, 2013.

Pender, Kelly. *Techne, from Neoclassicism to Postmodernism: Understanding Writing as a Useful Teachable Art*. Parlor Press, 2011.

Perelman, Chaim. "Rhetoric and Politics." *Philosophy and Rhetoric*, vol. 17, no. 3, 1984, pp. 129-34.

Perelman, Chaim, and L. Olbrechts-Tyteca. *The New Rhetoric: A Treatise on Argumentation*. Translated by John Wilkinson and Purcell Weaver, U of Notre Dame P, 1969.

Pepperberg, Irene M. *Alex and Me: How a Scientist and a Parrot Discovered a Hidden World of Animal Intelligence—and Formed a Deep Bond in the Process*. Harper, 2008.

Pflugfelder, Ehren Helmut. "Is No One at the Wheel? Nonhuman Agency and Agentive Movement." *Thinking with Bruno Latour in Rhetoric and Composition*, edited by Paul Lynch and Nathaniel Rivers, Southern Illinois UP, 2015, pp. 115-31.

Phelps, Louise Wetherbee. *Composition as a Human Science: Contributions to the Self-Understanding of a Discipline*. Oxford UP, 1988.

Pollan, Michael. *Second Nature: A Gardener's Education*. Grove Press, 1991.
Prigogine, Ilya, and Peter M. Allen. "The Challenge of Complexity." *Self-Organization and Dissipative Structures: Applications in the Physical and Social Sciences*, edited by William C. Schieve and Peter M. Allen, U of Texas P, 1982, pp. 3–39.
Prigogine, Ilya, and Isabelle Stengers. *Order out of Chaos: Man's New Dialogue with Nature*. Bantam, 1984.
Prior, Paul, and Jody Shipka. "Chronotopic Lamination: Tracing the Contours of Literate Activity." *Writing Selves/Writing Societies*, edited by Charles Bazerman and David Russell, 2003. www.wac.colostate.edu/books/selves_societies/.
Ratcliffe, Krista. *Rhetorical Listening: Identification, Gender, Whiteness*. Southern Illinois UP, 2005.
Remnick, David. *The Bridge: The Life and Rise of Barack Obama*. Knopf, 2010.
Rice, Jenny. *Distant Publics: Development Rhetoric and the Subject of Crisis*. U of Pittsburgh P, 2012.
Rickert, Thomas. *Acts of Enjoyment: Rhetoric, Zizek, and the Return of the Subject*. U of Pittsburgh P, 2007.
Rickert, Thomas. *Ambient Rhetoric: The Attunements of Rhetorical Being*. U of Pittsburgh P, 2013.
Rickert, Thomas. "Towards Ecosophy in a Participating World: Rhetoric and Cosmology in Heidegger's Fourfold and Empedocles' Four Roots." *Tracing Rhetoric and Material Life: Ecological Approaches*, edited by Bridie McGreavy et al., Palgrave Macmillan, 2017, pp. 59–83.
Rickert, Thomas. "Tuning: A Brief on Rhetoric, Relationality, and Attunement." *Rhetoric Society Quarterly*, vol. 47, no. 5, 2017, pp. 448–54.
Ricoeur, Paul. "The Hermeneutical Function of Distanciation." *Philosophy Today*, vol. 17, iss. 2, Summer 1973, pp. 129–41.
Roberts-Miller, Patricia. *Deliberate Conflict*. Southern Illinois UP, 2007.
Roberts-Miller, Patricia. "Fighting without Hatred: Hannah Arendt's Agonistic Rhetoric." *JAC*, vol. 22, no. 3, 2002, pp. 585–601.
Robinson, Keith. "Toward a Metaphysics of Complexity." *Interchange*, vol. 36, 2005, pp. 159–77.
Rohman, D. Gordon, and Albert O. Wlecke. *Prewriting: The Construction and Application of Models for Concept Formation in Writing*. Office of Education, U.S. Department of Health, Education, and Welfare, 1964.
Rorty, Richard. *Philosophy and the Mirror of Nature*. Princeton UP, 1979.
Sachs, Joe. "Introduction." Aristotle, *Nicomachean*, pp. xi–xxv.
Schultz, Connie. "His Grandmother, My Father, Your Uncle . . ." Sharpley-Whiting, pp. 102–12.
Schutz, Alfred. "Making Music Together: A Study in Social Relationship." *Social Research*, vol. 18, no. 1, Mar. 1951, pp. 76–97.

Schutz, Alfred. *The Problem of Social Reality: Collected Papers*. Vol. 1, edited by Maurice Natanson, Nijhoff, 1961.

Sennett, Richard. *The Craftsman*. Penguin/Allen Lane, 2008.

Shapiro, Lawrence. *Embodied Cognition*. Routledge, 2011.

Sharpley-Whiting, T. Denean. "Chloro from Morning Joe: Introduction." Sharpley-Whiting, pp.1–15.

Sharpley-Whiting, T. Denean, editor. *The Speech: Race and Barack Obama's "A More Perfect Union."* Bloomsbury, 2009.

Shaviro, Steven. *The Universe of Things: On Speculative Realism*. U of Minnesota P, 2014.

Shaviro, Steven. *Without Criteria: Kant, Whitehead, Deleuze, and Aesthetics*. MIT P, 2009.

Sheard, Cynthia Miecznikowski. "The Public Value of Epideictic Rhetoric." *College English*, vol. 58, no. 7, Nov. 1996, pp. 765–94.

Sicking, C. M. J. "The General Purport of Pericles' Funeral Oration." *Hermes*, vol. 123, 1995, pp. 404–25.

Simondon, Gilbert. "The Genesis of the Individual," translated by Mark Cohen and Sanford Kwinter. *Incorporations*, edited by Jonathan Crary and Sanford Kwinter, Zone, 1992, pp. 297–319.

Simondon, Gilbert. "Technical Mentality," translated by Arne De Boever. *Parrhesia*, vol. 7, 2009, pp. 17–27.

Smith, Erec. "The New Cultural Politics of Obama." Conference on College Composition and Communication. San Francisco. Mar. 2009. (Presentation.)

Smuts, Barbara. "Encounters with Animal Minds." *Journal of Consciousness Studies*, vol. 8, nos. 5–7, 2001, pp. 293–309.

Spinoza, Benedict de. *Ethics*. 1677. Edited and translated by Edwin Curley, Penguin, 1996.

Spuybroek, Lars. *The Symphony of Things: Ruskin and the Ecology of Design*. V_2 Publishing, 2011.

Stack, Liam. "When Robert F. Kennedy Told an Indianapolis Crowd of King's Assassination." *New York Times*, 4 April 2018.

Stengers, Isabelle. "Introductory Notes on an Ecology of Practices." *Cultural Studies Review*, vol. 11, iss. 1, Mar. 2013, pp. 183–96.

Stengers, Isabelle. *Thinking with Whitehead: A Free and Wild Creation of Concepts*. Translated by Michael Chase, Harvard UP, 2011.

Stengers, Isabelle. "Whitehead's Account of the Sixth Day." *Configurations*, vol. 13, no. 1, Winter 2005, pp. 35–55.

Stiegler, Bernard. *The Re-enchantment of the World: The Value of Spirit against Industrial Populism*. Translated by Trevor Arthur, Bloomsbury Academic, 2014.

Stiegler, Bernard. *Technics and Time, 1: The Fault of Epimetheus*. Translated by Richard Beardsworth and George Collins, Stanford UP, 1998.

Stiegler, Bernard. *Technics and Time, 2: Disorientation*. Translated by Stephen Barker, Stanford UP, 2009.

Stormer, Nathan, and Bridie McGreavy. "Thinking Ecologically about Rhetoric's Ontology: Capacity, Vulnerability, and Resilience." *Philosophy and Rhetoric*, 50, vol. 50, no. 1, 2017, pp. 1–25.

Suchman, Lucy A. *Plans and Situated Actions: The Problem of Human-Machine Communication*. Cambridge UP, 1987.

Sugrue, Thomas J. *Not Even Past: Barack Obama and the Burden of Race*. Princeton UP, 2010.

Sullivan, Dale. "A Closer Look at Education as Epideictic Rhetoric." *Rhetoric Society Quarterly*, vol. 23, no. 3–4, Summer–Autumn 1994, pp. 70–89.

Syverson, Margaret. *The Wealth of Reality: An Ecology of Composition*. Southern Illinois UP, 1999.

Taylor, Mark C. *The Moment of Complexity: Emerging Network Culture*. U of Chicago P, 2001.

Thompson, Evan. *Mind in Life: Biology, Phenomenology, and the Sciences of Mind*. Harvard UP, 2007.

Thucydides. "Pericles Funeral Oration." *Peloponnesian War*, Book 2.34–46. https://sourcebooks.fordham.edu/ancient/pericles-funeralspeech.asp.

Todd, Kim. "The Island Wolves." *Orion Magazine*, May/June 2017. www.orionmagazine.org/article/the-island-wolves/.

Trimbur, John. *The Call to Write*, 3rd ed. Pearson, 2005.

Tsing, Anna Lowenhaupt. *Friction: An Ethnography of Global Connection*. Princeton UP, 2005.

Tsing, Anna Lowenhaupt. *The Mushroom at the End of the World: On the Possibility of Life in Capitalist Ruins*. Princeton UP, 2015.

Turing, A.M. "Computing Machinery and Intelligence." *Mind*, vol. 59, no. 236, Oct. 1950, pp. 433–60.

Tye, Larry. *Bobby Kennedy: The Making of a Liberal Lion*. Random House, 2016.

Uexküll, Jakob von. *A Foray into the Worlds of Animals and Humans, with A Theory of Meaning*. Translated by Joseph D. O'Neil, U of Minnesota P, 2010.

Uexküll, Jakob von. *Theoretical Biology*. Kegan Paul, Trench, Trubner, 1926.

Varela, Francisco, Evan Thompson, and Eleanor Rosch. *The Embodied Mind: Cognitive Science and Human Experience*. MIT P, 1991.

Venn, Couze. "Individuation, Relationality, Affect: Rethinking the Human in Relation to the Living." *Body & Society*, vol. 16, no. 1, 2010, pp. 129–61.

Vitanza, Victor J. "Preface." *Writing Histories of Rhetoric*, edited by Victor J. Vitanza, Southern Illinois UP, 1994, pp. vii–xii.

Waldrop, M. Mitchell. *Complexity: The Emerging Science at the Edge of Order and Chaos*. Simon and Schuster, 1992.

Walker, Jeffrey. "Aristotle's Lyric: Re-Imagining the Rhetoric of Epideictic Song." *College English*, vol. 51, no.1, Jan. 1989, pp. 5–28.

Walker, Jeffrey. *The Genuine Teachers of This Art: Rhetorical Education in Antiquity*. U of South Carolina P, 2012.

Wegner, Daniel M. *The Illusion of Conscious Will*. MIT P, 2002.

Welch, Nancy. *Living Room: Teaching Public Writing in a Privatized World*. Heinemann/Boynton-Cook, 2008.

Weng, Juyang, James McClelland, Alex Pentland, Olaf Sporns, Ida Stockman, Mriganka Sur, and Esther Thelen. "Autonomous Mental Development by Robots and Animals." *Science*, vol. 291, 26 Jan. 2001, pp. 599–600.

Wertsch, James V. *Mind as Action*. Oxford UP, 1998.

Whitehead, Alfred North. *Adventures of Ideas*. 1933. Free Press, 1967.

Whitehead, Alfred North. *The Aims of Education and Other Essays*. 1929. Free Press, 1967.

Whitehead, Alfred North. *The Concept of Nature*. 1920. Prometheus Books, 2004.

Whitehead, Alfred North. *Modes of Thought*. Free Press, 1938.

Whitehead, Alfred North. *Process and Reality*. 1929. Corrected edition, edited by David Ray Griffin and Donald W. Sherburne, Free Press, 1978.

Whitehead, Alfred North. *Religion in the Making*. Fordham UP, 1926.

Whitehead, Alfred North. *Science and the Modern World*. 1925. Free Press, 1967.

Wiener, Norbert. *The Human Use of Human Beings: Cybernetics and Society*. Da Capo Press, 1954.

Wilde, Oscar. "The Decay of Lying." 1891. *The Artist as Critic: Critical Writings of Oscar Wilde*, edited by Richard Ellman, U of Chicago P, 1968, pp. 290–320.

Wittgenstein, Ludwig. *Philosophical Investigations*, 3rd ed. Translated by G. E. M. Anscombe, Macmillan, 1968.

Woodard, Colin. "Clever Canines: Did Domestication Make Dogs Smarter?" *Chronicle of Higher Education*, 15 Apr. 2005. www.chronicle.com/free/v51/i32/32a01201.htm.

Wray, Alison. "Holistic Utterances in Protolanguage: The Link from Primates to Humans." *The Evolutionary Emergence of Language: Social Function and the Origins of Linguistic Form*, edited by Chris Knight, Michael Studdert-Kennedy, and James R. Hurford, Cambridge UP, 2000, pp. 285–302.

Yong, Ed. "A Brainless Slime that Shares Memories by Fusing." *The Atlantic*, 21 Dec. 2016. www.theatlantic.com/science/archive/2016/12/the-brainless-slime-that-can-learn-by-fusing/511295/.

Young, Iris Marion. *Justice and the Politics of Difference*. Princeton UP, 1990.

Young, Richard E., Alton L. Becker, and Kenneth L. Pike. *Rhetoric: Discovery and Change*. Harcourt, Brace and World, 1970.

Zickefoose, Julie. *The Bluebird Effect: Uncommon Bonds with Common Birds*. Houghton Mifflin Harcourt, 2012.

Index

accountability, 6, 49, 130
actual entity, 22–23, 36, 115–17, 135, 154–55, 205, 207
Adorno, Theodor W. *See* Horkheimer and Adorno
adventure of ideas, 27, 158–59, 176, 180, 192, 202
affect, 25, 29, 107, 133–35, 247n10
agency: as common, 128; as distributed, 61; as emergent, 14, 23; productive, 137–39, 141–53; as a relation, 131, 137–38
agential cut, 11, 48, 107, 115, 130, 190. *See also* boundary drawing practices
agents: active, 132–36; autonomous, 113; as emergent, 13–14, 22; ethical, 134; as individuating entities, 126, 129–30; nonhuman, 64, 129, 242n2; postmodern, 131–32. *See also* subjects
al-Sādāt, Muḥammad Anwar, 230–31
anthropomorphism, 54, 66
appetition, 30, 135, 161
Arca, Rosemary, 8, 236n13
Arendt, Hannah, 16–17, 194, 197–98, 247n6

argument, 139, 191, 193, 217. *See also* persuasion
Aristotle, 9, 26, 38–39, 42, 77–80, 83–85, 87–89, 147, 149, 192, 194, 231
Atwill, Janet, 77–78, 90–92, 239n3
Austin, J. L., 29

Bacon, Nora, 8
Badiou, Alain, 246n1
Bakhtin, Mikhail, 65–66, 123–24, 178, 186–88
Barad, Karen, 235n5, 240n4; on agency, 129; on entanglement, 22; on ethics, 6, 10–11, 33, 92, 130, 189; on knowing, 48–49; on material-discursive practice, 190; on meaning, 49; on minds as material, 130; on phenomena, 35, 136, 241n8; on reality, 24, 48–49; on responsibility, 221. *See also* agential cut; boundary drawing practices; intra-action; mattering
Barbery, Muriel, 177
Barnett, Scot, and Boyle, "Introduction: Rhetorical Ontology," 5

Index

Bateson, Gregory, 47, 48, 61, 62, 126
Becker, Alton. *See* Young, Becker, and Pike
becoming: assumption of enchanted ontology, 22; and being, 77, 78, 79–81, 82, 84–86, 117, 241n8; and concrescence, 22–23; definition of, 12–13; and Enlightenment thought, 108–9
Benhabib, Seyla, 152
Bennett, Jane, 27, 139
Bergson, Henri, 25, 26, 244n5
Berlin, James, 229, 239n1
Bernard-Donals, Michael, 189–90, 194, 200–101, 246n1
Biesecker, Barbara, 129
bifurcation of nature, 12, 23, 78, 79–81, 82, 240n10
Bogdanov, Alexander, 27
Bohr, Niels, 34, 35, 48, 49, 190, 240n4
Bok, Gordon, 76
boundary drawing practices, 34, 36. *See also* agential cut; decision
Bourdieu, Pierre, 91
Boyle, Casey, 41, 43, 127. *See also* Barnett and Boyle
Bradshaw, John, 58
Braidotti, Rosi, 5
Brooke, Collin, and Rickert, "Being Delicious," 4, 5
Brooke, Robert, 128
Burke, Kenneth, 46, 67, 70, 71
Butler, Judith, 125

Capra, Fritjof, 27, 124
Carroll, Sean, 73

Carter, Michael, 15, 157, 164–70, 172–75, 245n14
causation, 112–13, 130, 153–54
de Certeau, Michel, 80
change, 25–26, 107–15, 233–34. *See also* permanence and change
choice, 141, 152–53, 155, 219–20
Chomsky, Noam. *See* Hauser, Chomsky, and Fitch
Chorost, Michael, 208–10
Clark, Andy, 46, 61, 62–63, 66, 238n19
Clark, Katerina, and Holquist, *Mikhail Bakhtin*, 65–66
Clifford, John, 128
cobalt, 212–13, 214
cochlear implant, 208–10
cognition: conscious, nonconscious, and unconscious, 55, 143; distributed 61–66; as enactive, 11, 47–48, 51–54; human and nonhuman, 46, 54–60
cognitive ecologies, 61–67. *See also* entanglement
collective, 136, 151, 243n13
community-managed forest campaign, 215–18
complex systems, 65, 109–12, 113–15, 119, 158, 164
complex system theory (complexity), 3, 4, 23, 27, 109
consciousness, 145, 165; shifts in, 155, 244n24
concrescence, 12–13, 22–23, 87, 107, 116–17, 134–35, 154, 160– 64, 241n7, 245n14; and the fourfold, 35–36; and Carter's beginnings, 169–73. *See also* correspondence; individuation; intra-action; reciprocal induction
Connolly, William, 25

consensus, 194, 201
contingency, 108, 110–12, 133–34, 199
contrast, 30–31, 139, 163, 192
Coole, Diana, and Frost, "Introducing the New Materialisms," 5
Corder, Jim, 194–95, 198–200
correspondence, 11–12, 20, 76, 84–85, 87, 89–90, 92–105, 223. *See also* concrescence; individuation; intra-action; reciprocal induction
cosmos, 9, 22, 157, 236n12
creativity: assumption of enchantment ontology, 9, 22; defined, 157–58, 159; as emergent, 23; more significant in living systems, 158; and permanence and change, 161; of the universe, 163–64
creatures, 17, 164, 189, 242–43n10, 247n2
Csányi, Vilmos, 57–58

Damasio, Antonio, 54, 144, 149
Darwin, Charles, 24, 26, 54, 112
Davis, Diane, 5, 60, 132, 219, 246n18, 247n10
decision, 35–36, 115, 154–55. *See also* boundary drawing practices; structural determination; "yuck" and "yum"
Deleuze, Gilles, 24, 25, 175, 240n4. *See also* Deleuze and Guattari
Deleuze and Guattari, *A Thousand Plateaus,* 12, 106–7, 119–20, 158, 185, 240n1, 244n24. *See also* wasp and orchid
Dennett, Daniel, 54–55
Derrida, Jacques, 45–46, 67, 70, 128, 193; on writing, 71–72

Descartes, René, 134
Despret, Vinciane, 208, 211–12, 240n4, 244n1
Detienne, Marcel, and Vernant, *Cunning Intelligence in Greek Culture and Society,* 7, 77, 78, 81–82, 86, 88
de Waal, Frans, 55
Diab, Rasha, 230–31
dialectic, 15, 27, 30, 31, 139, 166–67, 170, 172, 185, 240n9, 246n22
differánce, 72
disclosure, 32, 34, 40.
Dobrin, Sidney, 235n7
dogs, 181; and wolves, 57–58
dragonfly, 190–91, 205, 206, 213
Dreyfus, Hubert, 144
Dunne, Joseph, 12, 77, 78, 79, 83–84, 87–89, 226
duration, 25–26
dwelling, 32–33

education, 42–43, 222, 228. *See also* pedagogy; service learning
embodiment, 237n1
Emig, Janet. *See* Lauer, Montague, Lunsford, and Emig
emotions, 143–44, 146, 152
enactive approach to mind, 14, 47, 133, 140–47
enchantment ontology: assumptions of, 9, 21–24, 76; definition of, 6; distinct from social constructivism and postmodernism, 23–24; origins of, 24–27; and writing, 19, 166
endurance, 120–26
enjoyment, 30, 135, 161, 173–75
Enframing, 46, 74

entanglement: assumption of enchantment ontology, 22; definition of, 22
epideictic rhetoric, 18, 222, 228–30
epistéme, 12, 77
epistemology and ontology, 4, 5, 29
ethics, 9, 33, 130–31, 156
experience: habits of, 39–40, 202; hold on, 17, 202
expression, 205

fact, 7, 115, 117, 152, 160, 179
feedback, 62, 124–25, 142, 241n12, 241n13
Fitch, W. Tecumseh. *See* Hauser, Chomsky, and Fitch
Fiumara, Gemma, 193, 207
Fixer Upper (television series), 222–23
Ford, Lewis, 182, 241n7
Foucault, Michel, 14, 60, 75, 128, 137–39, 151, 184–85, 190, 220
the fourfold, 23, 33, 35–36
Framework for Success in Postsecondary Writing, 8–9, 44
free will, 130, 153–56
Freeman, Walter, 14, 140, 141–43, 145, 146, 153–54, 244n24
Frost, Samantha. *See* Coole and Frost

Garsten, Bryan, 147, 148, 151, 152, 190, 192, 204, 205, 244n22
Gee, James Paul, 59
Gibson, Kathleen, 66
Giddens, Anthony, 144
Gould, Stephen Jay, 74, 112
Graham, Scott, 127

Green, Bill, 212–13, 214, 247–48n15
Griffin, David Ray, 165, 245n8
Griffin, Donald, 54, 55
Gunn, Joshua, 133. *See also* Lundberg and Gunn

habits, 6, 8–9, 12, 14–15, 31, 38–44, 78, 88, 90, 144–45, 221, 243–44n20. *See also* hexis; writing, habits of
Hairston, Maxine, 229
Halasek, Kay, 186–87
Haraway, Donna, 16, 22, 32, 49, 61, 174, 191, 199, 210, 240n4. *See also* reciprocal induction
Harberd, Nicholas, 12, 93–105, 193
Harman, Graham, 35, 36, 126
Harrington, Anne, 25
Hauser, Mark, 59. *See also* Hauser, Chomsky, and Fitch
Hauser, Chomsky, and Fitch, "The Faculty of Language," 58, 66, 71, 72
Hawhee, Debra, 60, 88
Hawk, Byron, 4–5, 90, 91–92, 229, 239n6, 239n8, 240n9
Hayles, Katherine, 46–47, 55, 56, 61
Haynes, Cynthia, 233
Heidegger, Martin, 23, 25, 32–33, 46, 74–75, 155–56, 207. *See also* disclosure; dwelling; Enframing; the fourfold
Herndl, Carl, and Licona, "Shifting Agency," 14, 128, 131
hexis, 9, 38–39, 44, 78, 88, 221. *See also* habits
Hoagland, Edward, 3
Hofstadter, Douglas, 113
Holland, John, 13, 106, 109–10, 111, 240n4

Holquist, Michael, 123. *See also* Clark and Holquist
Horkheimer, Max, and Adorno, *Dialectic of Enlightenment,* 46
humans: distinct from other animals (or not), 45–46, 66–67, 68, 71, 72–73; evolution of, 73–74, 238n18; invention of, 70–71
humanism, 4, 5, 77
hummingbirds, 211–12
Hutchins, Edwin, 47–48, 61, 62–63
hylomorphism, 12, 76, 82–83, 85, 117
hypnosis, 15, 178, 246n18

importance, 15–16, 157, 167–68, 175, 176, 177, 180, 181, 222–24, 227–28. *See also* mattering
individuation, 13, 107, 117–18, 125–26, 129–30, 242n3. *See also* concrescence; correspondence; intra-action; reciprocal induction
Ingold, Tim: on cognition, 51; on foresight, 86–87; on skill as enactive, 59–60; on stories, 20–21, 89; on tools and speech, 67–68. *See also* correspondence; making
instinct, 52–53, 72–73
intention, 5, 113–14, 129–30, 133, 140, 141–44, 145, 146, 201, 243n14
interstices, 31
intra-action: definition of, 93, 235n3; as knowing, 11; as the process of emergence, 22, 107. *See also* concrescence; correspondence; individuation; reciprocal induction
Isocrates, 91

Jacobs, Jane, 110
James, William, 42, 43, 120, 171
Jarratt, Susan, 196–98
Johns, Jasper, 132–33, 242n8, 246n21
Johnson, Steven, 65

kairos, 78, 91
Kant, Immanuel, 25, 112, 134, 247n6
Kauffman, Stuart, 240n4; on autonomous agents, 129–30; on breaking symmetries, 246n16; on creativity, 164; on exaptation, 112; on novelty, 26; on sub- and supracriticality ("trading their stuff"), 121, 122–23, 235n3, 241n10. *See also* "yuck" and "yum"
Kennedy, George, 60
Kennedy, Robert, 17, 218–20, 230–31
Kennerly, Michele, and Woods, "Moving Rhetorica," 195–96, 197
Kent, Thomas, 4, 7
Kimmerer, Robin, 19–21, 22, 24, 39, 40, 41, 44, 179, 180, 202–3
Kress, Gunter, 13, 106, 119, 124

language: as arising in intra-action, 53–54, 114; consciousness of, 165; endurance of, 123–24; human and nonhuman animal, 58–60; and human exceptionalism, 46; recursion in, 58–59; and propositions, 41, 179–81, 213; system of, 30; and tools, 5, 67–68, 70–71, 102–3
Latour, Bruno, 240n4; on actors, 129, 135–36, 141; on cognition, 47–48; on facts, 7; on the good common world,

7, 243n13; on mode of existence, 63–64; on networks, 9, 67; on social constructionism, 236n3; on things, 36–37, 74–75. *See also* collective; matters of concern; speech prostheses
Lauer, Janice, Montague, Lunsford, and Emig, *Four Worlds of Writing*, 167
Leroi-Gourhan, André, 67, 68–70, 72
Levinas, Emmanuel, 201
Libet, Benjamin, 144
Licona, Adele. *See* Herndl and Licona
Lippi-Green, Rosina, 207
listening, 16–17, 198, 206–13
Luhmann, Niklas, 121
Lundberg, Christian, and Gunn, "Ouija Board, Are There Any Communications?" 128, 131
Lyotard, Jean-François, 247n7

making, definition of, 76, 77–78; and mētis, 78, 82–83, 86, 88–89; and phronetic technē, 78, 87–90; and habituation, 87–89; writing as, 6–7, 221–23. *See also* technē
Massumi, Brian, 215
mattering, 3, 6, 29, 34, 95, 103, 130. *See also* importance
matters of concern, 151, 244n23
Maturana, Humberto, 52–53, 119, 120, 151, 240n4. *See also* Maturana and Varela
Maturana and Varela, *Autopoesis and Cognition*, 51–52, 114, 118; *The Tree of Knowledge*, 24, 114, 118–19, 120. *See also* structural coupling; structural determination

Mazis, Glen, 46, 56, 155, 156, 208–10
McCloskey, Don, 229
McGreavy, Bridie. *See* Stormer and McGreavy
meaning: created in minds (meaning for free), 133, 140, 141–43, 151; as material, 123; and mattering, 29, 49, 103, 175; as use, 53, 115
Merleau-Ponty, Maurice, 25, 48, 141–42, 144, 155, 209, 240n4
mētis, 12, 77, 78, 80, 81, 91
Miller, Carolyn, 128, 131–32, 144, 181
Mindwalk (film), 236n13
miracle of creation (Ezekiel), 159, 175
Montague, Gene. *See* Lauer, Montague, Lunsford, and Emig
Muckelbauer, John, 138–39, 184–86, 192, 201
Murray, Donald, 167, 172

Nancy, Jean-Luc, 200–201
National Commission on Writing, 45
nature: and culture, 10, 23–24; disenchantment of, 46; as a garden, 10, 25; and technē, 83–84. *See also* bifurcation of nature
Nealon, Jeffrey, 14, 137–38
New London Group, 124
new materialism, 4, 5
nonhuman turn. *See* posthumanism
nonlinearity, 106, 108, 110–12

Obama, Barack, 9, 14, 140, 141, 143–44, 145–146, 147–53, 230–31, 243n12, 243–44n20

objects: as born things, 74; as emergent, 107; as open, 74; and relations, 36–37

order: out of chaos, 27, 107–9; not designed or planned, 113; for free, 23, 175; and novelty, 161. *See also* concrescence; creativity

the other, 6, 152, 189, 191, 207

Oyama, Susan, 73

parrots, 15–16, 17

paths: as foresight, 86–87; and hypnotism, 178; as invention, 92; and stories, 20–21, 89

patterns in time, 13, 106–9

pedagogy: critical, 31, 229; embodied, 88–89; ethics of, 228–29, 231–34. *See also* writing, pedagogy of

Pender, Kelly, 90, 91, 92, 239n7, 240n9

Pepperberg, Irene, 15–16, 17

Perelman, Chaim, 18, 222, 228, 229–30

Pericles, 195–96, 203–4, 230

permanence and change, 13, 27, 29, 30, 120–26, 160–64

persuadability, 4, 32

persuasion: as contingent, 205–6; ethical, 16–18, 151, 191–93, 221, 230–33; polite, 17, 37, 201–6; successful, 214–20; theories of, 193–206

Peterson, Rolf, 111

phase transition behavior, 124

Phelps, Louise, 28–30, 31

pigeons, 51–52, 238n14

Pike, Kenneth. *See* Young, Becker, and Pike

Plato, 77–78, 194

Pollan, Michael, 9–10

posthumanism, 4, 5

postmodernism, 23–24, 165, 166

practical knowledge (phronesis), 78–79, 80

predator-prey relations, 110–11

prehension, 192–93

prewriting, 224

Prigogine, Ilya, 158. *See also* Prigogine and Stengers

Prigogine and Stengers, *Order out of Chaos*, 27, 29, 109, 110, 240n4

process philosophy, 3, 24, 25, 109

productive knowledge (poiesis), 78–79

programs, 72–73

propositions, 15–16, 37, 40–41, 116–17, 175–81, 203, 213

public sphere, 199, 201, 246n1

quantum physics, 22, 28, 29, 34, 35, 171–72

rabbits, 180

Ratcliffe, Krista, 17, 206, 209, 223–24, 247n10

reality: as an intra-active process of creation, 26, 47–49, 89–90, 181; as single, 24–25, 28, 98

reciprocal induction, 22, 32, 135–36, 141, 159–60, 161–64, 166–67, 203, 236n2. *See also* concrescence, correspondence, individuation, intra-action

resistance, 137–39

responsibility, 6, 130, 151, 153, 202–3

rhetoric: agency required of, 128; as ambient, 32; animal, 60; deliberative, 147–48, 151; humanist, 131
Rice, Jenny, 247n13
Rickert, Thomas, 31–34, 35, 37, 126, 128, 129, 132–33, 235n4, 242n1. *See also* Brooke and Rickert
Ricoeur, Paul, 28, 29, 30
Roberts-Miller, Patricia, 16–17, 194, 197–98, 199
Robinson, Keith, 109
robots, 56
Rorty, Richard, 24, 37, 51
Rosch, Eleanor. *See* Varela, Thompson, and Rosch

Sachs, Joe, 9, 38–39, 40, 42, 149
Schrag, Calvin, 28
Schutz, Alfred, 87, 93
Sennett, Richard, 86
service learning, 8
Shaviro, Steven, 24, 25, 26, 112, 117, 135, 154, 155
Sheard, Cynthia, 229
Sherburne, Donald, 183
Simondon, Gilbert, 240n4; on creativity, 164; on falling out of step, 175; on technical mentality, 74; on transduction, 121, 126. *See also* individuation
skillful coping, 144–45, 156
slime mold, 55–56
Smith, Erec, 149
social constructionism, 23–24, 236n3
sophists, 80, 82, 88, 194, 196–97
space-time, 171–72, 174
speech act theory, 29

speech prostheses, 17, 208, 211–12
Spinoza, Benedict de, 26
Spuybroek, Lars, 86
Stengers, Isabelle, 240n4; on affect, 135; on creativity, 26, 178; on decision, 155; on education, 43; on ethics, 189; on God, 163, 244n3; on habits, 39–40, 43–44, 202; on hypnotism, 178; on interstices, 31; on objectification, 162–63; on particularity of experience, 207; on persuasion, 149, 192, 202–4, 205–6, 217–18; on physical and conceptual poles, 161; on presence of others as a test, 191; on process theology, 245n11; on propositions, 15, 41, 176–77; on politeness, 37; on souls and language, 130, 179–81; on thinking with Whitehead, 182–84; on the trick of evil, 6; on words, 103. *See also* cosmos, Prigogine and Stengers
Stiegler, Bernard, 11, 12, 70–71, 240n4
stories, 103–4, 150–51; as paths, 20–21, 37, 89, 192, 213
Stormer, Nathan, and McGreavy, "Thinking Ecologically about Rhetoric's Ontology," 132, 138
structural coupling, 52–53, 68, 120, 159, 237n8
structural determination, 118–19. *See also* decision, "yuck" and "yum"
subjective aim, 115, 154, 158, 171–72
subjects: animals as, 51; decentering of, 128; as emergent, 22, 107, 200–201; humanist, 4, 5, 91, 200–201;

posthumanist, 5, 129; social construction of, 128–29. *See also* agents

Suchman, Lucy, 56, 113–14

Sugrue, Thomas, 140

Syverson, Margaret, 47

tactics, 80, 81

technē: Atwill on, 77–78, 90–92; as correspondence, 11–12; as invention, 92; phronetic, 12, 78, 79–80, 83–84, 87–90; in rhetoric and composition, 90–92; as teachable, 90. *See also* making

technology, 6, 45, 46, 61, 62–63, 66, 67, 209–10; digital, 55, 65, 75

Terminator (films), 46

Thompson, Evan, 51, 57, 140, 145, 146. *See also* Varela, Thompson, and Rosch

the trace, 71–72

the trick of evil, 6, 31, 42, 138, 194

Trimbur, John, 115

Tsing, Anna Lowenhaupt, 21, 22, 214, 215–18

Turing, Alan, 75

2001: A Space Odyssey (film), 68

Uexküll, Jacob von, 11, 25, 51, 57

understanding, 27, 178, 186, 187–88

Varela, Francisco. *See* Maturana and Varela; Varela, Thompson, and Rosch

Varela, Francisco, Thompson, and Rosch, *The Embodied Mind*, 57, 239n2

Venn, Couze, 121–22, 126

Vernant, Jean-Pierre. *See* Detienne and Vernant

vitalism, 25, 27, 92

Walker, Jeffrey, 144, 222, 229, 243n15, 248n2

wasp and orchid, 107, 217

Wenger, Daniel, 156

"Wholeness" movement, 24–25

Weng, Juyang, 56

Whitehead, Alfred North, 240n4; on affect, 134; on becoming, 22–23, 35–36; on causation, 154; composing process of, 182, 185, 246n20; cosmology of, 161–64; on creativity, 26, 159, 160; on duration, 25–26; on education, 42–43; on embodiment, 147; on endurance, 120–21, 126; on eternal objects, 116–17; on ethics, 6, 12–13, 15, 17, 30–31, 130; on expression, 205; on God, 163–64, 244n3; on habits of experience, 39, 42; on language, 102, 179–81; on nature, 49; on order, 109, 203–4; on particularity of experience, 207; on permanence and change, 29, 126; on persuasion, 203–4; on subjects, 134–35; on time, 107, 171–72; on understanding, 27, 188; on wonder, 212; Uexküll's influence on, 25; on Wordsworth, 120, 205; and Young, Becker, and Pike, 167–68. *See also* actual entities; adventure of ideas; appetition; bifurcation of nature; concrescence; contrast; decision; enjoyment; importance; propositions; subjective aim; the trick of evil

Wiener, Norbert, 124

Wittgenstein, Ludwig, 53, 115

wolves: and dogs, 57–58; and moose, 110–11

Woods, Carly S. *See* Kennerly and Woods

wrangling, 194, 196–97

Wray, Alison, 53

writing: as adventure of ideas, 158–59, 181–82, 224; cognitive ecologies of, 64–66; as the composition of texts, 4, 7, 28; creativity in, 15, 163–64, 181–88; definition of, 4–7, 13, 18, 19, 45, 106, 125, 222–23, 235n2; enchanted, 37; ethical, 221; feedback in, 125; good, 8, 38, 44, 131, 222–24; habits of, 94–95, 147–53, 206–13, 226–27, 228, 248n6; as a material practice, 49–51; materials of, 94; pedagogy of, 18, 31, 186–88, 197, 224–29; postprocess, 4; process of, 4; public, 8; purposes and intentions in, 114–15; structural determination in, 119; students of, 8, 128, 157, 186–88; tools of, 102

Young, Iris Marion, 191, 200, 201

Young, Richard, 90, 91. *See also* Young, Becker, and Pike

Young, Becker, and Pike, *Rhetoric: Discovery and Change* 167–68

"yuck" and "yum," 112–13, 154, 243n14. *See also* decision; structural determination

Zickefoose, Julie, 210–12

www.ingramcontent.com/pod-product-compliance
Lightning Source LLC
Chambersburg PA
CBHW032030290426
44110CB00012B/742